# LSAT®
# LOGICAL REASONING
## STRATEGIES AND TACTICS

**100% OFFICIAL LSAT PREPTEST® QUESTIONS**

Deborah A. Katz, JD, PhD

Published by Kaplan Publishing, a division of Kaplan, Inc.
395 Hudson Street
New York, NY 10014

Printed in the United States of America

10 9 8 7 6 5 4 3 2 1

ISBN-13: 978-1-60978-150-7

Kaplan Publishing books are available at special quantity discounts to use for sales promotions, employee premiums, or educational purposes. For more information or to purchase books, please call the Simon & Schuster special sales department at 866-506-1949.

# Contents

# About the Author

**Deborah A. Katz, JD, PhD,** is an elite LSAT instructor and teacher trainer, honored in 2007 as the Columbus Teacher of the Year. Deborah has taught with Kaplan since 2002; in 2007, she was selected to participate in the inaugural Kaplan LSAT Summer Intensive program, and currently serves as Program Director.

Deborah holds both a JD and a PhD from The Ohio State University. She is a consultant for the American NewMedia Educational Foundation, where she consults with the education and athletic communities to evaluate NCAA compliance and develop rules, educational programs, and materials. She also serves as an adjunct professor for the Law of Amateur Sports at Capital University Law School.

# Introduction to the LSAT

The Law School Admissions Test (LSAT) is probably unlike any other test you've taken in your academic career. Most tests you've encountered in high school and college have been content based—that is, they have required you to recall facts, formulas, theorems, or other acquired knowledge.

The LSAT, however, is a skills-based test. It doesn't ask you to repeat memorized facts or to apply learned formulas to specific problems. In fact, all you'll be asked to do on the LSAT is think—thoroughly, quickly, and strategically. There's no required content to study.

But the lack of specific content to memorize is one of things that makes preparing for the LSAT so challenging. Before you get the idea that you can skate into the most important test of your life without preparing, remember that learning skills and improving performance take practice. You can't cram for the test.

## ABOUT THE LSAT

The LSAT is a standardized test written by the Law School Admissions Council (LSAC) and administered four times each year. The test is a required component of your application to all American Bar Association–approved law schools as well as some others.

The LSAT is designed to measure the skills necessary (according to the governing bodies of law schools) for success in your first year of law school, such as strategic reading, analyzing arguments, understanding formal logic, and making deductions. Because these skills will serve you well throughout law school and your professional life, consider your LSAT preparation an investment in your career.

You may already possess some level of proficiency with LSAT-tested skills. However, you probably haven't yet mastered how to use those skills to your advantage in the context of a standardized, skills-based test that requires careful time management.

The LSAT is also a test of endurance—five 35-minute blocks of multiple-choice testing plus a 35-minute writing sample. Add in the administrative tasks at both ends of the test and a 10- to 15-minute break midway through, and you can count on being in the test room for at least four and a half hours. It's a grueling experience, but it's not as bad if you are familiar with the test and ready to handle every section. You want to approach the test with confidence so that you can maintain your focus, limit your stress, and get your highest score on test day. That's why it's so important to take control of the test, just as you will take control of the rest of the application process.

Our material is as up-to-date as possible at the time of this printing, but test specifications may change at any time. Please visit our website at http://kaptest.com/LSAT for the latest news and updates.

## How Do I Register for the LSAT?

The LSAT is administered by the Law School Admissions Council (LSAC). Be sure to register as soon as possible, as your preferred test site can fill up quickly. You can register for the LSAT in three ways:

- Online: Sign up at http://lsac.org.
- Telephone: Call LSAC at (215) 968-1001.
- Email: Contact LSAC for a registration packet at lsacinfo@lsac.org.

If you have additional questions about registration, contact the LSAC by phone or by email.

## The LSAT Sections

The LSAT consists of five multiple-choice sections: two Logical Reasoning sections, one Logic Games section, one Reading Comprehension section, and one unscored "experimental" section that looks exactly like one of the other multiple-choice sections. At the end of the test, there is a Writing Sample section during which you'll write a short essay. Here's how the sections break down:

| Section | Number of Questions | Minutes |
|---|---|---|
| Logical Reasoning | 24–26 | 35 |
| Logical Reasoning | 24–26 | 35 |
| Logic Games | 22–24 | 35 |
| Reading Comprehension | 26–28 | 35 |
| "Experimental" | 23–28 | 35 |
| Writing Sample | n/a | 35 |

The five multiple-choice sections can appear in any order, but the Writing Sample is always last. You will also get a 10- or 15-minute break between the third and fourth sections of the test.

You'll be answering roughly 125 multiple-choice questions (101 of which are scored) over the course of three intense hours. Taking control of the LSAT means increasing your test speed only to the extent that you can do so without sacrificing accuracy.

First, just familiarize yourself with the sections and the kinds of questions asked in each one.

## Logical Reasoning

**WHAT IT IS:** The Logical Reasoning sections consist of 24–26 questions each that reward your ability to analyze a "stimulus" (a paragraph or a dialogue between two speakers) and make judgments accordingly. You will evaluate the logic and structure of arguments and make inferences from the statements as well as find underlying assumptions, strengthen and weaken arguments, determine logical flaws, and identify parallel argument structures.

**WHY IT'S ON THE TEST:** Law schools want to see whether you can understand, analyze, evaluate, and manipulate arguments, and draw reliable conclusions—as every law student and attorney must. This question type makes up half of your LSAT score, which means this is a valuable skill to master.

## Logic Games

**WHAT IT IS:** In the Logic Games (a.k.a. Analytical Reasoning) section, you'll find four games (aka critical-thinking puzzles) with five to seven questions each for a total of 22–24 questions. They reward your ability to make valid deductions from a set of rules or restrictions in order to determine what can, must, or cannot be true in various circumstances.

**WHY IT'S ON THE TEST:** In law school, your professors will have you read dozens of cases, extract their rules, and apply them to or distinguish them from hypothetical cases. The Logic Games section rewards the same skill set: attention to detail, rigorous deductive reasoning, an understanding of how rules limit and order behavior (the very definition of law), and the ability to discern the conditions under which those rules do and do not apply.

## Reading Comprehension

**WHAT IT IS:** The Reading Comprehension section consists of three passages, each 450–550 words, and a set of two short passages that total 450–550 words. Each passage is followed by five to eight questions. The topics may range from areas of social science, humanities, natural science, and law. Because content isn't tested, you won't need any outside knowledge.

**WHY IT'S ON THE TEST:** The Reading Comprehension section tests your ability to quickly understand the gist and structure of long, difficult prose—just as you'll have to do in law school and throughout your career.

### The Writing Sample

**WHAT IT IS:** During the Writing Sample section, you will read a paragraph that presents a problem and lists two possible solutions. Each solution will have strengths and weaknesses; you must argue in favor of one based on the given criteria. There is no right or wrong answer, and the writing sample is unscored. However, law schools will receive a copy of your essay along with your LSAT score.

**WHY IT'S ON THE TEST:** The Writing Sample shows law schools your ability to argue for a position while attacking an opposing argument under timed conditions. In addition, it may be used to verify that your writing style is similar to that in your personal statement.

## How the LSAT Is Scored

You'll receive one score for the LSAT ranging between 120 and 180 (no separate scores for Logical Reasoning, Logic Games, and Reading Comprehension). There are roughly 101 scored multiple-choice questions on each exam:

- About 52 from the two Logical Reasoning sections
- About 22 from the Logic Games section
- About 27 from the Reading Comprehension section

Your **raw score**, the number of questions that you answer correctly, will be multiplied by a complicated scoring formula (different for each test, to accommodate differences in difficulty level) to yield the **scaled score**—the one that will fall somewhere in that 120–180 range—which is reported to the schools.

Because the test is graded on a largely preset curve, the scaled score will always correspond to a certain percentile, also indicated on your score report. A score of 160, for instance, corresponds roughly to the 80th percentile, meaning that 80 percent of test takers scored at or below your level. The percentile figure is important because it allows law schools to see where you fall in the pool of applicants.

All scored questions are worth the same amount—one raw point—and there's no penalty for guessing. That means that you should always fill in an answer for every question, whether you get to that question or not.

## What's a "Good" LSAT Score?

What you consider a "good" LSAT score depends on your own expectations and goals, but here are a few interesting statistics.

If you got about half of all of the scored questions right (a raw score of roughly 50), you would earn a scaled score of roughly 147, putting you in about the 30th percentile—not a great performance. But on the LSAT, a little improvement goes a long way. In fact, getting only one additional question right every 10 minutes would give you a raw score of about 64, pushing you into the 60th percentile—a huge improvement.

| Sample Percentiles Approx. Scaled Score | | |
|---|---|---|
| Percentile | (Range 120–180) | Approx. Raw Score |
| 99th percentile | 174 | ~94 correct out of 101 |
| 95th percentile | 168 | ~88 correct out of 101 |
| 90th percentile | 164 | ~82 correct out of 101 |
| 80th percentile | 160 | ~76 correct out of 101 |
| 75th percentile | 157 | ~71 correct out of 101 |
| 50th percentile | 152 | ~61 correct out of 101 |

**Note:** Exact percentile-to-scaled-score relationships vary from test to test.

As you can see, you don't have to be perfect to do well. On most LSATs, you can get as many as 28 questions wrong and still remain in the 80th percentile or as many as 20 wrong and still be in the 90th percentile. Most students who score 180 get a handful of questions wrong.

Although many factors play a role in admissions decisions, the LSAT score is usually one of the most important. And—generally speaking—being average won't cut it. The median LSAT score is somewhere around 152. If you're aiming for the top, you've got to do even better.

By using the strategies in this book, you'll learn how to approach—and master—the test in a general way. As you'll see, knowing specific strategies for each type of question is only part of your task. To do your best, you have to approach the entire test with the proactive, take-control kind of thinking it inspires—the LSAT mindset.

For more information on the LSAT experience, see Part IV of this book.

# PART I

# HOW LOGICAL REASONING WORKS

# CHAPTER 1

# TESTING LOGICAL REASONING

## AN INTRODUCTION TO LOGICAL REASONING

Have you ever seen a Logical Reasoning question from the LSAT? Before I talk about methods and skills you will use to achieve your best score on test day, I'll show you what a Logical Reasoning question looks like.

The following two questions appeared on the September 2006 test. Read them over and see whether you can get the correct answer.

1.  Typically, people who have diets high in saturated fat have an increased risk of heart disease. Those who replace saturated fat in their diets with unsaturated fat decrease their risk of heart disease. Therefore, people who eat a lot of saturated fat can lower their risk of heart disease by increasing their intake of unsaturated fat.

    Which one of the following, if assumed, most helps to justify the reasoning above?

    (A)   People who add unsaturated fat to their diets will eat less food that is high in saturated fat.
    (B)   Adding unsaturated fat to a diet brings health benefits other than a reduced risk of heart disease.
    (C)   Diet is the most important factor in a person's risk of heart disease.
    (D)   Taking steps to prevent heart disease is one of the most effective ways of increasing life expectancy.
    (E)   It is difficult to move from a diet that is high in saturated fat to a diet that includes very little fat.

2.  Only people who are willing to compromise should undergo mediation to resolve their conflicts. Actual litigation should be pursued only when one is sure that one's position is correct. People whose conflicts are based on ideology are unwilling to compromise.

    If the statements above are true, then which one of the following must be true?

    (A)   People who do not undergo mediation to resolve their conflicts should be sure that their positions are correct.
    (B)   People whose conflicts are not based on ideology should attempt to resolve their conflicts by means of litigation.
    (C)   People whose conflicts are based on ideology are not always sure that their positions are correct.
    (D)   People who are sure of the correctness of their positions are not people who should undergo mediation to resolve their conflicts.
    (E)   People whose conflicts are based on ideology are not people who should undergo mediation to resolve their conflicts.[2]

Did you select choice (A) as your answer to question 1 and choice (E) for question 2?

If so, congratulations! Maybe you got both wrong or maybe one correct. Frankly, your specific response doesn't matter right now. What is most important is how you answered the questions,

---

[2]PrepTest 50, Sec. 4, Qs 9–10

why you chose the answers you did, and why you did not pick the other answers. If you follow the approach in this book, you'll learn how Logical Reasoning questions are put together and how you can take them apart efficiently, effectively, and routinely. If you practice the methods and strategies introduced here, you will maximize your Logical Reasoning performance and, in turn, your LSAT score.

## Logical Reasoning Tests Skills, Not Content

Logical Reasoning, like the other sections on the LSAT, is a skill-based exercise that requires no outside knowledge of the content. Unlike many of your academic endeavors, the test includes no subject matter to memorize and regurgitate. Instead, you use critical-thinking skills to answer the questions.

Starting now, you should think of logical reasoning as a skill, just like playing basketball, strumming the guitar, cooking, or even driving a car. As with any skill, your goal is to perform the activity proficiently at a high level. You may have some innate talent or even some beginner's luck; however, you must develop and practice your skills so you walk in on test day confident in your ability to answer any question put in front of you.

Think about this example: A basketball player first learns the fundamentals of the game by practicing dribbling, passing, and shooting drills. Then she runs through plays that put the skills together, and she adds scrimmages to simulate game situations. In the process, the player works out to improve strength, agility, and endurance. The more comfortable with the skills and the more fit the player becomes, the quicker she can "read" the situation on the floor, make decisions, and respond in a game. Just like the basketball player, you must practice the fundamentals, break down the activities, and put your "game" together for test day.

Part I of this book has three purposes: to familiarize you with the Logical Reasoning sections on the LSAT, to introduce you to the Kaplan Method for tackling any Logical Reasoning question, and to provide you with a chance to practice your fundamental logical reasoning skills.

Later, in Part II, you will apply your skills to the specific question types asked on every LSAT and then put your skills to the test on complete Logical Reasoning sections.

# LOGICAL REASONING SKILLS

Logical reasoning refers to the ability to identify, analyze, evaluate, and construct complex reasoning. The LSAT tests your ability to reason logically and critically by asking questions that require you to:

- Distinguish the parts of an argument and understand their relationships
- Recognize unstated assumptions
- Strengthen and weaken an argument

- Determine what must be true based on a set of assertions
- Identify argument flaws
- Identify similarities and differences between patterns of reasoning
- Recognize points of disagreement
- Identify principles and apply them to fact sets
- Detect a method of argument

## THE IMPORTANCE OF LOGICAL REASONING ON THE LSAT

Logical reasoning accounts for half your score and assesses critical-thinking skills that are vital to your success in law school and the legal profession. The LSAT is not an end unto itself. Lawyers need critical-thinking skills to meet their professional responsibilities, and a legal education is designed to develop, hone, and refine those skills. Therefore, the LSAT must test your logical reasoning skills. Law schools want to evaluate your ability to think critically, amongst other skills, and use the LSAT, in large part, to determine your fit with their program.

Regardless of the nature of a lawyer's practice, there are some basic analytic, communication, and problem-solving skills that are universal. Lawyers must be able to structure and evaluate arguments for and against propositions to persuade, negotiate, and conduct business. Lawyers must analyze legal issues in light of changing laws and public policy. They must be able to advocate the views of individuals and diverse interest groups within the context of the legal system. They must be able to synthesize and apply material that relates to multifaceted issues. Ultimately, they must give logically reasoned and sound counsel on the law's requirements.

## ANATOMY OF A LOGICAL REASONING QUESTION

How does the LSAT present logical reasoning and test the related skills? Every Logical Reasoning question begins with a stimulus: either a single paragraph or a dialogue between two speakers. Each stimulus presents an argument or a set of facts drawn from various sources, such as newspapers and magazines, academic journals, advertisements, and informal discourse. Regardless of whether the topic is art, medicine, or animals, remember that your knowledge of any particular content is not tested.

The stimulus is followed by a question that states your task—for example, to find the assumption, to strengthen the argument, or to identify parallel reasoning. Then, five multiple-choice answers are presented.

Table 1.1 is a breakdown by part of one of the September 2006 logical reasoning questions I showed you earlier:

**Table 1.1**

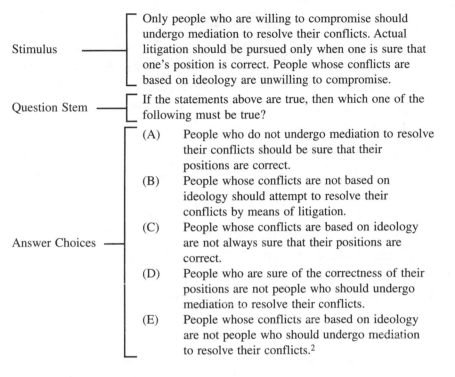

Stimulus — Only people who are willing to compromise should undergo mediation to resolve their conflicts. Actual litigation should be pursued only when one is sure that one's position is correct. People whose conflicts are based on ideology are unwilling to compromise.

Question Stem — If the statements above are true, then which one of the following must be true?

Answer Choices —

(A) People who do not undergo mediation to resolve their conflicts should be sure that their positions are correct.

(B) People whose conflicts are not based on ideology should attempt to resolve their conflicts by means of litigation.

(C) People whose conflicts are based on ideology are not always sure that their positions are correct.

(D) People who are sure of the correctness of their positions are not people who should undergo mediation to resolve their conflicts.

(E) People whose conflicts are based on ideology are not people who should undergo mediation to resolve their conflicts.[2]

## Breakdown of Question Types

The 24–26 questions in each Logical Reasoning section are drawn from 12 common question types asked consistently on past LSATs. Kaplan research shows that the number of questions from each category is predictable, although not exact.

Logical Reasoning will comprise two of the four scored sections on your LSAT. You will see a total of approximately 50 scored Logical Reasoning questions out of the 100–101 total scored questions on test day. Half the test! And far more than the 22–24 Logic Games questions.

I will extensively review each question type in Part II of this book. For now, I'll provide you with an introduction to give you some context for the strategies you'll be learning in the meantime. Ultimately, your goal is to integrate this information in your approach to Logical Reasoning and to become more efficient and accurate in completing the sections to increase your score.

In Table 1.2, I've identified the 12 common Logical Reasoning question types, what each question type asks, the number of questions of each type that typically appear, and a sample question for each type.

---

[2]PrepTest 50, Sec. 4, Q 10

Table 1.2

| Question Type | Task | Number of Questions | Sample Question |
|---|---|---|---|
| Assumption | Find the unstated assumption the author makes to go from the evidence provided to the conclusion reached. | 8 | Which one of the following is an assumption on which the argument depends? |
| Strengthen | Identify information that can be added to the argument to make it more likely to be so; in other words, to make the assumption of the argument more probable. | 8 (Strengthen and Weaken combined) | Which one of the following, if true, most supports the argument? |
| Weaken | Identify information that can be added to the argument to make it less likely to be so; in other words, to make the assumption of the argument less probable. | | Which one of the following, if true, most seriously weakens the argument? |
| Flaw | Determine the error the author makes in going from the evidence to the conclusion. | 8 | Which one of the following, if true, identifies a flaw in the plan for the program? |
| Inference | Find the answer that must be true based on the information provided in the stimulus. | 7 | If the statements above are true, then which one of the following must be true? |
| Principle | Identify a general rule that governs or matches a specific situation. | 5 | The situation described above most closely conforms to which one of the following principles? |
| Paradox | Provide an alternative explanation or factor to make sense of two facts that seem contradictory. | 4 | Which of the following would resolve the apparent discrepancy above? |
| Parallel Reasoning | Identify the choice that contains the same kind of reasoning as the stimulus. | 3 | The reasoning above is most closely paralleled in which one of the following? |
| Method of Argument | Explain how an author's argument is put together. | 2 | Which one of the following describes the author's argumentative strategy? |

(continued)

| Question Type | Task | Number of Questions | Sample Question |
|---|---|---|---|
| Point at Issue | Identify the issue on which two speakers present differing opinions. | 1 | Jack and Jeff disagree over whether . . . |
| Role of a Statement | Determine the function of a given statement in the argument. | 2 | The assertion that the company must increase production plays which of the following roles in the president's argument? |
| Main Point | Find the central claim presented in the author's argument. | 2 | Which one of the following most accurately expresses the main point of the argument? |

## LOGICAL REASONING SKILLS IN EVERYDAY LIFE

Over the years, most of my students have approached the Logical Reasoning section of the LSAT with some degree of trepidation. After all, the term "logical reasoning" sounds like some lofty endeavor, something practiced in the ivory towers of law schools or in judicial chambers. This couldn't be further from the truth. Logical reasoning is a common practice and something you use in your personal, academic, and professional lives. In fact, you've probably invoked logical reasoning before you had any inkling of what is was. Consider this scenario:

Parent: You can't go to the party tonight. You were out late last night.

Teenager: That's not fair! All my friends are going to the party. Even Andrew's mom is letting him go.

Does this sound familiar? It provides an excellent example of how pervasive logical reasoning is in everyday life. The point at issue between the parent and teenager is whether the teenager should be able to go to the party. Both sides present an argument. The parent concludes the teenager will miss the party and supports it with evidence that he was out late the previous evening. The teenager concludes the decision is not fair because all his friends will be there and he should be able to do what his friends do.

In this situation, the argument may continue in a variety of ways. The parent may come back with a statement like, "I don't care what your friends are doing. If they all shaved their heads, would you shave yours, too?" The teenager might try to negotiate and offer to do extra chores for the week. If a scenario such as this one were presented on the LSAT, you would not be asked to decide whether the parent's decision is fair or whether the teenager should be allowed to attend the party. Instead, you would be asked to analyze the arguments—possibly by identifying the parent's assumption (going to a party means the teenager will be out late), by finding the flaw in the teenager's argument (he shifts scope from staying out late to doing what his friends do, but does not address the argument at hand), or by describing the teenager's method of argument (presenting group behavior and referring to an "expert", i.e., his friend's mom).

Surely you've engaged in logical reasoning in some respect, so the concept is not completely foreign to you. The LSAT and your legal pursuits just require you to take it to a more sophisticated, purposeful level. You must be able to understand the structure of an argument or statement, break it down to its basic elements, and recognize the impact of additional information. To succeed in law school and a law-related profession, you must develop and improve your logical reasoning abilities. And to succeed on the LSAT, you need a plan of action. Fortunately for you, I'll show you the best way to handle anything the Logical Reasoning section can throw at you: the Kaplan Method.

# THE IMPORTANCE OF A STRATEGY

## The Kaplan Method for Logical Reasoning

Has this ever happened to you on a multiple-choice test? You read the text. You read the question. Then, you go back to reread the text looking for information to answer the question. You read the question again to remind yourself what was asked. Finally, you read each answer choice and check it once more against the paragraph. You rack your brain trying to find the right answer. When you look up at the clock you notice that five minutes have passed and you still have 20 more questions to answer in the final 18 minutes.

Ultimately, that "process" is time consuming and does not necessarily get you to the correct answer. Because you didn't have a plan of action, you probably felt rushed, frustrated, and anxious. I'm not going to let that happen to you again. I'm going to introduce you to the Kaplan Method, which has helped thousands of my students over the years improve their logical reasoning performance.

From now until test day, work through every Logical Reasoning question by taking the following steps:

## THE KAPLAN METHOD FOR LOGICAL REASONING

**STEP 1**  **Identify the Question Type**
READ the question stem to identify the question type and determine your task.

**STEP 2**  **Untangle the Stimulus**
READ the stimulus to find the information you need to answer the question.

**STEP 3**  **Make a Prediction**
USE the information to make effective predictions to locate the right answer quickly and efficiently.

**STEP 4**  **Evaluate the Answer Choices**
FIND the answer choice that best matches your prediction.

### Step 1. Identify the Question Type

Read the question stem to identify the question type. This step may seem counterintuitive because the question stem is presented after the stimulus. However, reading the question stem first lets you identify the question type and determine your task as you read the stimulus. It also allows you to read the stimulus actively by pulling specific information that will help you answer the question.

### Step 2. Untangle the Stimulus

Read the stimulus and examine it through the lens of the question type you identified in Step 1. In other words, as you read the stimulus, unpack it for the information you will need to answer the particular question. You will learn skills—analyzing arguments and using formal logic—in chapters 2 and 3 to help you complete this step. In Part II, you will apply your newly learned skills in the context of each Logical Reasoning question type and learn what information to read for based on the question type.

### Step 3. Make a Prediction

Now that you've analyzed the information from the question stem and stimulus, it's time to think critically about the answer. You don't need to use complete sentences or formal language. You just need enough to move to the next step and sort through the answers. You also have to be ready for an answer that is similar to, but not an exact replica of, your prediction. This step is very important and is the one you will be most likely to skip. Don't! It will feel awkward in the beginning, but give it a chance. Once you practice it and get better, it will actually improve your speed and efficiency. Without this step, you are more likely to get distracted by wrong answers and waste time analyzing each answer and rechecking it against the stimulus.

### Step 4. Evaluate the Answer Choices

Review the answer choices and determine which one best matches your prediction. Most often, one answer will stand out for you. If not, eliminate wrong answers and consider the common wrong answer traps. I'll have more on that later.

# THE KAPLAN METHOD IN ACTION

Now I'll walk you through the examples I provided at the beginning of the chapter to demonstrate the Kaplan Method for Logical Reasoning. Again, the Method remains the same regardless of the question type; however, the application may change. I'll continue to break down the steps in the chapters ahead.

1. Typically, people who have diets high in saturated fat have an increased risk of heart disease. Those who replace saturated fat in their diets with unsaturated fat decrease their risk of heart disease. Therefore, people who eat a lot of saturated fat can lower their risk of heart disease by increasing their intake of unsaturated fat.

   Which one of the following, if assumed, most helps to justify the reasoning above?

   (A) People who add unsaturated fat to their diets will eat less food that is high in saturated fat.
   (B) Adding unsaturated fat to a diet brings health benefits other than a reduced risk of heart disease.
   (C) Diet is the most important factor in a person's risk of heart disease.
   (D) Taking steps to prevent heart disease is one of the most effective ways of increasing life expectancy.
   (E) It is difficult to move from a diet that is high in saturated fat to a diet that includes very little fat.[3]

*[handwritten: stimulus]*
*[handwritten: Question stem]*
*[handwritten: Identify, Untangle, Predict, Evaluate]*

### Step 1. Identify the Question Type

Always start with the question stem. As you will learn, the phrase "justify the reasoning" identifies a Strengthen question.

### Step 2. Untangle the Stimulus

Because this is a Strengthen question, the stimulus presents an argument. So, read the stimulus to determine the conclusion and evidence. The conclusion is signaled by "Therefore" and

---

[3]PrepTest 50, Sec. 4, Q 9

reads "people who eat a lot of saturated fat can lower their risk of heart disease by increasing their intake of unsaturated fat."

How does the author know that saturated fat eaters can lower their risk of heart disease by eating more unsaturated fat? The author presents evidence saying that replacing saturated fat with unsaturated fat in one's diet decreases the risk of heart disease.

Don't worry if you weren't able to distinguish the conclusion from the evidence at this point. In the next chapter, I'll discuss the skill of analyzing arguments in detail.

### Step 3. Make a Prediction

Because a Strengthen question asks you to select an answer that makes the conclusion more likely to be true, you can confirm the assumption; in other words, state the gap that exists between the conclusion and evidence. Notice the subtle shift between the conclusion ("eating *more* unsaturated") and the evidence ("*replacing* saturated"). I can eat more unbuttered pop-corn without cutting back on my porkrinds, so the author is making an assumption that eating more good foods with unsaturated fats *replaces* bad foods with saturated fats, rather than just being *more*.

The correct answer should confirm that assumption or make it more likely that the saturated fats really are being *replaced*.

### Step 4. Evaluate the Answer Choices

Look over the answer choices to determine whether any match your prediction. Eureka! Choice (A) does perfectly. The more you practice the Logical Reasoning method before test day, the more confident you will be in your ability to spot the correct answer. You will be able to review answer choices quickly and move on when you've found the correct one.

It is also important to consider the wrong answer choices as you learn the Kaplan Method. So, why are the other answers wrong? The other benefits besides a reduced risk of heart disease, presented in choice (B), are outside the scope of the argument. Whether diet is the most important factor in a person's risk of heart disease, as stated in choice (C), is irrelevant to whether replacing saturated fats is one way to reduce the risk of heart disease. Life expectancy, discussed in choice (D), is also outside the scope of the argument. And choice (E)—whether it is difficult to switch from lots of saturated fats to very little fat—is not germane to the point; the argument talks about replacing one kind of fat for another, not cutting overall fat intake.

Now take a look at the second question.

2.  Only people who are willing to compromise should undergo mediation to resolve their conflicts. Actual litigation should be pursued only when one is sure that one's position is correct. People whose conflicts are based on ideology are unwilling to compromise.

    If the statements above are true, then which one of the following must be true?

    (A)  People who do not undergo mediation to resolve their conflicts should be sure that their positions are correct.

    (B)  People whose conflicts are not based on ideology should attempt to resolve their conflicts by means of litigation.

    (C)  People whose conflicts are based on ideology are not always sure that their positions are correct.

    (D)  People who are sure of the correctness of their positions are not people who should undergo mediation to resolve their conflicts.

    (E)  People whose conflicts are based on ideology are not people who should undergo mediation to resolve their conflicts.[4]

## Step 1. Identify the Question Type

You will come to learn that the phrase "must be true" indicates an Inference question.

## Step 2. Untangle the Stimulus

An Inference question typically presents a series of facts rather than an argument. Read the stimulus to make sure you understand each statement. The information is presented in formal logic, so you will need to translate the sentences and identify the contrapositive of each to best comprehend the statements.

I'll show you all the formal logic you need for the LSAT in chapter 3, but for now accept that the formal logic conversion goes like this:

Table 1.2

| Statement | Formal Logic Translation and Contrapositive |
|---|---|
| Only people who are willing to compromise should undergo mediation to resolve their conflicts. | • If you should undergo mediation → you are willing to compromise<br>• If you are not willing to compromise → you should not undergo mediation |
| Actual litigation should be pursued only when one is sure that one's position is correct. | • If you pursue litigation → you are sure your position is correct<br>• If you are not sure your position is correct → you will not pursue litigation |

**(continued)**

---

[4]PrepTest 50, Sec. 4, Q 10

| Statement | Formal Logic Translation and Contrapositive |
|---|---|
| People whose conflicts are based on ideology are unwilling to compromise. | • If your conflict is ideology-based → you are not willing to compromise<br>• If you are willing to compromise → your conflict is not ideology-based |

## Step 3. Make a Prediction

Inference questions often require you to combine two statements or make a deduction: formal logic is a ready tool on Inference questions to help you do just that. You can link the third and first statements from question 2 like so: If your conflict is ideology-based → you are not willing to compromise → you should not undergo mediation.

## Step 4. Evaluate the Answer Choices

As you review each answer choice, ask yourself whether it *must be true* based on the stimulus. If so, you have found the correct answer.

Choice (E) combines two of the formal logic statements and is the correct answer. If your conflict is ideology-based, then you are not willing to compromise; and if you are not willing to compromise, then you will not undergo mediation. Therefore, if your conflict is ideology-based, then you will not undergo mediation.

For choice (A), check the six formal logic statements you created. You know what happens if someone does undergo mediation, but not if they don't. Don't assume that people who do not undergo mediation must actually litigate, and thereby must be sure their positions are correct.

Choice (B) is wrong because based on the information, people whose conflicts are not based on ideology may be willing to compromise and thus maybe could use mediation.

Choice (C) tries to combine the statements about ideology-based conflict and litigation, but the terms of those statements don't allow us to make any such link.

Finally, in choice (D), even though sureness of belief in the correctness of one's position is necessary for litigation, there is not a statement that precludes people who are sure of their correctness from undergoing mediation, provided they are willing to compromise despite that sureness. You can't assume that people sure of their correctness will not be willing to compromise. Often on the LSAT, you will identify the assumptions of authors, but you must never make your own assumptions.

These steps may seem cumbersome now, but by learning the patterns of the LSAT and predicting what the correct answer should generally indicate, you will become a more efficient, effective, and accurate test taker, and not get distracted by complicated, yet erroneous, answers.

## THE IMPORTANCE OF PRACTICE

No one plays a good, complete game when they are handed a basketball for the first time. No one plays a full concert the first day they learn to play the guitar. The same goes with the LSAT. Only after you practice the fundamentals and learn the steps can you become a proficient test taker. Be patient with yourself so you can learn and practice the Kaplan Method and logical reasoning skills and ultimately put together your best score on test day.

# CHAPTER 2

# ANALYZING ARGUMENTS

## ARGUMENTS: THE FOUNDATION OF LEGAL STUDY

### Definition of a Legal Argument

Arguments are a fundamental part of the study and practice of law. The ability to analyze arguments is a critical skill for a legal professional to master, so it's no surprise that it's tested on the LSAT. You might think of an argument as a shouting match in which the participants are often more irrational than reasonable. But an argument on the LSAT is simply a process of reasoning; the author makes a point and supports it with relevant evidence. The argument is what the author is trying to convince you of in the form of a supported point of view.

### Components of an Argument

The majority of Logical Reasoning stimuli you'll see on test day will contain an argument. An argument consists of two parts: the conclusion—the main point the author is making—and the evidence—the information offered by the author to support the conclusion. Or, put more simply, the conclusion is the "what" of the argument and the first thing you will look for, and the evidence is the "why."

Look at this example from a previous LSAT and find the two parts of the argument:

> Having an efficient, attractive subway system makes
> good economic sense. So, the city needs to purchase new
> subway cars, since the city should always do what makes
> good economic sense.[1]

In the conclusion—signaled by the word "so"—the author declares that the city needs to purchase new subway cars. The author supports this course of action with evidence that answers the question, "Why does the city need to purchase new subway cars?" Here, the word "since" identifies the evidence—the city should always do what makes good economic sense. "Economic sense" is defined in the first sentence as having an efficient, attractive subway system.

Success in answering argument-based question types depends on your ability to break an argument down to its core components. In terms of the Kaplan Method you learned in the last chapter, once you identify the question as argument-based, you will analyze the argument in the second step.

In other words, you will read the stimulus specifically to identify the conclusion and the evidence. Consider the following statement:

Raymond should begin his LSAT preparation with Logical Reasoning.

Is it an argument? If you said no, then you're on the right track. This statement alone is not an argument. It is a recommendation to take a certain action, but no evidence is given to support it. Now, look at the next statement and decide whether it is an argument:

Logical Reasoning accounts for one-half of his LSAT score.

This statement is not an argument either. It could be used to support the previous recommendation, but by itself it does not form an argument. Only when the two statements are combined do you get a complete argument with a conclusion supported by evidence: Raymond should begin his LSAT preparation with Logical Reasoning because it accounts for one-half of his LSAT score.

## Keywords Show You the Way

Logical Reasoning questions will ask you to analyze, in some form, the process by which the author moves from the evidence to the conclusion. Therefore, the first step in an argument-based question is to break down the argument into the conclusion and the evidence. There isn't a general rule about where the conclusion and evidence always appear in an argument, so you can't use location to determine the components. The conclusion could be the first sentence, followed by the evidence; it could be the last sentence with the evidence preceding it; or, it could be any sentence in between. Placement of the conclusion and evidence is a stylistic issue and not necessarily indicative of the argument's structure.

---

[1]PrepTest 34, Sec. 2, Q 2

So how can you find the conclusion and evidence in an argument? The test makers commonly use certain words in Logical Reasoning stimuli to signal the conclusion and evidence. Here is a list of some common conclusion Keywords:

- Therefore
- Hence
- Thus
- As a result
- It follows that
- Clearly

Here are some common evidence Keywords:

- Because
- Since
- As
- After all
- For

Also look for structure phrases such as "This is made clear from the fact that . . ." The word "this" indicates that the conclusion is in the preceding sentence and the following fact is the evidence.

Obviously, these lists are not exhaustive, and you will run across other Keywords. A good way to help you keep track of them is to circle them when you see them in the stimulus. This action will draw your attention to them and help you pause to consider their purpose.

## No Keywords? No Problem

In a perfect world, you could identify the structure of every argument by using Keywords. However, it's not always that easy. Sometimes you won't have that luxury. If that is the case, don't worry.

There's another way to determine the argument's structure: It's called the one-sentence test. Ask yourself: What does the author want me to walk away thinking? In other words: Which sentence in the stimulus would the author choose to keep if limited to a single sentence? The answer to that question will be the conclusion. You can usually locate it by looking for a statement in which the author presents a recommendation, proposal, thesis, judgment, opinion, or disagreement.

Read the following stimulus and identify the conclusion and evidence:

> Clearly, State University's plan to renovate the football stadium must include additional construction to come into compliance with the Americans with Disabilities Act. After all, the building has no elevator, limiting access to the upper levels. In addition, it has no viewing areas for people in wheelchairs.

The word "clearly" points to the conclusion that the university's stadium renovation plans must include accommodations under the Americans with Disabilities Act (ADA). A piece of evidence is offered to support the conclusion—that the building does not have elevator access and lacks wheelchair viewing areas—and is signaled by "after all." The phrase "in addition" indicates that the sentence is continuing the thought before it and, in this case, is a piece of evidence.

Now suppose this argument appeared on test day without any Keywords.

> State University's plan to renovate the football stadium must include additional construction to come into compliance with the Americans with Disabilities Act. The building has no elevator, limiting access to the upper levels, and it has no viewing areas for people in wheelchairs.

Can you still identify the conclusion and evidence? Of course you can. The first sentence states the author's viewpoint and the following sentence provides reasons to support it. Try it another way. The stadium has no elevator and no viewing area; therefore, construction must include ADA accommodations. If you are still unsure, you can insert Keywords yourself to test your analysis of the argument. Or, try replacing the evidence with the conclusion: The stadium has no elevator and no viewing area because construction must include ADA accommodations. This does not make sense, so you know the first statement cannot be the evidence and the second cannot be the conclusion.

## Bracket the Conclusion

Now that you've identified the conclusion and evidence, you'll need an easy way to keep track of them. A simple, effective method is to place brackets around the conclusion. In the argument you just examined, it looks like this:

> <Clearly, State University's plan to renovate the football stadium must include additional construction to come into compliance with the Americans with Disabilities Act.> After all, the building has no elevator, limiting access to the upper levels. In addition, it has no viewing areas for people in wheelchairs.

That one simple step allows you to isolate the conclusion and quickly find it as you go through the questions. From now until test day, do this to every argument you see. It'll soon become a habit that will help improve your speed and efficiency, and—more importantly—add points to your score.

# DRILL: IDENTIFYING COMPONENTS OF AN ARGUMENT

Now that you've learned the difference between conclusions and evidence, it's time to practice on your own. Once you develop your argument-analysis skills, you'll be able to take on the questions in Part II.

On test day, you'll be using the Kaplan Method on every Logical Reasoning question you encounter. Here's where you are in the process now:

### Step 1. Identify the Question Type

For purposes of this drill, the question is argument-based.

### Step 2. Untangle the Stimulus

You are here.

### Step 3. Make a Prediction

### Step 4. Evaluate the Answer Choices

As you can see, there are two more steps. Step 1 has been done for you, as you'll be working with argument-based questions exclusively in this Drill. You'll learn about all the question types later in the book, but now, you're focusing on Step 2: Untangle the Stimulus.

Argument-based questions require you to read the stimulus and then break down the argument by looking for the conclusion and evidence. For the following LSAT arguments, (1) circle any Keywords, (2) bracket the conclusion, and (3) summarize the evidence. Detailed explanations follow.

1. Psychologist: There are theories that posit completely different causal mechanisms from those posited by Freudian psychological theory and that are more successful at predicting human behavior. Therefore, Freudian theories of behavior, no matter how suggestive or complex they are, ought to be abandoned in favor of these other theories.[2]

**Evidence:**

_____

_____

_____

2. Skeletal remains of early humans indicate clearly that our ancestors had fewer dental problems than we have. So, most likely, the diet of early humans was very different from ours.[3]

**Evidence:**

_____

_____

_____

3. Several legislators claim that the public finds many current movies so violent as to be morally offensive. However, these legislators have misrepresented public opinion. In a survey conducted by a movie industry guild, only 17 percent of respondents thought that movies are overly violent, and only 3 percent found any recent movie morally offensive. These low percentages are telling, because the respondents see far more current movies than does the average moviegoer.[4]

**Evidence:**

_____

_____

_____

4. In countries where government officials are neither selected by free elections nor open to criticism by a free press, the lives of citizens are controlled by policies they have had no role in creating. This is why such countries are prone to civil disorder, in spite of the veneer of calm such countries often present to a visitor. When people do not understand the purpose of the restrictions placed on their behavior they have a greater tendency to engage in civil disorder as an expression of their frustration.[5]

**Evidence:**

_____

_____

_____

5. Everyone likes repertory theater. Actors like it because playing different roles each night decreases their level of boredom. Stagehands like it because changing sets every night means more overtime and, thus, higher pay. Theater managers like it because, if plays that reflect audience demand are chosen for production, most performances generate large revenues. It is evident, therefore, that more theaters should change to repertory.[6]

**Evidence:**

_____

_____

_____

6. Investment banker: Democracies require free-market capitalist economies, because a more controlled economy is incompatible with complete democracy. But history shows that repressive measures against certain capitalistic developments are required during the transition from a totalitarian regime to a democracy. Thus, people who bemoan the seemingly anticapitalistic measures certain governments are currently taking are being hasty.[7]

**Evidence:**

_____

_____

_____

---

[2]PrepTest 40, Sec. 1, Q 5

[3]PrepTest 40, Sec. 1, Q 6

[4]PrepTest 40, Sec. 1, Q 12

[5]PrepTest 40, Sec. 1, Q 16

[6]PrepTest 40, Sec. 3, Q 8

[7]PrepTest 40, Sec. 3, Q 20

7. The number of applications for admission reported by North American Ph.D. programs in art history has declined in each of the last four years. We can conclude from this that interest among recent North American college and university graduates in choosing art history as a career has declined in the last four years.[8]

**Evidence:**

_____

_____

_____

8. Air traffic controllers and nuclear power plant operators are not allowed to work exceptionally long hours, because to do so would jeopardize lives. Yet physicians in residency training are typically required to work 80-hour weeks. The aforementioned restrictions on working exceptionally long hours should also be applied to resident physicians, since they too are engaged in work of a life-or-death nature.[9]

**Evidence:**

_____

_____

_____

9. Studies have shown that specialty sports foods contain exactly the same nutrients in the same quantities as do common foods from the grocery store. Moreover, sports foods cost from two to three times more than regular foods. So very few athletes would buy sports foods were it not for expensive advertising campaigns.[10]

**Evidence:**

_____

_____

_____

10. Traditionally, students at Kelly University have evaluated professors on the last day of class. But some professors at Kelly either do not distribute the paper evaluation forms or do so selectively, and many students cannot attend the last day of class. Soon, students will be able to use school computers to evaluate their professors at any time during the semester. Therefore, evaluations under the new system will accurately reflect the distribution of student opinion about teaching performance.[11]

**Evidence:**

_____

_____

_____

[8]PrepTest 40, Sec. 3, Q 26

[9]PrepTest 46, Sec. 2, Q 10

[10]PrepTest 46, Sec. 2, Q 25

[11]PrepTest 46, Sec. 3, Q 17

## Explanations

1. Psychologist: There are theories that posit completely different causal mechanisms from those posited by Freudian psychological theory and that are more successful at predicting human behavior. (Therefore,) <Freudian theories of behavior, no matter how suggestive or complex they are, ought to be abandoned in favor of these other theories.>[12]

The Keyword "therefore" directs you right to the conclusion. To find the evidence, all you need to do is ask yourself why the author recommends abandoning Freud's behavior theory.

**Evidence:** Some non-Freudian theories are better at predicting human behavior than Freudian theory.

Don't worry if you didn't phrase the evidence exactly like I did. As long as you got the gist of it, you're on the right track.

2. Skeletal remains of early humans indicate clearly that our ancestors had fewer dental problems than we have. (So,) <most likely, the diet of early humans was very different from ours.>[13]

The conclusion Keyword in this argument is "so," which points to the conclusion that early humans ate differently than we do.

**Evidence:** Our ancestors had fewer dental problems than we do.

3. Several legislators claim that the public finds many current movies so violent as to be morally offensive. (However,) <these legislators have misrepresented public opinion.> In a survey conducted by a movie industry guild, only 17 percent of respondents thought that movies are overly violent, and only 3 percent found any recent movie morally offensive. These low percentages are telling, because the respondents see far more current movies than does the average moviegoer.[14]

The author presents a claim in the first sentence and then signals his disagreement by using the word "however." He concludes that legislators misrepresented public opinion about current movies and uses a survey to defend his conclusion.

**Evidence:** A movie industry guild survey found that 17% of respondents found movies overly violent and 3% said any recent movie is morally offensive.

---

[12]PrepTest 40, Sec. 1, Q 5

[13]PrepTest 40, Sec. 1, Q 6

[14]PrepTest 40, Sec. 1, Q 12

4. In countries where government officials are neither
   selected by free elections nor open to criticism by a free
   press, the lives of citizens are controlled by policies they
   have had no role in creating. (This is why) <such countries
   are prone to civil disorder,> in spite of the veneer of calm
   such countries often present to a visitor. When people do
   not understand the purpose of the restrictions placed on
   their behavior, they have a greater tendency to engage in
   civil disorder as an expression of their frustration.[15]

Remember, evidence answers why the conclusion is so. When the author says "This is why,"
she is pointing to the conclusion. In this case, the conclusion splits the evidence. The first
sentence states that citizens have no input in governmental policies in despotic countries. The
last sentence explains that people who don't understand the policies that control their lives
tend to participate in civil disorder.

**Evidence:** Citizens in these countries have no input in policies that control their lives and they
don't understand the purpose of the laws that control them.

5. Everyone likes repertory theater. Actors like it because
   playing different roles each night decreases their level of
   boredom. Stagehands like it because changing sets every
   night means more overtime and, thus, higher pay.
   Theater managers like it because, if plays that reflect
   audience demand are chosen for production, most
   performances generate large revenues. (It is evident,)
   (therefore,) that <more theaters should change to repertory.>[16]

The author recommends that more theaters should change to repertory because everyone likes
it. He then lists different groups who like repertory theater and their rationale for enjoying it.

**Evidence:** Everyone likes repertory theater, although for different reasons.

6. Investment banker: Democracies require free-market
   capitalist economies, because a more controlled
   economy is incompatible with complete
   democracy. But history shows that repressive
   measures against certain capitalistic developments
   are required during the transition from a
   totalitarian regime to a democracy. (Thus,) <people
   who bemoan the seemingly anticapitalistic
   measures certain governments are currently taking
   are being hasty.>[17]

The investment banker concludes that complaints about certain governments' anticapitalistic
actions are premature. Why? Check the evidence statement below.

---

[15]PrepTest 40, Sec. 1, Q 16
[16]PrepTest 40, Sec. 3, Q 8
[17]PrepTest 40, Sec. 3, Q 20

**Evidence:** Anticapitalist measures are necessary during the transition from a totalitarian regime to a democracy.

7. The number of applications for admission reported by North American Ph.D. programs in art history has declined in each of the last four years. (We can conclude from this) that <interest among recent North American college and university graduates in choosing art history as a career has declined in the last four years.>[18]

The author directs you right to the conclusion with the Keywords "We can conclude from this." The author's conclusion is that interest in art history as a career is down among North American graduates. He bases this on the evidence that admission applications for North American doctoral programs in art history are down.

**Evidence:** Application numbers are down for North American Ph.D. art history programs over the past four years.

8. Air traffic controllers and nuclear power plant operators are not allowed to work exceptionally long hours, because to do so would jeopardize lives. Yet physicians in residency training are typically required to work 80-hour weeks. <The aforementioned restrictions on working exceptionally long hours should also be applied to resident physicians,> (since) they too are engaged in work of a life-or-death nature.[19]

Although the author doesn't use any conclusion Keywords, "since" points to the evidence in the argument that supports the statement preceding it. The author supports the conclusion that long work hours should be limited for resident physicians just like they are air traffic controllers and nuclear power plant operators with the evidence that they all face life-or-death issues at work.

**Evidence:** The work of residents, like air traffic controllers and nuclear plant operators, involves life-or-death decisions and responsibilities.

9. Studies have shown that specialty sports foods contain exactly the same nutrients in the same quantities as do common foods from the grocery store. Moreover, sports foods cost from two to three times more than regular foods. (So) <very few athletes would buy sports foods were it not for expensive advertising campaigns.>[20]

This argument determines that athletes buy sports foods because of the advertising. The author's rationale is that sports foods have the same nutrition as traditional groceries, but cost more.

---

[18]PrepTest 40, Sec. 3, Q 26
[19]PrepTest 46, Sec. 2, Q 10
[20]PrepTest 46, Sec. 2, Q 25

**Evidence:** Specialty sports foods have the same nutrients as common food from the grocery, yet they cost two to three times more.

10.  Traditionally, students at Kelly University have evaluated professors on the last day of class. But some professors at Kelly either do not distribute the paper evaluation forms or do so selectively, and many students cannot attend the last day of class. Soon, students will be able to use school computers to evaluate their professors at any time during the semester. (Therefore,) <evaluations under the new system will accurately reflect the distribution of student opinion about teaching performance.>[21]

The author predicts that the new evaluation system will be more accurate than the traditional process for a number of reasons. She cites problems with the paper system and notes that the new process will always be accessible.

**Evidence:** There are problems with the traditional policy of paper teacher evaluations distributed on the last day of class. Students will soon be able to complete teacher evaluations anytime via the computer.

## EFFECTIVELY ANALYZING ARGUMENTS EQUALS LSAT SUCCESS

You now have a good idea about what arguments are and how to identify their components. This is very important, because they form the foundation of the entire Kaplan Method for argument-based questions. You may be worried at this point that circling the Keywords and bracketing the conclusions will be too time-consuming to be useful on test day. But with practice, you'll soon find that marking up arguments becomes a natural and automatic part of your approach to Logical Reasoning. And as you'll see throughout the book, being able to quickly and effectively analyze an argument will significantly raise your LSAT score.

---

[21]PrepTest 46, Sec. 3, Q 17

# CHAPTER 3

# FORMAL LOGIC

If the economy is weak, then prices remain constant although unemployment rises. But unemployment rises only if investment decreases. Fortunately, investment is not decreasing.[1]

Formal logic, like this example, is prevalent on the LSAT, and your ability to identify and interpret formal logic statements is imperative for your success. Over the years, I've seen how a stimulus like this one can intimidate and frustrate students. Such formal logic appears in Logical Reasoning stimuli as well as in Logic Game rules. In this chapter, I will focus on helping you recognize and translate formal logic in the Logical Reasoning section.

Recognizing and translating formal logic is a skill that you use in Step 2 of the Kaplan Method for Logical Reasoning when you untangle the stimulus and extract information from it. You also use it in Step 3 when formulating a prediction for the correct answer. As you hone this skill, you'll be able to take complex statements and transform them into a more manageable format. A strong command of formal logic is critical to improving your accuracy and efficiency on the LSAT, and in this chapter I'll show you how to achieve it.

---

[1]PrepTest 28, Sec. 1, Q 20

Rather than something tested on the LSAT, formal logic is one of the tools you use to help you answer questions on the LSAT. Like a carpenter uses and loves his favorite hammer, use and love your formal logic!

# CONDITIONAL STATEMENTS
## Necessary vs. Sufficient

Formal logic is all about conditional if-then statements. Every LSAT formal logic statement includes a sufficient condition and a necessary condition. Don't let these terms intimidate you; just use their normal definitions: "Sufficient" means "enough by itself" and "necessary" means "you need it." If a sufficient condition occurs, then the necessary condition will result. If the necessary condition occurs, the sufficient condition could result but is not required. Take a look at a basic example of a formal logic statement:

If you are taking a test, then you turn off your cell phone.

I will discuss the language that signals sufficient and necessary clauses later in this chapter. For now, understand that the sufficient condition is taking a test. What happens when you take a test? You get the necessary condition every time: your cell phone is turned off. Now, what if you turn off your cell phone? Can you identify the necessary result? Does a turned off cell phone mean you are taking a test? No, you could be taking a test but you don't have to be. You could be watching a movie, taking a nap, riding in a car, or doing absolutely nothing. Therefore, turning off your cell phone is not sufficient to know the necessary result.

Now, you may be thinking of a time when you took a test with your cell phone on and want to contradict the formal logic statement. Don't. On the LSAT, the formal logic statement says exactly what it means. The way a statement appears on the test dictates its meaning. The test makers do not want you to supplement the text.

## If-then Statements

The most basic form of formal logic is an if-then statement. If X happens, then Y will result. The "if" (or the X) part of the statement is the sufficient condition, and the "then" (or the Y) part of the statement is the necessary condition. In other words, the "if" (X) part of the statement is sufficient for you to know that the "then" (Y) part of the statement will result. Therefore, you must be able to break statements down into their sufficient and necessary elements.

Consider the following example, and see whether you can identify the sufficient and necessary components:

If Riley travels to Europe, then he must have a valid passport.

The "if" identifies the "Riley travels to Europe" as the sufficient phrase, and the "then" identifies the "he must have a valid passport" as the necessary phrase. In other words, a valid passport is *necessary* for Riley's trip to Europe. Also, just knowing that Riley takes a trip to Europe is *sufficient* for you to know that he has a valid passport.

However, if Riley has a valid passport, does he have to take a trip to Europe? Not necessarily. He may or may not. Just knowing he has a valid passport does not tell us whether he takes a trip to Europe or anywhere. The valid passport is necessary, but not sufficient, for Riley to take a trip to Europe. Again, the result is necessary for the condition to occur, but the result is never sufficient by itself to know whether the condition must occur or has already.

## Conditional Statements Practice

To help you better understand the idea of sufficient and necessary conditions, consider the following example:

Scott wants to go to a music festival and a ticket costs $100.

Each of the following statements tells you something that is sufficient (but not necessary), necessary (but not sufficient), or both sufficient and necessary in order for Scott to purchase the ticket. Consider each statement and label it accordingly.

Scott has $65.    _____

Scott has $140.    _____

Scott has $100.    _____

Here are the answers:

Scott has $65. *Necessary, but not sufficient.* If Scott doesn't have at least $65, there's no way he can have $100. $65 is not enough for him to buy the ticket, so it's not sufficient.

Scott has $140. *Sufficient, but not necessary.* He could buy the ticket and plenty more. So, it's sufficient for Scott to have $140, but it's not necessary that Scott has so much in order to get the ticket.

Scott has $100. *Sufficient and necessary.* Knowing that Scott has $100 means he has enough to buy a ticket. It's also necessary. If he doesn't have $100, he can't buy the ticket.

# RECOGNIZING FORMAL LOGIC

Before you can use formal logic to help you untangle a stimulus, you must be able to recognize it on the test. An if-then statement is the most common form of formal logic, but formal logic can be stated in a variety of ways using different terms. On the Logical Reasoning section of the test, you must be prepared to recognize formal logic whenever it's used and in whatever form it is presented. But don't worry: there are Keywords to help you identify formal logic and determine which part of the statement is sufficient and which part is necessary. The following list of sufficient and necessary terms is by no means comprehensive, but it provides some of the most common indicators.

| If this happens . . . | → | Then this is the result |
|:---:|:---:|:---:|
| X<br>Sufficient words | → | Y<br>Necessary words |
| If<br>Any<br>All<br>Each<br>Every<br>When(ever)<br>Always<br>No<br>None<br>Never | → | Then<br>Only<br>Only if<br>Unless<br>Not/Never/No . . . unless<br>Not/Never/No . . . without<br>Necessary/Needed/Required<br>Effect<br>Result<br>Must |

Please note that the order of the terms in a statement does not indicate whether a term is sufficient or necessary. When evaluating a formal logic statement, always use the Keywords and the language of the terms to determine which clause is sufficient and which is necessary.

For example, "Every Friday night we order pizza for dinner" translates the same way as "We order pizza for dinner every Friday night." The sufficient term, "every Friday night," can appear in the beginning or at the end of the sentence. In either case, "every Friday night" is still the sufficient term.

Also, the chronology in which things happen doesn't determine the sufficient and necessary conditions. For example, consider the following statement: In order for it to rain, there must be clouds.

Even though the clouds appear in the sky before it starts raining, clouds are not the sufficient condition. Because clouds are necessary for rain, knowing that it is raining is sufficient for you to know that there are clouds.

# COMMON FORMAL LOGIC TRANSLATIONS

Once you recognize that a statement includes formal logic, your next job is to translate it into a formal logic "equation." There are five basic statement types in which the X is always the sufficient condition and Y is always the necessary result. Although they use different terminology, each of these statement types means the same thing. They are logically equivalent, and you can write them using a shorthand equation to help you quickly identify the X and Y terms.

For example, look at the first statement in the following table: If you apply to law school, then you have to take the LSAT. This is the most straightforward type of formal logic statement, as it is written in "if-then" language. The X term, the sufficient element, is applying to law school. The Y term, the necessary result, is taking the LSAT.

| Formal Logic in Text Form | Formal Logic Equation |
|---|---|
| *If* you apply to law school, then you have to take the LSAT. | If X, then Y |
| *All* students who apply to law school have to take the LSAT. | All X are Y |
| *Only* students who have taken the LSAT can apply to law school. | Only Y are X |
| You can apply to law school *only if* you have taken the LSAT. | X only if Y |
| No student can apply to law school *unless* he or she has taken the LSAT. | No X unless Y |

Now look at the second statement: All students who apply to law school have to take the LSAT. What word tells you this is a formal logic statement? Check the list of indicators for sufficient and necessary words, and you will find "All." Whenever you see "all," translate the statement to the corresponding formal logic equation. Here, it's "All X are Y." The purpose of this step is to specifically identify the X and the Y. What are they in this case? The X is "students who apply to law school," and the Y is "have to take the LSAT."

Now try the next statement: Only students who have taken the LSAT can apply to law school. The "Only" dictates that this is a formal logic statement. Since "only" is a necessary word, what follows "only" is the necessary term. When you see "only," translate the statement to the matching formal logic equation which is "Only Y are X." Again, "taken the LSAT" is the Y and "apply to law school" is the X.

The next statement is a little trickier in that "X only if Y" looks like it combines a sufficient (if) and a necessary (only) indicator. The general rule is easy though. "Only if" combined is always just a necessary term and the related formal logic equation is "X only if Y." Once again, the X is "apply to law school" and the Y is "taken the LSAT." What if you saw the same language on the test but the order was different? Only if you take the LSAT can you apply to law school. Would that change the identity of the terms? Absolutely not. Taking the LSAT still follows "only if" and remains the necessary condition. Just reorder the phrases to return to an "X only if Y" format.

The final statement, the one with "unless," is always the hardest for my students. Start with the basics. "Unless" tells you this is a formal logic statement and what follows "unless" is the necessary term. So the Y is "taken the LSAT." The matching formal logic equation is "No X unless Y." Here is where an "unless" statement differs from the other formal logic translations. To determine the X, you must negate the phrase in the text. In this case, negate the "no" in "no student applies to law school" and you get "student applies to law school." "Student applies to law school" is the X.

Try a few variations of "No student applies to law school unless he or she has taken the LSAT" to cement your understanding. What if the sentence said, "Unless he or she has taken the LSAT, no student applies to law school?" The "unless" identifies it as formal logic, and specifically signals the necessary condition. So change the order of the phrases. Remember, "No X unless Y" is the same as "If X, then Y."

Regardless of the formal logic words and format, each statement yields the same X and Y equations. You must be able to identify formal logic when you see it, and you must be able to translate the text into the corresponding formal logic equation and identify the X and the Y terms.

## Creating the "If X, then Y" Statement

Once you know the X and Y terms, your next step is to translate the statement into the basic "If X, then Y" format. When you write in this formal logic shorthand, use an arrow (→) to indicate "then." The phrase to the left of the arrow is the sufficient condition. The phrase to the right of the arrow is the necessary result. You can also drop "if" so you have less to write down.

Here are some examples from the sample formal logic statements you've seen in this chapter. Remember, first you identify formal logic language in the text. Next, you translate the statement into a formal logic equation and identify the X and Y terms. Then you create the basic X → Y statement.

| Formal Logic in Text Form | Formal Logic Equation | Formal Logic Shorthand |
|---|---|---|
| If you are taking a test, then you must turn off your cell phone. | If X, then Y | Taking test → cell phone off |
| If Riley travels to Europe, then he must have a valid passport. | If X, then Y | Europe → have passport |

(continued)

| Formal Logic in Text Form | Formal Logic Equation | Formal Logic Shorthand |
|---|---|---|
| If you apply to law school, then you take the LSAT. | If X, then Y | Apply to law school → take LSAT |
| All students who apply to law school have to take the LSAT. | All X are Y | |
| Only students who have taken the LSAT are applying to law school. | Only Y are X | |
| You are applying to law school only if you have taken the LSAT. | X only if Y | |
| No student applies to law school unless he or she has taken the LSAT. | No X unless Y | |

## Formal Logic Translation Practice

Here's the stimulus that opened the chapter. Take a minute and try to work through the translation process and determine the X → Y statements.

> If the economy is weak, then prices remain constant although unemployment rises. But unemployment rises only if investment decreases. Fortunately, investment is not decreasing.[2]

1. Identify Formal Logic Language

2. Determine the Matching Equation(s)

3. Translate the Formal Logic

Here are the answers:

1. Identify Formal Logic Language

Note the "if-then" language in the first sentence and "only if" in the second sentence. Move forward with those two sentences.

2. Determine the Matching Equations

"If the economy is weak, then prices remain constant although unemployment rises." The first sentence uses the basic "If X, then Y" format.

---

[2]PrepTest 28, Sec. 1, Q 20

"But unemployment rises *only if* investment decreases." The formal logic equation represented in the second sentence is "X only if Y".

3. Translate the Formal Logic

Now you want to translate the formal logic into a shorthand version of the X → Y statement:

Economy weak → prices constant and unemployment rises

Unemployment rises → investment decreases

I know it seems like a lot of work to untangle a Logical Reasoning stimulus. Keep in mind that the more you practice with formal logic, the faster you will be able to spot and translate the statements.

There's just one more step to complete a formal logic translation: forming the contrapositive.

# FORMING THE CONTRAPOSITIVE
## Simple If-Then Statements

After you've translated a statement into X → Y form, you will then write its contrapositive, a confusing-sounding aspect of formal logic that's actually quite straightforward.

A contrapositive is the logical equivalent of any conditional formal logic statement with the sufficient and necessary terms reversed and negated. Put simply, the contrapositive is equally valid as the original statement and is nothing more than another way to express the truth of the original statement. The reason you write the contrapositive is to complete your understanding of the formal logic statement. The X → Y statement provides a simpler version of the sentence, and the contrapositive is the only other statement you can know to be true about the statement.

While formal logic language can appear in any Logical Reasoning question type, it is most prevalent in Inference, Parallel Reasoning, and Principle questions. So, for example, an Inference question will ask you to identify the answer that *must be true* based on the information in the stimulus. If the stimulus is presented in formal logic terms, there are only two things that must be true from it, the X → Y statement and its contrapositive. You'll have an opportunity to work with formal logic in the context of different question types in Part II. For now, I'll show you how to form a statement's contrapositive.

Start with the statement in X → Y form

    If you apply to law school, then you take the LSAT.

    Apply to law school → take the LSAT

Then reverse and negate the sufficient and necessary terms.

Don't take LSAT → can't apply to law school

That's all you have to do in this case to form the contrapositive. One step and you're done. Now you try one. I'll give you a statement and then you reverse and negate it to form the contrapositive.

If you are taking a test, then you turn off your cell phone.

Translation: _____

Contrapositive: _____

Here's the answer:

Translation: Taking test → cell phone off

Contrapositive: Cell phone not off → not taking test

Did you get the right answer? If you did, congratulations! If not, don't worry. You'll have plenty of opportunities to practice. But remember, this is an important fundamental skill to master by test day. Rest assured that the test makers will design wrong answers to catch students who cannot correctly interpret and contrapose formal logic statements.

Before I go on, here's a big caution: Never ever reverse without negating or negate without reversing. Doing so confuses the sufficient and necessary terms in the rule and will lead straight to wrong answers. With that in mind, let me move on to complex "if-then" statements.

## Complex If-then Statements: Change "and" to "or"

When either of the clauses in a formal logic rule has more than one term linked with either "and" or "or," you have one more step in making the contrapositive. To see how it works, consider the following example:

If a play is by Shakespeare, then it is by a famous writer *and* it is by an English writer.

You can translate the formal logic statement this way: Play by Shakespeare → famous writer and English writer

Now, imagine you see a play and ask a friend, "Who wrote it?" Your friend answers, "I don't know the writer's name, but I know that he was relatively unknown." What can you infer? Right! The play isn't by Shakespeare.

Try it another way. This time, when you ask your friend who wrote the play, she says, "I don't know the writer's name, but I know he was Italian." Again, you can safely conclude that you're not looking at a work of Shakespeare.

Now put those two inferences together and compare them to the original statement. Here, you form the contrapositives by reversing and negating the terms and by changing "and" to "or." So, the contrapositive would be: Not famous writer or not an English writer → not a Play by Shakespeare

There are different ways to write the negation of a term. You could use words, such as "no", "don't", and "can't". You could also strike through the negative term or use a tilde (~). Use the symbols that are clearest to you, but whatever you choose to do, do it consistently.

That's what you need to know to form the correct contrapositives of any formal logic rule you will encounter on the LSAT. So remember the rules for forming the contrapositive of either a simple or complex formal logic statement.

## TO FORM THE CONTRAPOSITIVE

**STEP 1** Reverse and negate the sufficient and necessary terms.

**STEP 2** If needed, change "and" to "or," or vice versa.

## Using Contrapositives to Make Deductions

You must be clear on the deductions you can and can't make based on formal logic statements. Look at this statement:

Every Friday night we order pizza for dinner.

For this statement, the matching formal logic equation is "Every X is Y." So Friday night is the sufficient term (X) and pizza for dinner is the necessary term (Y). Knowing that it is Friday night is sufficient to know that pizza will be ordered for dinner. Knowing that pizza was ordered for dinner means it could be Friday, but it doesn't have to be. So here is the information I know:

**Statement:** Every Friday night we order pizza for dinner.

**Equation:** Every X is Y

**Shorthand:** Friday night → pizza dinner (X → Y)

**Contrapositive:** Not pizza dinner → not Friday night (Not Y → Not X)

Given that the previous statements are true, which one of the following statements must also be true?

> If it is not Friday night, then we don't eat pizza for dinner.
> If we eat pizza for dinner, then it is Friday night.
> If we don't have pizza for dinner, then it is not Friday night.

The third statement, the contrapositive, is the only one of the three that you can infer from the original statement. The first statement negates the terms without reversing. The second statement reverses the terms without negating. The terms "not Friday night" and "pizza for dinner" are not sufficient terms, so you can't know the necessary result if they happen.

I'll walk you through one more example. Read the following statement:

> If Jonathan votes, then he must be registered and 18 or older.

The "if" identifies Jonathan voting as the sufficient part of the statement. Jonathan voting is sufficient to know that he must be registered and he must be 18 or older. Being registered and 18 or older is the necessary result of the sufficient clause. Can you reverse the terms and say, "If Jonathan is registered and 18 or older, then he votes?" No. He could vote under those circumstances, but he doesn't have to.

So here's how you would work through this statement on the LSAT:

> If Jonathan votes, he is registered and he is 18 or older.

## Step 1. Identify Formal Logic Language

If Jonathan votes, he is registered and he is 18 or older.

## Step 2. Determine the Matching Equation

If X, then Y and Z

## Step 3. Translate the Formal Logic

Jonathan votes → registered and 18+ (X → Y and Z)

## Step 4. Form the Contrapositive

Not registered or not 18+ → Jonathan does not vote (No Y or no Z → no X)

So from the original statement and the contrapositive, you know what happens if Jonathan votes, and you know what the result is if Jonathan is not registered or if he's not 18 or older. That's it. You can't know the result if Jonathan does not vote. You also can't know the result if Jonathan is registered and he's 18 or older. Again, they are not sufficient terms.

# FORMAL LOGIC REVIEW

I've introduced a lot of material in this chapter, so here's a summary of the important points to remember regarding formal logic statements.

First, identify formal logic language in the stimulus. Then, determine the matching equation. Translate the statement to identify the X and the Y terms and form the X → Y statement. Finally, form the contrapositive by reversing and negating the sufficient and necessary terms, (and if needed, change "and" to "or," or vice versa).

Once again, return to the stimulus introduced at the beginning of this chapter to see this process in action.

> If the economy is weak, then prices remain constant
> although unemployment rises. But unemployment rises
> only if investment decreases. Fortunately, investment is
> not decreasing.[3]

You'll recall the first three steps of the transformation:

### Step 1. Identify Formal Logic Language

The if-then language in sentence one and the "only if" in sentence two signal formal logic.

### Step 2. Determine the Matching Equations

"If the economy is weak, then prices remain constant although unemployment rises." The first sentence is presented in the basic "If X, then Y" format.

"But unemployment rises *only* if investment decreases." The formal logic equation represented in the second sentence is "X only if Y."

### Step 3. Translate the Formal Logic

Now, translate the formal logic into a shorthand version of the X → Y statement:

Economy weak → prices constant and unemployment rises

Unemployment rises → investment decreases

### Step 4. Form the Contrapositive

Prices not constant or unemployment not rise → economy not weak

Investment does not decrease → unemployment does not rise

In the final sentence of the original stimulus, you are told that investment is not decreasing. So you can be assured from sentence two's contrapositive that unemployment does not rise. Therefore, you can use sentence one's contrapositive to determine that the economy is not weak.

Again, you've covered a lot of information here. The following two Drills will help you practice your formal logic skills.

---

[3]PrepTest 28, Sec. 1, Q 20

# DRILL: PRACTICING FORMAL LOGIC

Read the following statements, then underline the terms that indicate formal logic, identify the matching equation, write the formal logic translation, and then form the contrapositive. The first one has been done for you.

1. Statement: We have pizza for dinner <u>every</u> Friday night.

   Formal Logic Equation: Every X is Y

   Formal Logic Shorthand: Friday night → pizza for dinner

   Contrapositive: Not pizza for dinner → not Friday night

2. Statement: All employees must wash their hands.

   Formal Logic Equation: _____

   Formal Logic Shorthand: _____

   Contrapositive: _____

3. Statement: Use this product only if the seal is intact.

   Formal Logic Equation: _____

   Formal Logic Shorthand: _____

   Contrapositive: _____

4. Statement: Don't open the test unless the proctor says so.

   Formal Logic Equation: _____

   Formal Logic Shorthand: _____

   Contrapositive: _____

5. Statement: All children under 13 must be accompanied by an adult.

   Formal Logic Equation: _____

   Formal Logic Shorthand: _____

   Contrapositive: _____

6. Statement: Do not eat this product if you are allergic to peanuts.

   Formal Logic Equation: _____

   Formal Logic Shorthand: _____

   Contrapositive: _____

7.  Statement: Put your pencil down when the proctor calls time.

    Formal Logic Equation: _____

    Formal Logic Shorthand: _____

    Contrapositive: _____

8.  Statement: She drinks hot chocolate only when it is cold outside.

    Formal Logic Equation: _____

    Formal Logic Shorthand: _____

    Contrapositive: _____

9.  Statement: If you want to reach the operator or leave a message, press "0."

    Formal Logic Equation: _____

    Formal Logic Shorthand: _____

    Contrapositive: _____

10. Statement: Each graduate must wear a cap and gown.

    Formal Logic Equation: _____

    Formal Logic Shorthand: _____

    Contrapositive: _____

11. Statement: The President cannot go anywhere unless the secret service goes with her.

    Formal Logic Equation: _____

    Formal Logic Shorthand: _____

    Contrapositive: _____

12. Statement: No service without shirt and shoes.

    Formal Logic Equation: _____

    Formal Logic Shorthand: _____

    Contrapositive: _____

13. Statement: Only public libraries lend DVDs for free.

    Formal Logic Equation: _____

    Formal Logic Shorthand: _____

    Contrapositive: _____

14. Statement: Larry has tickets to each home football game.

    Formal Logic Equation: _____

    Formal Logic Shorthand: _____

    Contrapositive: _____

15. Statement: Whenever you're ready, give me a call.

    Formal Logic Equation: _____

    Formal Logic Shorthand: _____

    Contrapositive: _____

16. Statement: No employee took vacation in February.

    Formal Logic Equation: _____

    Formal Logic Shorthand: _____

    Contrapositive: _____

17. Statement: Charlie eats strawberries unless he eats bananas.

    Formal Logic Equation: _____

    Formal Logic Shorthand: _____

    Contrapositive: _____

18. Statement: Charlie does not eat strawberries unless he eats bananas.

    Formal Logic Equation: _____

    Formal Logic Shorthand: _____

    Contrapositive: _____

19. Statement: Scott drinks coffee and reads the newspaper every morning.

    Formal Logic Equation: _____

    Formal Logic Shorthand: _____

    Contrapositive: _____

20. Statement: Airplane travel requires a photo ID.

    Formal Logic Equation: _____

    Formal Logic Shorthand: _____

    Contrapositive: _____

## Explanations

1.  Statement: We have pizza for dinner every Friday night.

    Formal Logic Equation: Every X is Y

    Formal Logic Shorthand: Friday night → pizza for dinner

    Contrapositive: Not pizza for dinner → not Friday night

2.  Statement: <u>All</u> employees <u>must</u> wash their hands.

    Formal Logic Equation: All X must Y

    Formal Logic Shorthand: Employee → wash hands

    Contrapositive: Don't wash hands → not an employee

3.  Statement: Use this product <u>only if</u> the seal is intact.

    Formal Logic Equation: X only if Y

    Formal Logic Shorthand: Use product → seal is intact

    Contrapositive: Seal is not intact → don't use product

4.  Statement: <u>Don't</u> open the test <u>unless</u> the proctor says so.

    Formal Logic Equation: No X unless Y

    Formal Logic Shorthand: Test open → proctor says to open it

    Contrapositive: Proctor does not say to open the test → the test is not open

5.  Statement: <u>All</u> children under 13 <u>must</u> be accompanied by an adult.

    Formal Logic Equation: All X must Y

    Formal Logic Shorthand: Under 13 → with an adult

    Contrapositive: Not with an adult → not under 13

6.  Statement: Do not eat this product <u>if</u> you are allergic to peanuts.

    Formal Logic Equation: If X, then not Y

    Formal Logic Shorthand: Allergic to peanuts → do not eat this product

    Contrapositive: Eat this product → not allergic to peanuts

7.  Statement: Put your pencil down <u>when</u> the proctor calls time.

    Formal Logic Equation: If X, then Y

    Formal Logic Shorthand: Proctor calls time → put your pencil down

    Contrapositive: Pencil is not down → proctor has not called time

8.  Statement: She drinks hot chocolate <u>only when</u> it is cold outside.

    Formal Logic Equation: X only if Y

    Formal Logic Shorthand: Drinking hot chocolate → cold outside

    Contrapositive: Not cold outside → not drinking hot chocolate

9.  Statement: <u>If</u> you want to reach the operator or leave a message, press "0."

    Formal Logic Equation: If X or Y, then Z

    Formal Logic Shorthand: Operator or message → press "0"

    Contrapositive: Not press "0" → no operator and no message

10. Statement: <u>Each</u> graduate <u>must</u> wear a cap and gown to walk in the ceremony.

    Formal Logic Equation: Each X must Y and Z

    Formal Logic Shorthand: Graduate → wear cap and gown to walk in the ceremony

    Contrapositive: Don't wear a cap or don't wear a gown → not a graduate

11. Statement: The President cannot go anywhere <u>unless</u> the secret service goes with her.

    Formal Logic Equation: No X unless Y

    Formal Logic Shorthand: President goes anywhere → secret service is with her

    Contrapositive: Secret service is not with her → President cannot go

12. Statement: <u>No</u> service <u>without</u> shirt and shoes.

    Formal Logic Equation: No X unless Y and Z

    Formal Logic Shorthand: Service → shirt and shoes

    Contrapositive: If no shirt or no shoes → no service

13. Statement: <u>Only</u> public libraries lend DVDs for free.

    Formal Logic Equation: Only Y are X

    Formal Logic Shorthand: DVD lent for free → public library

    Contrapositive: Not public library → DVD not lent for free

14. Statement: Larry has tickets to <u>each</u> home football game.

    Formal Logic Equation: If X, then Y

    Formal Logic Shorthand: Home football game → Larry has tickets

    Contrapositive: Larry does not have tickets → not home football game

15. Statement: <u>Whenever</u> you're ready, give me a call.

    Formal Logic Equation: If X, then Y

    Formal Logic Shorthand: Ready → call me

    Contrapositive: Don't call me → not ready

16. Statement: <u>No</u> employee took vacation in February.

    Formal Logic Equation: "No X are Y" becomes "If X, then not Y"

    Formal Logic Shorthand: Employee → no vacation in February

    Contrapositive: Vacation in February → not an employee

17. Statement: Charlie eats strawberries <u>unless</u> he eats bananas.

    Formal Logic Equation: "X unless Y" becomes "If not X, then Y"

    Formal Logic Shorthand: No strawberries → bananas

    Contrapositive: No bananas → strawberries

18. Statement: Charlie does <u>not</u> eat strawberries <u>unless</u> he eats bananas.

    Formal Logic Equation: "No X unless Y" because "if X then Y"

    Formal Logic Shorthand: Strawberries → Bananas

    Contrapositive: no Bananas → no Strawberries

19. Statement: Scott drinks coffee and reads the newspaper <u>every</u> morning.

    Formal Logic Equation: Every X is Y and Z

    Formal Logic Shorthand: Morning → coffee and paper

    Contrapositive: Not coffee or not paper → not morning

20. Statement: Airplane travel <u>requires</u> a photo ID.

    Formal Logic Equation: X only if Y

    Formal Logic Shorthand: Airplane travel → photo ID

    Contrapositive: No photo ID → no airplane travel

# DRILL: IDENTIFYING FORMAL LOGIC AND FORMING CONTRAPOSITIVES

The following stimuli appeared on previously released LSATs. Underline the formal logic indicators. Then, write out the formal logic statements and form their contrapositives. Hint: Some stimuli may have more than one formal logic statement.

1.  If legislators are to enact laws that benefit constituents, they must be sure to consider what the consequences of enacting a proposed law will actually be. Contemporary legislatures fail to enact laws that benefit constituents. Concerned primarily with advancing their own political careers, legislators present legislation in polemical terms; this arouses in their colleagues either repugnance or enthusiasm for the legislation.[4]

2.  All works of art are beautiful and have something to teach us. Thus, since the natural world as a whole is both beautiful and instructive, it is a work of art.[5]

3.  Only people who are willing to compromise should undergo mediation to resolve their conflicts. Actual litigation should be pursued only when one is sure that one's position is correct. People whose conflicts are based on ideology are unwilling to compromise.[6]

4.  If Juan went to the party, it is highly unlikely that Maria would have enjoyed the party. But in fact it turned out that Maria did enjoy the party; therefore, it is highly unlikely that Juan was at the party.[7]

5.  Sonya: Anyone who lives without constant awareness of the fragility and precariousness of human life has a mind clouded by illusion. Yet those people who are perpetually cognizant of the fragility and precariousness of human life surely taint their emotional outlook on existence.[8]

6.  Philosopher: An action is morally good if it both achieves the agent's intended goal and benefits someone other than the agent.[9]

7.  Only experienced salespeople will be able to meet the company's selling quota. Thus, I must not count as an experienced salesperson, since I will be able to sell only half the quota.[10]

8.  Expert: What criteria distinguish addictive substances from nonaddictive ones? Some have suggested that any substance that at least some habitual users can cease to use is nonaddictive. However, if this is taken to be the sole criterion of nonaddictiveness, some substances that most medical experts classify as prime examples of addictive substances would be properly deemed nonaddictive. Any adequate set of criteria for determining a substance's addictiveness must embody the view, held by these medical experts, that a substance is addictive only if withdrawal from its habitual use causes most users extreme psychological and physiological difficulty.[11]

9.  Whoever murdered Jansen was undoubtedly in Jansen's office on the day of the murder, and both Samantha and Herbert were in Jansen's office on that day. If Herbert had committed the murder, the police would have found either his fingerprints or his footprints at the scene of the crime. But if Samantha was the murderer, she would have avoided leaving behind footprints or fingerprints. The police found fingerprints but no footprints at the scene of the crime. Since the fingerprints were not Herbert's, he is not the murderer. Thus Samantha must be the killer.[12]

10. Ecologists predict that the incidence of malaria will increase if global warming continues or if the use of pesticides is not expanded. But the use of pesticides is known to contribute to global warming, so it is inevitable that we will see an increase in malaria in the years to come.[13]

[4]PrepTest 50, Sec. 2, Q 14
[5]PrepTest 50, Sec. 4, Q 2
[6]PrepTest 50, Sec. 4, Q 10
[7]PrepTest 50, Sec. 4, Q 14
[8]PrepTest 50, Sec. 4, Q 15
[9]PrepTest 51, Sec. 1, Q 9

[10]PrepTest 51, Sec. 1, Q 20
[11]PrepTest 51, Sec. 3, Q 14
[12]PrepTest 51, Sec. 3, Q 20
[13]PrepTest 51, Sec. 3, Q 24

## Explanations

1. If legislators are to enact laws that benefit constituents, they <u>must</u> be sure to consider what the consequences of enacting a proposed law will actually be. Contemporary legislatures fail to enact laws that benefit constituents. Concerned primarily with advancing their own political careers, legislators present legislation in polemical terms; this arouses in their colleagues either repugnance or enthusiasm for the legislation.[14]

   Enact laws that benefit constituents → consider consequences of proposed law

   Don't consider consequences of proposed law → don't enact laws that benefit constituents

2. <u>All</u> works of art are beautiful and have something to teach us. Thus, since the natural world as a whole is both beautiful and instructive, it is a work of art.[15]

   Art → beautiful and teach us

   Not beautiful or not teach us → not art

3. <u>Only</u> people who are willing to compromise should undergo mediation to resolve their conflicts. Actual litigation should be pursued <u>only when</u> one is sure that one's position is correct. <u>People</u> whose conflicts are based on ideology are unwilling to compromise.[16]

   Undergo mediation → willing to compromise

   Not willing to compromise → not undergo mediation

   Litigation → position correct

   Position not correct → no litigation

   Conflict based on ideology → unwilling to compromise

   Willing to compromise → conflict not based on ideology

By connecting this string of logic, you can validly deduce the following:

Undergo mediation → willing to compromise → conflict not based on ideology

---

[14]PrepTest 50, Sec. 2, Q 14

[15]PrepTest 50, Sec. 4, Q 2

[16]PrepTest 50, Sec. 4, Q 10

4. <u>If</u> Juan went to the party, it is highly unlikely that Maria would have enjoyed the party. But in fact it turned out that Maria did enjoy the party; therefore, it is highly unlikely that Juan was at the party.[17]

| | | |
|---|---|---|
| Juan to party | → | Maria likely not enjoy party |
| Maria enjoy party | → | Juan likely not at party |

5. Sonya: <u>Anyone</u> who lives without constant awareness of the fragility and precariousness of human life has a mind clouded by illusion. Yet those <u>people</u> who are perpetually cognizant of the fragility and precariousness of human life surely taint their emotional outlook on existence.[18]

| | | |
|---|---|---|
| Live without constant awareness | → | mind clouded by illusion |
| Mind not clouded by illusion | → | live with constant awareness |

| | | |
|---|---|---|
| Live with constant awareness | → | taint emotional outlook |
| Don't taint emotional outlook | → | don't live with constant awareness |

By connecting this string of logic, you can validly deduce the following:

Don't taint emotional outlook → don't live with constant awareness → mind clouded by illusion

6. Philosopher: An action is morally good <u>if</u> it both achieves the agent's intended goal and benefits someone other than the agent.[19]

| | | |
|---|---|---|
| Action achieves intended goal and benefits someone else | → | action is morally good |
| Action not morally good | → | action doesn't achieve intended goal or doesn't benefit someone else |

7. <u>Only</u> experienced salespeople will be able to meet the company's selling quota. Thus, I must not count as an experienced salesperson, since I will be able to sell only half the quota.[20]

| | | |
|---|---|---|
| Meet sales quota | → | experienced salespeople |
| Not experienced sales people | → | does not meet sales quota |

---

[17]PrepTest 50, Sec. 4, Q 14
[18]PrepTest 50, Sec. 4, Q 15
[19]PrepTest 51, Sec. 1, Q 9
[20]PrepTest 51, Sec. 1, Q 20

8. Expert: What criteria distinguish addictive substances from nonaddictive ones? Some have suggested that any substance that at least some habitual users can cease to use is nonaddictive. However, if this is taken to be the sole criterion of nonaddictiveness, some substances that most medical experts classify as prime examples of addictive substances would be properly deemed nonaddictive. Any adequate set of criteria for determining a substance's addictiveness must embody the view, held by these medical experts, that a substance is addictive <u>only if</u> withdrawal from its habitual use causes most users extreme psychological and physiological difficulty.[21]

Addictive  →  withdrawal causes psychological and physiological difficulty in most users

Withdrawal does not cause psychological or physiological difficulty in most users  →  not addictive

9. Whoever murdered Jansen was undoubtedly in Jansen's office on the day of the murder, and both Samantha and Herbert were in Jansen's office on that day. <u>If</u> Herbert had committed the murder, the police would have found either his fingerprints or his footprints at the scene of the crime. But <u>if</u> Samantha was the murderer, she would have avoided leaving behind footprints or fingerprints. The police found fingerprints but no footprints at the scene of the crime. Since the fingerprints were not Herbert's, he is not the murderer. Thus Samantha must be the killer.[22]

Herbert did it  →  police would find his fingerprints or his footprints at the scene

Police find no fingerprints and no footprints from Herbert  →  Herbert did not do it

Samantha did it  →  she would leave no fingerprints and no footprints

Find fingerprints or footprints from Samantha  →  Samantha did not do it

Note: this is a tricky example with the "and" versus "or" in the second statement. Saying "If Samantha is the murderer then she would avoid leaving footprints or fingerprints" means that she would leave neither fingerprints nor footprints, so, that's why it's written as: Samantha did it ▢ she would leave no fingerprints *and* no footprints.

---

[21]PrepTest 51, Sec. 3, Q 14
[22]PrepTest 51, Sec. 3, Q 20

10. Ecologists predict that the incidence of malaria will increase <u>if</u> global warming continues or <u>if</u> the use of pesticides is not expanded. But the use of pesticides is known to contribute to global warming, so it is inevitable that we will see an increase in malaria in the years to come.[23]

| | | |
|---|---|---|
| Global warming continues or use of pesticides not expanded | → | incidence of malaria will increase |
| Incidence of malaria will not increase | → | global warming does not continue and use of pesticides not expanded |

---

[23]PrepTest 51, Sec. 3, Q 24

# PART II

# Logical
# Reasoning
# Question Types

# CHAPTER 4

# ASSUMPTION FAMILY OF QUESTIONS

The four question types that make up the Assumption family of questions (Assumption, Strengthen, Weaken, and Flaw) represent half of the points available in the two scored Logical Reasoning sections. So you can expect Assumption, Strengthen, Weaken, and Flaw questions to account for approximately 25 out of 50 scored Logical Reasoning questions, and 25 out of 100 total scored LSAT questions. As you can see, they're a big part of your score, so I'll get started!

## Family Members Linked by Arguments

The stimulus of any Assumption, Strengthen, Weaken, or Flaw question will always include an argument. To successfully answer these question types, you need to be able to break their arguments down to their core components: conclusion and evidence. Then, you identify and analyze the author's assumption, an unstated piece of evidence that links the evidence and the conclusion. In the following chapters, you will learn about the Assumption family of questions in greater depth. To provide some context, I'll show you how the questions are related before you begin to learn about each question type.

Consider the following stimulus:

> Companies wishing to boost sales of merchandise should use in-store displays to catch customers' attention. According to a marketing study, today's busy shoppers have less time for coupon-clipping and pay little attention to direct-mail advertising; instead, they make two-thirds of their buying decisions on the spot at the store.[1]

In this stimulus, the author presents an argument. He concludes that companies should use in-store displays to attract shoppers and increase sales because shoppers make their buying decisions in the store and not based on coupons and direct-mail advertising. Notice the mismatched terms: The conclusion talks about in-store displays, while the evidence refers to on-the-spot buying decisions. The assumption must connect these terms, so the author must assume that in-store displays will influence on-the-spot purchases.

I did not include a question because this stimulus presents an argument, while the question could be an Assumption, Strengthen, Weaken, or Flaw question. In fact, you could answer each question type with the information gleaned so far.

If the accompanying question to this stimulus asked for the author's assumption, you could predict that the correct answer will state something along the lines of "in-store displays impact in-store buying."

What if the question asked you to strengthen the argument—to make it more likely to happen? You could confirm the assumption or cite an example of customers buying on-the-spot because of the in-store displays.

How could you weaken the argument—to make it less likely to happen? You could say something like "in-store displays do not influence impulse buying," or you could provide an example of customers ignoring in-store displays.

Flaw questions ask you to identify the logical error the author makes in moving from the evidence to the conclusion. In this case, you could predict a faulty assumption and predict that the author has not made his case because he included no evidence that in-store displays affect impulse buying.

The point that I want you to take away from this is that by practicing these question types, you reinforce your ability to answer the other question types as well. Over the years, I have found that my students typically relate to one of the question types more than the others. If this turns out to be the case for you, start practicing with that question type and then bring your expertise to the other question types. In other words, focus on what you do best, especially in the initial stages of your practice, and then bring that momentum and skill to the rest of the questions.

After you have a chance to learn about the individual question types in the coming chapters, I'll give you an opportunity to review the Assumption family of questions together in one exercise. In the meantime, I'll introduce the first question type in this family: Assumption questions.

---

[1]PrepTest 46, Sec. 2, Q 13

# CHAPTER 5

# ASSUMPTION QUESTIONS

Assumption questions are the most important question type on the LSAT. You will see 6–8 scored assumption questions—sometimes more—on every test. Assumptions are also a key component of other question types, particularly Strengthen, Weaken, and Flaw. Therefore, your ability to identify the assumptions the authors make is critical for your success on test day.

## DEFINITION OF ASSUMPTION QUESTIONS

Assumption questions ask you to identify the unstated premise the author uses to move from the evidence he provides to his conclusion. In other words, you have to identify what the author is taking for granted—the assumption—in the argument.

Take a look at this example:

> Desserts are delicious.

> Therefore, chocolate cake is delicious.

The author concludes that chocolate cake is delicious based on evidence that desserts are delicious. The author's unstated assumption must logically connect them. So, in this case, the assumption is that chocolate cake is a dessert.

Some LSAT arguments may seem obvious like the previous example, or they may be longer and more complex. Regardless, your task remains the same: Identify the missing piece of the argument to bridge the gap between the evidence and the conclusion. Use the following example as a visual reference:

**Figure 5.1**

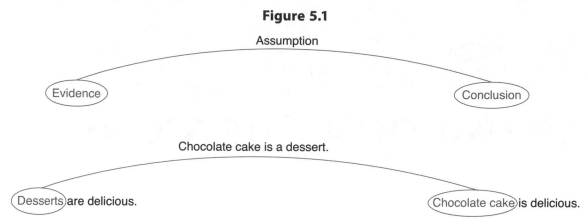

When you look for the author's assumption, it must come from the argument. This is what makes Assumption questions the most difficult Logical Reasoning question type for many students. Your comfort with the assumptions you make in everyday life is based on repetition and context. An LSAT assumption requires you to identify the author's thinking in constructing the argument and determine what is left unsaid.

Can you assume from the previous example that the author eats chocolate cake? No, not on the LSAT. Even though the author says chocolate cake is delicious, it doesn't mean that he eats it. After all, maybe the author is allergic to chocolate or on a diet. Whatever the case, you should never make your own assumptions on the LSAT; only identify the ones the authors must be making. Once you understand and accept that the assumption must remain within the scope of the author's argument, you will find it easier to identify assumptions.

## USE THE KAPLAN METHOD TO ANSWER ASSUMPTION QUESTIONS
### Identify the Question Type

There are certain words in the question stem that help you to recognize an Assumption question. Some of those include:

- Assumes
- Depends on
- Added to the premise
- Presupposes

The test makers word Assumption questions in a variety of ways, but here are some common Assumption question stems:

- Upon which one of the following assumptions does the author rely?
- Which one of the following, if added to the passage, will make the conclusion follow logically?

- The validity of the argument depends on which one of the following?
- The argument above is based on which one of the following assumptions?
- Her response depends on the presupposition that

As you read the question stem, look for indicator words to identify the question type. After you find Keywords, circle them in your test booklet. This gets you thinking about the question type and serves as a visual reminder of it to keep you from reading the question over and over again.

## Untangle the Stimulus

Once you identify a question as an Assumption question, your next step is to strategically read the argument in the stimulus and identify its components. Look for the conclusion by using Keywords or the one-sentence test, and bracket it for easy recall. (Go back to chapter 2 to review conclusion and evidence Keywords and the one-sentence test.) Then, determine and summarize the evidence the author uses to support the conclusion. Remember, don't get distracted by background information.

## Make a Prediction

Now, think about the assumption the author makes—the link between the evidence and conclusion. Ask yourself: What does the author take for granted to move from the evidence to the conclusion? What connects them? What words or concepts is the author comparing or treating as similar?

Making the assumption explicit by bridging the gap between the conclusion and evidence will improve your speed and accuracy—and help you score points—on test day. In the next section, I will show you how to use mismatched terms, ignored possibilities, the denial test, and formal logic to predict the author's assumption.

## Evaluate the Answer Choices

Finally, take your prediction and compare it to the answer choices. Find the choice that best matches your prediction—that one is your answer. Be sure to avoid comparing the answer choices to each other and picking an answer that is "true" or "sounds good." Those are common mistakes that I've seen my students make over the years, and I don't want you to fall into that trap.

Look again at the example from the beginning of this chapter:

Desserts are delicious.

Therefore, chocolate cake is delicious.

The author's assumption is "chocolate cake is a dessert" because it connects "chocolate cake" in the conclusion to "desserts" in the evidence. But what if you saw the following answer choice: Apple pie is delicious.

It may sound good because the evidence says that desserts are delicious and you know apple pie is a dessert. Apple pie may be your favorite dessert in the whole world, so you know that apple pie is delicious. But choosing this answer would be based on outside knowledge and the truth of the statement—which are not valid LSAT reasons. Apple pie is outside the scope of the argument and cannot be a part of the correct answer.

Like every other question on the LSAT, there is ALWAYS only one right answer. In fact, the test makers write wrong answers to be wrong for a particular reason. Think about why answers are wrong as you move through the practice drills. I will discuss common wrong answers used in Logical Reasoning in a later chapter. Understanding common wrong answers will help you quickly eliminate incorrect answer choices.

# THE KAPLAN METHOD IN ACTION

Now, it's time to practice the Kaplan Method by working through a few problems. In the process, I'll show you different techniques to help you identify the assumption in each argument.

## Mismatched Terms

The most powerful method to find the author's assumption is to identify the mismatched terms in the conclusion and evidence, and link them together. Consider this example:

Vanwilligan:  Some have argued that professional athletes receive unfairly high salaries. But in an unrestricted free market, such as the market these athletes compete in, salaries are determined by what someone else is willing to pay for their services. These athletes make enormous profits for their teams' owners, and that is why owners are willing to pay them extraordinary salaries. Thus the salaries they receive are fair.

Vanwilligan's conclusion follows logically if which one of the following is assumed?

(A)     The fairest economic system for a society is one in which the values of most goods and services are determined by the unrestricted free market.

(B)     If professional athletes were paid less for their services, then the teams for which they play would not make as much money.

(C)     The high level of competition in the marketplace forces the teams' owners to pay professional athletes high salaries.

(D)     Any salary that a team owner is willing to pay for the services of a professional athlete is a fair salary.

(E)     If a professional athlete's salary is fair, then that salary is determined by what an individual is willing to pay for the athlete's services in an unrestricted free market.[1]

## Step 1. Identify the Question Type

The word "assumed" tells you that this is an Assumption question.

## Step 2. Untangle the Stimulus

Find the components of the argument. The word "thus" reveals the conclusion, which states that salaries received by professional athletes are fair. Why are they fair? Because, Vanwilligan explains, the owners are willing to pay the salaries. Notice the gap between the conclusion and the evidence: The conclusion talks about fairness while the evidence talks about willingness to pay.

## Step 3. Make a Prediction

Look for terms that appear in the evidence but not the conclusion, and vice versa; the correct answer will link them together. In this case, the correct answer must connect the owners' willingness to pay high salaries (the evidence) with fairness (the conclusion). The new term that pops up in the conclusion ("fair") without mention in the evidence is usually the focus of the author's assumption.

---

[1]PrepTest 49, Sec. 2, Q 19

**Step 4. Evaluate the Answer Choices**

Choice (A) focuses on the fairest *economic system*, which is beyond the scope of this argument; this author merely concludes certain *salaries* are fair. Eliminate this choice.

Choice (B) discusses the result of paying athletes less money and does not address the issue of fairness, so this choice is out.

Choice (C) also ignores fairness and instead raises the irrelevant issue of why owners pay high salaries.

Choice (D) matches the prediction: If an owner is willing to pay the salary, then it must be fair. This is the correct answer.

Choice (E) uses a botched contrapositive by reversing the conditional terms without negating them. I hope you didn't fall for it. But if you did, don't worry. You'll have plenty of opportunity to practice and learn from your mistakes.

You can depend on the Kaplan Method to help you answer all Logical Reasoning question types regardless of their difficulty level. The important thing is to use the Method and to apply it consistently. Some students insist on using the Method only when they think they can't get the answer their own way. I can tell you from experience that is a big mistake. By using the Kaplan Method for every question, you will be prepared every time. If it is an easier question for you, you will just be able to work through the problem more quickly. Switching between different methods will only eat up your already short 35 minute time period.

## "Ignored" Possibilities

Another way the test makers present assumptions in arguments is the failure to consider—or mention—other possibilities (or other factors, explanations, causes, reasons, options, etc.) to their preferred possibility. Here's an example:

A certain credit-card company awards its customers bonus points for using its credit card. Customers can use accumulated points in the purchase of brand name merchandise by mail at prices lower than the manufacturers' suggested retail prices. At any given time, therefore, customers who purchase merchandise using the bonus points spend less than they would spend if they purchased the same merchandise in retail stores.

Which one of the following is an assumption on which the argument depends?

(A) The merchandise that can be ordered by mail using the bonus points is not offered at lower prices by other credit-card companies that award bonus points.

(B) The bonus points cannot be used by the credit-card customers in the purchase of brand name merchandise that is not available for purchase in retail stones.

(C) The credit-card company does not require its customers to accumulate a large number of bonus points before becoming eligible to order merchandise at prices lower than the manufacturers' suggested retail price.

(D) The amount credit-card customers pay for shipping the merchandise ordered by mail does not increase the amount customers spend to an amount greater than they would spend if they purchased the same merchandise in retail stores.

(E) The merchandise available to the company's credit-card customers using the bonus points is frequently sold in retail stores at prices that are higher than the manufacturers' suggested retail prices.[2]

## Step 1. Identify the Question Type

The word "assumption" identifies this stem as an Assumption question.

## Step 2. Untangle the Stimulus

The word "therefore" signals the author's conclusion that people who buy mail-order merchandise with bonus points spend less money than people who buy merchandise in retail stores. What is his evidence for that? The mail-order merchandise is offered at a lower cost than the store products.

## Step 3. Make a Prediction

The author says that mail-order merchandise is less expensive so customers spend less. The author ignores the possibility of other costs. He assumes the mail-order merchandise will present no additional costs to the customer, such as shipping or insurance, which would raise the price above the retail amount. The correct choice should address this assumption.

### Step 4. Evaluate the Answer Choices

Choice (A) wanders off point when it raises other credit card companies. The type of merchandise to be purchased using bonus points also strays from the argument. Eliminate this choice.

Choice (B) is outside the scope of the argument; the stimulus says nothing about restricting what customers can and can't buy. Move on to the next choice.

The discussion in choice (C) regarding when a customer can use her bonus points is also beyond the scope of the argument. This choice is out.

Choice (D) takes the general prediction and provides a specific example in which an added cost does not raise the mail-order price above the retail price. This is the correct answer.

Finally, you can eliminate choice (E) because the manufacturer's suggested retail price is irrelevant. This argument is only concerned with the mail-order price versus the retail price.

## Denial Test: Necessary Assumptions Only

Assumptions on the LSAT come in two varieties, necessary and sufficient. Necessary assumptions are subject to the denial test, which is one more way to determine if you have found the correct assumption. However, the denial test will not help you if the assumption is sufficient. Let's sort this out.

Necessary Assumption questions—the most common—ask for an unstated piece of evidence needed for the conclusion to be true. Specifically, the question stems ask for the assumption "required by" the author or that the author "depends on" or "relies on." It can also ask for the assumption the author "makes" or for what the "author assumes."

In the case of a necessary assumption, if you negate it, then the argument no longer makes sense.

To illustrate this, go back, again, to the chocolate cake stimulus:

Desserts are delicious.

Therefore, chocolate cake is delicious.

Now imagine that with this argument comes a question stem that asks for the assumption on which the argument depends; in other words, a necessary assumption. You've already identified the assumption as "chocolate cake is a dessert." If you deny the assumption and say "chocolate cake is not a dessert," then the argument makes no sense; "desserts are delicious and chocolate cake is not a dessert" does not lead to a conclusion that chocolate cake is delicious. So, if you deny an assumption that is necessary for the argument to work, the argument will fall apart. You can use this denial test to double-check your answer to a Necessary Assumption question. You don't need to use the denial test on every single answer in every Necessary Assumption question. Other methods may be more direct. However, the denial test is available to review your answer if you are not sure of it.

In contrast to Necessary Assumption questions, Sufficient Assumption questions typically ask for the assumption that "allows the conclusion to follow logically." They are not susceptible to the denial test.

Now I'll walk you through an LSAT example to show you how the denial test works:

> Proponents of organic farming claim that using chemical fertilizers and pesticides in farming is harmful to local wildlife. To produce the same amount of food, however, more land must be under cultivation when organic farming techniques are used than when chemicals are used. Therefore, organic farming leaves less land available as habitat for local wildlife.
>
> Which one of the following is an assumption on which the author's argument depends?
>
> (A)  Chemical fertilizers and pesticides pose no health threat to wildlife.
> (B)  Wildlife living near farms where chemicals are used will not ingest any food or water containing those chemicals.
> (C)  The only disadvantage to using chemicals in farming is their potential effect on wildlife.
> (D)  The same crops are grown on organic farms as on farms where chemicals are used.
> (E)  Land cultivated by organic farming methods no longer constitutes a habitat for wildlife.[3]

## Step 1. Identify the Question Type

Because of the phrase "assumption on which the author's argument depends," you know that this is a Necessary Assumption question.

## Step 2. Untangle the Stimulus

"Therefore" points out the conclusion to you, that organic farming means there is less land available for wildlife habitat. The reason, according to the author, is that organic farming means that more land must be cultivated. That's your evidence.

## Step 3. Make a Prediction

The argument presents mismatched terms in the evidence and conclusion. They both talk about organic farming; however, the evidence relates it to land cultivation and the conclusion connects it to wildlife habitat. The author must assume they are separate—land use is for either one or the other, not both.

---

[3]PrepTest 15, Sec. 3, Q 12

### Step 4. Evaluate the Answer Choices

The health threat posed by chemicals is not discussed in the argument, so choice (A) is outside the scope. Just to confirm this, try the denial test. Denying choice (A), chemicals do pose a threat to wildlife, has no effect on the conclusion regarding the impact of organic farming on wildlife habitat. So that answer choice is out.

Choice (B) has a similar problem, as the ingestion of the chemicals is also outside the scope of this problem. If you deny choice (B) and say that wildlife will ingest chemicals in their food and water, it bears no impact on the conclusion. Again, in the conclusion, the author says organic farming uses a wider area and reduces living space for wildlife.

Choice (C) presents another answer that is outside the scope of the argument. The author is not interested in the disadvantages of using chemicals in farming. Denying the answer results in saying the impact on wildlife is not the only disadvantage to using chemicals, and, in this case, other possible disadvantages have no affect on the conclusion.

Whether the same crops are grown is irrelevant to the argument, so you can quickly eliminate choice (D).

The author must assume choice (E), land used for organic farming can no longer be used as a wildlife habitat, which is the correct answer. If you're in doubt, try confirming the answer by using the denial test. Negate the statement and see what effect that has on the conclusion. It becomes "Land cultivated by organic farming can be used as a wildlife habitat." The assumption denied destroys the conclusion and therefore must be the correct answer.

One important lesson to take away from this exercise: While the mismatched terms in this argument lead you directly to answer choice (E), it is important to practice applying the denial test on "easier" questions like this at first. You'll likely find that the denial test is especially helpful on tough assumption questions, and you can count on the test makers giving you at least a couple of those on every test. The ability to answer the harder questions correctly is what sets the high scorers apart from the pack, and by practicing the Kaplan Method, you'll be one of those test takers.

## Formal Logic and Sufficient Assumptions

Here's a slightly trickier version of the Assumption question that the test makers can throw at you, but the Kaplan Method has an answer for it, too. If the stimulus includes formal logic, translate the formal logic into if-then statements. Then use the translations to identify the gap between the evidence and the conclusion. You'll find that Sufficient Assumption questions tend to use formal logic. They ask for an assumption that's enough to make an argument acceptable, unlike a necessary assumption required for the argument to make sense.

Marian Anderson, the famous contralto, did not take success for granted. We know this because Anderson had to struggle early in life, and anyone who has to struggle early in life is able to keep a good perspective on the world.

The conclusion of the argument follows logically if which one of the following is assumed?

(A) Anyone who succeeds takes success for granted.

(B) Anyone who is able to keep a good perspective on the world does not take success for granted.

(C) Anyone who is able to keep a good perspective on the world has to struggle early in life.

(D) Anyone who does not take success for granted has to struggle early in life.

(E) Anyone who does not take success for granted is able to keep a good perspective on the world.[4]

## Step 1. Identify the Question Type

The word "assumed" immediately tells you that this is an Assumption question.

## Step 2. Untangle the Stimulus

Although there is no conclusion Keyword, note the evidence phrase at the beginning of the second sentence: "We know this because" indicates that the author is about to provide evidence for a conclusion she just mentioned. Therefore, "Marian Anderson did not take success for granted" is the conclusion. Why didn't she take success for granted? She struggled and, according to the author, anyone who struggles has a good world perspective.

Do you notice anything else about the argument? Look at the language. Do you see "anyone"? You will recall from chapter 3 that "anyone" is an indicator of formal logic, specifically the sufficient term. If you spot formal logic in an assumption argument, translate it to help you find the gap between the conclusion and evidence and identify the assumption.

The basic components of this argument consist of two pieces of evidence and the conclusion. One piece of evidence is a formal logic rule that applies to everybody. There also is a factual piece of evidence specific to Marian Anderson, which is used to support a conclusion specific to Marian Anderson. Map it out as follows:

| **Formal Logic Evidence:** | **Struggle** | $\rightarrow$ | **good perspective** |
|---|---|---|---|
| **Factual Evidence:** | **Anderson struggled** | **(thus)** | **Conc: Anderson not take success for granted** |

With the common term "struggle" lined up on the left side, the assumption simply is to link the mismatched terms on the right side; link "good perspective" to "not take success for granted." Since this is a Sufficient Assumption question, your goal is to guarantee that the conclusion (Anderson did not take success for granted) is true, so the assumption must go from "good perspective" to "not take success for granted."

---

## Step 3. Make a Prediction

In this case, start with the obvious formal logic statement and translate it to the basic X → Y statement. Then, translate the other statements so you can find the gap. Here's what you'll get:

The evidence goes from A (Marian Anderson) → B (struggle) → C (good perspective), and then the conclusion jumps from A (Marian Anderson) → D (don't take success for granted). Let me show it to you in a picture:

Evidence:      A  →  B

                    B  →  C

Conclusion:     A ——————→  D

The gap exists between C and D, which gets you the assumption: If you keep a good perspective, then you don't take success for granted.

## Step 4. Evaluate the Answer Choices

What do you notice about all the answer choices? What do they all have in common? They all start with "anyone," which tells you to translate them into formal logic. By test day, your goal is to recognize the formal logic quickly and work through it without a mechanical process. For now, go ahead and translate each answer choice to the basic X → Y form. It's good practice while you are learning the skill:

Choice (A) translates to: Succeed → take success for granted. Succeeding is a new term in the argument and therefore outside the scope. Eliminate this choice.

Choice (B) matches the prediction exactly: Good perspective → not take success for granted. That's your answer.

Choice (C) translates to: Good perspective → struggle. Notice it reverses terms of the evidence without negating, which is a common wrong answer trap.

Choices (D), Not take success for granted → struggle, and (E), Not take success for granted → good perspective, also reverse terms without negating.

# ASSUMPTION QUESTIONS NOW YOU TRY IT

Now it's your turn to try a couple Assumption questions on your own. Use the template I've provided after each question to guide you through the four-step Kaplan Method.

(Note: On test day, you won't be writing out all the steps as you are in this exercise. However, as you are learning the Method, it's good practice to help it become second nature.) Remember to bracket the conclusions and circle Keywords.

1.  Barnes:  The two newest employees at this company have salaries that are too high for the simple tasks normally assigned to new employees and duties that are too complex for inexperienced workers. Hence, the salaries and the complexity of the duties of these two newest employees should be reduced.

    Which one of the following is an assumption on which Barnes's argument depends?

    (A)   The duties of the two newest employees are not less complex than any others in the company.
    (B)   It is because of the complex duties assigned that the two newest employees are being paid more than is usually paid to newly hired employees.
    (C)   The two newest employees are not experienced at their occupations.
    (D)   Barnes was not hired at a higher-than-average starting salary.
    (E)   The salaries of the two newest employees are no higher than the salaries that other companies pay for workers with a similar level of experience.[5]

## Step 1. Identify the Question Type

## Step 2. Untangle the Stimulus

## Step 3. Make a Prediction

## Step 4. Evaluate the Answer Choices

---

[5]PrepTest 29, Sec. 1, Q 5

2. Human beings can exhibit complex, goal-oriented behavior without conscious awareness of what they are doing. Thus, merely establishing that nonhuman animals are intelligent will not establish that they have consciousness.

Which one of the following is an assumption on which the argument depends?

(A) Complex, goal-oriented behavior requires intelligence.

(B) The possession of consciousness does not imply the possession of intelligence.

(C) All forms of conscious behavior involve the exercise of intelligence.

(D) The possession of intelligence entails the possession of consciousness.

(E) Some intelligent human behavior is neither complex nor goal-oriented.[6]

## Step 1. Identify the Question Type

_____

## Step 2. Untangle the Stimulus

_____

## Step 3. Make a Prediction

_____

## Step 4. Evaluate the Answer Choices

_____

_____

[6]PrepTest 49, Sec. 2, Q 17

# Explanations

## 1. (C)

Barnes: The two newest employees at this company have salaries that are too high for the simple tasks normally assigned to new employees and duties that are too complex for inexperienced workers. <(Hence) the salaries and the complexity of the duties of these two newest employees should be reduced.>

Which one of the following is an (assumption) on which Barnes's argument (depends)?

(A) The duties of the two newest employees are not less complex than any others in the company.

(B) It is because of the complex duties assigned that the two newest employees are being paid more than is usually paid to newly hired employees.

(C) The two newest employees are not experienced at their occupations.

(D) Barnes was not hired at a higher-than-average starting salary.

(E) The salaries of the two newest employees are no higher than the salaries that other companies pay for workers with a similar level of experience.[7]

## Step 1. Identify the Question Type

The question asks you directly for an assumption, so you will need to link the evidence to the conclusion. "Depends" indicates this is a necessary assumption, so remember you can confirm your answer with the denial test.

## Step 2. Untangle the Stimulus

"Hence" points to Barnes' conclusion that the salaries and complexity of the duties of the newest employees should be reduced. What evidence does Barnes give to support this conclusion? He says their salaries are too high for tasks assigned to new employees and their duties are too complex for inexperienced workers. In other words, new employees should have a certain salary based on their duties and inexperienced workers should have a certain level of complexity in their duties.

## Step 3. Make a Prediction

This is a classic example of mismatched terms. The conclusion is about the "newest employees," but right before "hence" the author refers to them as "inexperienced workers." So Barnes must assume that the two newest employees are inexperienced. It's certainly possible and sounds reasonable enough to read right over the difference. But couldn't they have experience from prior jobs? Of course! So Barnes is making an assumption. And you've identified it. Now find that assumption in the answer choices.

---

[7]PrepTest 29, Sec. 1, Q 5

## Step 4. Evaluate the Answer Choices

Choice (A) broadens the comparison group to all company employees, not just inexperienced workers. Barnes never discusses the complexity of job responsibilities for all company workers, so you cannot make any assumptions about them. This choice is out.

Choice (B) presents the opposite of what Barnes' assumes. It rationalizes the newest employees' higher salary based on the complexity of their job responsibilities. Eliminate this choice.

Choice (C) is correct because it confirms that the two newest employees are inexperienced at their jobs. Deny this choice and it states that the two newest employees have experience; then the argument falls apart, so this must be right.

Choice (D) is outside the scope of the argument. Barnes' salary has no bearing on the salary of the two newest employees.

Choice (E) presents an irrelevant comparison between the newest employees' salaries and salaries of workers outside the company. Pay practices of other companies are also beyond the scope of this argument.

## 2.　(A)

Human beings can exhibit complex, goal-oriented behavior without conscious awareness of what they are doing. Thus, merely establishing that nonhuman animals are intelligent will not establish that they have consciousness.>

Which one of the following is an assumption on which the argument depends?

(A)　Complex, goal-oriented behavior requires intelligence.
(B)　The possession of consciousness does not imply the possession of intelligence.
(C)　All forms of conscious behavior involve the exercise of intelligence.
(D)　The possession of intelligence entails the possession of consciousness.
(E)　Some intelligent human behavior is neither complex nor goal-oriented.[8]

## Step 1. Identify the Question Type

Again, the question stem tells you specifically to determine the assumption necessary to the argument.

## Step 2. Untangle the Stimulus

"Thus" points you right to the conclusion, where the author maintains that proving nonhumans are intelligent will not prove that they have consciousness. Why not? Because complex, goal-oriented behavior in humans is possible without consciousness. Intelligence, she says, does

---

[8]PrepTest 49, Sec. 2, Q 17

not demonstrate consciousness because complex, goal-oriented behavior is possible without consciousness.

### Step 3. Make a Prediction

Can you spot the mismatched terms? The author must connect intelligence, which only appears in the conclusion, to complex, goal-oriented behavior, found only in the evidence.

### Step 4. Evaluate the Answer Choices

Choice (A) is the only answer that links the two unique terms and is therefore the correct answer.

Choice (B) inverts the conclusion and does not connect the mismatched terms. Move on.

Choice (C) says that intelligence is required for conscious behavior. Obviously, this answer does not link the mismatched terms. But, it also doesn't represent the argument which concludes that intelligence does not require consciousness.

Choice (D) contradicts the author's conclusion.

Choice (E) has two problems. First, it distinguishes, rather than ties together, intelligence and complex and goal-oriented behavior. It also separates complex and goal-oriented behavior, which differs from the argument.

# DRILL: ANSWERING ASSUMPTION QUESTIONS

Use the Kaplan Method to answer the following Assumption questions. Take this opportunity to practice and apply the steps in the Method so you are comfortable using them on test day. Check your responses against the full explanations provided after the Drill.

1.  Braille is a method of producing text by means of raised dots that can be read by touch. A recent development in technology will allow flat computer screens to be made of a material that can be heated in patterns that replicate the patterns used in braille. Since the thermal device will utilize the same symbol system as braille, it follows that anyone who is accustomed to reading braille can easily adapt to the use of this electronic system.

    Which one of the following is an assumption on which the conclusion depends?

    (A)   Braille is the only symbol system that can be readily adapted for use with the new thermal screen.

    (B)   Only people who currently use braille as their sole medium for reading text will have the capacity to adapt to the use of the thermal screen.

    (C)   People with the tactile ability to discriminate symbols in braille have an ability to discriminate similar patterns on a flat heated surface.

    (D)   Some symbol systems encode a piece of text by using dots that replicate the shape of letters of the alphabet.

    (E)   Eventually it will be possible to train people to read braille by first training them in the use of the thermal screen.[9]

2.  Although the charter of Westside School states that the student body must include some students with special educational needs, no students with learning disabilities have yet enrolled in the school. Therefore, the school is currently in violation of its charter.

    The conclusion of the argument follows logically if which one of the following is assumed?

    (A)   All students with learning disabilities have special educational needs.

    (B)   The school currently has no student with learning disabilities.

    (C)   The school should enroll students with special educational needs.

    (D)   The only students with special educational needs are students with learning disabilities.

    (E)   The school's charter cannot be modified in order to avoid its being violated.[10]

3.  Robert:  Speed limits on residential streets in Crownsbury are routinely ignored by drivers. People crossing those streets are endangered by speeding drivers, yet the city does not have enough police officers to patrol every street. So the city should install speed bumps and signs warning of their presence on residential streets to slow down traffic.

    Sheila:  That is a bad idea. People who are driving too fast can easily lose control of their vehicles when they hit a speed bump.

    Sheila's response depends on the presupposition that

    (A)  problems of the kind that Robert describes are worse in Crownsbury than they are in other cities

    (B)  Robert's proposal is intended to address a problem that Robert does not in fact intend it to address

    (C)  with speed bumps and warning signs in place, there would still be drivers who would not slow down to a safe speed

    (D)  most of the people who are affected by the problem Robert describes would be harmed by the installation of speed bumps and warning signs

    (E)  problems of the kind that Robert describes do not occur on any nonresidential streets in Crownsbury[11]

4.  Physician:  Hatha yoga is a powerful tool for helping people quit smoking. In a clinical trial, those who practiced hatha yoga for 75 minutes once a week and received individual counseling reduced their smoking and cravings for tobacco as much as did those who went to traditional self-help groups once a week and had individual counseling.

    Which one of the following is an assumption on which the physician's argument relies?

    (A)  The individual counseling received by the smokers in the clinical trial who practiced hatha yoga did not help them quit smoking.

    (B)  Most smokers are able to practice hatha yoga more than once a week.

    (C)  Traditional self-help groups are powerful tools for helping people quit smoking.

    (D)  People who practice hatha yoga for 75 minutes once a week are not damaging themselves physically.

    (E)  Other forms of yoga are less effective than hatha yoga in helping people quit smoking.[12]

5.  We learn to use most of the machines in our lives through written instructions, without knowledge of the machines' inner workings, because most machines are specifically designed for use by nonexperts. So, in general, attaining technological expertise would prepare students for tomorrow's job market no better than would a more traditional education stressing verbal and quantitative skills.

    The argument depends on assuming which one of the following?

    (A)  Fewer people receive a traditional education stressing verbal and quantitative skills now than did 20 years ago.

    (B)  Facility in operating machines designed for use by nonexperts is almost never enhanced by expert knowledge of the machines' inner workings.

    (C)  Most jobs in tomorrow's job market will not demand the ability to operate many machines that are designed for use only by experts.

    (D)  Students cannot attain technological expertise and also receive an education that does not neglect verbal and quantitative skills.

    (E)  When learning to use a machine, technological expertise is never more important than verbal and quantitative skills.[13]

[11]PrepTest 37, Sec. 4, Q 23

[12]PrepTest 37, Sec. 4, Q 19
[13]PrepTest 36, Sec. 3, Q 14

6. Ann will either take a leave of absence from Technocomp and return in a year or else she will quit her job there; but she would not do either one unless she were offered a one-year teaching fellowship at a prestigious university. Technocomp will allow her to take a leave of absence if it does not find out that she has been offered the fellowship, but not otherwise. Therefore, Ann will quit her job at Technocomp only if Technocomp finds out she has been offered the fellowship.

Which one of the following, if assumed, allows the conclusion above to be properly drawn?

(A) Technocomp will find out about Ann being offered the fellowship only if someone informs on her.

(B) The reason Ann wants the fellowship is so she can quit her job at Technocomp.

(C) Technocomp does not allow any of its employees to take a leave of absence in order to work for one of its competitors.

(D) Ann will take a leave of absence if Technocomp allows her to take a leave of absence.

(E) Ann would be offered the fellowship only if she quit her job at Technocomp.[14]

7. Vague laws set vague limits on people's freedom, which makes it impossible for them to know for certain whether their actions are legal. Thus, under vague laws people cannot feel secure.

The conclusion follows logically if which one of the following is assumed?

(A) People can feel secure only if they know for certain whether their actions are legal.

(B) If people do not know for certain whether their actions are legal, then they might not feel secure.

(C) If people know for certain whether their actions are legal, they can feel secure.

(D) People can feel secure if they are governed by laws that are not vague.

(E) Only people who feel secure can know for certain whether their actions are legal.[15]

8. Publicity campaigns for endangered species are unlikely to have much impact on the most important environmental problems, for while the ease of attributing feelings to large mammals facilitates evoking sympathy for them, it is more difficult to elicit sympathy for other kinds of organisms, such as the soil microorganisms on which large ecosystems and agriculture depend.

Which one of the following is an assumption on which the argument depends?

(A) The most important environmental problems involve endangered species other than large mammals.

(B) Microorganisms cannot experience pain or have other feelings.

(C) Publicity campaigns for the environment are the most effective when they elicit sympathy for some organism.

(D) People ignore environmental problems unless they believe the problems will affect creatures with which they sympathize.

(E) An organism can be environmentally significant only if it affects large ecosystems or agriculture.[16]

9. Professor: Each government should do all that it can to improve the well-being of all the children in the society it governs. Therefore, governments should help finance high-quality day care since such day care will become available to families of all income levels if and only if it is subsidized.

Which one of the following is an assumption on which the professor's argument depends?

(A) Only governments that subsidize high-quality day care take an interest in the well-being of all the children in the societies they govern.

(B) Government subsidy of high-quality day care would not be so expensive that it would cause a government to eliminate benefits for adults.

(C) High-quality day care should be subsidized only for those who could not otherwise afford it.

(D) At least some children would benefit from high-quality day care.

(E) Government is a more efficient provider of certain services than is private enterprise.[17]

---

[14]PrepTest 21, Sec. 2, Q 20
[15]PrepTest 36, Sec. 3, Q 12

[16]PrepTest 35, Sec. 4, Q 16
[17]PrepTest 47, Sec. 1, Q 20

## Explanations

### 1.   (C)

Braille is a method of producing text by means of raised dots that can be read by touch. A recent development in technology will allow flat computer screens to be made of a material that can be heated in patterns that replicate the patterns used in braille. (Since) the thermal device will utilize the same symbol system as braille, <it follows that> anyone who is accustomed to reading braille can easily adapt to the use of this electronic system.>

Which one of the following is an (assumption) on which the conclusion (depends)?

(A)   Braille is the only symbol system that can be readily adapted for use with the new thermal screen.

(B)   Only people who currently use braille as their sole medium for reading text will have the capacity to adapt to the use of the thermal screen.

(C)   People with the tactile ability to discriminate symbols in braille have an ability to discriminate similar patterns on a flat heated surface.

(D)   Some symbol systems encode a piece of text by using dots that replicate the shape of letters of the alphabet.

(E)   Eventually it will be possible to train people to read braille by first training them in the use of the thermal screen.[18]

## Step 1. Identify the Question Type

The words "assumption and "depends" tell you that this question asks for a necessary assumption.

## Step 2. Untangle the Stimulus

The phrase "it follows that" signals the author's conclusion that anyone who can read braille can easily use the electronic system. "Since" identifies the evidence that says the thermal device will use the same symbol system as braille. So the braille symbols are the same, but the delivery system is different.

## Step 3. Make a Prediction

Since the symbols are the same, the only shift in the argument is from the raised dots to the thermal screen. The author must assume that anyone who can read braille in a traditional manner can transfer that skill to read the heated computer screen.

---

[18]PrepTest 22, Sec. 2, Q 1

## Step 4. Evaluate the Answer Choices

Choice (A) is too extreme, a common "necessary assumption" wrong answer type that can sound attractive, because it's on track, but you can easily eliminate it using the denial test, because it goes too far. Choice (A) indicates that "only" braille can be adapted to the thermal screen. Denied, choice (A) indicates that the thermal screens can be used for other systems besides braille; which in no way destroys the argument that the screen is good for braille users.

Choice (B) is also too extreme; it limits those who can adapt to the new technology to only people who use braille as their sole medium for reading text. Using the denial test, the possibility that additional people could adapt to the new technology in no way destroys the conclusion that current braille readers can.

Choice (C) matches the prediction by linking the evidence and conclusion: People who can read braille can read the same symbols on the heated computer surface. Remember, assumptions will always connect the existing points in an argument and not add new information. If you want additional confirmation that (C) is correct, try the denial test. If people who can read braille don't have an ability to read braille from a heated surface, then the conclusion makes no sense.

Choice (D) discusses symbol systems other than braille, so is out of scope.

Choice (E) talks about training people to read braille in the future, so it is way out of the scope of this argument, which is about what current braille users can do.

### 2.   **(D)**

Although the charter of Westside School states that the student body must include some students with special educational needs, no students with learning disabilities have yet enrolled in the school. <Therefore, the school is currently in violation of its charter.>

The conclusion of the argument follows logically if which one of the following is assumed?

(A)   All students with learning disabilities have special educational needs.

(B)   The school currently has no student with learning disabilities.

(C)   The school should enroll students with special educational needs.

(D)   The only students with special educational needs are students with learning disabilities.

(E)   The school's charter cannot be modified in order to avoid its being violated.[19]

---

[19]PrepTest 34, Sec. 2, Q 10

### Step 1. Identify the Question Type

This question asks you to identify a sufficient assumption.

### Step 2. Untangle the Stimulus

"Therefore" in the last sentence points to the conclusion, which states that if we have the current situation at the school, then the charter is violated. When the conclusion refers to a vague term, such a "this policy" or here "the charter," it is helpful to incorporate the definition of the policy or charter into the conclusion. The charter requires that the school must have special-needs students, so the conclusion really indicates that the current situation at the school violates the charter requirement to have special-needs students. So how does the author know the school is in violation of its charter? The Westside School charter requires that special-needs students be included in the student body, yet the school has no students with learning disabilities.

### Step 3. Make a Prediction

In this case, the mismatched terms are "learning disabilities" and "special needs." The correct answer should link those terms. If only one answer makes the link, then it will be correct. But if two answers make that connection, you need to determine whether the author assumes that all students with learning disabilities have special needs or conversely all special-needs students have learning disabilities. So the author assumes that if there are no students with learning disabilities then there are no special needs students:

Statement: No learning disabled students → no special-needs students

Contrapositive: Special need students → learning disabled

So the author assumes all special-needs students have learning disabilities.

### Step 4. Evaluate the Answer Choices

Choice (A) reverses the logic, so you can eliminate it.

Choice (B) repeats evidence stated in the argument rather than providing an unstated premise, a common wrong answer trap for Assumption questions. Move on to the next choice.

The recommendation in choice (C), that the school enroll special-needs students, is irrelevant to the argument; the charter requires enrollment of special-needs students.

Choice (D) is the only choice that correctly connects the two student groups in the evidence to make the conclusion valid.

Whether the school charter can be modified, as raised in choice (E), has no impact on the argument because the argument already concludes that the school is in violation of its charter.

### 3. (C)

Robert: Speed limits on residential streets in Crownsbury are routinely ignored by drivers. People crossing those streets are endangered by speeding drivers, yet the city does not have enough police officers to patrol every street. So the city should install speed bumps and signs warning of their presence on residential streets to slow down traffic.

Sheila: <That is a bad idea.> People who are driving too fast can easily lose control of their vehicles when they hit a speed bump.

Sheila's response depends on the presupposition that

(A) problems of the kind that Robert describes are worse in Crownsbury than they are in other cities

(B) Robert's proposal is intended to address a problem that Robert does not in fact intend it to address

(C) with speed bumps and warning signs in place, there would still be drivers who would not slow down to a safe speed

(D) most of the people who are affected by the problem Robert describes would be harmed by the installation of speed bumps and warning signs

(E) problems of the kind that Robert describes do not occur on any nonresidential streets in Crownsbury[20]

### Step 1. Identify the Question Type

"Depends on the presupposition" tells you that this answer requires a necessary assumption.

### Step 2. Untangle the Stimulus

Crownsbury has a problem with speeding drivers. Sheila concludes that Robert's recommendation to add speed bumps and warning signs is a bad idea. Her evidence is that speeding drivers will lose control of their cars when they hit a speed bump.

### Step 3. Make a Prediction

The purpose of the precautionary measures is to slow drivers down. If Sheila is concerned that drivers will continue to speed and create dangerous situations, she must not think the speed bumps and the warning signs will be effective to slow drivers down.

### Step 4. Evaluate the Answer Choices

The comparison of Crownsbury's problems to other cities in choice (A) is irrelevant in this argument.

---

[20]PrepTest 37, Sec. 4, Q 23

Choices (B) and (E) also raise irrelevant factors; neither Robert's intentions nor nonresidential streets are ever mentioned in the argument.

Choice (C) matches the prediction and is the correct answer.

Choice (D) talks about who would be hurt rather than drivers who continue to speed.

### 4. (C)

Physician: <Hatha yoga is a powerful tool for helping people quit smoking.> In a clinical trial, those who practiced hatha yoga for 75 minutes once a week and received individual counseling reduced their smoking and cravings for tobacco as much as did those who went to traditional self-help groups once a week and had individual counseling.

Which one of the following is an assumption on which the physician's argument relies?

(A) The individual counseling received by the smokers in the clinical trial who practiced hatha yoga did not help them quit smoking.
(B) Most smokers are able to practice hatha yoga more than once a week.
(C) Traditional self-help groups are powerful tools for helping people quit smoking.
(D) People who practice hatha yoga for 75 minutes once a week are not damaging themselves physically.
(E) Other forms of yoga are less effective than hatha yoga in helping people quit smoking.[21]

## Step 1. Identify the Question Type

It doesn't get any easier than this. This question uses "assumption," so you know what to do.

## Step 2. Untangle the Stimulus

The physician concludes that Hatha yoga is a powerful tool to help people quit smoking because when combined with individual counseling, it is just as effective as traditional self-help groups and individual counseling.

## Step 3. Make a Prediction

Individual counseling is common in both treatments, so to determine that Hatha yoga is powerful, the physician must assume that traditional self-help groups are also powerful.

## Step 4. Evaluate the Answer Choices

You can eliminate choice (A) because both groups received individual counseling and you have no way to differentiate the value added by the treatment.

---

[21]PrepTest 37, Sec. 4, Q 19

Choice (B) is outside the scope of the argument since you have no information about how often the smokers could practice yoga.

Choice (C) matches the prediction exactly and is the correct answer.

Choices (D) and (E) also add factors outside the scope of the argument; the physical effect of Hatha yoga and a comparison with other forms of yoga are never discussed.

## 5.  (C)

We learn to use most of the machines in our lives through written instructions, without knowledge of the machines' inner workings, because most machines are specifically designed for use by nonexperts. <So, in general, attaining technological expertise would prepare students for tomorrow's job market no better than would a more traditional education stressing verbal and quantitative skills.>

The argument depends on assuming which one of the following?

(A)    Fewer people receive a traditional education stressing verbal and quantitative skills now than did 20 years ago.

(B)    Facility in operating machines designed for use by nonexperts is almost never enhanced by expert knowledge of the machines' inner workings.

(C)    Most jobs in tomorrow's job market will not demand the ability to operate many machines that are designed for use only by experts.

(D)    Students cannot attain technological expertise and also receive an education that does not neglect verbal and quantitative skills.

(E)    When learning to use a machine, technological expertise is never more important than verbal and quantitative skills.[22]

## Step 1. Identify the Question Type

Again, the Assumption question is revealed directly by the language.

## Step 2. Untangle the Stimulus

The author concludes that technological training to prepare for the future job market has no value over a traditional education because most machines are designed to be used by non-experts. Notice the scope shift: The conclusion refers to machines in the workplace while the evidence refers to machines in our daily lives.

---

[22]PrepTest 36, Sec. 3, Q 14

### Step 3. Make a Prediction

The author assumes that tomorrow's jobs will use those machines designed for nonexperts discussed in the evidence.

### Step 4. Evaluate the Answer Choices

The number of students receiving an education is irrelevant in the argument, so choice (A) is out.

Choice (B) strengthens the conclusion that technological expertise won't generally help students, but is too extreme to be a necessary assumption. The denial test is a great way to eliminate answer choices that support the author's conclusion but are too extreme or restrictive to be necessary to the argument. Choice (B) denied indicates that periodically, technological expertise would be an advantage in utilizing those machines designed for nonexperts in the evidence, but that does not preclude the claim that generally students do not gain a significant advantage from a technological education.

Choice (C), the correct answer, does that by saying work-related machines can be operated by nonexperts just like the everyday machines. The other answer choices do not address the scope shift.

The author would disagree with choice (D) because the author denies the need for tech expertise.

Finally, you can eliminate choice (E) because the comparative value of tech expertise and verbal and quantitative skills is never discussed in the argument.

6.   **(D)**

Ann will either take a leave of absence from
Technocomp and return in a year or else she will quit her
job there; but she would not do either one unless she
were offered a one-year teaching fellowship at a
prestigious university. Technocomp will allow her to
take a leave of absence if it does not find out that she has
been offered the fellowship, but not otherwise.
<Therefore,> Ann will quit her job at Technocomp only if
Technocomp finds out she has been offered the
fellowship.>

Which one of the following, if <assumed,> allows the
conclusion above to be properly drawn?

(A)   Technocomp will find out about Ann being
offered the fellowship only if someone informs
on her.

(B)   The reason Ann wants the fellowship is so she can
quit her job at Technocomp.

(C)   Technocomp does not allow any of its employees
to take a leave of absence in order to work for
one of its competitors.

(D)   Ann will take a leave of absence if Technocomp
allows her to take a leave of absence.

(E)   Ann would be offered the fellowship only if she
quit her job at Technocomp.[23]

## Step 1. Identify the Question Type

The question clearly asks for an assumption.

## Step 2. Untangle the Stimulus

"Therefore" points to the formal logic conclusion that Ann will quit her job only if Technocomp finds out about the fellowship. The evidence indicates that she will either take a leave or quit her job. Also, the evidence indicates that if Technocomp does not find out about the fellowship, Ann will be able to take a leave of absence.

## Step 3. Make a Prediction

You know Ann has two potential options. The contrapositive of the conclusion is helpful to recognize; it states that if Technocomp does not find out about the fellowship, then Ann will not quit her job, indicating that she would opt to take the leave of absence. So the author assumes that if given a choice, Ann prefers the leave of absence. So look for the choice where Ann will take the leave of absence if allowed by Technocomp.

## Step 4. Evaluate the Answer Choices

Choice (A) talks about someone informing on Ann which is beyond the scope of the argument.

---

[23]PrepTest 21, Sec. 2, Q 20

Similarly, Ann's rationale for her actions are outside the scope of the argument, making choice (B) incorrect.

Choice (C) makes no sense in the context of the argument. Ann is planning to teach at a university, not work for a competitor.

Choice (D) matches the prediction and is the answer.

You can eliminate choice (E) because the circumstances under which she is offered the fellowship are immaterial.

### 7.  (A)

Vague laws set vague limits on people's freedom, which makes it impossible for them to know for certain whether their actions are legal. <Thus, under vague laws people cannot feel secure.>

The conclusion follows logically if which one of the following is assumed?

(A)  People can feel secure only if they know for certain whether their actions are legal.
(B)  If people do not know for certain whether their actions are legal, then they might not feel secure.
(C)  If people know for certain whether their actions are legal, they can feel secure.
(D)  People can feel secure if they are governed by laws that are not vague.
(E)  Only people who feel secure can know for certain whether their actions are legal.[24]

### Step 1. Identify the Question Type

The question again asks for an assumption.

### Step 2. Untangle the Stimulus

"Thus" introduces the conclusion and the new term "people cannot feel secure" under vague laws. The evidence states that people cannot know the legality of their actions under vague laws.

### Step 3. Make a Prediction

People's security must require knowing their actions are legal for the argument to work.

### Step 4. Evaluate the Answer Choices

Choice (A) matches the prediction: Certain knowledge of legality is necessary for people to feel secure. This is the correct answer.

---

[24]PrepTest 36, Sec. 3, Q 12

The timid tone of choice (C) represented by "they might not feel secure" takes it out of the running.

Choice (C) reverses the formal logic without negating, so you can eliminate it.

Choice (D) is out because the argument does not refer to laws that are not vague.

Choice (E), like choice (B), reverses the formal logic without negating and therefore mixes up the sufficient and necessary clauses.

8.   **(A)**

<Publicity campaigns for endangered species are unlikely to have much impact on the most important environmental problems,> (for) while the ease of attributing feelings to large mammals facilitates evoking sympathy for them, it is more difficult to elicit sympathy for other kinds of organisms, such as the soil microorganisms on which large ecosystems and agriculture depend.

Which one of the following is an (assumption) on which the argument (depends)?

(A)   The most important environmental problems involve endangered species other than large mammals.
(B)   Microorganisms cannot experience pain or have other feelings.
(C)   Publicity campaigns for the environment are the most effective when they elicit sympathy for some organism.
(D)   People ignore environmental problems unless they believe the problems will affect creatures with which they sympathize.
(E)   An organism can be environmentally significant only if it affects large ecosystems or agriculture.[25]

### Step 1. Identify the Question Type

The phrase "an assumption on which the argument depends" tells you this is a Necessary Assumption question.

### Step 2. Untangle the Stimulus

"For" points to the evidence. Since there is no conclusion Keyword, look at the evidence and determine what it must support. Here, the conclusion is that publicity campaigns aren't likely to work for the most important environmental problems and the evidence is that it is easy to get sympathy only for large mammals, not the smaller, slimy creatures.

---

[25]PrepTest 35, Sec. 4, Q 16

## Step 3. Make a Prediction

So, the author is making a couple of assumptions: 1) that eliciting sympathy is the likely way for a publicity campaign to be effective and 2) that most important environmental problems are the small organisms (not the large mammals for which the campaigns do work). Since the author is making a couple of assumptions, you can anticipate that there might be two or more answers that sound good and that you should be ready to use the denial test to confirm which is correct.

## Step 4. Evaluate the Answer Choices

Choice (A) makes the connection, and because this is a necessary assumption, you can double-check your answer using the denial test. If choice (A) were false, and most important environmental problems did involve large mammals, then the publicity campaigns for endangered species would have a greater impact. So by denying choice (A), the argument falls apart and you know it is the answer.

Choice (B) does not work because it distorts the idea of feelings. The author does not say the microorganisms cannot feel, but rather people have trouble attributing feelings to them.

Choice (C) is tempting. The author does assume some connection between the ability to elicit sympathy and the likelihood that a publicity campaign will be effective. Your first clue that (C) is incorrect is how absolute it is: "most effective." But use the denial test: Choice (C) denied indicates that some other tactic besides eliciting sympathy could be the most effective. That doesn't prevent the author from properly concluding that sympathy is the way that has the greatest likelihood of being effective. You need to distinguish between probability of being effective and relative level of effectiveness; winning the lottery may be the most effective way of getting really rich, really quick, but the likelihood of that happening is extremely small.

The people ignoring environmental problems in choice (D) are not mentioned in the argument and are therefore outside the scope of the argument.

Choice (E) confuses environmental significance with important problems.

9.   **(D)**

Professor:  Each government should do all that it can
to improve the well-being of all the children in
the society it governs. <Therefore, governments
should help finance high-quality day care since
such day care will become available to families
of all income levels if and only if it is
subsidized.>

Which one of the following is an assumption on
which the professor's argument depends?

(A)   Only governments that subsidize high-quality
day care take an interest in the well-being of
all the children in the societies they govern.
(B)   Government subsidy of high-quality day care
would not be so expensive that it would cause
a government to eliminate benefits for adults.
(C)   High-quality day care should be subsidized only
for those who could not otherwise afford it.
(D)   At least some children would benefit from
high-quality day care.
(E)   Government is a more efficient provider of
certain services than is private enterprise.[26]

## Step 1. Identify the Question Type

"Assumption on which the professor's argument depends" signals a Necessary Assumption
question.

## Step 2. Untangle the Stimulus

"Therefore" identifies the conclusion, which recommends that government help fund high-
quality day care. The professor reasons that government subsidization will make day care more
widely accessible and that government should do all it can to improve the well-being of children.

## Step 3. Make a Prediction

The author must assume that high-quality day care will improve the well-being of children.

## Step 4. Evaluate the Answer Choices

Choice (A) talks about government taking an interest in children's well-being, not improving
children's well-being. Cross out this choice.

Choice (B) is also out because it talks about benefits for adults, not benefits for children.

The need-based subsidy raised in choice (C) is outside the scope of the argument as is choice
(E)'s comparison of government versus private enterprise efficiency.

---

[26]PrepTest 47, Sec. 1, Q 20

Choice (D) matches the prediction and is the correct answer. Notice how modest it is. The author has to believe that at least one child would benefit from day care to recommend that the government finance day care in order to meet its mandate to improve the well-being of children.

## ASSUMPTION QUESTION REVIEW

Before you proceed to the next chapter, turn to Appendix A and complete the review exercise for Assumption questions. A completed chart is included in Appendix B.

# CHAPTER 6

# WEAKEN QUESTIONS

In the legal profession, you need to be able to identify an adversary's argument and weaken it. So it's no surprise that the LSAT includes a question type—Weaken questions—that tests your ability to do just that.

Weaken questions and Strengthen questions will account for approximately eight scored questions on test day, a sizeable chunk of the 50 scored Logical Reasoning questions. You can quickly earn valuable points on test day by mastering Weaken and Strengthen questions now.

## DEFINITION OF WEAKEN QUESTIONS

Weaken questions ask you to find the answer choice that makes the conclusion less likely to follow from the evidence. You don't need to prove or disprove the argument. Instead, your task is to loosen the connection between the evidence and conclusion—or, as the chapter title implies, make it a weaker argument. Look at this example:

> A determination by the university that a student-athlete has not taken enough credits to be progressing toward a degree renders that student-athlete academically ineligible to compete. Henry did not play in Saturday's football game. Therefore, he must not have the proper number of credits to be progressing toward a degree.

When the author claims that Henry "must not" have the necessary credits, she is assuming that a lack of credits is the only factor that would make Henry ineligible to compete. To weaken this argument, you don't need to prove that Henry is progressing toward a degree; any new information that makes it less likely that he did not play because he is having trouble progressing toward a degree would weaken the author's claim. Here are some possible statements that could weaken the argument:

- Henry shows up at the game with a cast on his leg.
- The academic advisors for the athletic department follow the student-athletes very closely to ensure they are taking the proper number of credits to meet all eligibility requirements.

Neither statement explicitly or implicitly says that Henry is progressing toward his degree. However, an alternative reason for why he is not in the game (injury) and an attack on the conclusion (close academic monitoring by advisors) reduce the possibility that Henry does not have enough academic credit to progress toward a degree. That's all you need to do to weaken an argument: Find an answer that makes it less likely that the conclusion is true.

# USE THE KAPLAN METHOD TO ANSWER WEAKEN QUESTIONS

## Identify the Question Type

Obviously, to answer a Weaken question you have to be able to recognize a Weaken question. But don't worry. There are words in the question stem that indicate it's a Weaken question. They include:

- Weaken
- Calls into question
- Casts doubt on
- Undermine
- Counter
- Damages

Here's how these phrases could appear in question stems:

- Which one of the following, if true, most weakens the argument?
- Which one of the following, if true, most seriously undermines the hypothesis?
- Of the following, which one, if true, is the logically strongest counter the legislator can make to the commentator's argument?
- Which one of the following, if true, most calls into question the nutritionist's argument?
- Which one of the following, if true, most weakens the case for the department chair's position?
- The prediction that ends the passage would be most seriously called into question if it were true that in the last few years
- Each of the following, if true, weakens the official's argument EXCEPT:

Don't let the "if true" part fool you. It just tells you to accept the truth of the choice right off the bat, no matter how unlikely it may sound to you. Don't argue with the answer choices.

## Untangle the Stimulus

Once you know you have a Weaken question, actively read the stimulus to determine the author's argument by finding the conclusion and the evidence. Just as you did with Assumption questions, circle any Keywords, bracket the conclusion, and then connect the evidence to the conclusion to find the assumption. Remember, to find the assumption, you need to either connect the mismatched terms or use formal logic, if applicable. If this was an Assumption question, you would stop here and compare your prediction to the answer choices. However, with a Weaken question you must use the conclusion, evidence, *and* the assumption to attack the argument and make the conclusion less likely to be true.

## Make a Prediction

The key to weakening an argument is by either attacking the conclusion directly or by denying the author's assumption. Both of these viable approaches result in the same prediction; they just take different paths to get there. Look at the following example and I'll demonstrate these two practical ways to weaken the argument.

> Ozzie only read one book in the same week his sister read four books. Obviously, he is a slow reader.

The author concludes that Ozzie reads slowly based on the fact that he read one book while his sister read four books in the same time frame. Notice the mismatched terms: slow reader and one book. The author assumes that the only reason Ozzie read one book is because he is a slow reader. Stated more generally, the author assumes no other explanations exist and considers no other reasons for why Ozzie read just one book.

To weaken the argument, you can:

1. Attack the conclusion: Determine what you can add to the argument to make it more likely that Ozzie is not a slow reader. For example, maybe Ozzie's book was a thousand pages long while his sister read four books under a hundred pages each. Even though Ozzie read just one book, he read more pages than his sister, which casts doubt on whether he really is a slow reader.

2. Deny the assumption: Consider that being a slow reader is not the only explanation for why Ozzie read just one book in the time allotted, and identify other possibilities. For example, maybe Ozzie had a busy week with work deadlines and family obligations to meet. He had little free time to read all week, while his sister was not as busy and could spend much more time reading.

The most common method of weakening an argument is to break down the assumption by considering any alternative possibilities. Regardless of an argument's persuasiveness, you need to think critically and remember that a Weaken question has an inherent problem: an unstated piece of evidence. You need to ask yourself whether the author has ruled out all other possibilities, because when an author ignores alternative explanations in an argument, you can attack that misstep and look for alternative possibilities to reach the same conclusion.

As you read the stimulus of a Weaken question, pay particular attention to argument patterns. You can find two particular patterns in Weaken questions to help you: causal arguments and predictions.

## Causality

Causal arguments are arguments in which the author asserts or denies a cause-and-effect relationship between two events or things. Causal arguments are frequently used on the LSAT, especially in Assumption family and Parallel Reasoning questions. Here are some examples:

- The potato chips he ate caused his face to break out.
- The new marketing plan is responsible for the company's rise in sales.
- The devastation in Haiti was brought about by the earthquake.
- Her sense of responsibility started when she got her first apartment.

Notice the explicit causation indicators like "caused," "responsible for," and "brought about by." You will also find more subtle terms, such as "started." Many of my students circle causation indicators to get in the habit of looking for causal arguments and to draw their attention to them. Give it a try as you practice untangling arguments. Here is a list of common of terms you can use to identify a cause-and-effect relationship:

- Caused
- Responsible for
- Brought about by
- Leads to
- Is a result of
- Produces
- Reason for
- Makes happen
- Starts
- Is an effect of
- Set off by

Also note that the causes and effects don't necessarily appear in the same order in every argument. From the previous examples, eating potato chips is the causal factor while breaking out is the result. Or, the marketing plan is identified as the cause of the resulting sales increase. However, the third and fourth examples puts the cause at the end of the sentence: The earthquake caused the devastation, and the first apartment caused the sense of responsibility, respectively. The point to take away is that just because a term comes first in a sentence does not mean it is the cause. You have to read the statement carefully and pay attention to causal indicators.

Recognizing causal arguments is important for Weaken questions because the LSAT offers three classic alternatives to undermine the claim. Take a look at this example:

> Amy got a camera for her birthday and always carries it with her. She wants to take pictures everywhere she goes. So, getting the camera must be the reason for her interest in photography.

Here, the author argues that Amy is interested in photography because she has a new camera. "Reason for" signals a causal relationship between the camera and photography. Notice, however, that the author tells you Amy got a new camera (X) and Amy wants to take pictures everywhere she goes (Y) and then assumes a causal relationship in which the camera is the cause and picture taking is the effect.

To weaken a causal argument, you have three options.

1. Reverse the causality (Y → X)

You know X and Y both happened, but the author assumed the direction of the causality flowed from X to Y. Maybe it's really reversed. Maybe Amy's interest in taking pictures caused her to get a camera.

2. Identify an independent alternative cause (Z → Y)

Maybe an outside factor, Z, caused Y to happen. For example, perhaps Amy wanted to share her travels with family and friends. So it wasn't the camera that sparked her interest in photography, but rather her wanting to show people the places she'd been.

3. Chalk it up to coincidence

The elements of the argument coincidentally happened together in time but there is no causal relationship. Amy got a camera and she took pictures but one did not cause the other.

## Predictions

If the conclusion is stated as a prediction—a judgment about what is likely to happen in the future based on what is true in the past or the present—then you can weaken the argument by changing the circumstances on which the prediction is based. You can do this by showing the premise that supports it is inaccurate or irrelevant.

When Pauline opened her pizzeria, she beat her competitors' prices and all my neighbors became loyal customers. I doubt any of us will buy our pizza anywhere besides Pauline's Pizzeria.

In this example, the author predicts that she and her neighbors will always get their pizza from Pauline's Pizzeria because Pauline's sold the pies below her competitors' prices. Well sure, Pauline's prices were the lowest when the restaurant first opened. However, the author assumes the prices will continue to be the lowest and circumstances won't change: Pauline will keep her prices below competitors and the competitors will maintain their prices above Pauline's.

So, to weaken a prediction-based argument like this one, you need to look for an answer choice that changes the circumstances on which the prediction was made. Here, a correct answer choice will make Pauline's prices the same or above her competitors, or it could make a competitor's price the same or lower than Pauline's. For example, The Pizza Slice, a local pizzeria, celebrated its 10th anniversary by charging $10 for any pizza on the menu, the lowest price in town. This statement tells you that The Pizza Slice's prices are now lower than Pauline's. So, it is less likely that diners will stay loyal to Pauline's.

The main point I'm illustrating with these examples is that to make your answer prediction, think about how the author could reach a different conclusion or find an alternative explanation for how the author reached the conclusion.

## Evaluate the Answer Choices

Finally, take your prediction and compare it to the answer choices; the selection that most closely matches your prediction is your answer.

It is unlikely you will find an answer that completely negates the conclusion and obliterates the argument. That type of obvious answer seldom occurs on the LSAT. The typical Weaken answer will hurt the conclusion, not destroy it.

Also, pay close attention to any new terminology introduced in the answer choices. Don't let that fool you. The test makers often include new terms in the correct answer to a Weaken question because they are necessary to effectively Weaken the stimulus. (Remember that this is not the case with an Assumption question; the answer to an Assumption question must come from the argument itself).

## THE KAPLAN METHOD IN ACTION

Now I'll walk you through a couple examples to show you how the Kaplan Method can help you efficiently solve any Weaken question you'll see on test day.

1.  The manager of a nuclear power plant defended the claim that the plant was safe by revealing its rate of injury for current workers: only 3.2 injuries per 200,000 hours of work, a rate less than half the national average for all industrial plants. The manager claimed that, therefore, by the standard of how many injuries occur, the plant was safer than most other plants where the employees could work.

    Which one of the following, if true, most calls into question the manager's claim?

    (A)  Workers at nuclear power plants are required to receive extra training in safety precautions on their own time and at their own expense.
    (B)  Workers at nuclear power plants are required to report to the manager any cases of accidental exposure to radiation.
    (C)  The exposure of the workers to radiation at nuclear power plants was within levels the government considers safe.
    (D)  Workers at nuclear power plants have filed only a few lawsuits against the management concerning unsafe working conditions.
    (E)  Medical problems arising from work at a nuclear power plant are unusual in that they are not likely to appear until after an employee has left employment at the plant.[1]

## Step 1. Identify the Question Type

The phrase "calls into question" tells you that this is a Weaken question. The question specifically directs you to find the manager's claim.

## Step 2. Untangle the Stimulus

The manager's claim in the last sentence coupled with "therefore" identifies the conclusion. The nuclear power plant was safer than most other plants. The evidence for the claim is the low injury rate compared to all industrial plants.

## Step 3. Make a Prediction

The manager is comparing injury rates of a nuclear power plant to all industrial plants. Since this is a Weaken question, look for the questionable assumption. Here, she must assume they are comparable. What if they're not? Look for an answer that affects the injury rate comparison and makes the nuclear plant's rate higher or all plants' rates lower.

## Step 4. Evaluate the Answer Choices

It's good to know, as choice (A) tells you, that nuclear-plant workers receive extra training and unfortunately they must train on their own time and at their own expense. However, that has no bearing on the manager's claim of a comparatively low injury rate. Eliminate this choice.

---

[1]PrepTest 25, Sec. 4, Q 3

Choice (B) states that nuclear plant workers must report any radiation exposure not just an actual injury, which implies the injury rate should be higher. Therefore, choice (B) strengthens the argument and is incorrect.

Choices (C) and (D) discuss safe radiation levels and lawsuits filed against the nuclear plant. They don't add any information regarding the rate of injury comparison, and thus, are out of scope.

Choice (E) implies that the lower injury rates at the nuclear plant are artificially low because medical problems are latent and appear after workers leave the plant and those injuries are not included. This is the correct answer.

2. Police commissioner:  Last year our city experienced a 15 percent decrease in the rate of violent crime. At the beginning of that year a new mandatory sentencing law was enacted, which requires that all violent criminals serve time in prison. Since no other major policy changes were made last year, the drop in the crime rate must have been due to the new mandatory sentencing law.

   Which one of the following, if true, most seriously weakens the police commissioner's argument?

   (A)  Studies of many other cities have shown a correlation between improving economic conditions and decreased crime rates.
   (B)  Prior to the enactment of the mandatory sentencing law, judges in the city had for many years already imposed unusually harsh penalties for some crimes.
   (C)  Last year, the city's overall crime rate decreased by only 5 percent.
   (D)  At the beginning of last year, the police department's definition of "violent crime" was broadened to include 2 crimes not previously classified as "violent."
   (E)  The city enacted a policy 2 years ago requiring that 100 new police officers be hired in each of the 3 subsequent years.[2]

## Step 1. Identify the Question Type

The phrase "most seriously weakens" tells you that this is a Weaken question.

## Step 2. Untangle the Stimulus

The police commissioner concludes that the 15 percent drop in the crime rate was due to the new mandatory sentencing law. He supports his statement with evidence that no other major policy change was made last year except for that mandatory sentencing law. Do you see the causal language in the conclusion? That's right, "must have been due to." What is the cause

---

[2]PrepTest 47, Sec. 3, Q 24

and what is the effect? The police commissioner indicates that the sentencing law caused the crime rate reduction.

### Step 3. Make a Prediction

To weaken a causal argument, look for the three classic alternatives: reverse the causal relationship, find an alternative cause, or chalk it up to coincidence. Remember, finding an alternative cause is always the most likely of the three alternatives.

In this case, the reversed relationship would mean that the reduced crime rate caused the mandatory sentencing law. But, that doesn't really make sense, so maybe there is another reason for reduction in the crime rate that the commissioner did not consider. Maybe the city added police officers on patrol or expanded neighborhood block watches. It could also be that the occurrence of the crime rate drop and the enactment of the mandatory sentencing laws is a mere coincidence. Keep those options in mind as you look over the answer choices.

### Step 4. Evaluate the Answer Choices

Choice (A) alludes to an alternative cause for the drop in crime rate: improved economic conditions. But the study of other cities—not the one in question—identifies a correlation—not a causal relationship—between economic improvement and lower crime rate. Without information about the economic trends in this cities, this answer could weaken *or* strengthen the argument; it is completely ambiguous without knowing what direction the economy is headed in this town. Cross out this choice.

If judges imposed harsh penalties prior to the enactment of the mandatory sentencing law as choice (B) suggests, maybe the law just codified what was already in place. In other words, maybe the law did not do anything new. However, this answer has a problem. It refers to "unusually harsh" punishment applied to "some crimes" (meaning at least one, and not necessarily any violent crimes) rather than all violent crimes, as the new legislation did. Therefore, it is possible the legislation did have a causal relationship with the drop in crime rate. Move on to the next choice.

Choice (C) mentions the city's overall crime rate as opposed to the violent crime rate discussed in the argument. Therefore, it takes you outside the scope. Eliminate this choice.

Choice (D) expands the definition of a violent crime with the addition of a few new crimes but does not indicate any affect on the causality. If the mandatory sentencing law lowered the rate of occurrence of these new violent crimes, then, if anything, it would strengthen the argument.

That leaves one choice, choice (E), which offers an alternative cause for the reduced crime rate. Two years ago, the city decided to hire an additional 100 police officers each year for the next three years. An expanded police force is a viable reason for the drop in crime rate and thus weakens the argument that the reduction is due solely to the mandatory sentencing law. This is the correct answer.

# WEAKEN QUESTIONS: NOW YOU TRY IT

Now it's your turn to try a Weaken question. Use the template I've provided after the question to guide you through the four-step Kaplan Method. (Note: On test day, you won't be writing out all the steps as you are in this exercise. However, as you are learning the Method, it's good practice to help it become second nature.) Remember to bracket the conclusion and circle Keywords.

1.  Nutritionist: Recently a craze has developed for home juicers, $300 machines that separate the pulp of fruits and vegetables from the juice they contain. Outrageous claims are being made about the benefits of these devices: drinking the juice they produce is said to help one lose weight or acquire a clear complexion, to aid digestion, and even to prevent cancer. But there is no indication that juice separated from the pulp of the fruit or vegetable has any properties that it does not have when unseparated. Save your money. If you want carrot juice, eat a carrot.

    Which one of the following, if true, most calls into question the nutritionist's argument?

    (A)     Most people find it much easier to consume a given quantity of nutrients in liquid form than to eat solid foods containing the same quantity of the same nutrients.

    (B)     Drinking juice from home juicers is less healthy than is eating fruits and vegetables because such juice does not contain the fiber that is eaten if one consumes the entire fruit or vegetable.

    (C)     To most people who would be tempted to buy a home juicer, $300 would not be a major expense.

    (D)     The nutritionist was a member of a panel that extensively evaluated early prototypes of home juicers.

    (E)     Vitamin pills that supposedly contain nutrients available elsewhere only in fruits and vegetables often contain a form of those compounds that cannot be as easily metabolized as the varieties found in fruits and vegetables.[3]

---

[3]PrepTest 36, Sec. 1, Q 2

**Step 1. Identify the Question Type**

_____

**Step 2. Untangle the Stimulus**

_____

**Step 3. Make a Prediction**

_____

**Step 4. Evaluate the Answer Choices**

_____

## Explanations

1.   **(A)**

Nutritionist:  Recently a craze has developed for home juicers, $300 machines that separate the pulp of fruits and vegetables from the juice they contain. Outrageous claims are being made about the benefits of these devices: drinking the juice they produce is said to help one lose weight or acquire a clear complexion, to aid digestion, and even to prevent cancer. (But) there is no indication that juice separated from the pulp of the fruit or vegetable has any properties that it does not have when unseparated. <Save your money.> If you want carrot juice, eat a carrot.

Which one of the following, if true, (most calls) into (question) the nutritionist's argument?

(A)   Most people find it much easier to consume a given quantity of nutrients in liquid form than to eat solid foods containing the same quantity of the same nutrients.

(B)   Drinking juice from home juicers is less healthy than is eating fruits and vegetables because such juice does not contain the fiber that is eaten if one consumes the entire fruit or vegetable.

(C)   To most people who would be tempted to buy a home juicer, $300 would not be a major expense.

(D)   The nutritionist was a member of a panel that extensively evaluated early prototypes of home juicers.

(E)   Vitamin pills that supposedly contain nutrients available elsewhere only in fruits and vegetables often contain a form of those compounds that cannot be as easily metabolized as the varieties found in fruits and vegetables.[4]

## Step 1. Identify the Question Type

The phrase "calls into question" is a common weaken indicator; not all Weaken question stems contain the work "weaken." The phrase "nutritionist's argument" directs you specifically to look for what he concluded and why.

## Step 2. Untangle the Stimulus

The first two sentences of this stimulus present background information about juicers: they work by separating the pulp of fruits and vegetables from their juice, and they have become quite popular for their health benefits. However, "but" signals that the nutritionist disagrees

---

[4]PrepTest 36, Sec. 1, Q 2

with these claims. The nutritionist concludes that potential juicer customers should save their $300 and eat the fruits and vegetables in their solid form.

## Step 3. Make a Prediction

The nutritionist assumes that there's no reason to drink the juice other than for health reasons. But what if there was? That is, look at the answer choices for alternative reasons to buy the juicer. The correct answer will make the conclusion less likely that customers should not buy the juicer; or, put more clearly, it will provide a reason why customers *should* buy the juicer.

## Step 4. Evaluate the Answer Choices

Choice (A) offers a reason to buy a juicer—nutrients in liquid form rather than solid are easier to consume for most people—and therefore is the correct answer.

Choice (B) strengthens the argument, so it is incorrect; the fact that the juice is less healthy supports the choice of not buying the juicer.

Choice (C) is wrong. The cost of the juicer is mentioned in the stimulus but is not a factor in the argument; the juicer's affordability is not the issue, its practical value is. The nutritionist's evaluation of the early juicer prototype, presented in choice (D) is irrelevant.

Choice (E) draws an irrelevant comparison between the nutrition in vitamin pills and fruits and vegetables which is outside the scope of the argument.

# DRILL: PRACTICING WEAKEN QUESTIONS

Use the Kaplan Method to answer the following Weaken questions. Take this opportunity to practice and apply the steps in the Method so you are comfortable using them on test day. Be sure to circle conclusion and evidence Keywords and bracket the conclusion. Check your responses against the full explanations provided after the Drill.

1. Opponents of allowing triple-trailer trucks to use the national highway system are wrong in claiming that these trucks are more dangerous than other commercial vehicles. In the western part of the country, in areas where triple-trailers are now permitted on some highways, for these vehicles the rate of road accident fatalities per mile of travel is lower than the national rate for other types of commercial vehicles. Clearly, triple-trailers are safer than other commercial vehicles.

   Which one of the following, if true, most substantially weakens the argument?

   (A) It takes two smaller semitrailers to haul as much weight as a single triple-trailer can.
   (B) Highways in the sparsely populated West are much less heavily traveled and consequently are far safer than highways in the national system as a whole.
   (C) Opponents of the triple-trailers also once opposed the shorter twin-trailers, which are now common on the nation's highways.
   (D) In areas where the triple-trailers are permitted, drivers need a special license to operate them.
   (E) For triple-trailers the rate of road accident fatalities per mile of travel was higher last year than in the two previous years.[5]

2. Compared to us, people who lived a century ago had very few diversions to amuse them. Therefore, they likely read much more than we do today.

   Which one of the following statements, if true, most weakens the argument?

   (A) Many of the books published a century ago were of low literary quality.
   (B) On average, people who lived a century ago had considerably less leisure time than we do today.
   (C) The number of books sold today is larger than it was a century ago.
   (D) On the average, books today cost slightly less in relation to other goods than they did a century ago.
   (E) One of the popular diversions of a century ago was horse racing.[6]

3. The play *Mankind* must have been written between 1431 and 1471. It cannot have been written before 1431, for in that year the rose noble, a coin mentioned in the play, was first circulated. The play cannot have been written after 1471, since in that year King Henry VI died, and he is mentioned as a living monarch in the play's dedication.

   The argument would be most seriously weakened if which one of the following were discovered?

   (A) The Royal Theatre Company includes the play on a list of those performed in 1480.
   (B) Another coin mentioned in the play was first minted in 1422.
   (C) The rose noble was neither minted nor circulated after 1468.
   (D) Although Henry VI was deposed in 1461, he was briefly restored to the throne in 1470.
   (E) In a letter written in early 1428, a merchant told of having seen the design for a much-discussed new coin called the "rose noble."[7]

4. It is probably not true that colic in infants is caused by the inability of those infants to tolerate certain antibodies found in cow's milk, since it is often the case that symptoms of colic are shown by infants that are fed breast milk exclusively.

Which one of the following, if true, most seriously weakens the argument?

(A) A study involving 500 sets of twins has found that if one infant has colic, its twin will probably also have colic.

(B) Symptoms of colic generally disappear as infants grow older, whether the infants have been fed breast milk exclusively or have been fed infant formula containing cow's milk.

(C) In a study of 5,000 infants who were fed only infant formula containing cow's milk, over 4,000 of the infants never displayed any symptoms of colic.

(D) When mothers of infants that are fed only breast milk eliminate cow's milk and all products made from cow's milk from their own diets, any colic symptoms that their infants have manifested quickly disappear.

(E) Infants that are fed breast milk develop mature digestive systems at an earlier age than do those that are fed infant formulas, and infants with mature digestive systems are better able to tolerate certain proteins and antibodies found in cow's milk.[8]

5. Parent P: Children will need computer skills to deal with tomorrow's world. Computers should be introduced in kindergarten, and computer languages should be required in high school.

Parent Q: That would be pointless. Technology advances so rapidly that the computers used by today's kindergartners and the computer languages taught in today's high schools would become obsolete by the time these children are adults.

Which one of the following, if true, is the strongest logical counter parent P can make to parent Q's objection?

(A) When technology is advancing rapidly, regular training is necessary to keep one's skills at a level proficient enough to deal with the society in which one lives.

(B) Throughout history people have adapted to change, and there is no reason to believe that today's children are not equally capable of adapting to technology as it advances.

(C) In the process of learning to work with any computer or computer language, children increase their ability to interact with computer technology.

(D) Automotive technology is continually advancing too, but that does not result in one's having to relearn to drive cars as the new advances are incorporated into new automobiles.

(E) Once people have graduated from high school, they have less time to learn about computers and technology than they had during their schooling years.[9]

6. Letter to the editor: After Baerton's factory closed, there was a sharp increase in the number of claims filed for job-related injury compensation by the factory's former employees. Hence there is reason to believe that most of those who filed for compensation after the factory closed were just out to gain benefits they did not deserve, and filed only to help them weather their job loss.

Each of the following, if true, weakens the argument above EXCEPT:

(A) Workers cannot file for compensation for many job-related injuries, such as hearing loss from factory noise, until they have left the job.

(B) In the years before the factory closed, the factory's managers dismissed several employees who had filed injury claims.

(C) Most workers who receive an injury on the job file for compensation on the day they suffer the injury.

(D) Workers who incur partial disabilities due to injuries on the job often do not file for compensation because they would have to stop working to receive compensation but cannot afford to live on that compensation alone.

(E) Workers who are aware that they will soon be laid off from a job often become depressed, making them more prone to job-related injuries.[10]

7. Several companies will soon offer personalized electronic news services, delivered via cable or telephone lines and displayed on a television. People using these services can view continually updated stories on those topics for which they subscribe. Since these services will provide people with the information they are looking for more quickly and efficiently than printed newspapers can, newspaper sales will decline drastically if these services become widely available.

Which one of the following, if true, most seriously weakens the argument?

(A) In reading newspapers, most people not only look for stories on specific topics but also like to idly browse through headlines or pictures for amusing stories on unfamiliar or unusual topics.

(B) Companies offering personalized electronic news services will differ greatly in what they charge for access to their services, depending on how wide a range of topics they cover.

(C) Approximately 30 percent of people have never relied on newspapers for information but instead have always relied on news programs broadcast on television and radio.

(D) The average monthly cost of subscribing to several channels on a personalized electronic news service will approximately equal the cost of a month's subscription to a newspaper.

(E) Most people who subscribe to personalized electronic news services will not have to pay extra costs for installation since the services will use connections installed by cable and telephone companies.[11]

# Explanations

## 1. (B)

<Opponents of allowing triple-trailer trucks to use the national highway system are wrong in claiming that these trucks are more dangerous than other commercial vehicles.> In the western part of the country, in areas where triple-trailers are now permitted on some highways, for these vehicles the rate of road accident fatalities per mile of travel is lower than the national rate for other types of commercial vehicles. <Clearly, triple-trailers are safer than other commercial vehicles.>

Which one of the following, if true, most substantially weakens the argument?

(A)  It takes two smaller semitrailers to haul as much weight as a single triple-trailer can.

(B)  Highways in the sparsely populated West are much less heavily traveled and consequently are far safer than highways in the national system as a whole.

(C)  Opponents of the triple-trailers also once opposed the shorter twin-trailers, which are now common on the nation's highways.

(D)  In areas where the triple-trailers are permitted, drivers need a special license to operate them.

(E)  For triple-trailers the rate of road accident fatalities per mile of travel was higher last year than in the two previous years.[12]

## Step 1. Identify the Question Type

The author uses the phrase "most substantially weakens," which is the language of a Weaken question.

## Step 2. Untangle the Stimulus

The author states his conclusion twice for emphasis. In the first sentence, he says people are wrong to say triple-trailer trucks (TTTs) are more dangerous than other commercial vehicles. In the last sentence, he adds the word "clearly" to emphasize the conclusive nature of a positive version of a similar statement: TTTs are safer than commercial vehicles. The author offers as evidence of TTT safety the western part of the country where the rate of road incident vehicles per mile of travel is lower than the national rate for other commercial vehicles. Do you see a pattern in the argument? The author says that TTTs are safer than commercial vehicles out West, therefore, TTTs are safer everywhere.

---

[12]PrepTest 20, Sec. 4, Q 3

### Step 3. Make a Prediction

The author assumes that TTT safety in the western part of the country is comparable to the whole country. To weaken the argument, you need to reduce the likelihood that western TTT safety would hold in other parts of the country.

### Step 4. Evaluate the Answer Choices

Choice (A) is outside the scope as it deals with the hauling capacity of a TTT rather than safety. This choice is out.

Choice (B) provides a rationale for a better safety record for western highways. This matches the prediction and is the correct answer.

The TTT opponents' past opposition to shorter twin-trailers as presented in choice (C) has no bearing on the argument.

Having a special license to drive a TTT as stated in choice (D) has no impact on the argument unless the license carries a requirement for special training that renders the TTTs safer on the road than other trucks. In that case, the special license would strengthen, not weaken, the argument.

The argument compares the TTT safety record to the safety record of other commercial vehicles. Choice (E), which addresses a rise in the TTT accident rate without comparison information about the other commercial vehicles, does not address whether the TTT is safer than other commercial vehicles.

2. **(B)**

Compared to us, people who lived a century ago had very few diversions to amuse them. ⟨Therefore,⟩ they likely read much more than we do today.⟩

Which one of the following statements, if true, most ⟨weakens⟩ the argument?

(A) Many of the books published a century ago were of low literary quality.
(B) On average, people who lived a century ago had considerably less leisure time than we do today.
(C) The number of books sold today is larger than it was a century ago.
(D) On the average, books today cost slightly less in relation to other goods than they did a century ago.
(E) One of the popular diversions of a century ago was horse racing.[13]

---

[13]PrepTest 37, Sec. 2, Q 4

### Step 1. Identify the Question Type

The question uses standard Weaken language.

### Step 2. Untangle the Stimulus

The word "Therefore" points you to the conclusion that people who lived a century ago probably read more than we do today. The author supports the claim with evidence that our ancestors had fewer diversions back then.

### Step 3. Make a Prediction

According to the author, those who lived a century ago had fewer things to do, so they read more than us. That seems like a big logical jump. For example, the few things they did might have left them no time for reading. Or maybe, they chose a different activity than reading. There are lots of opportunities here to loosen the connection between conclusion and evidence and weaken the argument.

### Step 4. Evaluate the Answer Choices

The low level of literary quality discussed in choice (A) does not affect the connection between fewer diversions and more reading. In fact, some might argue that low literary quality may not deter readers with time on their hands looking for anything to read. In that scenario, low literary quality would support the argument that our ancestors read more than us. Eliminate this choice.

Choice (B) matches the prediction. Without much leisure time, people 100 years ago didn't have time to read even if that was their only leisure activity option. This is the correct answer.

Choice (C) states that the number of books sold today is greater than 100 years ago. The implication is that more books sold means more books read. However, you don't know the number of book buyers or the number of books they bought. You also can't use this information to determine whether the buyers actually read the books let alone read more.

Choice (D) offers an irrelevant comparison between the cost of books and other goods. The answer choice insinuates that a lower book cost would influence readers to read. However, this statement does not tell us anything about the actual price, just that it is lower than other goods.

Choice (E) is equally problematic. It identifies horse racing as another diversion for people 100 years ago. However, it does not address the number of readers today compared to a century ago.

3.  **(E)**

<The play *Mankind* must have been written between 1431 and 1471.> It cannot have been written before 1431, (for) in that year the rose noble, a coin mentioned in the play, was first circulated. The play cannot have been written after 1471, (since) in that year King Henry VI died, and he is mentioned as a living monarch in the play's dedication.

The argument would be most seriously (weakened) if which one of the following were discovered?

(A)   The Royal Theatre Company includes the play on a list of those performed in 1480.

(B)   Another coin mentioned in the play was first minted in 1422.

(C)   The rose noble was neither minted nor circulated after 1468.

(D)   Although Henry VI was deposed in 1461, he was briefly restored to the throne in 1470.

(E)   In a letter written in early 1428, a merchant told of having seen the design for a much-discussed new coin called the "rose noble."[14]

## Step 1. Identify the Question Type

Again, this question uses standard Weaken language.

## Step 2. Untangle the Stimulus

In the first sentence, the author pinpoints the time period in which *Mankind* was written as between 1431 and 1471. The author presents two pieces of evidence to explain why the play must have been written during this span. First, she eliminates the possibility it was written before 1431 because a coin mentioned in the play was not circulated until after 1431. Then, she says 1471 had to be the latest year because the play mentions Henry VI as a living king, and he died in 1471.

## Step 3. Make a Prediction

The author assumes that a coin circulated after 1431 and the mention of a living king who died in 1471 absolutely set a boundary for the creation date of the play. The correct answer will attack the assumption and raise the possibility that the play was written before or after the speculated time period. This general prediction is enough to move forward and compare to the given answer choices. However, you may have predicted something more specific, such as "The exact year of King Henry VI's death is in dispute. While some claim he died in 1471, a growing number of historians believe he died in 1476." Whether your prediction is general or specific, it probably won't match the correct answer choice exactly. You must be flexible.

---

[14]PrepTest 24, Sec. 3, Q 9

## Step 4. Evaluate the Answer Choices

Choice (A) states the play was not performed until 1480. However, a 1480 play opening does not mean the play was written after 1471. The performance date is irrelevant in this argument. Cross out this choice.

Choice (B) discusses another coin mentioned in the play that was minted prior to 1431. This earlier-minted coin has no impact on the argument because it has nothing to do with the connection between the rose noble coin and the play's date of origin. Eliminate this choice.

The date of the rose noble coin's disappearance given in choice (C) does nothing to expand the play's time frame. The play could still have been written after 1431. This choice is wrong.

Choice (D) offers information about when King Henry VI was in power. The only important date is the year in which Henry died, 1471. Whether he was on the throne, Henry was a living monarch until he died in 1471. This choice is out, too.

Choice (E) essentially states that a circulation date of 1431 does not eliminate the possibility it was created prior to that year. You don't need to make it absolutely true the coin was created outside of the time frame, but just raise the possibility. That's what (E) does, and so it is the correct answer.

4. **(D)**

<It is probably not true that colic in infants is caused by the inability of those infants to tolerate certain antibodies found in cow's milk,> (since) it is often the case that symptoms of colic are shown by infants that are fed breast milk exclusively.

Which one of the following, if true, most seriously (weakens) the argument?

(A)   A study involving 500 sets of twins has found that if one infant has colic, its twin will probably also have colic.

(B)   Symptoms of colic generally disappear as infants grow older, whether the infants have been fed breast milk exclusively or have been fed infant formula containing cow's milk.

(C)    In a study of 5,000 infants who were fed only infant formula containing cow's milk, over 4,000 of the infants never displayed any symptoms of colic.

(D)   When mothers of infants that are fed only breast milk eliminate cow's milk and all products made from cow's milk from their own diets, any colic symptoms that their infants have manifested quickly disappear.

(E)   Infants that are fed breast milk develop mature digestive systems at an earlier age than do those that are fed infant formulas, and infants with mature digestive systems are better able to tolerate certain proteins and antibodies found in cow's milk.[15]

## Step 1. Identify the Question Type

"Weaken" signals a Weaken question.

## Step 2. Untangle the Stimulus

"Since" points to the evidence that infants fed only breast milk can show symptoms of colic. Based on this, the author disagrees with the thought that the inability to tolerate cow's milk causes colic in infants. In other words, the author concludes that cow's milk is not responsible for colic in infants because breast-fed infants also show signs of colic.

## Step 3. Make a Prediction

The author assumes that an infant raised exclusively on breast milk has no access to the antibodies in cow's milk. The access to cow's milk is certainly not direct, but is there any way a breast-fed infant could be exposed indirectly to cow's milk? If so, you will weaken the argument. Check the answers for any indication that cow's milk still plays some role in breast-fed infants who have colic.

---

[15]PrepTest 20, Sec. 1, Q 12

## Step 4. Evaluate the Answer Choices

Choice (A) does not weaken the argument because it ignores the type of milk the twin infants received. Cross out this choice.

Choice (B) focuses on the disappearance of colic while the argument discusses the cause of colic. So this answer is clearly outside the scope.

Choice (C) has the same problem. The argument is not about infants who don't develop colic, but rather infants who do. If anything, the answer strengthens the author's argument by indicating more than 80% of the infants in the study drank cow's milk and showed no signs of colic.

Choice (D) matches the prediction. When the breast-feeding mothers eliminate all forms of cow's milk from their diets, their infants' colic symptoms disappear. So the mothers may have indirectly exposed their infants to cow's milk. You still don't know if cow's milk definitely causes colic, but the author's conclusion that cow's milk probably does not cause colic is seriously weakened.

Choice (E) sheds no light on the connection between cow's milk and colic and therefore has no effect on the argument.

5.   **(C)**

Parent P: Children will need computer skills to deal with tomorrow's world. Computers should be introduced in kindergarten, and computer languages should be required in high school.
Parent Q: <That would be pointless.> Technology advances so rapidly that the computers used by today's kindergartners and the computer languages taught in today's high schools would become obsolete by the time these children are adults.

Which one of the following, if true, is the strongest logical counter parent P can make to parent Q's objection?

(A)   When technology is advancing rapidly, regular training is necessary to keep one's skills at a level proficient enough to deal with the society in which one lives.

(B)   Throughout history people have adapted to change, and there is no reason to believe that today's children are not equally capable of adapting to technology as it advances.

(C)   In the process of learning to work with any computer or computer language, children increase their ability to interact with computer technology.

(D)   Automotive technology is continually advancing too, but that does not result in one's having to relearn to drive cars as the new advances are incorporated into new automobiles.

(E)   Once people have graduated from high school, they have less time to learn about computers and technology than they had during their schooling years.[16]

## Step 1. Identify the Question Type

"Counter" indicates this is a Weaken question. You are asked to counter, or weaken, parent Q's objection.

## Step 2. Untangle the Stimulus

Start with Q's objection "That would be pointless" and determine what "That" is. Q is referring to P's proposal to introduce children to computers and computer language in school, and he concludes the proposal is pointless. His evidence is that the technology the schoolchildren learn will be obsolete by the time they reach adulthood.

## Step 3. Make a Prediction

Q assumes that any exposure to technology has no use or relevance in the future. The answer choice indicating that early exposure to technology supports future computer skills will weaken the argument.

---

[16]PrepTest 35, Sec. 1, Q 4

## Step 4. Evaluate the Answer Choices

Choice (A) raises the need for ongoing training as technology advances, which reduces the importance of early training. Go on to the next choice.

The ability to adapt to change discussed in choice (B) is outside the scope. Whether today's children can adapt to technology changes like people throughout history have adapted to change has no impact on the argument.

Choice (C) matches the prediction. It says that children who learn to work with computers and computer language are better able to interact with technology. In other words, early computer training benefits the children's future computer work. This is the correct answer.

Choice (D) makes an analogy to automotive technology based on an assumption that automotive technology and computer technology are comparable. Without establishing a direct connection between the two, knowing that early driving training was useful even as the industry instituted advances, does not help establish that the same will happen in the computer industry.

Choice (E) implies that computers and technology should be taught while children are in school because they have more time compared to after high school graduation. It does not address the value of early training, which the correct answer requires.

### 6.  (C)

Letter to the editor: After Baerton's factory closed, there was a sharp increase in the number of claims filed for job-related injury compensation by the factory's former employees. <Hence there is reason to believe that most of those who filed for compensation after the factory closed were just out to gain benefits they did not deserve, and filed only to help them weather their job loss.>

Each of the following, if true, weakens the argument above EXCEPT:

(A)  Workers cannot file for compensation for many job-related injuries, such as hearing loss from factory noise, until they have left the job.

(B)  In the years before the factory closed, the factory's managers dismissed several employees who had filed injury claims.

(C)  Most workers who receive an injury on the job file for compensation on the day they suffer the injury.

(D)  Workers who incur partial disabilities due to injuries on the job often do not file for compensation because they would have to stop working to receive compensation but cannot afford to live on that compensation alone.

(E)  Workers who are aware that they will soon be laid off from a job often become depressed, making them more prone to job-related injuries.[17]

---

[17]PrepTest 24, Sec. 3, Q 22

### Step 1. Identify the Question Type

The phrase "weakens the argument above EXCEPT" tells you the answer choices include four answers that weaken the argument and one answer—the correct answer—that either strengthens the argument or has no effect on the argument at all. Circling the word "EXCEPT" will help keep you from marking an answer choice that weakens the argument.

### Step 2. Untangle the Stimulus

"Hence" directs you to the conclusion that workers filed job-related injury claims seeking benefits they did not deserve after the factory closed. The letter writer's evidence is that there was a sharp increase in the number of job-related injury claims filed after the factory closed.

### Step 3. Make a Prediction

The letter writer jumps from evidence of an increase in claims to a conclusion of fraud and greed. So, he must assume that fraud and greed are the only explanation for the increase in claims after the factory closed. Because this is a Weaken . . . EXCEPT question, the four wrong answers will weaken the argument by presenting an alternative explanation for the increase in claims. As you find those weakeners, cross them out to eliminate them. The correct answer strengthens the argument or is completely irrelevant. Possible strengtheners would eliminate other explanations for the rise in filed claims or confirm that the workers are fraudulent and greedy.

### Step 4. Evaluate the Answer Choices

Choice (A) weakens the argument by requiring workers to file for many job-related injury benefits only after they have left the job. So, you would expect the number of filings to rise upon the closing of the factory since the end of the workers' jobs was a necessary condition for filing many injury claims.

Choice (B) provides another explanation for why factory workers would wait and file upon the closing of the factory: They no longer had jobs to lose and did not have to worry about retaliation from the factory managers.

Choice (C) has no weakening impact on the argument and is therefore the correct answer. That most workers file when they suffer an injury does nothing to explain why the workers at this factory would wait until the factory closed. By eliminating a potential alternative explanation for the timing of the claims—that workers typically wait to file a claim—this fact marginally strengthens the argument that greed is the explanation.

Choice (D) offers further incentive for workers to postpone filing injury claims. Filing under the circumstances means they would have to stop work and would receive inadequate compensation.

Choices (A), (B), and (D) all present viable reasons for the workers to file injury claims after the factory closed and thus raise the number of claims filed. In choice (E), workers aren't postponing the filing of a claim, but rather filing for claims that arise legitimately as the factory closes. It's not fraud or greed that causes the rise in filings. It's the injuries that occur as workers anticipate layoffs.

## 7.   **(A)**

Several companies will soon offer personalized electronic news services, delivered via cable or telephone lines and displayed on a television. People using these services can view continually updated stories on those topics for which they subscribe. (Since) these services will provide people with the information they are looking for more quickly and efficiently than printed newspapers can, <newspaper sales will decline drastically if these services become widely available.>

Which one of the following, if true, most seriously (weakens) the argument?

(A)   In reading newspapers, most people not only look for stories on specific topics but also like to idly browse through headlines or pictures for amusing stories on unfamiliar or unusual topics.

(B)   Companies offering personalized electronic news services will differ greatly in what they charge for access to their services, depending on how wide a range of topics they cover.

(C)   Approximately 30 percent of people have never relied on newspapers for information but instead have always relied on news programs broadcast on television and radio.

(D)   The average monthly cost of subscribing to several channels on a personalized electronic news service will approximately equal the cost of a month's subscription to a newspaper.

(E)   Most people who subscribe to personalized electronic news services will not have to pay extra costs for installation since the services will use connections installed by cable and telephone companies.[18]

## Step 1. Identify the Question Type

Again, "weakens" indicates that this a Weaken question.

## Step 2. Untangle the Stimulus

In the last half of the final sentence, the author concludes that newspaper sales will experience a drastic decline. The decline is based on evidence that electronic services are more efficient in providing information that people seek.

---

[18]PrepTest 36, Sec. 3, Q 2

### Step 3. Make a Prediction

The author assumes that providing information people want more efficiently is the only factor used to choose a news service and ignores other possibilities. The correct answer will provide an additional factor people use to select their news source.

### Step 4. Evaluate the Answer Choices

Choice (A) provides a feature that newspapers offer and that cannot be duplicated by the electronic media, and therefore, gives another reason the newspaper may remain attractive to readers. This is the correct answer.

The different prices of the electronic news services in choice (B) do nothing to make the printed newspaper more attractive or the electronic services less attractive to the reader.

Choice (C) refers to a group of people that don't read the newspapers, which is outside the scope of this argument. Additionally, the group of non-newspaper readers cannot contribute to a decline in newspaper sales.

Choice (D) strengthens the argument. If the subscription prices are the same for the printed and electronic news, cost cannot differentiate the two mediums and circumstances on which the prediction was made remains the same. So, the electronic news service remains more attractive to the reader than the printed service because it is faster and more efficient.

Choice (E) does not give enough information about the electronic compared to the printed news to determine if one service is more enticing to readers than the other. If anything, choice (E) strengthens the argument by making the cost of electronic service installation negligible.

## WEAKEN REVIEW

Before you proceed to the next chapter, turn to Appendix A and complete the review exercise for Weaken questions. A completed chart is included in Appendix B.

# CHAPTER 7

# STRENGTHEN QUESTIONS

Strengthen questions test your ability to identify an argument and add something to it to make it stronger. As a lawyer, you'll need to present your client's best case whether in negotiations or in trial, and so your ability to strengthen an argument is essential to this basic professional responsibility.

Consider the following scenario: A lawyer represents an experienced and highly successful college basketball coach in negotiations to extend his contract with a university. She plans to request a salary increase and additional retirement benefits. She will argue that her client is the best person for the job given his credentials, the job requirements, and the needs of the university. She will strengthen her argument by reminding the university officials of her client's tournament success, recruiting triumphs, and sellout crowds, as well as the difficulty and cost of replacing the coach. Because the lawyer was able to effectively present a strong argument, she increased the chances that the university would grant her client's requests. Now, this may be a simplified example, but I hope it illustrates how essential this skill is in the law profession.

Strengthen questions are similar to Weaken questions—just the opposite side of the coin. The two question types both require you to focus on the argument by identifying the conclusion and evidence and linking them with the assumption. However, they ask you to perform opposite tasks with these elements: Strengthen questions task you to use the elements to build support for an argument, while Weaken questions direct you to use the elements to undermine the argument.

Strengthen and Weaken questions together make up about eight out of 50 scored Logical Reasoning questions on the LSAT. They are also part of the Assumption family of questions, which accounts for half of the scored Logical Reasoning points. So, practicing and mastering Strengthen and Weaken questions can help you earn a substantial number of points on test day.

# DEFINITION OF STRENGTHEN QUESTIONS

As I mentioned before, Strengthen questions ask you to provide additional information to an argument to make the conclusion more likely to happen. Strengthening an argument does not mean you must make it true; rather, your job is to add information to bolster the argument so the conclusion is more likely to follow from the evidence.

Look at this example from the Weaken chapter:

> A determination by the university that a student-athlete has not taken enough credits to be progressing toward a degree renders that student-athlete academically ineligible to compete. Henry did not play in Saturday's football game. Therefore, he must not have the proper number of credits to be progressing toward a degree.

To strengthen this argument, you don't have to prove that Henry lacks the requisite number of credits to progress toward his degree, which is why he's not playing. Instead, you need to add something to the argument to make it more likely that Henry is missing credits, can't meet degree standards, and consequently can't compete. Can you think of anything to support the argument? Take a look at the following statements:

- When Henry got sick last semester, he had to drop a few courses in his psychology major.
- Henry is playing injury-free this season.
- Henry's coach reported no disciplinary problems to the pro scouts asking about him last week.
- Henry beat out all his competition for the starting running back position.

None of the statements specifically pinpoint that Henry failed to meet the progress toward degree requirements. However, dropping some courses for his major and eliminating other reasons for Henry to miss a game (injury, disciplinary problems, and competition) support the possibility that Henry missed the game because of academic ineligibility. That's all you need to do to strengthen an argument: Find an answer that makes it more likely that the conclusion is true.

An answer that essentially confirms the conclusion like "Henry, a senior, is five credits shy of the mandatory credits for a fourth year psychology major" would strengthen the argument, but seldom occurs on the LSAT. The typical strengthen answer will support the conclusion, not specifically confirm it. However, just as I discussed in the Weaken chapter, answers to Strengthen questions can include new terms. It's appropriate to look for information outside the argument to make the conclusion more likely to be true from the evidence.

# USE THE KAPLAN METHOD TO ANSWER STRENGTHEN QUESTIONS

## Identify the Question Type

As was the case with Weaken questions, there are certain words in the question stem that help you to recognize a Strengthen question. Some of those include:

- Strengthen
- Support
- Justify

In addition to those words, there are specific question stems that indicate a Strengthen question. They include:

- Which one of the following, if true, most strengthens the argument above?
- Which one of the following, if true, most strongly supports the claim above?
- Each of the following, if true, strengthens the argument EXCEPT:
- Which one of the following, if true, provides the strongest additional support for the hypotheses above?
- Which one of the following, if true, most helps to justify the company president's criticism of the human resources department's proposal?

Notice that Strengthen question stems typically begin with phrases such as, "Which of the following, if true, most…." Don't get hung up on the words "if true" and "most." Over thinking those terms is a common pitfall for students. "If true" tells you to accept the answer choice as true and not to argue with it. "Most" does not indicate a contest between the five answer choices in which you choose the best from amongst them—so don't approach the answer looking for the choice that best strengthens the argument. Rather, only the correct answer choice—the one you're looking for—will strengthen the argument, while the other four choices will not.

## Untangle the Stimulus

Just as you did with Assumption and Weaken questions, read a Strengthen stimulus to find the argument. First, circle any Keywords. Then find the conclusion, bracket it, and look for the evidence the author is using to support the conclusion. Next, connect the evidence to the conclusion to find the author's assumption. Finally, you use the conclusion, evidence, and the assumption to support the argument and make the conclusion more likely to be true.

## Make a Prediction

When predicting an answer choice that strengthens an argument, you need to think of ways to bolster the building blocks that make up the argument. You can do this in several different ways:

- Support the conclusion.
- Confirm the assumption.
- Discount objections to the argument.
- Eliminate alternative explanations.

Review the following example to see how this works:

> State University's Athletic Director wants the swimming and diving program to return to its glory days of conference championships and national record holders. Consequently, she committed to building a new, state-of-the-art aquatic facility.

The author concludes that the Athletic Director will build a new aquatic facility. The evidence provided is that she wants to improve the swimming and diving program's record. So, the author must assume that beating the competition requires a new facility.

To strengthen this argument, you can:

1. Support the conclusion: Determine what you can add to the argument to make it more likely that building a new aquatic center will meet the Athletic Director's competitive goal. For instance, the correct answer could cite another university that built a new aquatic facility and improved its competitive success.

2. Confirm the assumption: Determine what you can add to the argument to reinforce that competitive success requires a new aquatic facility. For example, you could indicate that new athletic facilities attract the best student-athletes. The correct answer could cite a study that shows the top collegiate swimming and diving programs in the country all added new facilities in the last five years. The right choice also could state something about how new pools are engineered to reduce waves and promote faster times.

3. Eliminate alternative explanations: Think of alternatives that could explain the argument, and look for an answer that eliminates them. Maybe there are other factors that could possibly contribute to a winning university swim team. If an answer choice disposes of one of those factors, the argument will be stronger. For example, the specific equipment and apparel sponsor of the athletic department is not a big consideration for student-athletes when they choose their schools.

### Causality

As I noted in the Weaken chapter, causal arguments—where the author asserts or denies a cause-and-effect relationship between two events or things—are common in the Assumption family of questions. So keep your eye out for causal indicators.

Consider the following example:

> Flo is playing better volleyball this year than in any other season before it. She's spiking harder, jumping higher, and responding quicker on the court. So, her off-season strength and conditioning program is responsible for her improvement.

The author claims that Flo's off-season workout program (X) caused her to be a better player (Y) because her volleyball skills have improved.

To strengthen a causal argument such as this one, you have three options (which are the opposite of those you use to Weaken an argument):

1. Support the causality (X → Y)

Here, you have two options to show that X caused Y—that the off-season workouts caused skill improvement. First, you could give another example of the cause producing the effect. In this example, that could be another player showing skill improvement because of her off-season workouts. Your second option is to support the causality by showing that without the cause the result doesn't happen. In this case, you could add that Flo did not work out last year and she showed no skill improvement.

2. Eliminate an alternative cause for the stated result (Z did not cause Y)

Remember, the author believes that X caused Y. By disposing of an alternative cause, the causal relationship between X and Y is that much closer and it's more likely that X caused Y. So, if you learn that Flo's coach remained the same over the past three years and that the coaching strategy has not changed, then the possibility that coaching was a factor in Flo's improvement is eliminated, and therefore the workout regimen is a stronger choice.

3. Eliminate the possibility of coincidence

The final way to strengthen an argument is to find an answer that proves that the relationship between X and Y was not because of coincidence. In this case, the elements of the argument did not coincidentally happen at the same time—Flo's workout preceded her improvement and the workout led to the improvement.

## Evaluate the Answer Choices

Armed with your prediction, review the answer choices and find the one that most closely matches. Remember that the match may not be exact; your prediction may be more specific or more general than the one correct answer, so you need to be open to different presentations.

# THE KAPLAN METHOD IN ACTION

Now I'll walk you through a couple examples to show you how the Kaplan Method can help you efficiently solve any Strengthen question you'll see on test day.

1.  Poor nutrition is at the root of the violent behavior of many young offenders. Researchers observed that in a certain institution for young offenders, the violent inmates among them consistently chose, from the food available, those items that were low in nutrients. In a subsequent experiment, some of the violent inmates were placed on a diet high in nutrients. There was a steady improvement in their behavior over the four months of the experiment. These results confirm the link between poor nutrition and violent behavior.

    Which one of the following, if true, most strengthens the argument?

    (A)   Some of the violent inmates who took part in the experiment had committed a large number of violent crimes.
    (B)   Dietary changes are easier and cheaper to implement than any other type of reform program in institutions for young offenders.
    (C)   Many young offenders have reported that they had consumed a low-nutrient food sometime in the days before they committed a violent crime.
    (D)   A further study investigated young offenders who chose a high-nutrient diet on their own and found that many of them were nonviolent.
    (E)   The violent inmates in the institution who were not placed on a high-nutrient diet did not show an improvement in behavior.[1]

## Step 1. Identify the Question Type

The word "strengthens" in the question stem indicates that this is a Strengthen question.

## Step 2. Untangle the Stimulus

The author makes a causal argument and begins the stimulus with the conclusion, using the words "is at the root of" to tell you that poor nutrition causes violent behavior in young offenders. She bases her conclusion on an experiment in which violent young offenders were given a high-nutrient diet and experienced steady improvement in behavior. So, in other words, poor nutrition causes violent behavior because good nutrition causes improved behavior.

## Step 3. Make a Prediction

The author must assume the causal relationship between nutrition and behavior. So to strengthen the argument, you need to find an answer that connects them. Possible correct

---

[1]PrepTest 41, Sec. 1, Q 12

answers may eliminate other explanations for the violent behavior, confirm the assumption, or provide additional research that achieved the same results. Another possibility is to show an absence of one factor is followed by the absence of the other.

## Step 4. Evaluate the Answer Choices

The number of violent crimes as discussed in choice (A) does not impact the relationship between nutrition and behavior, and thus it has no impact on the argument.

Likewise, the relative ease and low cost of dietary changes is not related to the effectiveness of the dietary changes, so you can eliminate choice (B).

Do the same with choice (C). Consuming a low-nutrient food sometime prior to a violent crime is too vague. You don't know how much low-nutrient food was consumed and in what proportion to healthy food. You also don't know when in time the low-nutrient food was eaten. So the relationship between food and behavior remains unchanged.

Whether the high-nutrient diet was a voluntary dining choice is also irrelevant and has no effect on the link between food and behavior. Cross out choice (D) as well.

Choice (E) matches the prediction by tying nutrition and behavior closer together. Without the high nutrition diet, violent inmates showed no behavioral improvement. This is the correct answer.

2.  Someone who gets sick from eating a meal will often develop a strong distaste for the one food in the meal that had the most distinctive flavor, whether or not that food caused the sickness. This phenomenon explains why children are especially likely to develop strong aversions to some foods.

    Which one of the following, if true, provides the strongest support for the explanation?

    (A)  Children are more likely than adults to be given meals composed of foods lacking especially distinctive flavors.
    (B)  Children are less likely than adults to see a connection between their health and the foods they eat.
    (C)  Children tend to have more acute taste and to become sick more often than adults do.
    (D)  Children typically recover more slowly than adults do from sickness caused by food.
    (E)  Children are more likely than are adults to refuse to eat unfamiliar foods.[2]

---

[2]PrepTest 20, Sec. 1, Q 9

### Step 1. Identify the Question Type

The word "support" in the question stem indicates you have either a Strengthen or an Inference question. To determine which question type you are dealing with, you need to determine which way the support travels. In this case, the question asks you to find the answer choice that supports the explanation—meaning that the support travels from the answer choice to stimulus. When the correct answer choice supports, or strengthens, the argument, you know you are dealing with a Strengthen question. Besides identifying a Strengthen question, this stem also tells you what to strengthen—the explanation in the argument.

### Step 2. Untangle the Stimulus

Once you identify a Strengthen question, read the stimulus to find the conclusion and the evidence. In this example, the stimulus presents a phenomenon in which people tend to dislike the most distinctive-tasting food in a meal from which they got sick, even if that particular food did not cause the illness. Note the phrase "this phenomenon explains why." Since the evidence explains the conclusion, the phenomenon is the evidence, and the conclusion—that children are especially likely to develop strong aversions to some food—must follow.

### Step 3. Make a Prediction

To strengthen the argument, you need to identify the assumption and confirm it. In this case, the argument talks about children hating food because some people hate the strongest flavor of a meal from which they get sick. The assumption must connect the children to the factors inherent in the phenomenon, getting sick and picking out a distinctive flavor.

### Step 4. Evaluate the Answer Choices

Choices (A) and (B) both weaken the argument by breaking down the assumption: Choice (A) loosens the connection between children and distinctive flavors, while choice (B) loosens the connection between children and linking food to sickness.

Choice (C) states that children have an acute sense of taste and connects that to getting sick. It also compares children to adults, saying children are more likely to pick out distinctive flavors and are more likely to get sick than adults. Therefore, children are more likely to develop a list of foods they dislike. This matches your prediction and makes choice (C) the correct answer.

Choices (D) and (E) are both outside the scope of the argument, which focuses on the development of food aversion at the onset of illness, not the pace of recovery mentioned in choice (D). You can eliminate choice (E) because whether the food is familiar is irrelevant; the argument focuses on the connection between getting sick and distinctive-tasting food.

# STRENGTHEN QUESTION: NOW YOU TRY IT

Now it's your turn to try a Strengthen question on your own. Use the template I've provided after the question to guide you through the four-step Kaplan Method. (Note: On test day, you won't be writing out all the steps as you are in this exercise. However, as you are learning the Method, it's good practice to help it become second nature.) Remember to bracket the conclusion and circle Keywords.

1. Ringtail opossums are an Australian wildlife species that is potentially endangered. A number of ringtail opossums that had been orphaned and subsequently raised in captivity were monitored after being returned to the wild. Seventy-five percent of these opossums were killed by foxes, a species not native to Australia. Conservationists concluded that the native ringtail opossum population was endangered not by a scarcity of food, as had been previously thought, but by non-native predator species against which the opossum had not developed natural defenses.

   Which one of the following, if true, most strongly supports the conservationists' argument?

   (A) There are fewer non-native predator species that prey on the ringtail opossum than there are native species that prey on the ringtail opossum.

   (B) Foxes, which were introduced into Australia over 200 years ago, adapted to the Australian climate less successfully than did some other foreign species.

   (C) The ringtail opossums that were raised in captivity were fed a diet similar to that which ringtail opossums typically eat in the wild.

   (D) Few of the species that compete with the ringtail opossum for food sources are native to Australia.

   (E) Ringtail opossums that grow to adulthood in the wild defend themselves against foxes no more successfully than do ringtail opossums raised in captivity.[3]

## Step 1. Identify the Question Type

_____

## Step 2. Untangle the Stimulus

_____

## Step 3. Make a Prediction

_____

## Step 4. Evaluate the Answer Choices

_____

_____

[3]PrepTest 34, Sec. 3, Q 24

# Explanations

## 1.   (E)

Ringtail opossums are an Australian wildlife species that is potentially endangered. A number of ringtail opossums that had been orphaned and subsequently raised in captivity were monitored after being returned to the wild. Seventy-five percent of these opossums were killed by foxes, a species not native to Australia. <Conservationists concluded that the native ringtail opossum population was endangered not by a scarcity of food, as had been previously thought, but by non-native predator species against which the opossum had not developed natural defenses.>

Which one of the following, if true, most strongly (supports) the conservationists' argument?

(A)   There are fewer non-native predator species that prey on the ringtail opossum than there are native species that prey on the ringtail opossum.

(B)   Foxes, which were introduced into Australia over 200 years ago, adapted to the Australian climate less successfully than did some other foreign species.

(C)   The ringtail opossums that were raised in captivity were fed a diet similar to that which ringtail opossums typically eat in the wild.

(D)   Few of the species that compete with the ringtail opossum for food sources are native to Australia.

(E)   Ringtail opossums that grow to adulthood in the wild defend themselves against foxes no more successfully than do ringtail opossums raised in captivity.[4]

## Step 1. Identify the Question Type

Since the question stem asks you for an answer that supports the conservationists' argument, this is a Strengthen question.

## Step 2. Untangle the Stimulus

You're given the conclusion in direct language: "Conservationists concluded that …" the native ringtail opossum population was endangered by non-native predators. This belief is based on evidence that 75 percent of opossums raised in captivity and returned to the wild were killed by the non-native predators.

## Step 3. Make a Prediction

Again, to strengthen the argument you must tighten the connection between the conclusion and the evidence. To identify the assumption, look for the mismatched terms between the

---

[4]PrepTest 34, Sec. 3, Q 24

conclusion and evidence. In this case, the conclusion applies to native opossums generally, while the evidence refers to a subset of the group, those opossums raised in captivity and later returned to the wild. To strengthen the link between the conclusion and evidence, you need an assumption that addresses this scope shift.

### Step 4. Evaluate the Answer Choices

Choice (A) talks about the number of non-native vs. native predators, which is out of scope.

In choice (B), foxes serve as an example of a non-native opossum predator. However, it provides only background information about them and does nothing to tie the two opossum groups together and strengthen the argument.

Although choice (C) identifies a shared diet between the two groups of opossums, the connection does not relate to the conclusion about opossums being threatened by non-native predators. Eliminate this choice.

Choice (D) is irrelevant. The origin of the species that compete with the opossum for food sources and the food sources themselves play no role in the argument.

Choice (E) asserts a similarity between the wild and captive opossums. It says the two groups are the same when it comes to their vulnerability to the predatory foxes, which strengthens the argument, and makes choice (E) the correct answer.

# DRILL: PRACTICING STRENGTHEN QUESTIONS

Use the Kaplan Method to answer the following Strengthen questions. Take this opportunity to practice and apply the steps in the Method so you are comfortable using them on test day. Check your responses against the full explanations provided after the Drill.

1. One year ago a local government initiated an antismoking advertising campaign in local newspapers, which it financed by imposing a tax on cigarettes of 20 cents per pack. One year later, the number of people in the locality who smoke cigarettes had declined by 3 percent. Clearly, what was said in the advertisements had an effect, although a small one, on the number of people in the locality who smoke cigarettes.

   Which one of the following, if true, most helps to strengthen the argument?

   (A) Residents of the locality have not increased their use of other tobacco products such as snuff and chewing tobacco since the campaign went into effect.
   (B) A substantial number of cigarette smokers in the locality who did not quit smoking during the campaign now smoke less than they did before it began.
   (C) Admissions to the local hospital for chronic respiratory ailments were down by 15 percent one year after the campaign began.
   (D) Merchants in the locality responded to the local tax by reducing the price at which they sold cigarettes by 20 cents per pack.
   (E) Smokers in the locality had incomes that on average were 25 percent lower than those of nonsmokers.[5]

2. Fossil-fuel producers say that it would be prohibitively expensive to reduce levels of carbon dioxide emitted by the use of fossil fuels enough to halt global warming. This claim is probably false. Several years ago, the chemical industry said that finding an economical alternative to the chlorofluorocarbons (CFCs) destroying the ozone layer would be impossible. Yet once the industry was forced, by international agreements, to find substitutes for CFCs, it managed to phase them out completely well before the mandated deadline, in many cases at a profit.

   Which one of the following, if true, most strengthens the argument?

   (A) In the time since the chemical industry phased out CFCs, the destruction of the ozone layer by CFCs has virtually halted, but the levels of carbon dioxide emitted by the use of fossil fuels have continued to increase.
   (B) In some countries, the amount of carbon dioxide emitted by the use of fossil fuels has already been reduced without prohibitive expense, but at some cost in convenience to the users of such fuels.
   (C) The use of CFCs never contributed as greatly to the destruction of the ozone layer as the carbon dioxide emitted by the use of fossil fuels currently contributes to global warming.
   (D) There are ways of reducing carbon dioxide emissions that could halt global warming without hurting profits of fossil-fuel producers significantly more than phasing out CFCs hurt those of the chemical industry.
   (E) If international agreements forced fossil-fuel producers to find ways to reduce carbon dioxide emissions enough to halt global warming, the fossil-fuel producers could find substitutes for fossil fuels.[6]

---

3.  Many scientific studies have suggested that taking melatonin tablets can induce sleep. But this does not mean that melatonin is helpful in treating insomnia. Most of the studies examined only people without insomnia, and in many of the studies, only a few of the subjects given melatonin appeared to be significantly affected by it.

    Which one of the following, if true, most strengthens the argument?

    (A)  A weaker correlation between taking melatonin and the inducement of sleep was found in the studies that included people with insomnia than in the studies that did not.

    (B)  None of the studies that suggested that taking melatonin tablets can induce sleep examined a fully representative sample of the human population.

    (C)  In the studies that included subjects with insomnia, only subjects without insomnia were significantly affected by doses of melatonin.

    (D)  Several people who were in control groups and only given placebos claimed that the tablets induced sleep.

    (E)  If melatonin were helpful in treating insomnia, then every person with insomnia who took doses of melatonin would appear to be significantly affected by it.[7]

4.  The supernova event of 1987 is interesting in that there is still no evidence of the neutron star that current theory says should have remained after a supernova of that size. This is in spite of the fact that many of the most sensitive instruments ever developed have searched for the tell-tale pulse of radiation that neutron stars emit. Thus, current theory is wrong in claiming that supernovas of a certain size always produce neutron stars.

    Which one of the following, if true, most strengthens the argument?

    (A)  Most supernova remnants that astronomers have detected have a neutron star nearby.

    (B)  Sensitive astronomical instruments have detected neutron stars much farther away than the location of the 1987 supernova.

    (C)  The supernova of 1987 was the first that scientists were able to observe in progress.

    (D)  Several important features of the 1987 supernova are correctly predicted by the current theory.

    (E)  Some neutron stars are known to have come into existence by a cause other than a supernova explosion.[8]

---

[7] PrepTest 50, Sec. 4, Q 23

[8] PrepTest 51, Sec. 1, Q 24

5. Modern navigation systems, which are found in most of today's commercial aircraft, are made with low-power circuitry, which is more susceptible to interference than the vacuum-tube circuitry found in older planes. During landing, navigation systems receive radio signals from the airport to guide the plane to the runway. Recently, one plane with low-power circuitry veered off course during landing, its dials dimming, when a passenger turned on a laptop computer. Clearly, modern aircraft navigation systems are being put at risk by the electronic devices that passengers carry on board, such as cassette players and laptop computers.

Which one of the following, if true, LEAST strengthens the argument above?

(A) After the laptop computer was turned off, the plane regained course and its navigation instruments and dials returned to normal.

(B) When in use, all electronic devices emit electromagnetic radiation, which is known to interfere with circuitry.

(C) No problems with navigational equipment or instrument dials have been reported on flights with no passenger-owned electronic devices on board.

(D) Significant electromagnetic radiation from portable electronic devices can travel up to eight meters, and some passenger seats on modern aircraft are located within four meters of the navigation systems.

(E) Planes were first equipped with low-power circuitry at about the same time portable electronic devices became popular.[9]

---

[9]PrepTest 28, Sec. 1, Q 26

## Explanations

### 1. (D)

One year ago a local government initiated an antismoking advertising campaign in local newspapers, which it financed by imposing a tax on cigarettes of 20 cents per pack. One year later, the number of people in the locality who smoke cigarettes had declined by 3 percent. ⟨Clearly⟩, what was said in the advertisements had an effect, although a small one, on the number of people in the locality who smoke cigarettes.⟩

Which one of the following, if true, most helps to ⟨strengthen⟩ the argument?

(A) Residents of the locality have not increased their use of other tobacco products such as snuff and chewing tobacco since the campaign went into effect.

(B) A substantial number of cigarette smokers in the locality who did not quit smoking during the campaign now smoke less than they did before it began.

(C) Admissions to the local hospital for chronic respiratory ailments were down by 15 percent one year after the campaign began.

(D) Merchants in the locality responded to the local tax by reducing the price at which they sold cigarettes by 20 cents per pack.

(E) Smokers in the locality had incomes that on average were 25 percent lower than those of nonsmokers.[10]

### Step 1. Identify the Question Type

"Strengthen" indicates this is a Strengthen question. Now, find the argument.

### Step 2. Untangle the Stimulus

Identified by the word "clearly," the conclusion states that the antismoking advertising campaign contributed to the decrease in the locality's number of smokers. The author uses the evidence that a local government initiated the advertising campaign and a small decline in the number of smokers followed. In the process of identifying this causal relationship, the author ignores the 20 cent increase in cigarette prices. So, he assumes the cost increase had no effect on the smoking decline.

### Step 3. Make a Prediction

Strengthening this argument requires confirmation of or additional support for the assumption. The correct answer will eliminate or reduce the price increase as a factor in the smoking

---

[10]PrepTest 17, Sec. 3, Q 12

decline. It may also provide additional support for the ad campaign as an influential factor in the reduction in smoking.

## Step 4. Evaluate the Answer Choices

Choice (A) is outside the scope. The argument is about smoking cigarettes, not the general use of tobacco products.

Choice (B) is also outside the scope. The argument refers to smokers who quit, not smokers who smoke less.

Choice (C) declares that hospital admissions for respiratory ailments are down, but it doesn't tie the information back to an explanation for the reduced number of smokers.

Choice (D) is the correct response. If local merchants responded to the tax by reducing the price of cigarettes by the exact amount of the tax, the price of cigarettes ultimately did not change. So, a tax increase with a consumer cost reduction cannot explain the smoking decline. The author's assumption is validated, and by eliminating a competing explanation for the smoking decline, the author's conclusion is strengthened.

Choice (E) tells you that smokers were generally poorer than nonsmokers. You can't know from that statement whether smokers are poor, just that they have less money than nonsmokers. If they are poor, they may be more sensitive to a cigarette price increase and be more inclined to stop smoking as a result. If that's the case, choice (E) weakens the argument. If it's not the case, choice (E) has no impact on the argument. Either way, it's incorrect.

2.  **(D)**

Fossil-fuel producers say that it would be prohibitively expensive to reduce levels of carbon dioxide emitted by the use of fossil fuels enough to halt global warming. <This claim is probably false.> Several years ago, the chemical industry said that finding an economical alternative to the chlorofluorocarbons (CFCs) destroying the ozone layer would be impossible. Yet once the industry was forced, by international agreements, to find substitutes for CFCs, it managed to phase them out completely well before the mandated deadline, in many cases at a profit.

Which one of the following, if true, most (strengthens) the argument?

(A)   In the time since the chemical industry phased out CFCs, the destruction of the ozone layer by CFCs has virtually halted, but the levels of carbon dioxide emitted by the use of fossil fuels have continued to increase.

(B)   In some countries, the amount of carbon dioxide emitted by the use of fossil fuels has already been reduced without prohibitive expense, but at some cost in convenience to the users of such fuels

(C)   The use of CFCs never contributed as greatly to the destruction of the ozone layer as the carbon dioxide emitted by the use of fossil fuels currently contributes to global warming.

(D)   There are ways of reducing carbon dioxide emissions that could halt global warming without hurting profits of fossil-fuel producers significantly more than phasing out CFCs hurt those of the chemical industry.

(E)   If international agreements forced fossil-fuel producers to find ways to reduce carbon dioxide emissions enough to halt global warming, the fossil-fuel producers could find substitutes for fossil fuels.[11]

## Step 1. Identify the Question Type

"Strengthens" tells you this is a Strengthen question. So now, as you should do with all Strengthen questions, look for the argument in the stimulus and find the answer choice that makes the conclusion more likely to be true from the evidence.

## Step 2. Untangle the Stimulus

Although there are no conclusion indicator words, any time the author tells you what others think and then says the others are wrong, then that is the conclusion. Here the author tells you

---

[11]PrepTest 50, Sec. 2, Q 13

the fossil fuel producers claim that it would be prohibitively expensive to reduce consumption to slow global warming. The author then says that the fossil fuel producers' claim is probably false. So the author's conclusion is that it is most likely not too expensive to reduce fossil fuel consumption to make a difference—it can be found affordably.

The author supports her conclusion with evidence in the form of an analogy. She says that the chemical industry made a similar claim about finding an alternative to CFCs. Not only was it a quicker process than expected, but the industry managed to make the substitution at a profit. Therefore, she concludes, it will work the same way with the reduction of carbon dioxide. When an author makes a conclusion based on an analogy, she assumes the analogy is sound and a comparison holds.

Notice you don't need to understand the technical information in this stimulus. Whether you know anything about carbon dioxide or fossil fuel is inconsequential to strengthening the argument. You only need to understand the pattern of the argument and how to strengthen it. Here, you are presented with two factors and asked to strengthen their bond.

### Step 3. Make a Prediction

To strengthen the argument, you need to look for an answer that supports the author's analogy and provides a strong link between the claims of the fossil-fuel producers and those of the chemical industry regarding CFCs.

### Step 4. Evaluate the Answer Choices

While it's nice to know the CFC regulations protected the environment, as mentioned in choice (A), the statement doesn't support the author's CFC analogy to show the reduction process is not expensive.

Choice (B) says a reduction in carbon dioxide emitted by the use of fossil fuels has occurred without great expense. However, the impact on global warming is unclear. Also, choice (B) doesn't connect to the CFC analogy.

Choice (C) is outside the scope, as it talks about the destruction caused by carbon dioxide and CFCs. The argument focuses on reducing these problems and the associated cost. Another problem with this answer choice is that it differentiates the two factors instead of bringing them together.

Choice (D) matches the prediction. It says not only can carbon dioxide emissions be reduced without hurting profits like phasing out CFCs, but it will be better at it. That makes choice (D) the correct answer.

While choice (E) tells you fossil fuels can be substituted, it is silent on whether the substitution would be prohibitively expensive, so you can eliminate it.

3.  **(C)**

Many scientific studies have suggested that taking melatonin tablets can induce sleep. <(But) this does not mean that melatonin is helpful in treating insomnia.> Most of the studies examined only people without insomnia, and in many of the studies, only a few of the subjects given melatonin appeared to be significantly affected by it.

Which one of the following, if true, most (strengthens) the argument?

(A)     A weaker correlation between taking melatonin and the inducement of sleep was found in the studies that included people with insomnia than in the studies that did not.

(B)     None of the studies that suggested that taking melatonin tablets can induce sleep examined a fully representative sample of the human population.

(C)     In the studies that included subjects with insomnia, only subjects without insomnia were significantly affected by doses of melatonin.

(D)     Several people who were in control groups and only given placebos claimed that the tablets induced sleep.

(E)     If melatonin were helpful in treating insomnia, then every person with insomnia who took doses of melatonin would appear to be significantly affected by it.[12]

## Step 1. Identify the Question Type

The word "strengthens" identifies this as a Strengthen question. Proceed to the stimulus and locate the conclusion and the evidence.

## Step 2. Untangle the Stimulus

"But" in the second sentence indicates a contradiction, which can point to a conclusion. In this case, it points to the conclusion that melatonin can induce sleep, but it won't help people with insomnia. The author says this because most of the studies included people without insomnia. So, the argument is that melatonin helped very few people without insomnia; therefore, it won't help people with insomnia.

## Step 3. Make a Prediction

Notice that the author bases her conclusion on "most studies" that didn't look at people with insomnia. The key is to recognize that "most" leaves open the possibility that there were other studies with insomniacs. To bolster the argument, you want to tie insomniacs to the studies and show they were unlikely to be helped by melatonin.

---

[12]PrepTest 50, Sec. 4, Q 23

## Step 4. Evaluate the Answer Choices

At first glance, choice (A) is tempting because you may think the weaker correlation between melatonin and inducement of sleep in studies with insomniacs argues that melatonin isn't as effective on people with insomnia. However, the source of the weaker correlation is unclear and the relationship between melatonin and inducement of sleep is not the issue here; the effect of melatonin on insomniacs is.

Choice (B) faults the studies for not including a fully representative sample of the human population and thereby weakens the argument. Eliminate this choice.

Choice (C) acknowledges there were some insomniacs included in the studies, and when they were, melatonin had no significant impact on them. Choice (C) matches the prediction and is the correct answer.

Choice (D) discusses the placebo effect and does not shed any light on the effects of melatonin on subjects with insomnia, so you can cross it out.

Choice (E) is an extreme answer because it suggests that if melatonin helps treat insomnia, then it is 100 percent effective with all insomnia sufferers. If anything, this answer weakens the argument. The correct answer connects insomniacs to the studies and makes it more likely they are not affected by melatonin, which this clearly doesn't.

4.   **(B)**

The supernova event of 1987 is interesting in that there is still no evidence of the neutron star that current theory says should have remained after a supernova of that size. This is in spite of the fact that many of the most sensitive instruments ever developed have searched for the tell-tale pulse of radiation that neutron stars emit. <Thus, current theory is wrong in claiming that supernovas of a certain size always produce neutron stars.>

Which one of the following, if true, most strengthens the argument?

(A)   Most supernova remnants that astronomers have detected have a neutron star nearby.

(B)   Sensitive astronomical instruments have detected neutron stars much farther away than the location of the 1987 supernova.

(C)   The supernova of 1987 was the first that scientists were able to observe in progress.

(D)   Several important features of the 1987 supernova are correctly predicted by the current theory.

(E)   Some neutron stars are known to have come into existence by a cause other than a supernova explosion.[13]

---

[13]PrepTest 51, Sec. 1, Q 24

### Step 1. Identify the Question Type

The word "strengthens" tells you this is a Strengthen question.

### Step 2. Untangle the Stimulus

The evidence states that the most sensitive instruments have looked for the neutron star that should have remained after the 1987 supernova event but have found no evidence of it. "Thus", the author concludes in the last sentence, the current theory that supernovas of a certain size always produce neutron stars is wrong.

### Step 3. Make a Prediction

To connect the evidence to the conclusion, the author assumes that "no evidence of the supernova" means the supernova does not exist. The correct answer will support this assumption.

### Step 4. Evaluate the Answer Choices

Choice (A) repeats current theory already stated in the evidence. Restating evidence never strengthens an argument. Move on to the next choice.

Choice (B) is the correct answer. It makes clear that the instruments were powerful enough to find neutron stars farther away than the 1987 supernova. Consequently, it eliminates an alternative explanation that the instruments were defective or problematic in some way. Remember, you don't need to prove that supernovas don't always produce neutron stars, you just need to make it more likely that they don't.

Choice (C) is irrelevant. Whether the supernova of 1987 was the first that scientists were able to observe in progress has no impact on the correctness of the current theory.

The production of neutron stars, not other features of the 1987 supernova, is your focus. So choice (D) is outside the scope. However, even if you thought (D) was relevant, the fact that the current theory correctly predicted several features of the 1987 supernova makes the theory look better, not worse.

The cause of neutron stars other than a supernova is outside the scope of the argument, so you can eliminate choice (E).

## 5. **(E)**

Modern navigation systems, which are found in most of today's commercial aircraft, are made with low-power circuitry, which is more susceptible to interference than the vacuum-tube circuitry found in older planes. During landing, navigation systems receive radio signals from the airport to guide the plane to the runway. Recently, one plane with low-power circuitry veered off course during landing, its dials dimming, when a passenger turned on a laptop computer. ⟨Clearly,⟩ modern aircraft navigation systems are being put at risk by the electronic devices that passengers carry on board,⟩ such as cassette players and laptop computers.

Which one of the following, if true, ⟨LEAST strengthens⟩ the argument above?

(A)    After the laptop computer was turned off, the plane regained course and its navigation instruments and dials returned to normal.

(B)    When in use, all electronic devices emit electromagnetic radiation, which is known to interfere with circuitry.

(C)    No problems with navigational equipment or instrument dials have been reported on flights with no passenger-owned electronic devices on board.

(D)    Significant electromagnetic radiation from portable electronic devices can travel up to eight meters, and some passenger seats on modern aircraft are located within four meters of the navigation systems.

(E)    Planes were first equipped with low-power circuitry at about the same time portable electronic devices became popular.[14]

## Step 1. Identify the Question Type

This question uses the word "strengthens," so you know it is a Strengthen question. However, notice the twist: It asks for the answer that "LEAST" strengthens the argument. An answer that does not strengthen an argument could make it weaker, but it doesn't have to; it could also be outside the scope of the argument. So, for this question, the four wrong answers will strengthen the argument, and the correct answer will not.

Under the pressure of test day, it's easy to skip a word in the question or to misread the question. Be sure to read the question carefully so you answer the question asked.

## Step 2. Untangle the Stimulus

"Clearly" in the last sentence indicates the author's conclusion, that electronic devices brought on airplanes by passengers endanger the navigation system. The author provides evidence that

---

[14]PrepTest 28, Sec. 1, Q 26

is full of technical language, but don't let that distract you; you just want to find out why the author thinks the electronic devices put the navigation system at risk. Essentially, the author is basing this sweeping conclusion on a single instance in which a passenger happened to use an electronic device around the same time that a plane malfunctioned.

### Step 3. Make a Prediction

The author assumes there is a causal connection between the electronic devices and the plane's malfunctioning. So, any answers that connect electronic devices to plane problems strengthens the argument. The one that weakens the argument or has no effect on the argument is the correct answer.

### Step 4. Evaluate the Answer Choices

Choice (A) gives one example of a laptop affecting a navigation system, which strengthens the argument. Eliminate choice (A).

Choice (B) states that all electronic devices interfere with circuitry, which confirms the assumption and strengthens the argument. Move on to the next choice.

To strengthen an argument, an answer need not prove an argument, just make it more likely. Choice (C) is a great example of that concept, indicating that without electronic devices on board, navigational systems did not experience any problems. This strengthens the argument, and is therefore incorrect.

Choice (D) ties electronic devices closer to navigation systems by declaring they have the range and proximity to interfere with navigation systems. This strengthens the argument, so it's incorrect.

Choice (E) indicates that low-power circuitry and electronic devices were both introduced to airplanes around the same time, which raises the possibility of a coincidental relationship between navigation systems and electronic devices. It does nothing to bring the relationship closer or strengthen the argument, so it is the correct answer.

## STRENGTHEN REVIEW

Before you proceed to the next chapter, turn to Appendix A and complete the review exercise for Strengthen questions. A completed chart is included in Appendix B.

# CHAPTER 8

# FLAW QUESTIONS

Many arguments presented on the LSAT are flawed—that is the evidence is inadequate to support the conclusion reached by the author. Your ability to spot and describe a defective argument will lead directly to points on test day.

Flaw questions—like the other members of the Assumption family of questions—are prevalent on the LSAT. In fact, you will see approximately eight scored Flaw questions out of the 50 scored Logical Reasoning questions on the LSAT. Because of their frequency, your grasp of Flaw questions is especially important.

## DEFINITION OF FLAW QUESTIONS

Flaw questions ask you to recognize a problem with an argument. Usually, you will point out a fallacy in the argument that prevents the evidence from logically establishing the conclusion. Whereas Weaken questions ask you to add something to the argument to damage it, Flaw questions ask you to determine how an argument is already damaged. It's a small distinction, but a very important one.

In this chapter, I will present the classic logical errors that have appeared on LSATs over the years. Knowing the types of flawed reasoning that you will see on test day and being able to quickly and confidently identify them will give you a distinct advantage over your competition.

# USE THE KAPLAN METHOD TO ANSWER FLAW QUESTIONS

## Identify the Question Type

As is always the case, remember to read the question stem first. After you identify the question as a Flaw question, you can focus on *how* the argument is flawed and not waste any time figuring out *whether* the argument is flawed. The following words and phrases will help you identify a Flaw question:

- Flaw
- Error in reasoning
- Vulnerable to criticism
- Questionable because
- Overlooks the possibility that
- Fails to demonstrate

When you see these phrases in a question, the argument is flawed and your job is to identify the error in reasoning. However, the wording of the question will determine whether your answer will be a general description of a flaw or whether it will point out flawed content. For example, the following question stems ask you to identify the flaw:

- Which one of the following describes a reasoning flaw in the letter's argument?
- The reasoning in the argument is most vulnerable to criticism on the grounds that it
- Which one of the following best describes an error in reasoning in the passage?

However, sometimes the question stem will acknowledge the specific flaw and ask you to point out the flawed content:

- The reasoning in Rebecca's argument is questionable in that she takes for granted that
- Jim's reasoning is questionable in that it fails to consider the possibility that

## Untangle the Stimulus

Flaw questions are part of the Assumption family of questions. So, as you would with any other Assumption family question, read the stimulus to locate the argument. As you read, circle any Keywords to help you find the conclusion and evidence. Then, bracket the conclusion.

## Make a Prediction

Flaw questions, like Assumption questions, focus on the disconnect between the evidence and conclusion. So, identifying the author's assumption will always lead you to the correct answer in a Flaw question. However, certain logical flaws have repeatedly appeared on the LSAT. Recognizing these recurring flaws can help you identify the author's assumption and, consequently, more efficiently and accurately answer Flaw questions.

## Common Flaws

The following is a list of common flaws that appear on the LSAT and an example of each type:

### Overlooked Possibilities

Definition: The author assumes only one possible explanation and fails to see that the evidence can lead to multiple possible conclusions. Be on the lookout for forceful, absolute conclusion language that indicates the author is ignoring other possibilities.

Example: If Olivia is in class, she turns her cell phone off. So if her phone is off, she must be in class. (The author errantly assumes Olivia turns off her cell phone only because she is in class, but she may also turn her phone off for other reasons.)

### Necessity v. Sufficiency

Definition: The author confuses a sufficient condition for a necessary one. The better you understand the relationship between sufficiency and necessity in formal logic, the easier it will be to spot an error when the author gets the relationship wrong.

The flaws of overlooked possibility and necessity v. sufficiency are similar. In both cases, the author disregards alternative explanations and reverses the formal logic.

Example: If we have dinner at home, then Mike went to the grocery store. I saw Mike picking up groceries today, so we must be having dinner at home. (You can state this formal logic statement in two different ways to highlight the sufficient and necessary terms: Dinner at home necessitates Mike's shopping, and having dinner at home is sufficient to know that Mike went to the grocery store. However, Mike's shopping is sufficient to indicate we could have dinner at home, but it is not necessary. For example, if he shops, we may still go out for dinner.)

### Causation v. Correlation

Definition: The author assumes that a correlation (two things happening at the same time) between events means one causes the other to occur. In other words, because two things happen at the same time, the author assumes a causal relationship between them.

Example: In the summer, the Osborn family goes swimming often. They also eat a lot of ice cream in the summer. Therefore, swimming causes the family to eat ice cream. (Swimming and eating ice cream may be related as summer activities, but the argument does not tell us anything about causation.)

### Scope Shift

Definition: The author changes the focus of the argument, talking about one thing in the evidence and something else in the conclusion, so the conclusion goes beyond the scope of the evidence.

Certain kinds of scope shifts are quite common on the LSAT: a shift from numbers to percentages (or vice versa), equivocation of a key term or phrase in an argument in two different ways without acknowledging the distinction, a shift from opinion to fact, a shift from possibility to certainty, and a shift from individual factors to generalizing about a group (or vice versa)

Example: Only 15 percent of the school's children have been to Washington DC. Therefore, the school children must not know a lot about our government. (General scope shift: The evidence talks about traveling to our nation's capital, and the conclusion talks about knowledge of government.)

Example: The new vice president for marketing wants to eliminate half of the manager positions and a quarter of the assistant positions. Therefore, she is getting rid of more manager spots than assistant jobs. (Number v. percentage: She could be eliminating 50 percent of ten manager spots and 25 percent of 100 assistant jobs.)

Example: Giving money to charity is the right thing to do. So, charities have the right to our money. (Equivocation: The author changes the meaning of a key term by using "right" to mean appropriate in the first clause and "entitlement" in the second clause.)

Example: The restaurant reviewer said this restaurant has great food. So, it must be great. (Opinion v. fact)

Example: Drugs and alcohol may have been involved in the actor's death. So, he must have overdosed. (Possibility v. certainty)

Example: Maya often wears clothes that have jewel-tone colors like deep red, blue, or green. So, she'll like that scarf with all three colors in it. (Group v. member)

## Less-Common Flaws

The following flaws can appear on the LSAT, although they are less common as a correct answer choice and more likely to appear in wrong answers choices.

### Analogy

Definition: The author incorrectly assumes that two things are similar enough to draw a valid comparison between them.

Example: Water is a liquid and is good for you. Therefore, soda pop, which is a liquid, is also good for you.

### Representativeness

Definition: The author draws a conclusion based on evidence regarding an unrepresentative sample, incorrectly assuming that the one group can represent the other.

Example: When I was your age, mint chocolate chip was my favorite ice cream flavor. So, I'll serve mint chocolate ice cream at your birthday party. (My ice cream preference may not be representative of what you and your friends like.)

### Ad hominem

Definition: The author responds to the argument by attacking the arguer rather than focusing on the logic of the argument itself.

Example: Bill is out of work, so you can't believe him when he says the proposed policy would help the economy.

### Circular Reasoning

Definition: The author's evidence and conclusion are the same. It is often presented on the LSAT by presupposing what the argument sets out to prove.

Example: The talk show host claims that Taylor's new mystery is the best book of the year because no other book is as well-written.

This list is not exhaustive but it does give you a place to start when thinking about what's gone wrong in an argument. If a question does not fit neatly into a classic flaw category, take a good look at the argument, accept that there is a logical flaw that prevents the evidence from supporting that conclusion, and find what it is.

## Evaluate the Answer Choices

Take your prediction and compare it to the answer choices. Be flexible as you review each choice, because the same flaw can be expressed in different ways. If you are unable to match your prediction after initially looking through the answer choices, use your knowledge of common flaws to help you eliminate incorrect answer choices and find the correct answer.

# THE KAPLAN METHOD IN ACTION

Now I'll walk you through a couple examples to show you how the Kaplan Method can help you efficiently solve any Flaw question you'll see on test day.

1. Researcher: People with certain personality disorders have more theta brain waves than those without such disorders. But my data show that the amount of one's theta brain waves increases while watching TV. So watching too much TV increases one's risk of developing personality disorders.

   A questionable aspect of the reasoning above is that it

   (A) uses the phrase "personality disorders" ambiguously
   (B) fails to define the phrase "theta brain waves"
   (C) takes correlation to imply a causal connection
   (D) draws a conclusion from an unrepresentative sample of data
   (E) infers that watching TV is a consequence of a personality disorder[1]

## Step 1. Identify the Question Type

The phrase "questionable aspect of the reasoning" tells you the researcher made an error in moving from the evidence to the conclusion in this argument, which means this is a Flaw question.

## Step 2. Untangle the Stimulus

Once you identify a Flaw question, read the stimulus to identify the conclusion and the evidence. The researcher's conclusion appears in the last sentence identified by the word "so." He states that watching too much TV increases the risk of developing personality disorders. He supports the conclusion with the evidence that people with certain disorders also have a higher number of theta brain waves, which increases when watching TV.

## Step 3. Make a Prediction

The researcher presents a correlation between personality disorders and theta brain waves that increase when watching TV. From that correlation, he concludes that watching TV causes an increase in the risk of developing personality disorders. He makes the faulty assumption that correlation between two things means that one caused the other. You are looking for an answer that generally identifies the causation v. correlation flaw.

## Step 4. Evaluate the Answer Choices

Look at the answer choices and determine which one most closely resembles your prediction.

Choice (A) is false. A phrase or word is used ambiguously when it has more than one meaning, which is not the case in this argument. Eliminate this choice.

Choice (B) is true, in a way—the researcher does not define theta brain waves. However, the lack of definition does not affect the argument at all and certainly does not point to a flaw. Eliminate this choice as well.

---

[1]PrepTest 41, Sec. 3, Q 13

Answer choice (C) matches the prediction exactly, and so it is the correct answer.

Choice (D) raises the flaw of representativeness but there is no sample data presented in the argument to be unrepresentative.

Finally, choice (E) is the opposite of what the researcher said in the argument.

2.  It is widely believed that by age 80, perception and memory are each significantly reduced from their functioning levels at age 30. However, a recent study showed no difference in the abilities of 80-year-olds and 30-year-olds to play a card game devised to test perception and memory. Therefore, the belief that perception and memory are significantly reduced by age 80 is false.

The reasoning above is most vulnerable to criticism on the grounds that it fails to consider the possibility that

(A)   the study's card game does not test cognitive abilities other than perception and memory

(B)   card games are among the most difficult cognitive tasks one can attempt to perform

(C)   perception and memory are interrelated in ways of which we are not currently aware

(D)   the belief that 80-year-olds' perception and memory are reduced results from prejudice against senior citizens

(E)   playing the study's card game perfectly requires fairly low levels of perception and memory[2]

## Step 1. Identify the Question Type

The phrase "reasoning above is most vulnerable to criticism" identifies this as a Flaw question. The phrase "fails to consider the possibility" tells you specifically that the flaw is an overlooked possibility. Since you already know what the flaw is, your task is to look for alternative possibilities as you analyze the argument to predict an answer using content from the stimulus.

## Step 2. Untangle the Stimulus

The author concludes that perception and memory are not significantly reduced by age 80 from age 30, as is widely believed. She bases her conclusion on evidence that 30- and 80-year-olds display the same abilities to play a card game designed to test perception and memory. At quick glance, the argument may seem plausible, but it can't be because it's part of a Flaw question that told you specifically the argument fails to consider something. So, you need to determine what the author overlooks in reaching that conclusion from that evidence.

[2]PrepTest 35, Sec. 4, Q 8

## Step 3. Make a Prediction

You are looking for a possible explanation as to why 30- and 80-year-olds have the same abilities to play a card game designed to test perception and memory. One reason could be that the card game does not demand a high level of perception and memory.

Often when there is technical evidence (e.g., a survey, study, or experiment), there is a built in assumption that the survey, study, test, or in this case card game, is accurate and adequate for the task. So, a problem with the test will weaken the argument and the author's failure to consider that problem is the flaw. Here, the flaw is simply that the test doesn't work as "devised."

## Step 4. Evaluate the Answer Choices

You can eliminate choice (A), as other cognitive abilities besides perception and memory are outside the scope of the argument.

If card games are the most difficult cognitive tasks, then choice (B) strengthens the author's argument and does not identify a flaw. Move on to the next choice.

Choice (C) raises an interrelationship between perception and memory that is irrelevant to the argument. This choice is also incorrect.

Choice (D) mentions a prejudice against senior citizens, which is also irrelevant. This choice is incorrect, which leaves only one.

Choice (E) provides the predicted overlooked possibility, and is the correct answer.

# FLAW QUESTIONS: NOW YOU TRY IT

It's now your turn to try a Flaw question on your own. Use the template I've provided after the question to guide you through the four-step Kaplan Method. (Note: On test day, you won't be writing out all the steps as you are in this exercise. However, as you are learning the Method, it's good practice to help it become second nature.) Remember to bracket the conclusion and circle Keywords.

1.  Consumer advocate: Last year's worldwide alarm about a computer "virus"—a surreptitiously introduced computer program that can destroy other programs and data—was a fraud. Companies selling programs to protect computers against such viruses raised worldwide concern about the possibility that a destructive virus would be activated on a certain date. There was more smoke than fire, however; only about a thousand cases of damage were reported around the world. Multitudes of antivirus programs were sold, so the companies' warning was clearly only an effort to stimulate sales.

    The reasoning in the consumer advocate's argument is flawed because this argument

    (A)  restates its conclusion without attempting to offer a reason to accept it
    (B)  fails to acknowledge that antivirus programs might protect against viruses other than the particular one described
    (C)  asserts that the occurrence of one event after another shows that the earlier event was the cause of the later one
    (D)  uses inflammatory language as a substitute for providing any evidence
    (E)  overlooks the possibility that the protective steps taken did work and, for many computers, prevented the virus from causing damage[3]

## Step 1. Identify the Question Type

_____

## Step 2. Untangle the Stimulus

_____

## Step 3. Make a Prediction

_____

## Step 4. Evaluate the Answer Choices

_____

_____

[3]PrepTest 25, Sec. 2, Q 9

## Explanations

### 1. (E)

Consumer advocate: <Last year's worldwide alarm about a computer "virus"—a surreptitiously introduced computer program that can destroy other programs and data—was a fraud.> Companies selling programs to protect computers against such viruses raised worldwide concern about the possibility that a destructive virus would be activated on a certain date. There was more smoke than fire, however; only about a thousand cases of damage were reported around the world. Multitudes of antivirus programs were sold, so the companies' warning was clearly only an effort to stimulate sales.

The reasoning in the consumer advocate's argument is (flawed) because this argument

(A) restates its conclusion without attempting to offer a reason to accept it

(B) fails to acknowledge that antivirus programs might protect against viruses other than the particular one described

(C) asserts that the occurrence of one event after another shows that the earlier event was the cause of the later one

(D) uses inflammatory language as a substitute for providing any evidence

(E) overlooks the possibility that the protective steps taken did work and, for many computers, prevented the virus from causing damage[4]

### Step 1. Identify the Question Type

The question stem tells you specifically that the reasoning is "flawed," so this is a Flaw question.

### Step 2. Untangle the Stimulus

The consumer advocate concludes that the worldwide alarm sounded by companies that sold virus protection regarding a destructive virus was a fraud—it was designed only to stimulate antivirus software sales. The author bases this claim on the fact that a relatively small number of cases of damage from the virus were reported.

### Step 3. Make a Prediction

This argument assumes only one explanation for the minimal damage reports—that the virus report was a fraud. In making this argument, the author commits the classic flaw of ignoring alternative explanations. So, your job now is to find an answer that presents a possible

---

alternative to explain the low number of reports. You don't need to predict the exact alternative; you just need to be on the lookout for a plausible possibility.

### Step 4. Evaluate the Answer Choices

Choice (A) is wrong because the advocate does offer a reason—limited damage caused by the virus—to accept the conclusion of fraud. The problem is that the advocate assumes it is the only explanation and ignores other possibilities.

Choice (B) is irrelevant. Protection against other viruses does not address the issue at hand—that virus protection companies sounded the alarm for fraudulent reasons.

Choice (C) is incorrect because the advocate does not present a causal argument. He does not assert that the sale of antivirus programs is responsible for the limited damage from the virus. Rather, he claims the limited damage means there was no threat for the software to fix at all.

The advocate doesn't really use any inflammatory language as evidence as stated by choice (D). The evidence for fraud is based on the limited amount of damage caused by the virus.

Choice (E) fits the bill. It suggests that computer owners responded to the alarm and bought virus protection that limited the amount of damage.

# DRILL: PRACTICING FLAW QUESTIONS

Use the Kaplan Method to answer the following Flaw questions. Take this opportunity to practice and apply the steps in the Method so you are comfortable using them on test day. Be sure to circle conclusion and evidence Keywords and bracket the conclusion. Check your responses against the full explanations provided after the Drill.

1.  Formal performance evaluations in the professional world are conducted using realistic situations. Physicians are allowed to consult medical texts freely, attorneys may refer to law books and case records, and physicists and engineers have their manuals at hand for ready reference. Students, then, should likewise have access to their textbooks whenever they take examinations.

    The reasoning in the argument is questionable because the argument

    (A)   cites examples that are insufficient to support the generalization that performance evaluations in the professional world are conducted in realistic situations

    (B)   fails to consider the possibility that adopting its recommendation will not significantly increase most students' test scores

    (C)   neglects to take into account the fact that professionals were once students who also did not have access to textbooks during examinations

    (D)   neglects to take into account the fact that, unlike students, professionals have devoted many years of study to one subject

    (E)   fails to consider the possibility that the purposes of evaluation in the professional world and in school situations are quite dissimilar[5]

2.  In determining the authenticity of a painting, connoisseurs claim to be guided by the emotional impact the work has on them. For example, if a painting purportedly by Rembrandt is expressive and emotionally moving in a certain way, then this is supposedly evidence that the work was created by Rembrandt himself, and not by one of his students. But the degree to which an artwork has an emotional impact differs wildly from person to person. So a connoisseur's assessment cannot be given credence.

    The reasoning in the argument is most vulnerable to criticism on the grounds that the argument

    (A)   ignores the fact that anybody, not just a connoisseur, can give an assessment of the emotional impact of a painting

    (B)   is based on the consideration of the nature of just one painter's works, even though the conclusion is about paintings in general

    (C)   neglects the possibility that there may be widespread agreement among connoisseurs about emotional impact even when the public's assessment varies wildly

    (D)   presumes, without giving justification, that a painting's emotional impact is irrelevant to the determination of that painting's authenticity

    (E)   presumes, without offering evidence, that Rembrandt was better at conveying emotions in painting than were other painters[6]

3.  A group of 1,000 students was randomly selected from three high schools in a medium-sized city and asked the question, "Do you plan to finish your high school education?" More than 89 percent answered "Yes." This shows that the overwhelming majority of students want to finish high school, and that if the national dropout rate among high school students is high, it cannot be due to a lack of desire on the part of the students.

The reasoning of the argument above is questionable because the argument

(A)  fails to justify its presumption that 89 percent is an overwhelming majority
(B)  attempts to draw two conflicting conclusions from the results of one survey
(C)  overlooks the possibility that there may in fact not be a high dropout rate among high school students
(D)  contradicts itself by admitting that there may be a high dropout rate among students while claiming that most students want to finish high school
(E)  treats high school students from a particular medium-sized city as if they are representative of high school students nationwide[7]

4.  The people most likely to watch a televised debate between political candidates are the most committed members of the electorate and thus the most likely to have already made up their minds about whom to support. Furthermore, following a debate, uncommitted viewers are generally undecided about who won the debate. Hence, winning a televised debate does little to bolster one's chances of winning an election.

The reasoning in the argument is most vulnerable to criticism because the argument fails to consider the possibility that

(A)  watching an exciting debate makes people more likely to vote in an election
(B)  the voting behavior of people who do not watch a televised debate is influenced by reports about the debate
(C)  there are differences of opinion about what constitutes winning or losing a debate
(D)  people's voting behavior may be influenced in unpredictable ways by comments made by the participants in a televised debate
(E)  people who are committed to a particular candidate will vote even if their candidate is perceived as having lost a televised debate[8]

5.  The typological theory of species classification, which has few adherents today, distinguishes species solely on the basis of observable physical characteristics, such as plumage color, adult size, or dental structure. However, there are many so-called "sibling species," which are indistinguishable on the basis of their appearance but cannot interbreed and thus, according to the mainstream biological theory of species classification, are separate species. Since the typological theory does not count sibling species as separate species, it is unacceptable.

The reasoning in the argument is most vulnerable to criticism on the grounds that

(A)  the argument does not evaluate all aspects of the typological theory
(B)  the argument confuses a necessary condition for species distinction with a sufficient condition for species distinction
(C)  the argument, in its attempt to refute one theory of species classification, presupposes the truth of an opposing theory
(D)  the argument takes a single fact that is incompatible with a theory as enough to show that theory to be false
(E)  the argument does not explain why sibling species cannot interbreed[9]

---

[7]PrepTest 34, Sec. 3, Q 4

[8]PrepTest 41, Sec. 1, Q 20

[9]PrepTest 51, Sec. 1, Q 15

# Explanations

1.  **(E)**

Formal performance evaluations in the professional world are conducted using realistic situations. Physicians are allowed to consult medical texts freely, attorneys may refer to law books and case records, and physicists and engineers have their manuals at hand for ready reference. <Students, (then) should likewise have access to their textbooks whenever they take examinations.>

The reasoning in the argument is (questionable because) the argument

(A)  cites examples that are insufficient to support the generalization that performance evaluations in the professional world are conducted in realistic situations

(B)  fails to consider the possibility that adopting its recommendation will not significantly increase most students' test scores

(C)  neglects to take into account the fact that professionals were once students who also did not have access to textbooks during examinations

(D)  neglects to take into account the fact that, unlike students, professionals have devoted many years of study to one subject

(E)  fails to consider the possibility that the purposes of evaluation in the professional world and in school situations are quite dissimilar[10]

## Step 1. Identify the Question Type

The phrase "questionable because" signals a Flaw question.

## Step 2. Untangle the Stimulus

The author concludes that students should be able to have open-book tests because physicians, attorneys, and other professionals are allowed to consult their books during performance evaluations.

## Step 3. Make a Prediction

The author uses evidence about professionals to form a conclusion about students, so she must assume they are comparable and makes her argument by analogy. The correct answer will point out the flawed comparison between professionals and students.

## Step 4. Evaluate the Answer Choices

You can eliminate choice (A) because the argument states specifically that performance evaluations in the professional world are conducted in realistic situations.

---

[10]PrepTest 29, Sec. 4, Q 25

Choice (B) is outside the scope because the argument is about access to books during test evaluation and not about score improvement.

Whether the professionals took closed-book exams when they were students as presented in choice (C) is of no consequence to the argument. The argument focuses on the comparison between professional evaluations and student evaluations, so you need an answer to address that comparison.

Choice (D) has the same problem. Even if it is true that professionals devote many years of study to one subject, choice (D) does not address whether closed-book exams are appropriate for students.

Choice (E) matches the prediction by distinguishing the two groups and raising the possibility that a professional and a student evaluation could serve different purposes. This is the correct answer.

## 2. (C)

In determining the authenticity of a painting, connoisseurs claim to be guided by the emotional impact the work has on them. For example, if a painting purportedly by Rembrandt is expressive and emotionally moving in a certain way, then this is supposedly evidence that the work was created by Rembrandt himself, and not by one of his students. But the degree to which an artwork has an emotional impact differs wildly from person to person. <So a connoisseur's assessment cannot be given credence.>

The reasoning in the argument is most vulnerable to criticism on the grounds that the argument

(A) ignores the fact that anybody, not just a connoisseur, can give an assessment of the emotional impact of a painting

(B) is based on the consideration of the nature of just one painter's works, even though the conclusion is about paintings in general

(C) neglects the possibility that there may be widespread agreement among connoisseurs about emotional impact even when the public's assessment varies wildly

(D) presumes, without giving justification, that a painting's emotional impact is irrelevant to the determination of that painting's authenticity

(E) presumes, without offering evidence, that Rembrandt was better at conveying emotions in painting than were other painters[11]

---

[11]PrepTest 37, Sec. 4, Q 16

### Step 1. Identify the Question Type

The "vulnerable to criticism" language identifies this as a Flaw question.

### Step 2. Untangle the Stimulus

The author determines that a connoisseur's assessment of a painting's authenticity is not credible. He reaches this conclusion with evidence that the emotional impact of a painting, which connoisseurs use to determine a painting's authenticity, differs from person to person.

### Step 3. Make a Prediction

Notice the author uses evidence about people in general to form a conclusion about connoisseurs, thus committing a scope shift. Although people may have different kinds of emotional reactions, it's possible the connoisseurs agree among each other. If so, then you can trust their authentication.

### Step 4. Evaluate the Answer Choices

Choice (A) is not true. The author argues that everyone can have an emotional response to a painting; it's the degree of impact that varies.

Choice (B) confuses the purpose of the Rembrandt example, which the author uses as one example of a painter, not as the basis of his argument.

Choice (C) points out the flaw and is the correct answer.

Choice (D) is incorrect; the author does provide justification that a painting's emotional impact is irrelevant to the determination of that painting's authenticity.

Whether Rembrandt was better at conveying emotions in painting than other painters is irrelevant in the argument. Again, Rembrandt serves as an example of painters, not the point of the argument. Cross out choice (E).

## 3.  (E)

A group of 1,000 students was randomly selected from three high schools in a medium-sized city and asked the question, "Do you plan to finish your high school education?" More than 89 percent answered "Yes." ⟨This shows that⟩ the overwhelming majority of students want to finish high school, and that if the national dropout rate among high school students is high, it cannot be due to a lack of desire on the part of the students.⟩

The reasoning of the argument above is ⟨questionable⟩ ⟨because⟩ the argument

(A)   fails to justify its presumption that 89 percent is an overwhelming majority

(B)   attempts to draw two conflicting conclusions from the results of one survey

(C)   overlooks the possibility that there may in fact not be a high dropout rate among high school students

(D)   contradicts itself by admitting that there may be a high dropout rate among students while claiming that most students want to finish high school

(E)   treats high school students from a particular medium-sized city as if they are representative of high school students nationwide[12]

## Step 1. Identify the Question Type

The phrase "questionable because" signals a Flaw question.

## Step 2. Untangle the Stimulus

You can identify the author's conclusion—that the majority of students want to complete high school, and a large number of high school dropouts does not indicate students' lack of interest in finishing school—by the phrase "this shows that." The evidence refers to a study of a thousand students from a medium-sized city, 89 percent of whom said they planned to finish high school.

## Step 3. Make a Prediction

The author uses a study about one group of students from one place in the country to form a conclusion about all students nationwide. Whenever an argument is based on research, a study, or an experiment, consider the flaw of representativeness. In this case, the author mistakenly assumes the single group can represent all high school students across the country.

## Step 4. Evaluate the Answer Choices

You can rule out choice (A), as the definition of "overwhelming majority" is not at issue in this argument. Even if it was, most people would agree 89 percent could pass for the overwhelming majority.

---

[12]PrepTest 34, Sec. 3, Q 4

The two points made in the conclusion are not contradictory, as choice (B) would have you believe. Rather, it makes sense that students say they want to finish high school, and then if and when they don't, say they had the desire to finish.

The author concedes a high national high school dropout rate, but questions its size. So, choice (C) does not work.

As already mentioned in (B), the notions that the dropout rate can be high and most students want to finish high school can coexist. So, choice (D) doesn't present a contradiction.

Choice (E) correctly identifies the flaw as lack of representativeness, and is your correct answer.

4.   **(B)**

The people most likely to watch a televised debate between political candidates are the most committed members of the electorate and thus the most likely to have already made up their minds about whom to support. Furthermore, following a debate, uncommitted viewers are generally undecided about who won the debate. <Hence, winning a televised debate does little to bolster one's chances of winning an election.>

The reasoning in the argument is most vulnerable to criticism because the argument fails to consider the possibility that

(A)   watching an exciting debate makes people more likely to vote in an election

(B)   the voting behavior of people who do not watch a televised debate is influenced by reports about the debate

(C)   there are differences of opinion about what constitutes winning or losing a debate

(D)   people's voting behavior may be influenced in unpredictable ways by comments made by the participants in a televised debate

(E)   people who are committed to a particular candidate will vote even if their candidate is perceived as having lost a televised debate[13]

## Step 1. Identify the Question Type

The phrase "vulnerable to criticism" is a common indicator of a Flaw question. Additionally, the question stem identifies the flaw as something the argument "fails to consider." Your job is to describe what the author overlooked in content-specific terms.

[13]PrepTest 41, Sec. 1, Q 20

### Step 2. Untangle the Stimulus

"Hence" points you to the conclusion, which states that winning a TV debate does little to improve a candidate's chances of winning an election. The author's evidence is that the people most likely to watch the debate are already committed to a candidate and that voters who are undecided aren't persuaded by the debate to support one candidate or another.

### Step 3. Make a Prediction

The author says the people who are either committed to a candidate or undecided will not be affected by the debate. Notice the author presents two extreme groups in the evidence, the fully committed and the uncommitted, and ignores the possibility of a middle ground. The failure to consider there might be some other people to consider is a basic LSAT pattern. Here, the author ignores the potential voters who do not see the debate; can they be influenced by the debate without watching it? The answer is yes. They could be persuaded indirectly by other influences, such as follow-up conversations and media reviews of the debate. The author fails to consider that possibility in reaching her conclusion.

### Step 4. Evaluate the Answer Choices

Choice (A) is out; the argument is about who the debate watchers would vote for, not their likelihood of voting.

Choice (B) matches the prediction and is the correct answer.

Choice (C) is outside the scope because the conclusion is about a winning debate candidate.

The determination of what constitutes a winning and losing debate is not relevant. The author's argument—that debate watchers are generally not influenced by the debate—specifically contradicts choice (D). Even if a small number of watchers are affected in an unpredictable way, the argument remains unchanged.

Choice (E) deals with the prospect of voting, not voting behavior. So, like choice (A), you can dismiss this answer.

5.    **(C)**

The typological theory of species classification, which has few adherents today, distinguishes species solely on the basis of observable physical characteristics, such as plumage color, adult size, or dental structure. However, there are many so-called "sibling species," which are indistinguishable on the basis of their appearance but cannot interbreed and thus, according to the mainstream biological theory of species classification, are separate species. (Since) the typological theory does not count sibling species as separate species, <it is unacceptable.>

The reasoning in the argument is most (vulnerable to) (criticism) on the grounds that

(A)    the argument does not evaluate all aspects of the typological theory

(B)    the argument confuses a necessary condition for species distinction with a sufficient condition for species distinction

(C)    the argument, in its attempt to refute one theory of species classification, presupposes the truth of an opposing theory

(D)    the argument takes a single fact that is incompatible with a theory as enough to show that theory to be false

(E)    the argument does not explain why sibling species cannot interbreed[14]

## Step 1. Identify the Question Type

The phrase "vulnerable to criticism" identifies this as a Flaw question.

## Step 2. Untangle the Stimulus

The author introduces two different theories of species classification—typological theory and mainstream biological theory. The mainstream biological theory considers sibling species to be separate species. In the evidence, identified by the word "since," the author states that the typological theory does not count sibling species as separate species. Therefore, the author concludes, the theory is unacceptable.

## Step 3. Make a Prediction

Don't let complicated or unfamiliar language intimidate you. The LSAT does not test content, so you don't need to understand the different theories and how they work. You need only to simplify the text and find any patterns to help you answer the questions.

Look at this argument in simpler terms: The MB (mainstream biological) theory says X, and the T (typological) theory says not X; and so the T theory is wrong. If the T theory is wrong because it doesn't agree with the MB theory, the author must assume that the MB theory is correct.

---

[14]PrepTest 51, Sec. 1, Q 15

Because this is a Flaw question, review the answers to find one that describes a faulty assumption.

### Step 4. Evaluate the Answer Choices

Choice (A) is true in that the argument does not evaluate all aspects of the typological theory. But it is not the correct answer. Even a complete evaluation of the typological theory would not address the real problem in the argument, the author's dismissal of typological theory because it doesn't meet a requirement of a different theory.

Eliminate choice (B). The argument does not confuse a necessary or sufficient condition for species distinction.

Choice (C) describes a faulty assumption; it says the argument assumes one theory is true to prove the other theory is false. This is the correct answer.

Cross out choice (D) because the author gives you no information that the ability to interbreed is incompatible with the typological theory.

Again, choice (E) may be true, but it doesn't match the author's faulty assumption. In fact, an explanation for why sibling species cannot interbreed will have no effect on the argument at all.

## FLAW REVIEW

Before you proceed to the next chapter, turn to Appendix A and complete the review exercise for Flaw questions. A completed chart is included in Appendix B.

# CHAPTER 9

# ASSUMPTION FAMILY OF QUESTIONS IN REVIEW

The Assumption family of questions consists of four members: Assumption, Strengthen, Weaken, and Flaw questions. These questions are related through their common components, and they also have a common purpose—to test your ability to analyze an argument.

## COMMON ELEMENTS

Every Assumption family argument shares two explicit components: a conclusion and evidence. The conclusion is the author's main point, and identifying it first helps you to determine the evidence used to reach it and evaluate the argument as a whole. The evidence is the information given by the author to support the conclusion. The argument's assumption is the implicit part that bridges the gap between the two and that must be true for the argument to be valid.

Each Assumption family question tests your ability to analyze an argument but in slightly different ways. Some questions directly ask you to identify the assumption while others ask you to weaken or strengthen an argument. This means you have to loosen or tighten the connection between the evidence and conclusion, typically, by undermining or affirming the assumption. Other questions will ask you to determine the flaw committed by the author. Since a flaw is an unwarranted gap in reasoning between the evidence and the conclusion, flaws typically stem from faulty assumptions. Notice that each question type comes back to finding the assumption, a skill that will help you earn a lot of points on test day.

# COMMON ARGUMENT STRUCTURES

The common elements of an argument often present themselves in common patterns. While the specifics change from question to question, there are certain argument structures that appear repeatedly on the LSAT. When you recognize them, you'll have a ready-made prediction of the assumption, strengthener, weakener, and flaw.

The following LSAT questions illustrate three of the most prominent argument patterns: recommendation, causal relationship, and prediction. Then I provided a breakdown of the argument elements for each Assumption family question type. Use these examples to revisit Assumption family questions from previous chapters, locate the patterns, and perform the same exercise. Practicing each question type in relation to a single stimulus will improve your argument-analysis skills and ultimately your ability to answer each Assumption family question type.

1. Medical doctor: Sleep deprivation is the cause of many social ills, ranging from irritability to potentially dangerous instances of impaired decision making. Most people today suffer from sleep deprivation to some degree. Therefore, we should restructure the workday to allow people flexibility in scheduling their work hours.[1]

**Table 9.1**

| | Recommendation | |
|---|---|---|
| | **General** | **Specific** |
| Conclusion | We should/should not adopt the proposal. | (Therefore), we (should) restructure the workday to allow people flexibility in scheduling their work hours. |
| Evidence | One reason a proposal is good/bad or needed/not needed. | Sleep deprivation causes many problems. |
| Assumption | There are no other considerations to take into account or the recommendation can/cannot address the problem. | Flexible scheduling can help reduce sleep deprivation and the accompanying effects. |
| Strengthener | This reason is particularly important/ eliminating another possible factor. | • Employees reported two extra hours of sleep when they had greater latitude in scheduling their work hours.<br>• Employees' healthier eating habits have not had any impact on employees' reduced sleep. |
| Weakener | There is another factor that's relevant. | • Adding fifteen minutes of exercise daily has been shown to reduce sleep deprivation.<br>• The primary cause of sleep deprivation is overwork. |
| Flaw | Alternative possibilities | The medical doctor ignores the possibility that something else could cause the sleep deprivation. |

---

[1]PrepTest 36, Sec. 3, Q 7

2. Galanin is a protein found in the brain. In an experiment, rats that consistently chose to eat fatty foods when offered a choice between lean and fatty foods were found to have significantly higher concentrations of galanin in their brains than did rats that consistently chose lean over fatty foods. These facts strongly support the conclusion that galanin causes rats to crave fatty foods.[2]

**Table 9.2**

| | Causal Relationship | |
| | General | Specific |
| --- | --- | --- |
| Conclusion | One thing (X) caused another (Y). | These facts strongly support the conclusion that galanin causes rats to crave fatty foods. |
| Evidence | Two things are correlated (X and Y happen to occur together). | Rats who chose fatty foods had a higher concentration of galanin than rats who chose lean foods. |
| Assumption | Assume the correlation was not a coincidence, not due to a third factor, or not due to reversed causation; or assume a causal relationship from X to Y. | • The relationship is not a coincidence.<br>• A genetic predisposition did not cause the fatty food cravings.<br>• Fatty food cravings do not result in a build-up of galanin.<br>• A causal relationship does exist from galanin to fatty food craving. |
| Strengthener | Eliminate the possibility of coincidence, third factor, or reversal; or strengthen the likelihood that the first really causes the second. | • Bright lights do not cause fatty food cravings in rats.<br>• The rats that preferred fatty foods had the higher concentrations of galanin in their brains before they were offered fatty foods.<br>• A second study confirmed the findings that galanin does cause rats to crave fatty foods. |

(continued)

| Weakener | Provide evidence that the correlation may really be just a coincidence, due to a third factor, or reversed; or weaken the likelihood that the first really causes the second. | • Sugar causes rats to crave fatty foods.<br>• The rats that preferred fatty foods did not have higher concentrations of galanin in their brains before they were offered fatty foods.<br>• The crucial experiment could not be repeated. |
| Flaw | Ignore the possibility that the correlation was a coincidence, there was an alternate cause, or causation was reversed. | Ignore the possibility that the correlation was a coincidence, there was an alternate cause, or causation was reversed. |

3.  Three major laundry detergent manufacturers have concentrated their powdered detergents by reducing the proportion of inactive ingredients in the detergent formulas. The concentrated detergents will be sold in smaller packages. In explaining the change, the manufacturers cited the desire to reduce cardboard packaging and other production costs. Market analysts predict that the decision of these three manufacturers, who control 80 percent of the laundry detergent market, will eventually bring about the virtual disappearance of old-style bulky detergents.[3]

**Table 9.3**

|  | Prediction | |
|---|---|---|
|  | **General** | **Specific** |
| Conclusion | Something will/will not occur | Market analysts (predict) that the decision of these three manufacturers, who control 80 percent of the laundry detergent market, (will) eventually bring about the virtual disappearance of old-style bulky detergents. |
| Evidence | Reasons something will/will not occur | Manufacturers want to reduce cardboard packaging and other production costs. |
| Assumption | The evidence is relevant to the prediction/no other factor is being ignored. | What the manufacturers want will happen and no other factor influences the prediction. |

(continued)

---

[3]PrepTest 17, Sec. 3, Q 6

| Strengthener | The basis for the prediction is more relevant. | When available, consumers are increasingly persuaded by environmental concerns to buy concentrated detergents in order to reduce cardboard waste. |
|---|---|---|
| Weakener | Some other factor that makes the given basis for the prediction less important/less relevant. | Switching the machines to produce the smaller packages is environmentally hazardous. |
| Flaw | Overlooks the possibility that the evidence is irrelevant/that another factor does have relevance | • The manufacturers don't always get what they want.<br>• Consumers prefer the larger packaging. |

# CHAPTER 10

# INFERENCE QUESTIONS

If a famous actor is spotted looking at rings in a fancy jewelry store, the tabloids might print pictures that imply he's shopping for an engagement ring for his long-time girlfriend. The tabloid editors and the readers don't know for sure what he was shopping for, but they could make a reasonable inference. While that definition of "inference" is probably the one with which you're most familiar, the LSAT definition is much more specific. For an inference to be valid on the LSAT, it *must be true* based on the information provided in the stimulus.

Try another example. Let's say you offer Jesse a slice of your pepperoni pizza and he says, "No thanks, I'm good." What could you infer about Jesse? He's not hungry? He doesn't like pizza? He is a vegetarian? He's lactose intolerant? He doesn't want to eat with you? There are lots of possible inferences you can make in everyday life, but they would be incorrect on the LSAT.

Inferences in everyday life are essentially educated guesses usually based on experience. LSAT inferences must be 100 percent true based on the information provided.

You will find approximately seven scored Inference questions on the LSAT. Because Inference questions also appear in the Reading Comprehension section, it is especially worthwhile to practice Inference questions to maximize your score on test day.

## DEFINITION OF INFERENCE QUESTIONS

Inference questions are different from the question types you've seen so far. Assumption, Strengthen, Weaken, and Flaw questions are all based on an argument and the relationship between the evidence and conclusion. Inference questions don't test the connection between the evidence and the conclusion. In fact, Inference stimuli typically don't contain an argument at all, but rather a set of facts. Your job is to inventory the facts provided and draw a logical conclusion from them. Given the difference between argument-based stimuli and Inference stimuli, you will have to modify your approach to an Inference question, but you will still follow the Kaplan Method.

## USE THE KAPLAN METHOD TO ANSWER INFERENCE QUESTIONS

### Identify the Question Type

As always, read the question stem first to identify the question type and note any relevant clues. You can identify an Inference question from words and phrases like:

- Must be true
- Logically follows
- Can be inferred
- Supports

You may remember that you already saw "support" as an indicator of a Strengthen question. To differentiate between a Strengthen question and an Inference question, you need to determine the direction of the support. If the stimulus supports the answer, it is an Inference question. If the answer supports the stimulus, it is a Strengthen question.

Here's some typical Inference question stems:

- Which one of the following is most strongly supported by the information above?
- Which one of the following most logically completes the argument?
- If the statements above are true, which one of the following must be true?
- Which one of the following can be properly inferred from the argument above?

Besides recognizing the question type as an Inference, pay close attention to how the answer choices are characterized. Read the stem to determine whether you need an answer that *must be true*, *must be false*, *could be true*, or *could be false*. This seems like an obvious step, but you don't get any points for answering the wrong question.

Most Inference questions ask for an answer that *must be true*. In that case, identify what must be true and eliminate any answer choice that *could be false*. If the question asks for what *must be false*, mark the answer that is always false and eliminate the four wrong answers that *could be true*. By taking a moment to characterize the answer choices, you know what you're looking for in a correct answer, which helps you to answer questions quickly and confidently.

## Untangle the Stimulus

Inference stimuli differ from the argument-based stimuli you've seen so far in that they don't typically contain a full argument. Instead, they will almost always be a set of facts. So, after you identify an Inference question, don't spend any time looking for a conclusion or identifying an assumption.

As you read the stimulus for an Inference question, you need to accept each statement as true, summarize each new piece of information, and translate any formal logic statements (formal logic shows up in Inference questions more often than any other question type). In other words, you need to get a basic understanding of what the stimulus says. In addition, you should circle qualifying language like "some," "most," and "all," as well as emphasis and opinion Keywords, just as you would on the Reading Comprehension section.

## Make a Prediction

This step is where you'll find the biggest difference between Inference questions and all other Logical Reasoning question types. Generally speaking, you won't be able to predict an answer for Inference questions. You'll find that many things *must be true* based on the statements in the stimulus, so it'll be hard to pre-phrase an answer. In that case, move on to step four.

However, if the stimulus includes formal logic or statements that you can combine, the correct answer choice will often be the outcome of the linked statements. In that case, take a moment in this step to combine the statements. For example, if an Inference stimulus states "if A, then B and if B, then C," combining the statements indicates "if A, then C," and that is a prediction you can make.

## Evaluate the Answer Choices

As you proceed to the answer choices, remember to characterize them—if the correct answer *must be true*, then the wrong answers *could be false*, and so on. After you know the characteristics of the right and wrong answers, you can assess the answer choices. As you do so, keep the following basic principles in mind:

- The correct answer to an Inference question will not require any information beyond what is provided in the stimulus. So, resist the temptation to add any outside knowledge to the stimulus. The further an answer choice gets from the stimulus and the harder you have to work to prove it is valid, the more likely that it is wrong.
- A valid inference may be a simple summary of the stimulus. Don't eliminate an answer just because you think it's too obvious. Sometimes, it's just that easy.

- The correct answer choice must be indisputable, not just possible or reasonable. So, look out for extreme wording in Inference answers. The correct answer cannot be more extreme than the stimulus. For example, the stimulus states that *some* students got an A in the class, and an answer choice indicates *everyone* got an A—this is extreme and incorrect. On the other hand, if the stimulus states that everybody received an A in the class, and an answer choice indicates a majority of the students (or even just one) got an A, it is within the scope of the stimulus. Look out for words like "never," "always," "some," and "must" so you can make sure the scope of the stimulus matches that of the answer choices.

- The correct inference need not come from the entire stimulus. It may just be a rephrasing of one sentence or a combination of sentences.

## THE KAPLAN METHOD IN ACTION

Now I'll walk you through a couple examples to show you how the Kaplan Method can help you efficiently solve any Inference question you see on test day.

1.  Having lived through extraordinary childhood circumstances, Robin has no conception of the moral difference between right and wrong, only between what is legally permitted and what is not. When Robin committed an offense, Robin did not recognize the fact that it was a morally wrong act, despite knowing that it was illegal.

    From the statements above, which one of the following can be properly inferred?

    (A)  Robin committed no offense that was not legally permissible.
    (B)  Robin did something that was morally wrong.
    (C)  Moral ignorance is never excusable in the eyes of the law.
    (D)  Robin's childhood could have provided more adequate moral training even in the circumstances.
    (E)  Robin could now be brought to see the moral difference between right and wrong.[1]

### Step 1. Identify the Question Type

The phrase "properly inferred" identifies this as an Inference question. Next, you need to read the stimulus and decide which answer *must be true* based on the information provided.

---

[1]PrepTest 40, Sec. 1, Q 3

## Step 2. Untangle the Stimulus

Read the stimulus to get a handle on the basic facts of the statement. Here, you learn that Robin doesn't know the difference between morally right and morally wrong, but she does know the difference between legally right and legally wrong. She committed an offense that she did not know was immoral, but did know it was illegal. Remember, that's all you need to do with an Inference stimulus: You don't need to find the argument or identify the evidence or conclusion.

## Step 3. Make a Prediction

Now that you have reviewed the facts of the statement and characterized the correct answer as one that *must be true* (and conversely, the wrong answers *could be false*), move on to the answer choices.

## Step 4. Evaluate the Answer Choices

The stimulus says that Robin committed an illegal offense, and choice (A) says the exact opposite, so you can eliminate this answer.

According to the stimulus, Robin did commit an immoral offense, she just didn't know it. So choice (B) must be true and is the correct answer.

Choice (C) raises the topic of moral ignorance as an excuse, which is not discussed in the stimulus. So, choice (C) is outside the scope and you can eliminate it. Also, the word "never" should set off an alarm as an extreme concept that does not fit with the stimulus.

Whether Robin's upbringing could have provided more moral training is not addressed in the stimulus. Therefore, choice (D) is outside the scope of the argument and is incorrect.

Choice (E) is also outside the scope of the stimulus. You can't know Robin's potential to learn the moral difference between right and wrong from the stimulus.

2. Essayist: Every contract negotiator has been lied to by someone or other, and whoever lies to anyone is practicing deception. But, of course, anyone who has been lied to has also lied to someone or other.

If the essayist's statements are true, which one of the following must also be true?

(A) Every contract negotiator has practiced deception.
(B) Not everyone who practices deception is lying to someone.
(C) Not everyone who lies to someone is practicing deception.
(D) Whoever lies to a contract negotiator has been lied to by a contract negotiator.
(E) Whoever lies to anyone is lied to by someone.[2]

---

[2]PrepTest 22, Sec. 4, Q 25

## Step 1. Identify the Question Type

The phrase "must also be true" tells you this is an Inference question. Also, note that you are looking for an answer that *must be true*.

## Step 2. Untangle the Stimulus

Words such as "every," "whoever," and "anyone" identify formal logic. When formal logic is present in a stimulus, expect the test makers to assess your understanding of what must be true on the basis of these statements. So, as with any formal logic statement, you will need to translate them and form their contrapositives.

The first statement says every contract negotiator has been lied to by someone or other. The matching formal logic equation is "Every X is Y." The translation and contrapositive are:

$$\text{Contract negotiator} \rightarrow \text{lied to}$$
$$\text{Not lied to} \rightarrow \text{not a contract negotiator}$$

The second statement says that whoever lies to anyone is practicing deception. The matching formal logic equation is "Whoever X is Y." The translation and contrapositive are:

$$\text{Liar} \rightarrow \text{deceptive}$$
$$\text{Not deceptive} \rightarrow \text{not liar}$$

The third statement says that anyone who has been lied to has also lied to someone or other. The matching formal logic equation is "Any X is Y." The translation and contrapositive are:

$$\text{Lied to} \rightarrow \text{liar}$$
$$\text{Not liar} \rightarrow \text{not lied to}$$

## Step 3. Make a Prediction

You can connect the formal logic statements in the following way: Contract negotiator → lied to → Liar → Deceptive. Proceed to the answer choices to determine which one you can infer from the stimulus.

## Step 4. Evaluate the Answer Choices

Each answer is presented in formal logic language. So, be prepared to translate each statement and compare it to the stimulus. When you find a match, you have the correct answer. And remember, you're looking for the correct answer that *must be true* and avoiding the four wrong answers that *could be false*.

Choice (A) says that every contract negotiator practices deception, which in formal logic terms is: Contract negotiator → deceptive. The stimulus does not have a statement that says this directly; however, this formal logic statement is a summary of the connected statements. Every contract negotiator has been lied to, and anyone who has been lied to also has lied to someone. So, every contract negotiator has lied to someone else. Whoever lies to anyone is practicing deception, so every contract negotiator has practiced deception. The equation form looks like this: Contract negotiator → lied to → lies → deceives. In summary, if you are a contract negotiator, then you practice deception. This matches the prediction, so mark choice (A) as the correct answer.

Choice (B) says that not everyone who practices deception is lying to someone. Practicing deception does not trigger a result in this stimulus. You cannot infer anything from practicing deception.

Choice (C) says not everyone who lies to someone is practicing deception. It directly contradicts the stimulus, which states that whoever lies to anyone is practicing deception.

Choice (D) says that whoever lies to a contract negotiator has been lied to by a contract negotiator. The stimulus never mentions what happens if you lie to a contract negotiator, so you can't know it to be true. Eliminate it.

Choice (E) says whoever lies has been lied to. Again, the stimulus never tells you the result of lying. So, it could be true because it's not contradicted by the stimulus, but it also *could be false*, making it a wrong answer.

# INFERENCE QUESTIONS: NOW YOU TRY IT

Now it's your turn to try an Inference question on your own. Use the template I've provided after the question to guide you through the four-step Kaplan Method. (Note: On test day, you won't be writing out all the steps as you are in this exercise. However, as you are learning the Method, it's good practice to help it become second nature.)

1.  Professor: The best users of a language are its great authors. However, these authors often use language in ways that are innovative and idiosyncratic, and are therefore less respectful of the strictures of proper usage than most of us are.

    The Professor's statements, if true, most support which one of the following?

    (A)    People who want to become great writers should not imitate great authors' use of language.
    (B)    Writers who do not observe proper language usage risk developing a peculiar or idiosyncratic style.
    (C)    Those most talented at using a language are not as likely as most other people to observe proper language usage.
    (D)    People who use an innovative or idiosyncratic writing style often incur criticism of their language usage.
    (E)    The standard for what constitutes proper language usage should be set by the best users of a language.[3]

## Step 1. Identify the Question Type

_____

## Step 2. Untangle the Stimulus

_____

## Step 3. Make a Prediction

_____

## Step 4. Evaluate the Answer Choices

_____

---

[3]PrepTest 40, Sec. 3, Q 3

## Explanations

### 1. **(C)**

Professor: The best users of a language are its great
authors. However, these authors often use
language in ways that are innovative and
idiosyncratic, and are therefore less respectful of
the strictures of proper usage than most of us are.

The Professor's statements, if true, (most support) which
one of the following?

(A)  People who want to become great writers should
     not imitate great authors' use of language.
(B)  Writers who do not observe proper language
     usage risk developing a peculiar or idiosyncratic
     style.
(C)  Those most talented at using a language are not as
     likely as most other people to observe proper
     language usage.
(D)  People who use an innovative or idiosyncratic
     writing style often incur criticism of their
     language usage.
(E)  The standard for what constitutes proper language
     usage should be set by the best users of a
     language.[4]

### Step 1. Identify the Question Type

The phrase "most support" coupled with the downward direction of the support makes this
an Inference question. The question stem tells you specifically that the Professor's statements
in the stimulus will support the correct answer.

### Step 2. Untangle the Stimulus

Paraphrase the stimulus so you have a handle on what it says: Great authors may be the best
users of a language, says the Professor, but they have less respect for the proper use of language than the rest of us.

### Step 3. Make a Prediction

The summary is straightforward, with no formal logic or statements to connect. Move on to
the answer choices and look for the one that *must be true*.

### Step 4. Evaluate the Answer Choices

Cross out choice (A), as the Professor gives no career advice in her statement.

Likewise, get rid of choice (B). The Professor does not discuss any negative impact of improp-
erly using language.

---

[4]PrepTest 40, Sec. 3, Q 3

Choice (C) closely matches the summary and is the correct answer. Those most talented or the best users of language are less likely to properly use language.

No mention of criticism is made in the stimulus, so choice (D) won't work.

Choice (E) is out as well because the stimulus does not talk about the origin of proper language use.

# DRILL: PRACTICING INFERENCE QUESTIONS

Use the Kaplan Method to answer the following Inference questions. Take this opportunity to practice and apply the steps in the Method so you are comfortable using them on test day. Be sure to circle conclusion and evidence Keywords and bracket the conclusion. Check your responses against the full explanations provided after the Drill.

1. Commentator: Recently, articles criticizing the environmental movement have been appearing regularly in newspapers. According to Winslow, this is due not so much to an antienvironmental bias among the media as to a preference on the part of newspaper editors for articles that seem "daring" in that they seem to challenge prevailing political positions. It is true that editors like to run antienvironmental pieces mainly because they seem to challenge the political orthodoxy. But serious environmentalism is by no means politically orthodox, and antienvironmentalists can hardly claim to be dissidents, however much they may have succeeded in selling themselves as renegades.

The commentator's statements, if true, most strongly support which one of the following?

(A) Winslow is correct about the preference of newspaper editors for controversial articles.
(B) Critics of environmentalism have not successfully promoted themselves as renegades.
(C) Winslow's explanation is not consonant with the frequency with which critiques of environmentalism are published.
(D) The position attacked by critics of environmentalism is actually the prevailing political position.
(E) Serious environmentalism will eventually become a prevailing political position.[5]

2. Among a sample of diverse coins from an unfamiliar country, each face of any coin portrays one of four things: a judge's head, an explorer's head, a building, or a tree. By examining the coins, a collector determines that none of them have heads on both sides and that all coins in the sample with a judge's head on one side have a tree on the other.

If the statements above are true, which one of the following must be true of the coins in the sample?

(A) All those with an explorer's head on one side have a building on the other.
(B) All those with a tree on one side have a judge's head on the other.
(C) None of those with a tree on one side have an explorer's head on the other.
(D) None of those with a building on one side have a judge's head on the other.
(E) None of those with an explorer's head on one side have a building on the other.[6]

3.  False chicory's taproot is always one half as long as the plant is tall. Furthermore, the more rain false chicory receives, the taller it tends to grow. In fact, false chicory plants that receive greater than twice the average rainfall of the species' usual habitat always reach above-average heights for false chicory.

    If the statements above are true, then which one of the following must also be true?

    (A)  If two false chicory plants differ in height, then it is likely that the one with the shorter taproot has received less than twice the average rainfall of the species' usual habitat.

    (B)  If a false chicory plant has a longer-than-average taproot, then it is likely to have received more than twice the average rainfall of the species' usual habitat.

    (C)  It is not possible for a false chicory plant to receive only the average amount of rainfall of the species' usual habitat and be of above-average height.

    (D)  If the plants in one group of false chicory are not taller than those in another group of false chicory, then the two groups must have received the same amount of rainfall.

    (E)  If a false chicory plant receives greater than twice the average rainfall of the species' usual habitat, then it will have a longer taproot than that of an average-sized false chicory plant.[7]

4.  All highly successful salespersons are both well organized and self-motivated, characteristics absent from many salespersons who are not highly successful. Further, although only those who are highly successful are well known among their peers, no salespersons who are self-motivated regret their career choices.

    If all of the statements above are true, which one of the following must be true?

    (A)  No self-motivated salespersons who are not highly successful are well organized.

    (B)  All salespersons who are well organized but not highly successful are self-motivated.

    (C)  No salespersons who are well known among their peers regret their career choices.

    (D)  All salespersons who are not well organized regret their career choices.

    (E)  All salespersons who do not regret their career choices are highly successful.[8]

5.  Journalist: Recent studies have demonstrated that a regular smoker who has just smoked a cigarette will typically display significantly better short-term memory skills than a nonsmoker, whether or not the nonsmoker has also just smoked a cigarette for the purposes of the study. Moreover, the majority of those smokers who exhibit this superiority in short-term memory skills will do so for at least eight hours after having last smoked.

    If the journalist's statements are true, then each of the following could be true EXCEPT:

    (A)  The short-term memory skills exhibited by a nonsmoker who has just smoked a cigarette are usually substantially worse than the short-term memory skills exhibited by a nonsmoker who has not recently smoked a cigarette.

    (B)  The short-term memory skills exhibited by a nonsmoker who has just smoked a cigarette are typically superior to those exhibited by a regular smoker who has just smoked a cigarette.

    (C)  The short-term memory skills exhibited by a nonsmoker who has just smoked a cigarette are typically superior to those exhibited by a regular smoker who has not smoked for more than eight hours.

    (D)  A regular smoker who, immediately after smoking a cigarette, exhibits short-term memory skills no better than those typically exhibited by a nonsmoker is nevertheless likely to exhibit superior short-term memory skills in the hours following a period of heavy smoking.

    (E)  The short-term memory skills exhibited by a regular smoker who last smoked a cigarette five hours ago are typically superior to those exhibited by a regular smoker who has just smoked a cigarette.[9]

---

[7]PrepTest 46, Sec. 3, Q 25

[8]PrepTest 40, Sec. 1, Q 22

[9]PrepTest 52, Sec. 1, Q 18

# Explanations

## 1.   **(A)**

Commentator: Recently, articles criticizing the environmental movement have been appearing regularly in newspapers. According to Winslow, this is due not so much to an antienvironmental bias among the media as to a preference on the part of newspaper editors for articles that seem "daring" in that they seem to challenge prevailing political positions. It is true that editors like to run antienvironmental pieces mainly because they seem to challenge the political orthodoxy. But serious environmentalism is by no means politically orthodox, and antienvironmentalists can hardly claim to be dissidents, however much they may have succeeded in selling themselves as renegades.

The commentator's statements, if true, most strongly support which one of the following?

(A)   Winslow is correct about the preference of newspaper editors for controversial articles.
(B)   Critics of environmentalism have not successfully promoted themselves as renegades.
(C)   Winslow's explanation is not consonant with the frequency with which critiques of environmentalism are published.
(D)   The position attacked by critics of environmentalism is actually the prevailing political position.
(E)   Serious environmentalism will eventually become a prevailing political position.[10]

## Step 1. Identify the Question Type

After you combine the phrase "most strongly support" and the fact that the stimulus supports the correct answer, you know that this stem asks an Inference question.

## Step 2. Untangle the Stimulus

Don't let the length of the stimulus bog you down. Get the basics: The commentator reports on recent criticism of the environmental movement in newspapers. Someone named Winslow claims the reason is not antienvironmental bias, but the editors interest in challenging the status quo. The commentator then says that editors may like to challenge the prevailing environmental attitudes as Winslow says, but environmentalism is not the commonly accepted view.

## Step 3. Make a Prediction

Don't stop to predict an answer for this Inference question. It includes no formal logic or statements to combine. Go right to the answers and determine which choice *must be true.*

---

[10]PrepTest 51, Sec. 3, Q 12

## Step 4. Evaluate the Answer Choices

Choice (A) notes the one point of agreement between Winslow and the commentator, newspaper editors like to challenge the status quo, and thus is correct.

Choice (B) is out because it directly contradicts the last two lines of the stimulus, where the commentator says antienvironmentalists "have succeeded in selling themselves as renegades."

The commentator never mentions the consistency of Winslow's explanation with the frequency of published environmental critiques, so you can't know them to be true from the stimulus. Get rid of choice (C).

Choice (D) won't work either because the stimulus does not identify environmentalism as the prevailing attitude.

The stimulus is set in the present, while choice (E) makes a prediction about environmentalism becoming the mainstream belief. Eliminate it, too.

### 2. **(D)**

Among a sample of diverse coins from an unfamiliar country, each face of any coin portrays one of four things: a judge's head, an explorer's head, a building, or a tree. By examining the coins, a collector determines that (none) of them have heads on both sides and that (all) coins in the sample with a judge's head on one side have a tree on the other.

If the statements above are true, which one of the following (must be true) of the coins in the sample?

(A)   All those with an explorer's head on one side have a building on the other.
(B)   All those with a tree on one side have a judge's head on the other.
(C)   None of those with a tree on one side have an explorer's head on the other.
(D)   None of those with a building on one side have a judge's head on the other.
(E)   None of those with an explorer's head on one side have a building on the other.[11]

## Step 1. Identify the Question Type

The phrase "must be true" signals an Inference question.

## Step 2. Untangle the Stimulus

The stimulus describes a sample of diverse coins in formal logic language signaled by the words "none" and "all." When an Inference question includes formal logic, the correct answer often requires you to translate the statements and form the contrapositives.

---

[11]PrepTest 48, Sec. 1, Q 14

The first statement says that no coins have heads on both sides. The matching formal logic equation is "No Y are X." The translation and contrapositive are:

$$\text{Coin} \rightarrow \text{no two heads}$$
$$\text{Two heads} \rightarrow \text{not a coin}$$

You can simplify those statements by specifically applying them to the stimulus with the following:

$$\text{Judge} \rightarrow \text{not explorer}$$
$$\text{Explorer} \rightarrow \text{not judge}$$

The second statement says that all coins with a judge's head on one side have a tree on the other side. The matching formal logic equation is "All X are Y." The translation and contrapositive are:

$$\text{Judge} \rightarrow \text{tree}$$
$$\text{No tree} \rightarrow \text{no Judge}$$

## Step 3. Make a Prediction

Because the stimulus contains formal logic, look for any statements to combine. In this case, the formal logic states that if the judge is on one side of a coin, then a tree is on the other side and not an explorer. Because the tree is necessary when the judge is on the coin, you can also infer that there is no building either.

In all likelihood, the wrong answers will confuse the formal logic statements.

## Step 4. Evaluate the Answer Choices

Choice (A) says in formal logic terms that coins with an explorer's head on one side have a building on the other (Explorer $\rightarrow$ building). This could be true, but you don't know anything from the stimulus about the explorer's head except that another head can't be on the other side. Eliminate it.

Choice (B) commits a classic mistake by reversing a formal logic statement without negating and says: Tree $\rightarrow$ judge. You can't determine it from the stimulus. Cross it out.

Choice (C) translates to Tree $\rightarrow$ explorer, and having a tree on one side of the coin does not necessitate anything. This one's out as well.

Choice (D) translates to Building $\rightarrow$ no judge, and its contrapositive is Judge $\rightarrow$ no building. This must be true because you know from the stimulus that Judge $\rightarrow$ tree, and since only one thing can be on each side of coin, there can't be a building on this coin. So, choice (D) is correct.

Choice (E) translates as Explorer $\rightarrow$ no building, and it is wrong. Nothing in the stimulus contradicts it so it could be true, but nothing in the stimulus confirms it. So, it does not have to be true.

3.  **(E)**

False chicory's taproot is (always) one half as long as the plant is tall. Furthermore, the more rain false chicory receives, the taller it tends to grow. In fact, false chicory plants that receive greater than twice the average rainfall of the species' usual habitat (always) reach above-average heights for false chicory.

If the statements above are true, then which one of the following (must also be true)?

(A)    If two false chicory plants differ in height, then it is likely that the one with the shorter taproot has received less than twice the average rainfall of the species' usual habitat.

(B)    If a false chicory plant has a longer-than-average taproot, then it is likely to have received more than twice the average rainfall of the species' usual habitat.

(C)    It is not possible for a false chicory plant to receive only the average amount of rainfall of the species' usual habitat and be of above-average height.

(D)    If the plants in one group of false chicory are not taller than those in another group of false chicory, then the two groups must have received the same amount of rainfall.

(E)    If a false chicory plant receives greater than twice the average rainfall of the species' usual habitat, then it will have a longer taproot than that of an average-sized false chicory plant.[12]

## Step 1. Identify the Question Type

The phrase "must also be true" tells you this is an Inference question.

## Step 2. Untangle the Stimulus

Extreme wording should always get your attention. Here, the word "always" is used in two different sentences. First, false chicory's taproot is always one half as long as the plant is tall. Second, if false chicory receives greater than twice the average rainfall, the plant will always reach above-average height.

## Step 3. Make a Prediction

Putting these two statements together, you can infer that when there's greater than twice the average rainfall, the false chicory taproot must have above-average length. And remember, the correct answer *must be true*, and so the wrong answers *could be false*.

## Step 4. Evaluate the Answer Choices

Choice (A) identifies a difference in rainfall as the reason for the height difference between two false chicory plants. The stimulus does not. Cross out choice (A).

---

[12]PrepTest 46, Sec. 3, Q 25

Choice (B) refers to rainfall as the likeliest way to get a longer than average taproot, but the stimulus does not address this. Choice (B) is out as well.

The stimulus also does not discuss whether it's possible for a false chicory plant to receive only the average amount of rainfall and be of above-average height. You only know that the more rain false chicory receives, the taller it tends to grow. That eliminates choice (C).

Choice (D) compares groups of false chicory and concludes a specific relationship between the amount of rainfall and plant growth, which is not supported by the stimulus. That only leaves one more choice.

Choice (E) reflects a combination of two statements from the stimulus and is the correct answer. You know that false chicory's taproot is always one half as long as the plant is tall. You also know that when false chicory receives greater than twice the average rainfall the plant will always reach above-average height. Since the plant will be above-average height and the length is always in the same proportion to the height, you can infer the plant will have a longer taproot than that of an average-sized false chicory plant.

4.   **(C)**

(All) highly successful salespersons are both well organized and self-motivated, characteristics absent from many salespersons who are not highly successful. Further, although (only) those who are highly successful are well known among their peers, (no) salespersons who are self-motivated regret their career choices.

If all of the statements above are true, which one of the following (must be true)?

(A)   No self-motivated salespersons who are not highly successful are well organized.
(B)   All salespersons who are well organized but not highly successful are self-motivated.
(C)   No salespersons who are well known among their peers regret their career choices.
(D)   All salespersons who are not well organized regret their career choices.
(E)   All salespersons who do not regret their career choices are highly successful.[13]

## Step 1. Identify the Question Type

The question asks for a statement that "must be true" based on the stimulus, signaling that it is an Inference question.

## Step 2. Untangle the Stimulus

The words "all," "only," and "no" signal formal logic language throughout the stimulus. Translate each statement and form the contrapositive.

---

[13]PrepTest 40, Sec. 1, Q 22

The first statement says that all highly successful (HS) salespersons are both well-organized (WO) and self-motivated (SM). The matching formal logic equation is "All X are Y." The translation and contrapositive are:

$$HS \rightarrow WO \text{ and } SM$$
$$\text{Not WO or not SM} \rightarrow \text{not HS}$$

The second statement says that only highly successful (HS) salespersons are well-known (WK). The matching formal logic equation is "Only Y are X." The translation and contrapositive are:

$$WK \rightarrow HS$$
$$\text{Not HS} \rightarrow \text{not WK}$$

The third statement says that no salespersons who are self-motivated (SM) regret their career choices (RC). The matching formal logic equation is "No Y are X." The translation and contrapositive are:

$$SM \rightarrow \text{not RC}$$
$$RC \rightarrow \text{not SM}$$

## Step 3. Make a Prediction

The three statements connect in the following way: WK → HS → WO and SM → not RC. Armed with the formal logic statements, you are ready to move on to the answer choices.

## Step 4. Evaluate the Answer Choices

Notice that each answer is presented in formal logic terms. You will need to translate them and compare them to the formal logic in the stimulus.

Choice (A) says SM and not HS → not WO. While "SM" and "not HS" appear in an "if" or sufficient clause in the stimulus, they do not individually or combined result in "not WO." So according to the stimulus, "SM" and "not HS" both trigger a result. But the result is never "not WO." Cross out this choice.

Choice (B) says WO and not HS → SM. WO is never part of a sufficient clause in the stimulus, so you can eliminate (B).

Choice (C) says WK → not RC. While it does not match an individual translation or contrapositive from the stimulus, it is a summary of the linked statement, and is a valid inference. This is the correct answer.

Choice (D) says not WO → RC. You can find a sufficient clause with "not WO," but there is no way to reach RC as the result. Choice (D) cannot be a valid inference.

Choice (E) says not RC → HS. Once again, check the translations and contrapositives. You will not find "not RC" in the sufficient clause, so you can't know what happens if salespeople don't regret their career choices.

5.    **(B)**

Journalist: Recent studies have demonstrated that a regular smoker who has just smoked a cigarette will typically display significantly better short-term memory skills than a nonsmoker, whether or not the nonsmoker has also just smoked a cigarette for the purposes of the study. Moreover, the majority of those smokers who exhibit this superiority in short-term memory skills will do so for at least eight hours after having last smoked.

If the journalist's statements are true, then each of the following could be true EXCEPT:

(A)    The short-term memory skills exhibited by a nonsmoker who has just smoked a cigarette are usually substantially worse than the short-term memory skills exhibited by a nonsmoker who has not recently smoked a cigarette.

(B)    The short-term memory skills exhibited by a nonsmoker who has just smoked a cigarette are typically superior to those exhibited by a regular smoker who has just smoked a cigarette.

(C)    The short-term memory skills exhibited by a nonsmoker who has just smoked a cigarette are typically superior to those exhibited by a regular smoker who has not smoked for more than eight hours.

(D)    A regular smoker who, immediately after smoking a cigarette, exhibits short-term memory skills no better than those typically exhibited by a nonsmoker is nevertheless likely to exhibit superior short-term memory skills in the hours following a period of heavy smoking.

(E)    The short-term memory skills exhibited by a regular smoker who last smoked a cigarette five hours ago are typically superior to those exhibited by a regular smoker who has just smoked a cigarette.[14]

### Step 1. Identify the Question Type

The language "could be true EXCEPT" tells you this is an Inference question with a twist, so it's important to make sure you know what the question is really asking you to find. An Inference... EXCEPT question directs you to identify the one answer choice that *must be false* according

---

[14]PrepTest 52, Sec. 1, Q 18

to the stimulus. That is, it can't be true if the stimulus is true. All four wrong answers *could be true*—they need not be valid inferences from the stimulus; they just can't contradict the stimulus.

### Step 2. Untangle the Stimulus

The journalist reports that regular smokers who smoked within the last eight hours typically display better short-term memory skills than a nonsmoker, even if the nonsmoker just smoked a cigarette for the study.

### Step 3. Make a Prediction

Pause for a moment to remind yourself that the correct answer *must be false* according to the stimulus and proceed to the answer choices.

### Step 4. Evaluate the Answer Choices

Choice (A) compares two groups of nonsmokers who are not addressed in the stimulus. Because you can't know whether the comparison is correct, the statement is possible. So you can eliminate (A). Remember, if the stimulus does not indicate specifically that an answer is false, it remains possible.

Choice (B) says the nonsmoker who just smoked has better short-term memory skills than a regular smoker. The stimulus says the exact opposite, that regular smokers have better short-term memory skills than a nonsmoker even if he just smoked for the study. Choice (B) contradicts the stimulus; therefore it *must be false* and is the correct answer.

Choice (C) makes a comparison between a nonsmoker who has just smoked and a regular smoker who has not smoked for more than eight hours. These two groups are never compared in the stimulus. Therefore, the stimulus does not confirm or contradict it and the answer remains a possibility. Cross it out.

The journalist never discusses the result of heavy smoking so you can't know it to be true or false according to the stimulus. Choice (D) is still a possibility and therefore can be eliminated.

Choice (E) also raises a point that is never made in the stimulus. The journalist never distinguishes the memory skill level at different points in the eight-hour time period. Choice (E) is not dismissed in the stimulus and is therefore still possible. Eliminate it.

## INFERENCE REVIEW

Before you proceed to the next chapter, turn to Appendix A and complete the review exercise for Inference questions.  A completed chart is included in Appendix B.

# CHAPTER 11

# Principle Questions

You're probably most familiar with the general definition of "principle"—a moral code of conduct or a foundation of a belief system. The term "principle" on the LSAT, however, specifically refers to a broad standard or rule that guides the decision-maker or actor in the stimulus and that directs her to follow a similar path in other similar situations. Principle questions model how the law actually works.

Principle questions have become increasingly important on the LSAT. Historically, tests have averaged five scored Principle questions; however more recent tests have had as many as seven. Principle questions are also important because they mimic other question types, which means they are amenable to the skills and strategies you've already learned for each question type. So, having a good grasp of the other question types will help you quickly and confidently handle any Principle question you see on test day.

## DEFINITION OF PRINCIPLE QUESTIONS

Principle questions ask you to find a general rule and match it to a specific factual situation. The wording of the question determines where the principle appears, either in the stimulus or the answer choices.

# USE THE KAPLAN METHOD TO ANSWER PRINCIPLE QUESTIONS

## Identify the Question Type

Just as you've done with all other Logical Reasoning question types, read the question stem first to determine the question type. The following terms denote a Principle question:

- Principle (this is used most often)
- Policy
- Proposition
- Generalization

Here's how some of those phrases could appear in a question stem:

- Which one of the following principles, if valid, most helps to justify the reasoning in the argument?
- The passage conforms most closely to which one of the following propositions?
- Which one of the following arguments illustrates a principle most similar to the principle underlying the argument above?
- Which one of the following principles most strongly supports the reasoning above?
- Which one of the following principles underlies the argument above?
- Of the following, which one illustrates a principle that is most similar to the principle illustrated by the passage?
- The situation described above most closely conforms to which one of the following generalizations?

## Principle Questions Can Mimic Other Logical Reasoning Question Types

Some Principle questions are just straightforward Principle questions. Others include additional language in the stem that makes them resemble other Logical Reasoning question types.

For example, you may be asked for a principle that justifies (Strengthens) the author's argument, that underlies the argument (Assumption), that comes from the stimulus and is parallel to the principle illustrated by the answer (Parallel Reasoning), or that must be true (Inference). If you recognize the wording of another question type in a Principle question, use that knowledge to help you untangle the stimulus.

Consider the following example:

> Which one of the following principles, if valid, most helps to justify the reasoning in the argument?

The word "principles" signals a Principle question, but "most helps to justify" makes it sound like a Strengthen question.

Try another example:

> Which one of the following principles underlies the argument above?

Again, you see the word "principles" to identify the Principle question. But "underlies" indicates that the Principle question acts like an Assumption question.

Here is a Parallel Reasoning example:

> Which one of the following arguments illustrates a principle most similar to the principle underlying the argument above?

"Principle" tells you this is a Principle question, while "most similar to" tells you the unstated Principle exemplified by the stimulus is parallel to the unstated Principle exemplified by the correct answer choice.

Finally, look at an Inference example:

> Which one of the following must be true based on the policy stated above?

"Policy" identifies a Principle question that asks you to identify what "must be true" or can be inferred from the stimulus.

## Find the Principle

After you identify a Principle question and another question type it may mimic, use the language of the question stem to determine the location of the principle. The LSAT asks Principle questions in three different ways. You may be asked to:

- Identify the Principle: Most Principle questions present an argument in the stimulus and ask you to identify the principle in the answer choices that is similar to the stimulus, yet broader in scope. It shifts from narrow reasoning in the stimulus to a broad focus in the answers.
  Example: Which one of the following principles most strongly supports the reasoning above?

- Apply the Principle: Here, you'll find the principle in the stimulus and different scenarios in the answer choices. Your task is to find an example that is covered by the principle but is narrower in scope. Keep your eye out for formal logic in these Principle question types.
  Example: Which one of the following most closely conforms to the principle stated above?

- Identify and Apply the Principle: In this Principle question type, you won't find the principle in the stimulus or in the answer choices. Instead, the stimulus presents a situation and the answer choices each provide a different scenario. Your job is to find a specific situation in the correct answer that falls under the same general rule exemplified by the situation in the stimulus. The principle is unstated, yet both the stimulus and the answer must follow the same principle.

  Example: Of the following, which one illustrates a principle that is most similar to the principle illustrated by the passage?

## Untangle the Stimulus

Since Principle questions resemble Strengthen, Assumption, Parallel Reasoning, and Inference questions, you can use those strategies to untangle the stimulus of a Principle question. Simply read a Principle stimulus like the question type it mimics.

For example, if the question resembles a Strengthen question, find the conclusion and evidence, determine the assumption, and make the argument more likely to be so. For an Assumption question, locate the conclusion and evidence and determine what links them together. With a Parallel Reasoning question, look for the same kind of evidence to support the same kind of conclusion in the stimulus and the correct answer choice. And for an Inference question, determine what you can know from the stimulus and evaluate the answer choices, looking for what must be true based on it.

## Make a Prediction

Think critically about the answer in the manner you would for the corresponding question type, and phrase the prediction as a broad principle or a narrow situation, depending on what the question calls for.

## Evaluate the Answer Choices

Find an answer choice that matches your prediction.

# THE KAPLAN METHOD IN ACTION

Now I'll walk you through a couple examples to show you how the Kaplan Method can help you efficiently solve any Principle question you'll see on test day.

1. Philosopher: Some of the most ardent philosophical opponents of democracy have rightly noted that both the inherently best and the inherently worst possible forms of government are those that concentrate political power in the hands of a few. Thus, since democracy is a consistently mediocre form of government, it is a better choice than rule by the few.

   Which one of the following principles, if valid, most helps to justify the philosopher's argument?

   (A) A society should adopt a democratic form of government if and only if most members of the society prefer a democratic form of government.
   (B) In choosing a form of government, it is better for a society to avoid the inherently worst than to seek to attain the best.
   (C) The best form of government is the one that is most likely to produce an outcome that is on the whole good.
   (D) Democratic governments are not truly equitable unless they are designed to prevent interest groups from exerting undue influence on the political process.
   (E) It is better to choose a form of government on the basis of sound philosophical reasons than on the basis of popular preference.[1]

## Step 1. Identify the Question Type

There are three important things to note in this question stem. First, the word "principle" identifies it as a Principle question. Second, the "most helps to justify" language tells you the question will behave like a Strengthen question. Third, you're asked about "the following principles," so you know that the principles are in the answer choices.

## Step 2. Untangle the Stimulus

Approach this as you would a Strengthen question and look for the conclusion and evidence in the stimulus. The philosopher says that the best and worst governments are those in which power is held by a few. With "Thus," he concludes that democracy is a better form of government than rule by a few because democracy is always mediocre.

## Step 3. Make a Prediction

Your task is to find the principle that makes the argument more likely to be so. The philosopher chooses mediocrity over other forms of government that could be the inherently best or the inherently worst. In his eyes, the risk of the worst government does not outweigh the possibility of the best government, so he chooses the safer route: mediocrity. He assumes it's better to be safe than sorry.

---

[1]PrepTest 51, Sec. 3, Q 13

## Step 4. Evaluate the Answer Choices

Choice (A) states that societal preference for a democratic government is both sufficient and necessary to adopt a democratic form of government. However, in the stimulus the philosopher never considers the majority preference in determining which form of government to adopt. Eliminate this choice.

Choice (B) matches the prediction and is the correct answer.

Choice (C) raises the likelihood of producing a good outcome, but the stimulus never discusses which form of government is most likely to produce a good outcome.

Choice (D) discusses the components of an equitable democratic government, which is outside the scope of the argument.

Choice (E) compares philosophical reasons to popular preference as a means to choose a form of government. However, the author's argument is concerned with the form of government that is chosen, not how it is chosen, so this choice is out.

2.  Any museum that owns the rare stamp that features an airplane printed upside down should not display it. Ultraviolet light causes red ink to fade, and a substantial portion of the stamp is red. If the stamp is displayed, it will be damaged. It should be kept safely locked away, even though this will deny the public the chance to see it.

The reasoning above most closely conforms to which one of the following principles?

(A) The public should judge the quality of a museum by the rarity of the objects in its collection.

(B) Museum display cases should protect their contents from damage caused by ultraviolet light.

(C) Red ink should not be used on items that will not be exposed to ultraviolet light.

(D) A museum piece that would be damaged by display should not be displayed.

(E) The primary purpose of a museum is to educate the public.[2]

## Step 1. Identify the Question Type

The phrase "following principles" tells you this is a Principle question and that the principle is in the answer choices. Your job is to make it parallel to (as indicated by "conforms to") the reasoning in the stimulus.

---

[2]PrepTest 52, Sec. 3, Q 1

### Step 2. Untangle the Stimulus

The author states that a museum with a rare stamp should not display the stamp because it will become damaged. He concludes with a recommendation to lock up the stamp rather than make it available for public display.

### Step 3. Make a Prediction

In broad terms, the author says that preserving museum pieces is more important than allowing the public to see the museum pieces.

### Step 4. Evaluate the Answer Choices

Choice (A) discusses how the public should judge the quality of museum objects, a topic never broached in the stimulus and therefore outside the scope. Eliminate this choice.

Choice (B) makes a recommendation to protect the museum objects from damage. However, you're not looking for a solution to the problem; you want a principle that is parallel to the stimulus' argument. So, this answer is out of scope.

Choice (C) has two problems. First, it talks about whether to use red ink, which has no bearing on the predicted principle. Second, the stimulus doesn't mention anything about items that will not be exposed to ultraviolet light. So, you can't know whether red ink would be a problem here. Cross this choice out and move on to the next one.

Choice (D) matches the prediction that if displaying the item would damage it, then it shouldn't be displayed, and thus it is the correct answer.

Choice (E) raises the purpose of a museum, which is irrelevant in the argument, so it is incorrect.

# PRINCIPLE QUESTIONS: NOW YOU TRY IT

It's now your turn to try a Principle question on your own. Use the template I've provided after the question to guide you through the four-step Kaplan Method. (Note: On test day, you won't be writing out all the steps as you are in this exercise. However, as you are learning the Method, it's good practice to help it become second nature.) Remember to bracket conclusions and circle Keywords.

1.  Consumer advocate:  One advertisement that is deceptive, and thus morally wrong, states that "gram for gram, the refined sugar used in our chocolate pies is no more fattening than the sugars found in fruits and vegetables." This is like trying to persuade someone that chocolate pies are not fattening by saying that, calorie for calorie, they are no more fattening than celery. True, but it would take a whole shopping cart full of celery to equal a chocolate pie's worth of calories.

    Advertiser:  This advertisement cannot be called deceptive. It is, after all, true.

    Which one of the following principles, if established, would do most to support the consumer advocate's position against the advertiser's response?

    (A)    It is morally wrong to seek to persuade by use of deceptive statements.

    (B)    A true statement should be regarded as deceptive only if the person making the statement believes it to be false, and thus intends the people reading or hearing it to acquire a false belief.

    (C)    To make statements that impart only a small proportion of the information in one's possession should not necessarily be regarded as deceptive.

    (D)    It is morally wrong to make a true statement in a manner that will deceive hearers or readers of the statement into believing that it is false.

    (E)    A true statement should be regarded as deceptive if it is made with the expectation that people hearing or reading the statement will draw a false conclusion from it.[3]

---

[3]PrepTest 21, Sec. 2, Q 16

**Step 1. Identify the Question Type**

_____

**Step 2. Untangle the Stimulus**

_____

**Step 3. Make a Prediction**

_____

**Step 4. Evaluate the Answer Choices**

_____

## Explanations

### 1.    (E)

Consumer advocate: <One advertisement that is deceptive, and (thus) morally wrong,> states that "gram for gram, the refined sugar used in our chocolate pies is no more fattening than the sugars found in fruits and vegetables." This is like trying to persuade someone that chocolate pies are not fattening by saying that, calorie for calorie, they are no more fattening than celery. True, but it would take a whole shopping cart full of celery to equal a chocolate pie's worth of calories.

Advertiser: <This advertisement cannot be called deceptive.> It is, after all, true.

Which one of the following (principles) if established, would do most to (support) the consumer advocate's position against the advertiser's response?

(A)    It is morally wrong to seek to persuade by use of deceptive statements.

(B)    A true statement should be regarded as deceptive only if the person making the statement believes it to be false, and thus intends the people reading or hearing it to acquire a false belief.

(C)    To make statements that impart only a small proportion of the information in one's possession should not necessarily be regarded as deceptive.

(D)    It is morally wrong to make a true statement in a manner that will deceive hearers or readers of the statement into believing that it is false.

(E)    A true statement should be regarded as deceptive if it is made with the expectation that people hearing or reading the statement will draw a false conclusion from it.[4]

### Step 1. Identify the Question Type

The phrase "which one of the following principles" indicates that this is a Principle question in which the principle will be in the answer choices. The question also asks you to use the principle answer to "support"—or strengthen—the consumer advocate's position.

### Step 2. Untangle the Stimulus

The consumer advocate argues that the advertisement is deceptive even though it is true, and the advertiser argues that the ad is not deceptive because it is true.

### Step 3. Make a Prediction

To strengthen the argument, the correct answer choice must define "deception" beyond the truth or falsity of the statement.

---

[4]PrepTest 21, Sec. 2, Q 16

## Step 4. Evaluate the Answer Choices

The basis of the dispute between the advocate and the advertiser is the definition of deception. Choice (A) focuses on morality, which the advertiser never mentions. Cross this choice out.

There is no indication the pie manufacturer believes the claim about the pie's sugar content to be false. So, you can discard choice (B).

Choice (C) raises the amount of information revealed, which does not address the advocate's meaning of deception. Eliminate this choice.

Choice (D) provides a definition for morally wrong, not deception. Like choice (A), the focus is on the wrong concept, so you can cross out (D).

By process of elimination you can arrive at choice (E) as the right answer. Choice (E) says a true statement is deceptive if the intent is to mislead. It strengthens the argument that the advertisement is deceptive by dismissing the advertiser's truth standard and by saying that a true statement is still deceptive if it was made with the expectation to mislead.

# DRILL: PRACTICING PRINCIPLE QUESTIONS

Use the Kaplan Method to answer the following Principle questions. Take this opportunity to practice and apply the steps in the Method so you are comfortable using them on test day. Be sure to circle conclusion and evidence Keywords and bracket the conclusion. Check your responses against the full explanations provided after the Drill.

1. Jablonski, who owns a car dealership, has donated cars to driver education programs at area schools for over five years. She found the statistics on car accidents to be disturbing, and she wanted to do something to encourage better driving in young drivers. Some members of the community have shown their support for this action by purchasing cars from Jablonski's dealership.

   Which one of the following propositions is best illustrated by the passage?

   (A) The only way to reduce traffic accidents is through driver education programs.

   (B) Altruistic actions sometimes have positive consequences for those who perform them.

   (C) Young drivers are the group most likely to benefit from driver education programs.

   (D) It is usually in one's best interest to perform actions that benefit others.

   (E) An action must have broad community support if it is to be successful.[5]

2. Environmentalists who seek stricter governmental regulations controlling water pollution should be certain to have their facts straight. For if it turns out, for example, that water pollution is a lesser threat than they proclaimed, then there will be a backlash and the public will not listen to them even when dire threats exist.

   Which one of the following best illustrates the principle illustrated by the argument above?

   (A) Middle-level managers who ask their companies to hire additional employees should have strong evidence that doing so will benefit the company; otherwise, higher-level managers will refuse to follow their suggestions to hire additional employees even when doing so really would benefit the company.

   (B) Politicians who defend the rights of unpopular constituencies ought to see to it that they use cool, dispassionate rhetoric in their appeals. Even if they have their facts straight, inflammatory rhetoric can cause a backlash that results in more negative reactions to these constituencies, whether or not they are deserving of more rights.

   (C) People who are trying to convince others to take some sort of action should make every effort to present evidence that is emotionally compelling. Such evidence is invariably more persuasive than dry, technical data, even when the data strongly support their claims.

   (D) Whoever wants to advance a political agenda ought to take the time to convince legislators that their own political careers are at stake in the matter at hand; otherwise, the agenda will simply be ignored.

   (E) Activists who want to prevent excessive globalization of the economy should assign top priority to an appeal to the economic self-interest of those who would be adversely affected by it, for if they fail in such an appeal, extreme economic globalization is inevitable.[6]

3. We have a moral obligation not to destroy books, even if they belong to us. The reason is quite simple: If preserved, books will almost certainly contribute to the intellectual and emotional enrichment of future generations.

   Which one of the following most accurately expresses the principle underlying the argument?

   (A) It is morally incumbent upon us to devote effort to performing actions that have at least some chance of improving other people's lives.

   (B) We are morally obligated to preserve anything that past generations had preserved for our intellectual and emotional enrichment.

   (C) The moral commitments we have to future generations supersede the moral commitments we have to the present generation.

   (D) We are morally obligated not to destroy anything that will most likely enrich, either intellectually or emotionally, for posterity.

   (E) Being morally obligated not to destroy something requires that we be reasonably assured that that thing will lead to the betterment of someone we know.[7]

4. If one does not have enough information to make a well-informed decision, one should not make a decision solely on the basis of the information one does possess. Instead, one should continue to seek information until a well-informed decision can be made.

   Of the following, which one most closely conforms to the principle stated above?

   (A) Economists should not believe the predictions of an economic model simply because it is based on information about the current economy. Many conflicting models are based on such information, and they cannot all be accurate.

   (B) When deciding which career to pursue, one needs to consider carefully all of the information one has. One should not choose a career solely on the basis of financial compensation; instead, one should consider other factors such as how likely one is to succeed at the career and how much one would enjoy it.

   (C) Though a researcher may know a great deal about a topic, she or he should not assume that all information relevant to the research is already in her or his possession. A good researcher always looks for further relevant information.

   (D) When one wants to buy a reliable car, one should not choose which car to buy just on the inadequate basis of one's personal experience with cars. Rather, one should study various models' reliability histories that summarize many owners' experiences.

   (E) When there is not enough information available to determine the meaning of a line of poetry, one should not form an opinion based on the insufficient information. Instead, one should simply acknowledge that it is impossible to determine what the line means.[8]

---

# Explanations

## 1. **(B)**

Jablonski, who owns a car dealership, has donated cars to driver education programs at area schools for over five years. She found the statistics on car accidents to be disturbing, and she wanted to do something to encourage better driving in young drivers. Some members of the community have shown their support for this action by purchasing cars from Jablonski's dealership.

Which one of the following propositions is best illustrated by the passage?

(A) The only way to reduce traffic accidents is through driver education programs.

(B) Altruistic actions sometimes have positive consequences for those who perform them.

(C) Young drivers are the group most likely to benefit from driver education programs.

(D) It is usually in one's best interest to perform actions that benefit others.

(E) An action must have broad community support if it is to be successful.[9]

## Step 1. Identify the Question Type

The phrase "Which of the following propositions" indicates that this is a Principle question and also that the principle is in the answer choices. Your task is to identify the principle that is parallel to the stimulus.

## Step 2. Untangle the Stimulus

Note the key points in the stimulus. Jablonski saw a problem with car accidents and donated cars to local driving schools to help address the problem. Community members supported Jablonski's cause by purchasing cars from her dealership.

## Step 3. Make a Prediction

The correct answer will be a broad statement of the situation described in the stimulus, probably about good deeds being rewarded.

## Step 4. Evaluate the Answer Choices

Don't let the content of choice (A) fool you. Using the same topic in the answer as in the stimulus in a Principle question is often a wrong answer trap. Choice (A) makes no mention of good deeds being rewarded. Cross this choice out and move on to the next one.

Choice (B) is an exact match of the prediction—altruistic actions and positive consequences. This is the correct answer.

Choice (C) presents no good act and no reward. Again, the subject matter is familiar but it certainly doesn't identify the correct answer.

---

[9]PrepTest June 2007, Sec. 3, Q 6

Choice (D) comes close to the answer but is not an exact match. The stimulus provides one example of a good deed being rewarded—that doesn't mean it "usually" works that way as choice (D) states.

Choice (E) asserts that an action must have broad support to be successful, but this falls outside of the scope of the stimulus. It also ignores the good deed–reward principle established in the stimulus. These reasons make this answer incorrect.

### 2. **(A)**

<Environmentalists who seek stricter governmental regulations controlling water pollution should be certain to have their facts straight.> For if it turns out, for example, that water pollution is a lesser threat than they proclaimed, then there will be a backlash and the public will not listen to them even when dire threats exist.

Which one of the following best illustrates the principle illustrated by the argument above?

(A)    Middle-level managers who ask their companies to hire additional employees should have strong evidence that doing so will benefit the company; otherwise, higher-level managers will refuse to follow their suggestions to hire additional employees even when doing so really would benefit the company.

(B)    Politicians who defend the rights of unpopular constituencies ought to see to it that they use cool, dispassionate rhetoric in their appeals. Even if they have their facts straight, inflammatory rhetoric can cause a backlash that results in more negative reactions to these constituencies, whether or not they are deserving of more rights.

(C)    People who are trying to convince others to take some sort of action should make every effort to present evidence that is emotionally compelling. Such evidence is invariably more persuasive than dry, technical data, even when the data strongly support their claims.

(D)    Whoever wants to advance a political agenda ought to take the time to convince legislators that their own political careers are at stake in the matter at hand; otherwise, the agenda will simply be ignored.

(E)    Activists who want to prevent excessive globalization of the economy should assign top priority to an appeal to the economic self-interest of those who would be adversely affected by it, for if they fail in such an appeal, extreme economic globalization is inevitable.[10]

---

[10]PrepTest 36, Sec. 3, Q 13

### Step 1. Identify the Question Type

The term "principle" tells you that this is a Principle question. Additionally, statements like "following best illustrates" and "illustrated by the argument above" let you know that the principle isn't in the stimulus or the answer choices. Instead, you must identify and apply the principle that is illustrated—not stated—in the stimulus. This Principle/Parallel Reasoning question stem tells you that the correct answer will use the same type of evidence to reach the same kind of conclusion used in the stimulus.

### Step 2. Untangle the Stimulus

The author recommends that environmentalists be certain of their claims before they seek tougher regulation of water pollution. Otherwise, their claims will be ignored even in the face of disaster.

### Step 3. Make a Prediction

Broadly stated, the author says that people should make sure a claim is solid before they ask for something, or else their claim will be ignored.

### Step 4. Evaluate the Answer Choices

Choice (A) recommends that managers have a solid case before asking for additional employees or else they'll be ignored even if their idea is beneficial, which is almost an exact match of the prediction. On the test, you might mark this answer and move on to the next question to save time. Right now, you can take the time to check the other answers.

Choice (B) may seem superficially parallel because it makes a recommendation and then lays out consequences if the recommendation is not followed. However, the recommendation to use specific language and the negative consequences don't match those presented in the stimulus.

Choice (C) makes a recommendation, but it's to present an emotionally compelling case, not necessarily a stronger case. The biggest problem with this answer is that it doesn't list any consequences for not following the recommendation.

Choice (D) also makes a recommendation to those with a political agenda, but it's to take time to make their case, not to make the case stronger, which shifts the scope.

Choice (E) recommends that activists assign top priority to a particular issue, not make a stronger case. The consequences of not following the recommendation are the opposite result of the activists' appeal, not that the activists will be ignored, which makes this answer out of scope.

### 3. **(D)**

<We have a moral obligation not to destroy books,> even if they belong to us. The (reason) is quite simple: If preserved, books will almost certainly contribute to the intellectual and emotional enrichment of future generations.

Which one of the following most accurately expresses the (principle underlying) the argument?

(A)  It is morally incumbent upon us to devote effort to performing actions that have at least some chance of improving other people's lives.

(B)  We are morally obligated to preserve anything that past generations had preserved for our intellectual and emotional enrichment.

(C)  The moral commitments we have to future generations supersede the moral commitments we have to the present generation.

(D)  We are morally obligated not to destroy anything that will most likely enrich, either intellectually or emotionally, for posterity.

(E)  Being morally obligated not to destroy something requires that we be reasonably assured that that thing will lead to the betterment of someone we know.[11]

## Step 1. Identify the Question Type

The word "principle" tells you that this is a Principle question, and the phrase "which one of the following," directs you to find the principle in the answer choices. Also, the term "underlying" suggests that the question resembles an Assumption question, so untangle the stimulus by identifying the conclusion and evidence.

## Step 2. Untangle the Stimulus

The author concludes that we should not destroy books, and he bases this on the evidence that preserved books can contribute to the enrichment of future generations.

## Step 3. Make a Prediction

To identify an underlying principle, phrase the gist of this argument in general terms. Essentially, the author is saying that we have a moral obligation not to destroy things that can contribute to the enrichment of future generations.

## Step 4. Evaluate the Answer Choices

Choice (A) states we must devote "effort to performing actions" rather than focusing on the need not to destroy things. Also, "have at least some chance" is too weak compared to "will almost certainly contribute to" in the stimulus. Cross this choice out.

Choice (B) confuses the generations, directing us to preserve anything from past generations, while the stimulus directs us to preserve for future generations. This choice is out as well.

---

[11]PrepTest 25, Sec. 4, Q 14

Choice (C) adds a comparison between the commitment owed to future versus present generations and is thus beyond the scope of the stimulus. Move on to the next choice.

Choice (D) matches the prediction and is the correct answer.

Choice (E) requires reasonable assurance that not destroying something will lead to the betterment of someone we know. In the stimulus, the obligation not to destroy books is aimed at the betterment of future generations. So, the target of our moral obligation does not match between choice (E) and the stimulus.

### 4.    **(D)**

If one does not have enough information to make a well-informed decision, one should not make a decision solely on the basis of the information one does possess. Instead, one should continue to seek information until a well-informed decision can be made.

Of the following, which one most closely conforms to the principle stated above?

(A)    Economists should not believe the predictions of an economic model simply because it is based on information about the current economy. Many conflicting models are based on such information, and they cannot all be accurate.

(B)    When deciding which career to pursue, one needs to consider carefully all of the information one has. One should not choose a career solely on the basis of financial compensation; instead, one should consider other factors such as how likely one is to succeed at the career and how much one would enjoy it.

(C)    Though a researcher may know a great deal about a topic, she or he should not assume that all information relevant to the research is already in her or his possession. A good researcher always looks for further relevant information.

(D)    When one wants to buy a reliable car, one should not choose which car to buy just on the inadequate basis of one's personal experience with cars. Rather, one should study various models' reliability histories that summarize many owners' experiences.

(E)    When there is not enough information available to determine the meaning of a line of poetry, one should not form an opinion based on the insufficient information. Instead, one should simply acknowledge that it is impossible to determine what the line means.[12]

---

[12]PrepTest 47, Sec. 3, Q 22

### Step 1. Identify the Question Type

The word "principle" tells you that this is a Principle question, and "the principle stated above" tells you that the principle is in the stimulus. "Most closely conforms" tells you to find an answer choice with a specific situation that parallels the principle.

### Step 2. Untangle the Stimulus

In simplest terms, this stimulus recommends that you should not make a decision unless you have enough information, and you should keep researching until you can make a good decision.

### Step 3. Make a Prediction

The correct answer must exemplify the principle given in the stimulus and match up on all parts. In this case, look for an answer that properly illustrates when not to reach a decision and what to do to make an informed decision.

### Step 4. Evaluate the Answer Choices

Choice (A) talks about believing information rather than gathering enough information to make a good decision, which is out of scope. Eliminate this choice.

Choice (B) contradicts the stimulus by saying that you should choose a career based on "all of the information one has." The stimulus directs us to look beyond "the information one does possess," so this choice is out as well.

Choice (C) acknowledges there is always more information to learn about a topic. However, choice (C) neglects the issue of when to come to a decision. Move on to the next choice.

Choice (D) tells you to look beyond what you know about cars if you don't know enough and to learn more before you buy one. That matches the prediction and is the correct answer.

Choice (E) starts off on the right track—if you don't have enough information about a line of poetry, don't form an opinion. To be parallel, the next statement would have to be about continuing to collect more information to make an informed decision. Instead, choice (E) says the opposite—don't look for additional information and accept you can't determine the poetry's meaning. Therefore, you can confidently eliminate this answer.

## PRINCIPLE REVIEW

Before you proceed to the next chapter, turn to Appendix A and complete the review exercise for Principle questions. A completed chart is included in Appendix B.

# CHAPTER 12

# PARALLEL REASONING QUESTIONS

At a glance, Parallel Reasoning questions can be daunting. Over the years, I've seen a countless number of my students, as they prepare for the LSAT, try to skip Parallel Reasoning questions altogether. They would look at the length of the stimuli and the length of the answer choices and decide that the questions must be too difficult or too time consuming to handle. I don't want this to happen to you. Don't let the length of Parallel Reasoning questions intimidate you. Parallel Reasoning questions, like every other question type you've examined thus far, are subject to a strategy that allows you to quickly and confidently handle every question you'll see on test day: the Kaplan Method.

You'll see approximately three to four scored Parallel Reasoning questions on the LSAT. While I know that doesn't sound like a lot of points in the big scheme of things, many students will opt not to do these questions at all. As a Kaplan-trained student, however, you will have the opportunity to start a few points ahead of your peers.

# DEFINITION OF PARALLEL REASONING QUESTIONS

Parallel Reasoning questions ask you to identify the answer that has the same argument structure as the stimulus. That is, your task is to find the answer that uses the same kind of evidence to reach the same kind of conclusion as the stimulus.

The correct answer of a Parallel Reasoning question is not based on argument content or placement of the conclusion and evidence. The stimulus may talk about international relations with China, and the correct answer may discuss the price of vegetables at the grocery store. That's okay because the subject matter is irrelevant. The stimulus may have its conclusion in the beginning and the correct answer may have its conclusion at that end. The arrangement is irrelevant. Keep your focus on the underlying structure of the argument.

# USE THE KAPLAN METHOD TO ANSWER PARALLEL REASONING QUESTIONS
## Identify the Question Type

Just as you've done with all other Logical Reasoning question types, read the question stem first to determine the question type. The following terms denote a Parallel Reasoning question:

- Parallel to
- Similar to
- Pattern of reasoning

Here's how some of those phrases could appear in a question stem:

- The reasoning above is most closely paralleled in which one of the following?
- Which one of the following arguments is most similar in its reasoning to the argument above?
- Which one of the following arguments has a pattern of reasoning most like the one in the argument above?
- The pattern of flawed reasoning in which one of the following is most similar to that in the argument above?
- Which one of the following most closely parallels the questionable reasoning cited above?

## Untangle the Stimulus

Every Parallel Reasoning stimulus contains an argument. As you would with the Assumption family of questions, read the stimulus to identify the author's conclusion. For some Parallel Reasoning questions, that's all you'll need from the argument to hone in on the correct answer.

## Types of Conclusions

Next, characterize the conclusion and then compare it to the conclusion types presented in the answer choices. Cross out the answer choices that have a different kind of conclusion. If you find only one answer choice with the same conclusion type, you have the correct answer and can move on to the next question. If the process of comparing conclusion types eliminates only some of the wrong answer choices, you then have to compare the type of evidence used to support the conclusion in the stimulus to the type of evidence used in the remaining answer choices.

You will see six basic types of conclusions on the LSAT, which are listed in Table 12.1. You can use the pneumonic "CAPRI V" or CAPRI Five to remember them.

**Table 12.1**

| Conclusion Types | Definition | Example |
|---|---|---|
| **C**omparison | Weighs one thing against another | In conclusion, Haley's LSAT practice went better today than it did yesterday. |
| **A**ssertion of fact | States what the author believes is or isn't so | Therefore, Haley benefited from practicing for the LSAT in the building she will take the actual test. |
| **P**rediction | Makes a claim about the future (often identified by "will" or "will not") | We can conclude that Haley will improve her LSAT score by practicing more questions. |
| **R**ecommendation | Advocates or discourages a course of action (often identified by "should" or "should not") | So, Haley should practice more to improve her LSAT score. |
| **I**f-then | Forms a conditional statement in any formal logic format | Thus, Haley won't improve her LSAT score unless she practices more Logical Reasoning questions. |
| **V**alue Judgment | Presents the author's subjective evaluation of the argument subject | Hence, making sure you get enough uninterrupted sleep during the week of the LSAT is good test-taking strategy. |

Most of the time, these broad conclusion types won't be enough to identify the matching conclusion in the correct answer choice, and you'll have to consider other factors such as:

Table 12.2

| Additional Conclusion Factors | Description |
| --- | --- |
| Positive or negative status | Pay attention to the positive or negative status of the conclusion. A recommendation to do something is different from a recommendation not to do something. |
| | But don't just rely on the wording and dismiss an answer because a conclusion in the stimulus is positive and the conclusion in the answer choice is negative. For example, a conclusion might say, "The LSAT taker must have picture identification to register at the test site." The conclusion also could have been stated as "The LSAT taker must not forget to bring picture identification to register at the test site." |
| | Remember to think about what the conclusion means, regardless of whether it is stated in positive or negative terms. |
| Level of certainty | An argument qualified by words such as "possibly," "likely," and "probably" is weaker than a claim about something that is "definitely" true or "impossible," and therefore, is different. For example, a claim that Haley will *definitely* achieve her goal LSAT score is different from a claim that Haley will *probably* get her goal LSAT score. |
| | So, be sure to find an answer choice that matches the level of certainty presented in the argument's conclusion. |
| Mix of conclusion types | A conclusion may include a combination of types. For example, "So, if you follow the Kaplan Method, you will become more efficient and accurate in answering LSAT questions." This conclusion is both an if-then statement and a prediction. The correct answer will have to follow suit. |

The more precisely you characterize the stimulus conclusion, the easier it will be to match in the answer.

## Check the Evidence

If more than one answer's conclusion matches the argument structure of the stimulus' conclusion type, you'll need to characterize the evidence as well. Ask yourself, "Does the author provide evidence in the form of an opinion, causation, necessary condition, numbers, examples, etc.?" If so, you'll need to find evidence in the answer choice that matches that structure.

### Characterize the Stimulus

If you've characterized and compared the conclusion and the evidence and you still haven't found the correct answer choice, then you will need to characterize the whole stimulus and analyze its form of reasoning. For example, it could present a formal logic statement and its contrapositive, or it could use an analogy or make a causal argument. The correct answer must also follow the same form of reasoning. So, check the answer choices to determine and compare their form of reasoning with the stimulus'.

### Look for Flaws

Sometimes the test makers will ask you not for an answer with Parallel Reasoning but rather a Parallel Flaw. In that case, the stimulus contains a flawed argument, and your job is to find an argument in the answer that is not only flawed, but flawed in the same manner as the argument in the stimulus. Use your knowledge of common flaw types to quickly characterize the flaws you find, and keep in mind that some of the wrong answers may not contain a flaw at all.

## Make a Prediction

Take the information you've learned about the stimulus and compare it to the answer choices. Make the first comparison between the stimulus and the answer choices after you characterize the conclusion to hopefully eliminate some answers. If necessary, check the evidence, flaw, and/or entire stimulus.

## Evaluate the Answer Choices

Match the correct answer to your summary of the argument's structure. First, find the conclusion of each answer to determine whether it is a match. If not, eliminate it—there is no need to check the rest of that answer. If you have more than one answer left after checking the conclusions, go back to those and compare the evidence structure.

# THE KAPLAN METHOD IN ACTION

Now I'll walk you through a couple examples to show you how the Kaplan Method can help you efficiently solve any Parallel Reasoning question you'll see on test day.

1. Often, a product popularly believed to be the best of its type is no better than any other; rather, the product's reputation, which may be independent of its quality, provides its owner with status. Thus, although there is no harm in paying for status if that is what one wants, one should know that one is paying for prestige, not quality.

Which one of the following arguments is most similar in its reasoning to the argument above?

(A) Often, choosing the best job offer is a matter of comparing the undesirable features of the different jobs. Thus, those who choose a job because it has a desirable location should know that they might be unhappy with its hours.

(B) Most people have little tolerance for boastfulness. Thus, although one's friends may react positively when hearing the details of one's accomplishments, it is unlikely that their reactions are entirely honest.

(C) Those beginning a new hobby sometimes quit it because of the frustrations involved in learning a new skill. Thus, although it is fine to try to learn a skill quickly, one is more likely to learn a skill if one first learns to enjoy the process of acquiring it.

(D) Personal charm is often confused with virtue. Thus, while there is nothing wrong with befriending a charming person, anyone who does so should realize that a charming friend is not necessarily a good and loyal friend.

(E) Many theatrical actors cannot enjoy watching a play because when they watch others, they yearn to be on stage themselves. Thus, although there is no harm in yearning to perform, such performers should, for their own sakes, learn to suppress that yearning.[1]

## Step 1. Identify the Question Type

The phrase "most similar in its reasoning" is typical of a Parallel Reasoning question.

## Step 2. Untangle the Stimulus

Read the stimulus to determine the argument's structure. Start by identifying the conclusion, which is signaled by the Keyword "Thus." Next, characterize the conclusion. The word "should" tells you that it's a recommendation. Notice the exact formation of the recommendation: It's OK to pay for status (X), but you should know you're paying for status (X) and not quality (not Y).

---

[1]PrepTest 47, Sec. 1, Q 15

### Step 3. Make a Prediction

A parallel answer will have a conclusion in the form of a positive recommendation that matches the conclusion structure. So, start by evaluating the conclusion in each answer choice.

### Step 4. Evaluate the Answer Choices

Choice (A)'s conclusion, identified by "Thus," is a recommendation because of "should." But the recommendation pattern does not match the stimulus. Choice (A) recommends awareness of a possible negative aspect of something you choose, but the stimulus recommends awareness that you're doing X and not Y.

Choice (B)'s conclusion is not a recommendation, it's a qualified assertion of fact—the fact that friends' reactions to boasting probably aren't all that honest. Eliminate this choice.

Choice (C)'s conclusion is an if-then statement about the likelihood of learning a skill. Choice (C) is not a match. Cross it out.

Choice (D)'s conclusion—signaled by "Thus"—is a recommendation that it's OK to be friends with a charming person (X) as long as you know the friend is charming (X) and not good and loyal (not Y). Choice (D) seems promising; it's a recommendation with the same pattern as the stimulus' conclusion. But you need to check the last answer choice before you can say it's the right answer. If any others match the conclusion, you'll have to compare the evidence as well.

Choice (E)'s conclusion, noted by "Thus," is also a recommendation. But it's a recommendation to take action, to learn to suppress that yearning. The stimulus recommends awareness, not action.

Choice (D) is the only answer with a matching conclusion. So you don't need to review and compare any other part of the stimulus. Mark choice (D) and move on.

2.  People who are good at playing the game Drackedary are invariably skilled with their hands. Mary is a very competent watchmaker. Therefore, Mary would make a good Drackedary player.

The flawed pattern of reasoning in the argument above is most similar to that in which one of the following?

(A)  People with long legs make good runners. Everyone in Daryl's family has long legs. Therefore, Daryl would make a good runner.

(B)  People who write for a living invariably enjoy reading. Julie has been a published novelist for many years. Therefore, Julie enjoys reading.

(C)  All race car drivers have good reflexes. Chris is a champion table tennis player. Therefore, Chris would make a good race car driver.

(D)  The role of Santa Claus in a shopping mall is often played by an experienced actor. Erwin has played Santa Claus in shopping malls for years. Therefore, Erwin must be an experienced actor.

(E)  Any good skier can learn to ice-skate eventually. Erica is a world-class skier. Therefore, Erica could learn to ice-skate in a day or two.[2]

## Step 1. Identify the Question Type

The phrases "flawed pattern of reasoning" and "most similar to" identify this as a Parallel Flaw question.

## Step 2. Untangle the Stimulus

The complete argument in the stimulus must match the complete argument in the correct answer choice. Before you determine the flaw in the argument, you need to evaluate the conclusion. The word "Therefore" leads you right to the conclusion of the argument; in this case, the author makes a value judgment. The author subjectively evaluates Mary and says that she would make a good Drackedary player.

## Step 3. Make a Prediction

Move to the answer choices to determine whether any of them have a similar conclusion. If more than one answer choice does, return to the stimulus to determine the flaw and look for a parallel flaw in the remaining answer choices.

## Step 4. Evaluate the Answer Choices

Quickly scan the answer choices. All five of them have the word "Therefore" in the statement, so you can go right to the conclusions and compare them to the stimulus conclusion.

Choice (A)'s conclusion is an exact structural match with the stimulus. It's a value judgment that states Daryl would make a good runner. Because you haven't checked the complete argument yet, you can't mark this as the right answer. Check the other conclusions to see whether you find any more matches. If so, you'll come back to this answer and analyze the flaw in the argument.

Choice (B)'s conclusion is an assertion of fact. "Julie enjoys reading" is a statement of what the author believes to be true. It doesn't match the stimulus' conclusion, so you can cross it out.

Choice (C)'s conclusion also makes a value judgment that Chris would make a good race car driver. It's a parallel conclusion, so keep it and check choices (D) and (E) for any other matches.

Choice (D)'s conclusion is a strong assertion of fact, not a value judgment. Eliminate this choice.

Choice (E)'s conclusion is a weak prediction. The author doesn't state what will happen; instead she states what could happen, that Erica could learn to ice-skate in a day or two. This choice is out.

You are now down to choices (A) and (C). In addition to having the same conclusion structure as the stimulus, they both have the same positive tone. You can't use the conclusion to identify the correct answer, so go back to the stimulus to determine the flaw in the argument.

### Repeat Step 2. Untangle the Stimulus

In the stimulus, the author claims Mary would make a good Drackedary player because people who are good at Drackedary are skilled with their hands, and Mary is a competent watchmaker. In formal logic terms, the argument looks like this:

| | | | |
|---|---|---|---|
| Conclusion: | | Mary $\rightarrow$ | good Drackedary player (X) |
| Evidence: | Good Drackedary player (X) | $\rightarrow$ | skilled with hands (Y) |
| Evidence: | | Mary $\rightarrow$ | competent watchmaker (Z) |
| Assumption: | Competent watchmaker (Z) | $\rightarrow$ | good Drackedary player (X) |

The author must be connecting the evidence in the following way to reach the given conclusion.

Mary $\rightarrow$ Z $\rightarrow$ X $\rightarrow$ Y and assuming Z $\rightarrow$ Y. Because this is a Parallel Flaw question, the assumption must be considered unwarranted.

### Repeat Step 3. Make a Prediction

Go back to choices (A) and (C) to look for similar formal logic and a similar flaw.

### Repeat Step 4. Evaluate the Answer Choices

In choice (A), the author states that Daryl would make a good runner (Y) because people with long legs (X) make good runners (Y). Everyone in Daryl's family has long legs (X). The argument's formal logic shows a valid argument, and thus does not match the stimulus' format.

| | | | |
|---|---|---|---|
| Conclusion: | Daryl | $\rightarrow$ | Y |
| Evidence: | | X $\rightarrow$ | Y |
| Evidence: | Daryl and family | $\rightarrow$ | X |

Eliminate this choice.

You are safe to mark choice (C) and move on to the next question. Choice (C) presents the same structure and makes the same unwarranted assumption as the stimulus:

All race car drivers (X) have good reflexes (Y). Chris is a champion table tennis player (Z). Therefore, Chris would make a good race car driver (X).

| Conclusion: | Chris | → | Y |
|---|---|---|---|
| Evidence: | X | → | Y |
| Evidence: | Chris | → | Z |
| Assumption: | Z | → | X |

# PARALLEL REASONING QUESTIONS: NOW YOU TRY IT

It's now your turn to try a Parallel Reasoning question on your own. Use the template I've provided after the question to guide you through the four-step Kaplan Method. (Note: On test day, you won't be writing out all the steps as you are in this exercise. However, as you are learning the Method, it's good practice to help it become second nature.) Remember to bracket the conclusions and circle Keywords.

1. It is inaccurate to say that a diet high in refined sugar cannot cause adult-onset diabetes, since a diet high in refined sugar can make a person overweight, and being overweight can predispose a person to adult-onset diabetes.

   The argument is most parallel, in its logical structure, to which one of the following?

   (A) It is inaccurate to say that being in cold air can cause a person to catch a cold, since colds are caused by viruses, and viruses flourish in warm, crowded places.

   (B) It is accurate to say that no airline flies from Halifax to Washington. No airline offers a direct flight, although some airlines have flights from Halifax to Boston and others have flights from Boston to Washington.

   (C) It is correct to say that overfertilization is the primary cause of lawn disease, since fertilizer causes lawn grass to grow rapidly and rapidly growing grass has little resistance to disease.

   (D) It is incorrect to say that inferior motor oil cannot cause a car to get poorer gasoline mileage, since inferior motor oil can cause engine valve deterioration, and engine valve deterioration can lead to poorer gasoline mileage.

   (E) It is inaccurate to say that Alexander the Great was a student of Plato; Alexander was a student of Aristotle and Aristotle was a student of Plato.[3]

## Step 1. Identify the Question Type

_____

## Step 2. Untangle the Stimulus

_____

## Step 3. Make a Prediction

_____

## Step 4. Evaluate the Answer Choices

_____

---

[3]PrepTest 30, Sec. 2, Q 14

# Explanations

### 1.    (D)

<It is inaccurate to say that a diet high in refined sugar cannot cause adult-onset diabetes,> (since) a diet high in refined sugar can make a person overweight, and being overweight can predispose a person to adult-onset diabetes.

The argument is (most parallel) in its logical structure, (to) which one of the following?

(A)    It is inaccurate to say that being in cold air can cause a person to catch a cold, since colds are caused by viruses, and viruses flourish in warm, crowded places.

(B)    It is accurate to say that no airline flies from Halifax to Washington. No airline offers a direct flight, although some airlines have flights from Halifax to Boston and others have flights from Boston to Washington.

(C)    It is correct to say that overfertilization is the primary cause of lawn disease, since fertilizer causes lawn grass to grow rapidly and rapidly growing grass has little resistance to disease.

(D)    It is incorrect to say that inferior motor oil cannot cause a car to get poorer gasoline mileage, since inferior motor oil can cause engine valve deterioration, and engine valve deterioration can lead to poorer gasoline mileage.

(E)        It is inaccurate to say that Alexander the Great was a student of Plato; Alexander was a student of Aristotle and Aristotle was a student of Plato.[4]

## Step 1. Identify the Question Type

The language "most parallel…to" signals a Parallel Reasoning question. Your job is to find an answer that has a logical structure parallel to that of the stimulus.

## Step 2. Untangle the Stimulus

The author concludes that it is not accurate to claim that a diet high in refined sugar can't cause diabetes. Or, in other words, that refined sugar CAN cause diabetes. The author's assertion of fact is based on evidence, identified by "since," that a diet high in refined sugar can make a person overweight, which leads to diabetes. You can symbolize the argument as: It's wrong to say that X can't cause Y, because X can lead to Z, which in turn can lead to Y.

## Step 3. Make a Prediction

The correct answer must present an assertion of fact with a parallel argument structure. Start by analyzing the conclusions of the answer choices.

---

[4]PrepTest 30, Sec. 2, Q 14

## Step 4. Evaluate the Answer Choices

Choice (A)'s conclusion is an assertion of fact, but it's not parallel to the stimulus. Choice (A) asserts a statement of no causation: that it's wrong to say that cold air can lead to colds. In the stimulus, the author asserts a statement of causation, once you eliminate the negative phrasing.

Choice (B)'s conclusion is also an assertion of fact, but it's problematic because it lacks a causal relationship in the conclusion. Keep moving.

Choice (C)'s conclusion goes wrong by making an assertion of fact referring to the "primary" cause of an effect. Eliminate choice (C).

In choice (D), you find an assertion of fact conclusion of what is not correct. So far so good. Specifically, what's incorrect is to say inferior motor oil (X) can't cause poorer gas mileage (Y), because inferior motor oil (X) can cause engine valve deterioration (Z) and lead to poorer gas mileage (Y). This answer looks pretty good, but you have to check choice (E).

Choice (E) starts out okay, stating that it's inaccurate to say Alexander the Great was a student of Plato, but there isn't a causal statement in the conclusion. Eliminate this choice and mark choice (D) as the correct answer.

# DRILL: PRACTICING PARALLEL REASONING QUESTIONS

Use the Kaplan Method to answer the following Parallel Reasoning questions. Take this opportunity to practice and apply the steps in the Method so you are comfortable using them on test day. Be sure to circle conclusion and evidence Keywords and bracket the conclusion. Check your responses against the full explanations provided after the Drill.

1. K, a research scientist, was accused of having falsified laboratory data. Although the original data in question have disappeared, data from K's more recent experiments have been examined and clearly none of them were falsified. Therefore, the accusation should be dismissed.

Which one of the following contains questionable reasoning that is most similar to that in the argument above?

(A) L, an accountant, was charged with having embezzled funds from a client. The charge should be ignored, however, because although the records that might reveal this embezzlement have been destroyed, records of L's current clients show clearly that there has never been any embezzlement from them.

(B) M, a factory supervisor, was accused of failing to enforce safety standards. This accusation should be discussed, because although the identity of the accuser was not revealed, a survey of factory personnel revealed that some violations of the standards have occurred.

(C) N, a social scientist, was charged with plagiarism. The charge is without foundation because although strong similarities between N's book and the work of another scholar have been discovered, the other scholar's work was written after N's work was published.

(D) O, an auto mechanic, has been accused of selling stolen auto parts. The accusation seems to be justified since although no evidence links O directly to these sales, the pattern of distribution of the auto parts points of O as the source.

(E) P, a politician, has been accused of failing to protect the public interest. From at least some points of view, however, the accusation will undoubtedly be considered false, because there is clearly disagreement about where the public interest lies.[5]

2. A worker for a power company trims the branches of trees that overhang power lines as a prevention against damage to the lines anticipated because of the impending stormy season. The worker reasons that there will be no need for her to trim the overhanging branches of a certain tree because the owners of the tree have indicated that they might cut it down anyway.

Which one of the following decisions is based on flawed reasoning that is most similar to the worker's flawed reasoning?

(A) A well inspector has a limited amount of time to inspect the wells of a town. The inspector reasons that the wells should be inspected in the order of most used to least used, because there might not be enough time to inspect them all.

(B) All sewage and incoming water pipes in a house must be replaced. The plumber reasons that the cheaper polyvinyl chloride pipes should be used for sewage rather than copper pipes, since the money saved might be used to replace worn fixtures.

(C) A mechanic must replace the worn brakes on a company's vans that are used each weekday. The mechanic reasons that since one of the vans is tentatively scheduled to be junked, he will not have to replace its brakes.

(D) A candidate decides to campaign in the areas of the city where the most new votes are concentrated. The candidate reasons that campaigning in other areas is unnecessary because in those areas the candidate's message is actually liable to alienate voters.

(E) None of the children in a certain kindergarten class will take responsibility for the crayon drawing on the classroom wall. The teacher reasons that it is best to keep all the kindergarten children in during recess in order to be certain to punish the one who did the drawing on the wall.[6]

---

3. The fact that politicians in a certain country are trying to reduce government spending does not by itself explain why they have voted to eliminate all government-supported scholarship programs. Government spending could have been reduced even more if instead they had cut back on military spending.

Which one of the following arguments is most similar in its reasoning to the argument above?

(A) The fact that Phyllis does not make much money at her new job does not by itself explain why she refuses to buy expensive clothing. Phyllis has always bought only inexpensive clothing even though she used to make a lot of money.

(B) The fact that Brooks has a part-time job does not by itself explain why he is doing poorly in school. Many students with part-time jobs are able to set aside enough time for study and thus maintain high grades.

(C) The fact that Sallie and Jim have different work styles does not by itself explain why they could not work together. Sallie and Jim could have resolved their differences if they had communicated more with one another when they began to work together.

(D) The fact that Roger wanted more companionship does not by itself explain why he adopted ten cats last year. He would not have adopted them all if anyone else had been willing to adopt some of them.

(E) The fact that Thelma's goal is to become famous does not by itself explain why she took up theatrical acting. It is easier to become famous through writing or directing plays than through theatrical acting.[7]

4. From the fact that people who studied music as children frequently are quite proficient at mathematics, it cannot be concluded that the skills required for mathematics are acquired by studying music: it is equally likely that proficiency in mathematics and studying music are both the result of growing up in a family that encourages its children to excel at all intellectual and artistic endeavors.

The pattern of reasoning in which one of the following arguments is most parallel to that in the argument above?

(A) Although children who fail to pay attention tend to perform poorly in school, it should not necessarily be thought that their poor performance is caused by their failure to pay attention, for it is always possible that their failure to pay attention is due to undiagnosed hearing problems that can also lead to poor performance in school.

(B) People who attend a university in a foreign country are usually among the top students from their native country. It would therefore be wrong to conclude from the fact that many foreign students perform better academically than others in this country that secondary schools in other countries are superior to those in this country; it may be that evaluation standards are different.

(C) People whose diet includes relatively large quantities of certain fruits and vegetables have a slightly lower than average incidence of heart disease. But it would be premature to conclude that consuming these fruits and vegetables prevents heart disease, for this correlation may be merely coincidental.

(D) Those who apply to medical school are required to study biology and chemistry. It would be a mistake, however, to conclude that those who have mastered chemistry and biology will succeed as physicians, for the practical application of knowledge is different from its acquisition.

(E) Those who engage in vigorous exercise tend to be very healthy. But it would be silly to conclude that vigorous exercise is healthful simply because people who are healthy exercise vigorously, since it is possible that exercise that is less vigorous also has beneficial results.[8]

5. Opposition leader: Our country has the least fair
   court system of any country on the continent
   and ought not to be the model for others.
   Thus, our highest court is the least fair of any
   on the continent and ought not to be emulated
   by other countries.

   The flawed reasoning in which one of the following
   arguments is most similar to that in the opposition
   leader's argument?

   (A)  The residents of medium-sized towns are, on
        average, more highly educated than people
        who do not live in such towns. Therefore,
        Maureen, who was born in a medium-sized
        town, is more highly educated than Monica,
        who has just moved to such a town.

   (B)  At a certain college, either philosophy or
        engineering is the most demanding major.
        Therefore, either the introductory course in
        philosophy or the introductory course in
        engineering is the most demanding
        introductory-level course at that college.

   (C)  For many years its superior engineering has
        enabled the Lawson Automobile Company to
        make the best racing cars. Therefore, its
        passenger cars, which use many of the same parts,
        are unmatched by those of any other
        company.

   (D)  Domestic cats are closely related to tigers.
        Therefore, even though they are far smaller
        than tigers, their eating habits are almost the
        same as those of tigers.

   (E)  If a suit of questionable merit is brought in the
        first district rather than the second district, its
        chances of being immediately thrown out are
        greater. Therefore, to have the best chance of
        winning the case, the lawyers will bring the
        suit in the second district.[9]

---

[9]PrepTest 47, Sec. 1, Q 21

## Explanations

### 1. (A)

K, a research scientist, was accused of having falsified laboratory data. Although the original data in question have disappeared, data from K's more recent experiments have been examined and clearly none of them were falsified. <Therefore, the accusation should be dismissed.>

Which one of the following contains questionable reasoning that is most similar to that in the argument above?

(A) L, an accountant, was charged with having embezzled funds from a client. The charge should be ignored, however, because although the records that might reveal this embezzlement have been destroyed, records of L's current clients show clearly that there has never been any embezzlement from them.

(B) M, a factory supervisor, was accused of failing to enforce safety standards. This accusation should be discussed, because although the identity of the accuser was not revealed, a survey of factory personnel revealed that some violations of the standards have occurred.

(C) N, a social scientist, was charged with plagiarism. The charge is without foundation because although strong similarities between N's book and the work of another scholar have been discovered, the other scholar's work was written after N's work was published.

(D) O, an auto mechanic, has been accused of selling stolen auto parts. The accusation seems to be justified since although no evidence links O directly to these sales, the pattern of distribution of the auto parts points of O as the source.

(E) P, a politician, has been accused of failing to protect the public interest. From at least some points of view, however, the accusation will undoubtedly be considered false, because there is clearly disagreement about where the public interest lies.[10]

### Step 1. Identify the Question Type

The question is asking for an argument with "questionable reasoning" that is "most similar to" the stimulus, making this is a Parallel Flaw question. The correct answer will have the same argument structure and the flaw that the stimulus has.

---

[10]PrepTest 24, Sec. 3, Q 16

### Step 2. Untangle the Stimulus

The word "Therefore" in the last sentence identifies the conclusion, that the accusation should be dismissed. The "should" tells you it's a recommendation, specifically, to throw something out.

### Step 3. Make a Prediction

First, find and characterize the conclusions in the answer choices to determine whether they are recommendations to throw something out as in the stimulus. If not, you can discard those choices right away. If you get more than one match, you will take the next step and compare the evidence.

### Step 4. Evaluate the Answer Choices

In choice (A), the conclusion recommends that "the charge should be ignored." That sounds like a match, so keep it as a possibility and check the other choices for any other recommendations to do something.

The conclusion in choice (B) is also a recommendation to do something, to discuss the accusation. Put it aside as well and keep checking the other choices.

Choice (C)'s conclusion, "the charge is without foundation," is an assertion of fact, so you can discard this choice.

Choice (D)'s conclusion presents a weak assertion of fact that "the accusation seems to be justified." Dismiss this choice as well.

The conclusion of choice (E), that the accusation will undoubtedly be considered false, is a prediction with strong conviction. This is another unparalleled conclusion, so you can cross it out. If the conclusion is not similar to the stimulus, there is no point to analyze the rest of the argument.

### Repeat Step 2. Untangle the Stimulus

With just (A) and (B) remaining, go back to the stimulus and quickly assess the evidence. The author recommends dismissal of data falsification charges because current records show no data falsification. The records in question are missing, but current records are clean. So, the author, in error, uses current, unrelated data as evidence and assumes they indicate the truth of past records.

### Repeat Step 3. Make a Prediction

Return to choices (A) and (B) to see which one matches the pattern of evidence and flaw.

### Repeat Step 4. Evaluate the Answer Choices

Choice (A) also recommends dismissal of charges, this time for embezzlement. Current records show no indication of embezzlement and should be used in place of the missing, relevant records. Again, the author, in error, uses current, unrelated data as evidence and assumes they indicate the truth of past records. It's like saying someone's not guilty for one crime because he didn't commit another one.

Check choice (B) quickly, but you can feel confident that choice (A) is the correct answer. Choice (B) fails on the evidence. The relevant evidence is available.

## 2. **(C)**

A worker for a power company trims the branches of trees that overhang power lines as a prevention against damage to the lines anticipated because of the impending stormy season. <The worker reasons that there will be no need for her to trim the overhanging branches of a certain tree> because the owners of the tree have indicated that they might cut it down anyway.

Which one of the following decisions is based on flawed reasoning that is most similar to the worker's flawed reasoning?

(A) A well inspector has a limited amount of time to inspect the wells of a town. The inspector reasons that the wells should be inspected in the order of most used to least used, because there might not be enough time to inspect them all.

(B) All sewage and incoming water pipes in a house must be replaced. The plumber reasons that the cheaper polyvinyl chloride pipes should be used for sewage rather than copper pipes, since the money saved might be used to replace worn fixtures.

(C) A mechanic must replace the worn brakes on a company's vans that are used each weekday. The mechanic reasons that since one of the vans is tentatively scheduled to be junked, he will not have to replace its brakes.

(D) A candidate decides to campaign in the areas of the city where the most new votes are concentrated. The candidate reasons that campaigning in other areas is unnecessary because in those areas the candidate's message is actually liable to alienate voters.

(E) None of the children in a certain kindergarten class will take responsibility for the crayon drawing on the classroom wall. The teacher reasons that it is best to keep all the kindergarten children in during recess in order to be certain to punish the one who did the drawing on the wall.[11]

## Step 1. Identify the Question Type

The question asks for "flawed reasoning" in the answer that is "most similar to" the stimulus. Therefore, it is a Parallel Flaw question.

---

[11]PrepTest 22, Sec. 4, Q 6

### Step 2. Untangle the Stimulus

The worker predicts there will be no need to trim the branches because the owners might take the tree down anyway. So, generally speaking, someone decides that taking a specific action is not necessary because something that would preclude the need to perform the action might happen.

### Step 3. Make a Prediction

Check the answer choices for an argument with a structure similar to that of the stimulus.

### Step 4. Evaluate the Answer Choices

Choice (A) recommends a course of action (to inspect wells) to serve a particular purpose (optimize available time). This is not a match, so you can dismiss choice (A).

Choice (B) also recommends a course of action (to use cheaper pipe instead of copper) to achieve a goal (save money and use it elsewhere). Eliminate this choice.

Choice (C) predicts that an action will not need to be taken (that tires won't need to be changed) because another action might happen (the van might be junked). This sounds promising, so hold on to choice (C) and check the other answers.

Choice (D) asserts that an action is not necessary (that campaigning in other areas is unnecessary) because it is counterproductive, not because of something that might happen. No match here, so cross this choice out.

Quickly eliminate choice (E). Like choices (A) and (B), it recommends a course of action (to keep all the kindergarten children in during recess) to achieve a particular goal (punish). Go with choice (C), the correct answer.

### 3. **(E)**

The fact that politicians in a certain country are trying to reduce government spending does not by itself explain why they have voted to eliminate all government-supported scholarship programs. Government spending could have been reduced even more if instead they had cut back on military spending.

Which one of the following arguments is (most similar) in its reasoning (to) the argument above?

(A)   The fact that Phyllis does not make much money at her new job does not by itself explain why she refuses to buy expensive clothing. Phyllis has always bought only inexpensive clothing even though she used to make a lot of money.

(B)   The fact that Brooks has a part-time job does not by itself explain why he is doing poorly in school. Many students with part-time jobs are able to set aside enough time for study and thus maintain high grades.

(C)   The fact that Sallie and Jim have different work styles does not by itself explain why they could not work together. Sallie and Jim could have resolved their differences if they had communicated more with one another when they began to work together.

(D)   The fact that Roger wanted more companionship does not by itself explain why he adopted ten cats last year. He would not have adopted them all if anyone else had been willing to adopt some of them.

(E)   The fact that Thelma's goal is to become famous does not by itself explain why she took up theatrical acting. It is easier to become famous through writing or directing plays than through theatrical acting.[12]

## Step 1. Identify the Question Type

The phrase "most similar...to" identifies this as a Parallel Reasoning question.

## Step 2. Untangle the Stimulus

The stimulus does not present a clear argument with a conclusion and evidence, so the best course of action is to paraphrase the stimulus in general terms and compare the summary to the answer choices.

The author states that politicians are trying to achieve a goal (to reduce government spending), but that does not explain why they took a particular action (voted to eliminate all government-

---

[12]PrepTest 37, Sec. 4, Q 14

supported scholarship programs). The author then states that politicians could have achieved the goal with better results if they would have taken another action (cut back on military spending).

## Step 3. Make a Prediction

Look for the choice that matches the general summary of the stimulus.

## Step 4. Evaluate the Answer Choices

Choice (A) doesn't work. It doesn't even present a goal. Instead, it ponders the motive behind the refusal to do something (buy expensive clothes) and doesn't offer a better alternative.

Choices (B) and (C) aren't parallel either. Like choice (A), they don't present a goal. Go on to the next choice.

Choice (D) starts out promising. It presents Roger's goal (more companionship) and says the goal does not explain why Roger took a particular action (adopted ten cats). However, this is where choice (D) goes wrong. Instead of offering a better way to achieve the goal (like get a roommate) to make the rest of the answer parallel with the stimulus, choice (D) explains why the action taken would not have been taken under other circumstances. That leaves only one choice.

By process of elimination, it looks like choice (E) is the correct answer. Let's find out why. Like the stimulus, choice (E) presents Thelma's goal (to become famous), which does not explain why she took a particular action (took up acting). The goal could have been achieved with better results if Thelma did something different (wrote or directed). We have a winner.

## 4. **(A)**

From the fact that people who studied music as children frequently are quite proficient at mathematics, <it cannot be concluded that the skills required for mathematics are acquired by studying music>: it is equally likely that proficiency in mathematics and studying music are both the result of growing up in a family that encourages its children to excel at all intellectual and artistic endeavors.

The (pattern of reasoning) in which one of the following arguments is (most parallel to) that in the argument above?

(A)    Although children who fail to pay attention tend to perform poorly in school, it should not necessarily be thought that their poor performance is caused by their failure to pay attention, for it is always possible that their failure to pay attention is due to undiagnosed hearing problems that can also lead to poor performance in school.

(B)    People who attend a university in a foreign country are usually among the top students from their native country. It would therefore be wrong to conclude from the fact that many foreign students perform better academically than others in this country that secondary schools in other countries are superior to those in this country; it may be that evaluation standards are different.

(C)    People whose diet includes relatively large quantities of certain fruits and vegetables have a slightly lower than average incidence of heart disease. But it would be premature to conclude that consuming these fruits and vegetables prevents heart disease, for this correlation may be merely coincidental.

(D)    Those who apply to medical school are required to study biology and chemistry. It would be a mistake, however, to conclude that those who have mastered chemistry and biology will succeed as physicians, for the practical application of knowledge is different from its acquisition.

(E)    Those who engage in vigorous exercise tend to be very healthy. But it would be silly to conclude that vigorous exercise is healthful simply because people who are healthy exercise vigorously, since it is possible that exercise that is less vigorous also has beneficial results.[13]

---

[13]PrepTest 49, Sec. 4, Q 17

## Step 1. Identify the Question Type

The phrases "pattern of reasoning" and "most parallel to" tell you that this is a Parallel Reasoning question.

## Step 2. Untangle the Stimulus

The author concludes it can't be said that studying music (X) causes better math skills (Y). He also states that it's possible that growing up in a family that encourages intellectual and artistic endeavors (Z) causes proficiency in music and math (X and Y). In other words, X did not necessarily cause Y because Z could have caused X and Y.

## Step 3. Make a Prediction

Check the answer choices for that pattern.

## Step 4. Evaluate the Answer Choices

Choice (A) concludes that children's failure to pay attention in school (X) does not necessarily cause their poor performance (Y), because undiagnosed hearing problems (Z) may be the cause of their failure to pay attention (X) and their poor performance (Y). Choice (A) looks like a match. Let's check the other answers.

Choice (B) starts strong, with evidence of a correlation between people who attend a university in a foreign country and their status as a top student from their native country. However, choice (B) veers off course with a discussion of the superiority of secondary schools that is not part of the causal relationship. Eliminate this choice.

Choice (C) is problematic from the beginning. It says it's too early to tell whether consuming fruits and vegetables prevents heart disease and that the relationship may just be coincidence. This is not parallel to the structure of the stimulus, so dismiss this choice and keep going.

Choice (D) also misses the pattern. While it says you can't conclude that mastering biology and chemistry (X) will lead to success as a physician (Y), it doesn't present another possible factor (Z) that could cause X and Y.

Choice (E) reaches a conclusion against a causal relationship between vigorous exercise and good health by suggesting that maybe less-vigorous exercise may be as effective as vigorous exercise. Cross this choice out and stick with choice (A).

5.  **(B)**

Opposition leader: Our country has the least fair
court system of any country on the continent
and ought not to be the model for others.
〈Thus〉 our highest court is the least fair of any
on the continent and ought not to be emulated
by other countries.〉

The ⟨flawed reasoning⟩ in which one of the following
arguments is ⟨most similar to⟩ that in the opposition
leader's argument?

(A)  The residents of medium-sized towns are, on
     average, more highly educated than people
     who do not live in such towns. Therefore,
     Maureen, who was born in a medium-sized
     town, is more highly educated than Monica,
     who has just moved to such a town.

(B)  At a certain college, either philosophy or
     engineering is the most demanding major.
     Therefore, either the introductory course in
     philosophy or the introductory course in
     engineering is the most demanding
     introductory-level course at that college.

(C)  For many years its superior engineering has
     enabled the Lawson Automobile Company to
     make the best racing cars. Therefore, its
     passenger cars, which use many of the same parts,
     are unmatched by those of any other
     company.

(D)  Domestic cats are closely related to tigers.
     Therefore, even though they are far smaller
     than tigers, their eating habits are almost the
     same as those of tigers.

(E)  If a suit of questionable merit is brought in the
     first district rather than the second district, its
     chances of being immediately thrown out are
     greater. Therefore, to have the best chance of
     winning the case, the lawyers will bring the
     suit in the second district.[14]

## Step 1. Identify the Question Type

The phrases "flawed reasoning" and "most similar to" identify this as a Parallel Flaw question.

## Step 2. Untangle the Stimulus

The opposition leader concludes that his country's highest court is the least fair on the continent because his country has the least fair court system of any country on the continent.
In other words, a single member of a group (the country's highest court) has X characteristic

---

[14]PrepTest 47, Sec. 1, Q 21

because the large group (country's court system) has X characteristic. The opposition commits a classic scope-shift flaw.

### Step 3. Make a Prediction

Check the answer choices for a scope shift between a group and an individual.

### Step 4. Evaluate the Answer Choices

Choice (A) does have a scope shift, but not the same kind as that in the stimulus. While the argument looks at a group (residents of medium-sized towns) and Maureen and Monica (two group members), the conclusion adds another scope shift of whether someone was born in or moved to a small town. Eliminate this choice.

Choice (B) reaches a conclusion about the difficulty of individual classes based on the difficulty of the related major. Don't let the "either…or" language confuse you. Choice (B) takes a group characteristic and says the characteristic applies to individual members of the group. You have the correct answer here. Keep going to find out why the last three choices are wrong.

Choice (C) commits a scope shift, but the wrong kind. The shift occurs between two different groups: Racing cars and passenger cars.

Choice (D) differs from the stimulus in that the individual member and group have the same characteristic. Here, the conclusion qualifies the similar eating habits of cats and tigers with "almost."

Choice (E) presents a scope shift but again, it's different from the stimulus. It shifts scope between a case getting thrown out and winning a case, which is not the same as shifting between a member and a group.

## PARALLEL REASONING REVIEW

Before you proceed to the next chapter, turn to Appendix A and complete the review exercise for Parallel Reasoning questions. A completed chart is included in Appendix B.

# CHAPTER 13

# METHOD OF ARGUMENT QUESTIONS

You learned in previous chapters that LSAT arguments consist of a conclusion and evidence, and they are connected by an unstated assumption. While every argument has the same building blocks, they can be structured in a variety of different ways. For example, they may present expert testimony or the results of a study, or they may question the motives behind a recommendation or propose alternative explanations. On the LSAT, Method of Argument questions test your ability to analyze how an argument is put together.

You can expect to see approximately two scored Method of Argument questions on an LSAT. Although this question type doesn't account for a large number of points, you'll still need to effectively handle them on test day to maximize your score. Fortunately for you, the Kaplan Method can help you do this.

## DEFINITION OF METHOD OF ARGUMENT QUESTIONS

Method of Argument questions ask you to identify the approach used to make an argument. You will not be asked for the facts of the argument, but rather for a general description of the argument's organization or for the type of evidence the author relies upon.

# USE THE KAPLAN METHOD TO ANSWER METHOD OF ARGUMENT QUESTIONS

## Identify the Question Type

Just as you've done with all other Logical Reasoning question types, read the question stem first to determine the question type. The following terms denote a Method of Argument question:

- Argumentative technique
- Method
- Process
- Argumentative strategy
- Responds to . . . by

Here's how some of those phrases could appear in a question stem:

- The argument proceeds by presenting evidence that
- Which one of the following most accurately describes the method of reasoning used in the argument?
- The economist's argument employs which one of the following techniques?
- The argument does which one of the following?
- Which one of the following describes the author's argumentative strategy?
- Ralph responds to Laura by pointing out that

## Untangle the Stimulus

A Method of Argument stimulus will be presented either as a paragraph or as a conversation between two people. As you read the stimulus, look for the conclusion and evidence, and look for how they are connected.

## Make a Prediction

Summarize the argument in general terms and characterize the type of evidentiary support the author uses (e.g., expert testimony or a research study).

## Evaluate the Answer Choices

Review the answer choices and select the one that matches your prediction. The correct answer to a Method of Argument question will have a 1:1 matchup with the stimulus. As you read each answer choice, ask yourself: Does the author do this? Then, match up the action in the answer choice with the components of the stimulus, especially the type of evidence upon which the author relies.

# THE KAPLAN METHOD IN ACTION

Now I'll walk you through a couple examples to show you how the Kaplan Method can help you efficiently solve any Method of Argument question you'll see on test day.

1. Lahar: We must now settle on a procedure for deciding on meeting agendas. Our club's constitution allows three options: unanimous consent, majority vote, or assigning the task to a committee. Unanimous consent is unlikely. Forming a committee has usually led to factionalism and secret deals. <(Clearly) we should subject meeting agendas to majority vote.>

   Lahar's argument does which one of the following?

   (A)  rejects suggested procedures on constitutional grounds
   (B)  claims that one procedure is the appropriate method for reaching every decision in the club
   (C)  suggests a change to a constitution on the basis of practical considerations
   (D)  recommends a choice based on the elimination of alternative options
   (E)  supports one preference by arguing against those who have advocated alternatives[1]

## Step 1. Identify the Question Type

The phrase "does which one of the following" indicates that this is a Method of Argument question. You want to determine how the author uses her evidence to build up to the conclusion.

## Step 2. Untangle the Stimulus

Lahar says there are three possible ways to determine the club's meeting agenda. He then eliminates two options and concludes that the third option should be used.

## Step 3. Make a Prediction

Here, Lahar reaches a conclusion by eliminating two other possibilities. So, the correct answer will do this as well. As you read the answer choices, ask yourself: Does the author do this?

## Step 4. Evaluate the Answer Choices

Choice (A) is wrong according to the stimulus, as Lahar doesn't reject any option based on constitutional grounds. In fact, all three options are allowed under the club's constitution.

Choice (B) starts off on the right track but takes a wrong turn. Lahar does recommend one procedure, just not as a way to reach every club decision. The recommendation is narrowly directed at developing the club's meeting agenda. Cross this choice out.

---

[1]PrepTest 52, Sec. 3, Q 5

You can also eliminate choice (C). Lahar doesn't mention anything about changing the club's constitution. Again, he says all three options are allowed by the constitution.

Choice (D) matches the prediction and is the correct answer.

Choice (E) adds information that's not included in the stimulus. Lahar doesn't argue against those who advocate alternatives; he argues against the alternatives.

2. According to the proposed Factory Safety Act, a company may operate an automobile factory only if that factory is registered as a class B factory. In addressing whether a factory may postpone its safety inspections, this Act also stipulates that no factory can be class B without punctual inspections. ⟨Thus⟩ under the Factory Safety Act, a factory that manufactures automobiles would not be able to postpone its safety inspections.⟩

The argument proceeds by

(A) pointing out how two provisions of the proposed Factory Safety Act jointly entail the unacceptability of a certain state of affairs

(B) considering two possible interpretations of a proposed legal regulation and eliminating the less plausible one

(C) showing that the terms of the proposed Factory Safety Act are incompatible with existing legislation

(D) showing that two different provisions of the proposed Factory Safety Act conflict and thus cannot apply to a particular situation

(E) pointing out that if a provision applies in a specific situation, it must apply in any analogous situation[2]

## Step 1. Identify the Question Type

The phrase "proceeds by" tells you that this is a Method of Argument question. As was the case in the previous example, your task is to untangle the structure of the argument.

## Step 2. Untangle the Stimulus

This argument concludes in the last sentence that a factory that manufactures automobiles would not be able to postpone its safety inspections under the Factory Safety Act. The evidence used to support it is presented in formal logic language signaled by "only if" and "no . . . without."

Translate the formal logic to determine the argument's structure.

---

[2]PrepTest 49, Sec. 4, Q 15

The first sentence says that if a company operates an auto factory, it must register that facility as a class B factory. The second statement says that if a factory is class B, then it must have punctual inspections. The argument concludes that under the Factory Safety Act, auto factories could not postpone inspections. Combine the negatives and the result is that auto factories must have punctual inspections. Note the classic formal logic statements and the more general equations depicted in the stimulus.

| Auto factory → class B | Class B → punctual inspections | Auto factory → punctual inspections |
|---|---|---|
| A → B | B → C | A → C |

### Step 3. Make a Prediction

The correct answer will describe the argument in structural terms. In this case, you have two statements from a piece of legislation that combine to indicate that something must happen.

### Step 4. Evaluate the Answer Choices

Choice (A) matches the prediction by pointing out two provisions of the Factory Safety Act that combine to produce a certain result. This is the correct answer.

Choice (B) is incorrect because the argument does not consider two interpretations of the Factory Safety Act. There is only one interpretation of the Act given in the stimulus, and it's reached by combining two provisions.

Choice (C) brings in existing legislation that is never mentioned in the stimulus or compared to the proposed Factory Safety Act.

Choice (D) is also wrong because the two provisions of the proposed Factory Safety Act don't conflict at all. Actually, they combine to produce a certain result.

Choice (E) discusses an analogy that does not exist in the stimulus. The provisions of the Factory Safety Act are only applied to a single situation.

# METHOD OF ARGUMENT QUESTIONS: NOW YOU TRY IT

It's now your turn to try a Method of Argument question on your own. Use the template I've provided after the question to guide you through the four-step Kaplan Method. (Note: On test day, you won't be writing out all the steps as you are in this exercise. However, as you are learning the Method, it's good practice to help it become second nature.) Remember to bracket conclusions and circle Keywords.

1. Xavier: Demand by tourists in Nepal for inexpensive thangka paintings has resulted in the proliferation of inferior thangkas containing symbolic inaccuracies—a sure sign of a dying art form. Nepal should prohibit sales of thangkas to tourists, for such a prohibition will induce artists to create thangkas that meet traditional standards.

   Yvette: An art form without dedicated young artists will decay and die. If tourists were forbidden to buy thangkas, young artists would cease making thangkas and concentrate instead on an art form tourists can buy.

   Yvette responds to Xavier by

   (A) denying the existence of the problem that Xavier's proposal is designed to ameliorate
   (B) challenging the integrity of Xavier's sources of information
   (C) arguing that Xavier's proposal, if implemented, would result in the very consequences it is meant to prevent
   (D) using an analogy to draw a conclusion that is inconsistent with the conclusion drawn by Xavier
   (E) showing that the evidence presented by Xavier has no bearing on the point at issue[3]

## Step 1. Identify the Question Type

_____

## Step 2. Untangle the Stimulus

_____

## Step 3. Make a Prediction

_____

## Step 4. Evaluate the Answer Choices

_____

---

[3] PrepTest 41, Sec. 1, Q 3

**Answer Explanations follow on the next page.**

# Explanations

### 1. **(C)**

Xavier: Demand by tourists in Nepal for inexpensive thangka paintings has resulted in the proliferation of inferior thangkas containing symbolic inaccuracies—a sure sign of a dying art form. <Nepal should prohibit sales of thangkas to tourists,> for such a prohibition will induce artists to create thangkas that meet traditional standards.

Yvette: An art form without dedicated young artists will decay and die. <If tourists were forbidden to buy thangkas, young artists would cease making thangkas and concentrate instead on an art form tourists can buy.>

Yvette responds to Xavier by

(A)  denying the existence of the problem that Xavier's proposal is designed to ameliorate

(B)  challenging the integrity of Xavier's sources of information

(C)  arguing that Xavier's proposal, if implemented, would result in the very consequences it is meant to prevent

(D)  using an analogy to draw a conclusion that is inconsistent with the conclusion drawn by Xavier

(E)  showing that the evidence presented by Xavier has no bearing on the point at issue[4]

## Step 1. Identify the Question Type

The phrase "responds to . . . by" is a common indicator of a Method of Argument question in which there is a dialogue between two people and you are asked to describe how the second speaker responds to the first speaker. In this case, you're asked to describe the structure of Yvette's response to Xavier.

## Step 2. Untangle the Stimulus

While it is tempting to go right to Yvette's response, never skip the first speaker's argument in a Method of Argument stimulus presented as a dialogue. You must summarize both speakers' arguments to know whether Yvette agrees or disagrees with Xavier and on what grounds.

Xavier recommends that Nepal prohibit tourist sales of thangkas to encourage young artists to create the traditional ones rather than inferior versions. Yvette says that young people are necessary to prevent the disappearance of an art form and raises her concern that if Nepal does prohibit tourist sales of thangkas, young people won't make them at all.

---

[4]PrepTest 41, Sec. 1, Q 3

### Step 3. Make a Prediction

Xavier wants to solve a problem (artists have stopped making traditional thangkas; they make inferior thangkas for tourists) and proposes a solution (prohibit thangka sales to tourists). Yvette points out that Xavier's solution will achieve the result he wants to avoid (artists will stop making thangkas; they will make something else for the tourists).

### Step 4. Evaluate the Answer Choices

Choice (A) is an inaccurate description because Yvette does not deny the existence of a problem. In fact, she shows concern for the same problem raised by Xavier, the decay and death of the traditional thangka as an art form. Cross out this answer.

Choice (B) is simply not something that Yvette says anywhere in her statement. Xavier's sources of information are never raised in the stimulus, and the integrity of these sources is never challenged. Move on to the next choice.

Choice (C) matches the prediction and is the correct answer.

Choice (D) is outside the scope in that Yvette never presents any kind of analogy. She identifies a necessary condition for an art form to thrive and then speculates on an unwanted result of Xavier's plan.

Choice (E) is outside the scope as well. Yvette does not argue with Xavier's evidence. She points out that the proposed solution will not achieve the desired results and ultimately contribute to the problem.

# DRILL: PRACTICING METHOD OF ARGUMENT QUESTIONS

Use the Kaplan Method to answer the following Method of Argument questions. Take this opportunity to practice and apply the steps in the Method so you are comfortable using them on test day. Be sure to circle conclusion and evidence Keywords and bracket the conclusion. Check your responses against the full explanations provided after the Drill.

1. Yang: Yeast has long been known to be a leaven, that is, a substance used in baking to make breads rise. Since biblical evidence ties the use of leavens to events dating back to 1,200 B.C., we can infer that yeast was already known to be a leaven at that time.

   Campisi: I find your inference unconvincing; several leavens other than yeast could have been known in 1,200 B.C.

   Campisi counters Yang's argument by

   (A) suggesting that an alternative set of evidence better supports Yang's conclusion
   (B) questioning the truth of a presumption underlying Yang's argument
   (C) denying the truth of Yang's conclusion without considering the reason given for that conclusion
   (D) pointing out that the premises of Yang's argument more strongly support a contrary conclusion
   (E) calling into question the truth of the evidence presented in Yang's argument[5]

2. Zachary: The term "fresco" refers to paint that has been applied to wet plaster. Once dried, a fresco indelibly preserves the paint that a painter has applied in this way. Unfortunately, additions known to have been made by later painters have obscured the original fresco work done by Michelangelo in the Sistine Chapel. Therefore, in order to restore Michelangelo's Sistine Chapel paintings to the appearance that Michelangelo intended them to have, everything except the original fresco work must be stripped away.

   Stephen: But it was extremely common for painters of Michelangelo's era to add painted details to their own fresco work after the frescos had dried.

   Stephen's response to Zachary proceeds by

   (A) calling into question an assumption on which Zachary's conclusion depends
   (B) challenging the definition of a key term in Zachary's argument
   (C) drawing a conclusion other than the one that Zachary reaches
   (D) denying the truth of one of the stated premises of Zachary's argument
   (E) demonstrating that Zachary's conclusion is not consistent with the premises he uses to support it[6]

3. Gamba: Muñoz claims that the Southwest Hopeville Neighbors Association overwhelmingly opposes the new water system, citing this as evidence of citywide opposition. The association did pass a resolution opposing the new water system, but only 25 of 350 members voted, with 10 in favor of the system. Furthermore, the 15 opposing votes represent far less than 1 percent of Hopeville's population. One should not assume that so few votes represent the view of the majority of Hopeville's residents.

Of the following, which one most accurately describes Gamba's strategy of argumentation?

(A) questioning a conclusion based on the results of a vote, on the grounds that people with certain views are more likely to vote

(B) questioning a claim supported by statistical data by arguing that statistical data can be manipulated to support whatever view the interpreter wants to support

(C) attempting to refute an argument by showing that, contrary to what has been claimed, the truth of the premises does not guarantee the truth of the conclusion

(D) criticizing a view on the grounds that the view is based on evidence that is in principle impossible to disconfirm

(E) attempting to cast doubt on a conclusion by claiming that the statistical sample on which the conclusion is based is too small to be dependable[7]

---

[7]PrepTest June 2007, Sec. 2, Q 20

## Explanations

### 1. **(B)**

Yang: Yeast has long been known to be a leaven, that is, a substance used in baking to make breads rise. Since biblical evidence ties the use of leavens to events dating back to 1,200 B.C., <we can infer that yeast was already known to be a leaven at that time.>

Campisi: <I find your inference unconvincing;> several leavens other than yeast could have been known in 1,200 B.C.

Campisi (counters) Yang's argument (by)

(A)     suggesting that an alternative set of evidence better supports Yang's conclusion

(B)     questioning the truth of a presumption underlying Yang's argument

(C)     denying the truth of Yang's conclusion without considering the reason given for that conclusion

(D)     pointing out that the premises of Yang's argument more strongly support a contrary conclusion

(E)     calling into question the truth of the evidence presented in Yang's argument[8]

### Step 1. Identify the Question Type

Typically, the term "counter" indicates a Weaken question. However, in this case, the phrase "counters . . . by" identifies a Method of Argument question asking how Campisi attempted to weaken Yang's argument. So, rather than adding a new fact that would weaken the argument, the correct answer will describe what Campisi does to attack Yang's argument.

### Step 2. Untangle the Stimulus

Yang concludes that because leavens were used at that time, yeast was a known leavening agent in the year 1,200 B.C. Notice the scope shift in Yang's argument from "leavens" generally to "yeast" specifically. Campisi recognizes that assumption and goes right at it: Yang assumes that the leaven was yeast, but other types of leavens could have existed at the time.

### Step 3. Make a Prediction

Campisi challenges an assumption that Yang makes, so the correct answer should reflect this approach.

### Step 4. Evaluate the Answer Choices

Choice (A) brings in an alternative set of evidence that is outside the scope of the argument. Campisi doesn't add anything to the argument or support Yang's conclusion. Rather, he questions Yang's argument and offers no support for Yang's conclusion. Eliminate this answer

---

[8]PrepTest 41, Sec. 3, Q 12

Choice (B), the correct answer, identifies the problem Campisi raised regarding Yang's assumption.

Choice (C) uses extreme language and is outside the scope. Campisi doesn't deny the truth of Yang's conclusion; he merely finds Yang's assumption unconvincing. In addition, Campisi does consider the reason given and argues that it fails to prove Yang's point.

Choice (D) is outside the scope because Campisi never discusses a contrary conclusion nor does he mention Yang's evidence supporting a contrary conclusion.

Choice (E) contradicts Campisi's response. He challenges Yang's assumption, not his evidence.

## 2.   (A)

Zachary: The term "fresco" refers to paint that has been applied to wet plaster. Once dried, a fresco indelibly preserves the paint that a painter has applied in this way. Unfortunately, additions known to have been made by later painters have obscured the original fresco work done by Michelangelo in the Sistine Chapel. ⟨Therefore⟩ in order to restore Michelangelo's Sistine Chapel paintings to the appearance that Michelangelo intended them to have, everything except the original fresco work must be stripped away.⟩

Stephen: ⟨But⟩ it was extremely common for painters of Michelangelo's era to add painted details to their own fresco work after the frescos had dried.

Stephen's ⟨response⟩ to Zachary ⟨proceeds by⟩

(A)   calling into question an assumption on which Zachary's conclusion depends

(B)   challenging the definition of a key term in Zachary's argument

(C)   drawing a conclusion other than the one that Zachary reaches

(D)   denying the truth of one of the stated premises of Zachary's argument

(E)   demonstrating that Zachary's conclusion is not consistent with the premises he uses to support it[9]

## Step 1. Identify the Question Type

The phrase "response . . . proceeds by" tells you that this is a Method of Argument question.

## Step 2. Untangle the Stimulus

Zachary concludes in his last sentence that to restore the Sistine Chapel paintings to what Michelangelo intended, everything except the original fresco work must be stripped away. He supports his conclusion with evidence that later painters made additions to the paintings.

---

[9]PrepTest 35, Sec. 4, Q 25

Zachary must assume that Michelangelo did not himself make any additions to his original work to fulfill his intentions.

Notice the "but" in Stephen's response, which indicates Stephen's disagreement with Zachary. Stephen points out a gap between the evidence and conclusion and questions it. He raises the possibility that Michelangelo added paint to his own original work, so stripping away everything except the original work would not achieve Michelangelo's intentions at all.

### Step 3. Make a Prediction

In general terms, Stephen casts doubt on Zachary's assumption.

### Step 4. Evaluate the Answer Choices

Correct choice (A) matches the prediction that Stephen would question Zachary's assumption.

Choice (B) is wrong because Stephen never challenges Zachary's terminology.

Choice (C) incorrectly indicates that Stephen reached a conclusion of his own. He did question Zachary's assumption, which could ultimately endanger Zachary's conclusion. However, he never reached a conclusion of his own.

Choice (D) is also wrong because Stephen never attacks the premises of Zachary's argument. Instead, he questions the unstated assumption.

Choice (E) is out. Stephen never demonstrates an inconsistency between Zachary's evidence and conclusion. He adds information that raises doubt about Zachary's assumption.

## 3.   **(E)**

Gamba: Muñoz claims that the Southwest Hopeville Neighbors Association overwhelmingly opposes the new water system, citing this as evidence of citywide opposition. The association did pass a resolution opposing the new water system, but only 25 of 350 members voted, with 10 in favor of the system. Furthermore, the 15 opposing votes represent far less than 1 percent of Hopeville's population. <One should not assume that so few votes represent the view of the majority of Hopeville's residents.>

Of the following, which one most accurately describes Gamba's ⟨strategy of argumentation⟩?

(A)   questioning a conclusion based on the results of a vote, on the grounds that people with certain views are more likely to vote

(B)   questioning a claim supported by statistical data by arguing that statistical data can be manipulated to support whatever view the interpreter wants to support

(C)   attempting to refute an argument by showing that, contrary to what has been claimed, the truth of the premises does not guarantee the truth of the conclusion

(D)   criticizing a view on the grounds that the view is based on evidence that is in principle impossible to disconfirm

(E)   attempting to cast doubt on a conclusion by claiming that the statistical sample on which the conclusion is based is too small to be dependable[10]

## Step 1. Identify the Question Type

The phrase "strategy of argumentation" tells you that this is a Method of Argument question.

## Step 2. Untangle the Stimulus

Gamba begins by noting Muñoz's claim, that the Southwest Hopeville Neighbors Association opposes the new water system, so the opposition is citywide. Typically, when an author mentions someone else' claim, you can expect the author to disagree with that claim. That's exactly what happens here. Gamba proceeds to discredit Muñoz's claim by pointing out the small size of the sample, which he says doesn't accurately represent the Association, let alone the whole city. Gamba concludes by noting that the small number of votes doesn't necessarily represent the views of the city's residents. Notice the word "represent" in the conclusion; it points out where Gamba identifies the flaw of representativeness in Muñoz's argument.

---

[10]PrepTest June 2007, Sec. 2, Q 20

### Step 3. Make a Prediction

Gamba questions Muñoz's claim by pointing out that the study sample is not representative of the larger population.

### Step 4. Evaluate the Answer Choices

All the answer choices begin by noting in some form that Gamba does not believe Muñoz's claim, but the answers differ based on the reason for Gamba's concern. You are looking for the answer choice that questions the sample size, as predicted.

Choice (A) raises an issue that is not addressed in the stimulus, as Gamba doesn't question whether people with certain views were more likely to vote.

Choice (B) also brings up a point that Gamba never mentions; he does not talk about the possibility of statistical manipulation.

Choice (C) adds another contention not discussed in the stimulus. Gamba is not concerned with whether the truth of the premises guarantees the truth of the conclusion. He questions the representativeness of the evidence altogether.

Choice (D) also falls outside the scope. Gamba says the evidence is not representative. He never claims the evidence is impossible to disconfirm.

Finally, you get to choice (E), which matches the prediction by questioning the sample size. This is the correct answer.

## METHOD OF ARGUMENT REVIEW

Before you proceed to the next chapter, turn to Appendix A and complete the review exercise for Method of Argument questions. A completed chart is included in Appendix B.

# CHAPTER 14

# PARADOX QUESTIONS

Paradox questions ask you to make something that does not appear to make sense into something that does. A Paradox question presents you with two statements that contradict each other, but are nonetheless both true. While a real-life paradox may not have a simple resolution, an LSAT paradox can always be resolved with the correct answer. You will see about four scored Paradox questions on test day.

## DEFINITION OF PARADOX QUESTIONS

On the LSAT, a paradox exists when a stimulus contains two inconsistent ideas or situations. The correct answer will reconcile the seemingly incompatible statements while allowing them both to remain true. Essentially, each question asks you to fix a problem.

## USE THE KAPLAN METHOD TO ANSWER PARADOX QUESTIONS

### Identify the Question Type

As always, read the question stem first to identify the question type and note any relevant clues. You can identify a Paradox question from words and phrases like:

- Solve the apparent paradox
- Resolve the discrepancy
- Explain
- Solve the mystery

Here's how some of those phrases could appear in a question stem:

- Which one of the following, if true, most helps to resolve the apparent paradox described above?
- Which one of the following, if true, most helps to account for the apparent discrepancy in the students' preferences?
- Which one of the following, if true, most helps to explain the facts cited above?
- Which one of the following solves the mystery presented above?

## Untangle the Stimulus

A Paradox stimulus does not present an argument. Instead, you're given information that sets up a contradiction, so read the stimulus looking for that paradox. Ask yourself: What doesn't make sense? Your task is to identify the statements that are at odds with each other.

## Make a Prediction

Think about how to reconcile the paradox. You need to provide an explanation or an alternative factor that accounts for the contradictory elements and makes them consistent.

## Evaluate the Answer Choices

Compare your prediction to the answer choices and choose the match.

# THE KAPLAN METHOD IN ACTION

Now I'll walk you through a couple examples to show you how the Kaplan Method can help you efficiently solve any Paradox question you'll see on test day.

1. In a study, shoppers who shopped in a grocery store without a shopping list and bought only items that were on sale for half price or less spent far more money on a comparable number of items than did shoppers in the same store who used a list and bought no sale items.

   Which one of the following, if true, most helps to explain the apparent paradox in the study's results?

   (A) Only the shoppers who used a list used a shopping cart.
   (B) The shoppers who did not use lists bought many unnecessary items.
   (C) Usually, only the most expensive items go on sale in grocery stores.
   (D) The grocery store in the study carries many expensive items that few other grocery stores carry.
   (E) The grocery store in the study places relatively few items on sale.[1]

---

[1]PrepTest 50, Sec. 4, Q 16

### Step 1. Identify the Question Type

Because the question asks you for an answer that "most helps to explain the apparent paradox," this is a Paradox question. Look for the paradox in the study's results.

### Step 2. Untangle the Stimulus

The stimulus presents two groups of shoppers who purchased the same number of items at the same grocery store. One group had no list and bought only sale items (half price or less), while the other group used a list and bought no sale items at all. The latter group spent less money than the former.

### Step 3. Make a Prediction

You would have expected the sale items to be less expensive than the full-price items; therein lies the paradox. To resolve it, the answer must explain why sale items cost more than the full-price items. Let that principle guide you as you evaluate the answer choices.

### Step 4. Evaluate the Answer Choices

Choice (A) is out of scope; shopping carts don't have any apparent impact on the amount of money spent, so they can't help resolve the paradox. Eliminate this choice.

Choice (B) has the same problem. Whether items were necessary does not address the amount of money spent. At first glance, you might think unnecessary means the shoppers splurged, but the answer doesn't tie price to it. You still don't know how the sale shoppers spent more money. Move on to the next choice.

Choice (C) explains the paradox. If the sale items were originally the most expensive items in the store, they could still cost more on sale than other items at full price. This is the correct answer.

Choice (D) mentions cost but doesn't identify which group buys the expensive items. So, choice (D) doesn't add anything to help explain why the sale items cost more than the full price items.

Choice (E) doesn't address the cost issue either. The number of items on sale does not explain the higher grocery bill of those who only bought sale items.

2.   After replacing his old gas water heater with a new,
     pilotless, gas water heater that is rated as highly
     efficient, Jimmy's gas bills increased.

Each of the following, if true, contributes to an
explanation of the increase mentioned above EXCEPT:

(A)   The new water heater uses a smaller percentage
      of the gas used by Jimmy's household than did
      the old one.
(B)   Shortly after the new water heater was installed,
      Jimmy's uncle came to live with him, doubling
      the size of the household.
(C)   After having done his laundry at a laundromat,
      Jimmy bought and started using a gas dryer
      when he replaced his water heater.
(D)   Jimmy's utility company raised the rates for gas
      consumption following installation of the new
      water heater.
(E)   Unusually cold weather following installation of
      the new water heater resulted in heavy gas
      usage.[2]

## Step 1. Identify the Question Type

The phrase "contributes to an explanation" signals a Paradox question. Be careful with this question; make sure you know what kind of answer you're looking for. The "EXCEPT" in this stem means that four answers will reconcile the paradox, while the one right answer—the one you're looking for—will not. It will have no effect at all, or it will contribute to the paradox. Now that you know what you're looking for, read the stimulus.

## Step 2. Untangle the Stimulus

Jimmy's gas bills went up after he installed a new, highly efficient gas water heater.

## Step 3. Make a Prediction

You would expect the bill to go down with a new, efficient heater. So, either the new water heater is less efficient than the old one, or some other factor is driving up his gas bills. Remember: The four wrong answers will explain why the gas bills rose. The correct answer will not.

## Step 4. Evaluate the Answer Choices

Choice (A) says the new heater really does use less gas. Rather than explain why the gas bill went up, it leaves you wondering why the gas bill did not go down. This answer doesn't solve the paradox, and is therefore the correct answer.

Choice (B) adds Jimmy's uncle as a user of the new heater. Additional usage could explain an increase in the gas bill.

---

[2]PrepTest June 2007, Sec. 3, Q 2

Choice (C) also shows increased use of the new heater and supports an explanation for an increase in the gas bill.

Choice (D) raises the gas rates. So, even if Jimmy used less gas, his gas bill could increase.

Choice (E) gives another reason for increased use of the new heater and thereby contributes to an explanation for the higher gas bill.

# PARADOX QUESTIONS: NOW YOU TRY IT

It's now your turn to try a Paradox question on your own. Use the template I've provided after the question to guide you through the four-step Kaplan Method. (Note: On test day, you won't be writing out all the steps as you are in this exercise. However, as you are learning the Method, it's good practice to help it become second nature.) Remember to circle Keywords.

1.  Recent investigations of earthquakes have turned up a previously unknown type of seismic shock, known as a displacement pulse, which is believed to be present in all earthquakes. Alarmingly, high-rise buildings are especially vulnerable to displacement pulses, according to computer models. Yet examination of high-rises within cities damaged by recent powerful earthquakes indicates little significant damage to these structures.

    Which one of the following, if true, contributes to a resolution of the apparent paradox?

    (A) Displacement pulses travel longer distances than other types of seismic shock.

    (B) Scientific predictions based on computer models often fail when tested in the field.

    (C) While displacement pulses have only recently been discovered, they have accompanied all earthquakes that have ever occurred.

    (D) The displacement pulses made by low- and medium-intensity earthquakes are much less powerful than those made by the strongest earthquakes.

    (E) Computer models have been very successful in predicting the effects of other types of seismic shock.[3]

## Step 1. Identify the Question Type

_____

## Step 2. Untangle the Stimulus

_____

## Step 3. Make a Prediction

_____

## Step 4. Evaluate the Answer Choices

_____

---

[3] PrepTest 47, Sec. 1, Q 6

**Answer Explanations follow on the next page.**

# Explanations

### 1. **(B)**

Recent investigations of earthquakes have turned up a previously unknown type of seismic shock, known as a displacement pulse, which is believed to be present in all earthquakes. Alarmingly, high-rise buildings are especially vulnerable to displacement pulses, according to computer models. Yet examination of high-rises within cities damaged by recent powerful earthquakes indicates little significant damage to these structures.

Which one of the following, if true, contributes to a resolution of the apparent paradox?

- (A) Displacement pulses travel longer distances than other types of seismic shock.
- (B) Scientific predictions based on computer models often fail when tested in the field.
- (C) While displacement pulses have only recently been discovered, they have accompanied all earthquakes that have ever occurred.
- (D) The displacement pulses made by low- and medium-intensity earthquakes are much less powerful than those made by the strongest earthquakes.
- (E) Computer models have been very successful in predicting the effects of other types of seismic shock.[4]

## Step 1. Identify the Question Type

The phrase "contributes to a resolution of the apparent paradox" indicates that this is a Paradox question.

## Step 2. Untangle the Stimulus

Displacement pulses occur in all earthquakes and are especially dangerous to high-rise buildings, according to computer simulations. However, high-rises located in cities recently hit by earthquakes show little damage. The paradox is the discrepancy between the computer model and actual results.

## Step 3. Make a Prediction

The correct answer will explain why in reality there was only minor damage from earthquakes despite computer models predicting major damage.

---

[4] PrepTest 47, Sec. 1, Q 6

## Step 4. Evaluate the Answer Choices

Choice (A) provides information that would make the displacement pulses more dangerous to high-rises and thus deepens the discrepancy between the computer model and reality. Cross this choice out.

Choice (B) helps explain the discrepancy and is the correct answer. If computer models often fail in the field, it's possible the displacement pulse models are not accurate.

Choice (C) doesn't help resolve the paradox. Knowing that the recently discovered displacement pulses have always accompanied earthquakes doesn't explain the discrepancy between the computer model and the actual earthquake results.

Choice (D) also doesn't explain why the high-rises weren't damaged. They were hit by "powerful" earthquakes, which supposedly would have stronger displacement pulses.

Choice (E) extends the paradox by saying computer models are accurate in predicting the effects of seismic shock. In other words, it would make less sense that successful computer models show earthquake damage to high-rises when in reality the high-rises show little damage.

# DRILL: PRACTICING PARADOX QUESTIONS

Use the Kaplan Method to answer the following Paradox questions. Take this opportunity to practice and apply the steps in the Method so you are comfortable using them on test day. Be sure to circle conclusion and evidence Keywords and bracket the conclusion. Check your responses against the full explanations provided after the Drill.

1. Most economists believe that reducing the price of any product generally stimulates demand for it. However, most wine merchants have found that reducing the price of domestic wines to make them more competitive with imported wines with which they were previously comparably priced is frequently followed by an increase in sales of those imported wines.

   Which one of the following, if true, most helps to reconcile the belief of most economists with the consequences observed by most wine merchants?

   (A) Economists' studies of the prices of grocery items and their rates of sales rarely cover alcoholic beverages.

   (B) Few merchants of any kind have detailed knowledge of economic theories about the relationship between item prices and sales rates.

   (C) Consumers are generally willing to forgo purchasing other items they desire in order to purchase a superior wine.

   (D) Imported wines in all price ranges are comparable in quality to domestic wines that cost less.

   (E) An increase in the demand for a consumer product is compatible with an increase in demand for a competing product.[5]

2. A recent study revealed that the percentage of people treated at large, urban hospitals who recover from their illnesses is lower than the percentage for people treated at smaller, rural hospitals.

   Each of the following, if true, contributes to an explanation of the difference in recovery rates EXCEPT:

   (A) Because there are fewer patients to feed, nutritionists at small hospitals are better able to tailor meals to the dietary needs of each patient.

   (B) The less friendly, more impersonal atmosphere of large hospitals can be a source of stress for patients at those hospitals.

   (C) Although large hospitals tend to draw doctors trained at the more prestigious schools, no correlation has been found between the prestige of a doctor's school and patients' recovery rate.

   (D) Because space is relatively scarce in large hospitals, doctors are encouraged to minimize the length of time that patients are held for observation following a medical procedure.

   (E) Doctors at large hospitals tend to have a greater number of patients and consequently less time to explain to staff and to patients how medications are to be administered.[6]

3.  When companies' profits would otherwise be reduced by
    an increase in the minimum wage (a wage rate set by the
    government as the lowest that companies are allowed to
    pay), the companies often reduce the number of workers
    they employ. Yet a recent increase in the minimum wage
    did not result in job cutbacks in the fast-food industry,
    where most workers are paid the minimum wage.

    Which one of the following, if true, most helps to
    explain why the increase in the minimum wage did not
    affect the number of jobs in the fast-food industry?

    (A)  After the recent increase in the minimum wage,
         decreased job turnover in the fast-food industry
         allowed employers of fast-food workers to save
         enough on recruiting costs to cover the cost of
         the wage increase.
    (B)  If, in any industry, an increase in the minimum
         wage leads to the elimination of many jobs that
         pay the minimum wage, then higher-paying
         supervisory positions will also be eliminated in
         that industry.
    (C)  With respect to its response to increases in the
         minimum wage, the fast-food industry does not
         differ significantly from other industries that
         employ many workers at the minimum wage.
    (D)  A few employees in the fast-food industry were
         already earning more than the new, higher
         minimum wage before the new minimum wage
         was established.
    (E)  Sales of fast food to workers who are paid the
         minimum wage did not increase following the
         recent change in the minimum wage.[7]

---

[7]PrepTest 50, Sec. 2, Q 8

## Explanations

### 1.   **(E)**

Most economists believe that reducing the price of any product generally stimulates demand for it. However, most wine merchants have found that reducing the price of domestic wines to make them more competitive with imported wines with which they were previously comparably priced is frequently followed by an increase in sales of those imported wines.

Which one of the following, if true, most helps to reconcile the belief of most economists with the consequences observed by most wine merchants?

- (A)   Economists' studies of the prices of grocery items and their rates of sales rarely cover alcoholic beverages.
- (B)   Few merchants of any kind have detailed knowledge of economic theories about the relationship between item prices and sales rates.
- (C)   Consumers are generally willing to forgo purchasing other items they desire in order to purchase a superior wine.
- (D)   Imported wines in all price ranges are comparable in quality to domestic wines that cost less.
- (E)   An increase in the demand for a consumer product is compatible with an increase in demand for a competing product.[8]

## Step 1. Identify the Question Type

Because the question asks for something that "most helps to reconcile," this is a Paradox question. The stem also directs you to the paradox: Something will not make sense between "the belief of most economists with the consequences observed by most wine merchants."

## Step 2. Untangle the Stimulus

Most economists believe that reducing the price of an item increases demand. Yet, most wine sellers find that reducing the price of domestic wines increases sales of similarly priced imported wines. So what's the paradox? You'd expect domestic wine sales to rise. But the stimulus doesn't say what happened to demand for domestic wine, just that imported wine sales went up. How can sales increase for a competing imported product when the price of a domestic product decreases?

## Step 3. Make a Prediction

You need to reconcile the belief of economists with the experience of wine sellers. The correct answer will explain how a price reduction of a domestic wine followed by increased demand

---

[8]PrepTest 52, Sec. 3, Q 22

for a competing imported wine remains consistent with the belief that price reductions increase demand for a product. In this case, maybe lowering the price of domestic wine increases demand for wine in general.

### Step 4. Evaluate the Answer Choices

Choice (A) doesn't reconcile the wine sellers' experience with the economists' belief, but rather explains why the wine sellers' experience doesn't fit the theory. Cross this choice out.

Choice (B) is irrelevant. The merchants' knowledge of economics has no bearing on the occurrence of economic forces. Move on to the next choice.

Choice (C) explains why domestic wine sales might decrease if you assume imported items are superior to domestic. However, it doesn't explain a sales increase. This choice is out.

Choice (D) is also incorrect, because it furthers the paradox. An increase in imported wine sales doesn't make sense if domestic wines are similar in quality and less expensive.

Choice (E) is the winner by explaining that demand for a competing product, in this case imported wine, does not indicate a demand reduction for a consumer product, the domestic wine. Consequently, the wine sellers' experience is not incompatible with the economists' theory.

## 2.  **(C)**

A recent study revealed that the percentage of people treated at large, urban hospitals who recover from their illnesses is lower than the percentage for people treated at smaller, rural hospitals.

Each of the following, if true, contributes to an explanation of the difference in recovery rates EXCEPT:

(A)  Because there are fewer patients to feed, nutritionists at small hospitals are better able to tailor meals to the dietary needs of each patient.

(B)  The less friendly, more impersonal atmosphere of large hospitals can be a source of stress for patients at those hospitals.

(C)  Although large hospitals tend to draw doctors trained at the more prestigious schools, no correlation has been found between the prestige of a doctor's school and patients' recovery rate.

(D)  Because space is relatively scarce in large hospitals, doctors are encouraged to minimize the length of time that patients are held for observation following a medical procedure.

(E)  Doctors at large hospitals tend to have a greater number of patients and consequently less time to explain to staff and to patients how medications are to be administered.[9]

---

[9]PrepTest 52, Sec. 1, Q 11

## Step 1. Identify the Question Type

The phrase "contributes to an explanation," indicates a Paradox question. This is an "EXCEPT" question, so be careful. The four wrong answers will resolve the paradox. The correct answer will have no effect on the paradox or will deepen the mystery.

## Step 2. Untangle the Stimulus

The stimulus says that people treated at large, urban hospitals are less likely to recover from their illnesses than people treated at smaller, rural hospitals. The four wrong answer choices will explain why that might be.

## Step 3. Make a Prediction

Generally, it is assumed that a bigger hospital with more resources will be better for recovery. To resolve this paradox, the four wrong answer choices will provide another factor that is good about small, rural hospitals or bad about large, urban hospitals.

## Step 4. Evaluate the Answer Choices

Choice (A) discusses the ability of patients at small hospitals to get nutrition better tailored to their needs. Such individualized attention from the nutritionist could certainly explain better recovery at a small hospital. This is a positive factor about small hospitals that helps to resolve the mystery, so this choice is incorrect.

Choice (B) says that large hospitals put stress on patients which could also explain why they are less likely to recover there. This is a negative factor about large hospitals, which also helps resolve the paradox. Eliminate this choice.

Choice (C) does not address the different recovery rates between large hospital and small hospital patients, and therefore doesn't resolve the paradox. So, in this "EXCEPT" question, it is the correct answer.

Choice (D) indicates that patients in large hospitals tend to have shorter hospital stays which could certainly hurt their recovery. Again, this is a negative factor about large hospitals and helps resolve the mystery.

Choice (E) tells you that doctors at large hospitals have less time to explain to staff and patients how to best administer medication. Consequently, patients at large hospitals may not receive their medication under the best circumstances, which is another reason why patients are less likely to recover at large hospitals. This is yet another negative factor about large hospitals that helps to resolve the paradox.

### 3. **(A)**

When companies' profits would otherwise be reduced by an increase in the minimum wage (a wage rate set by the government as the lowest that companies are allowed to pay), the companies often reduce the number of workers they employ. Yet a recent increase in the minimum wage did not result in job cutbacks in the fast-food industry, where most workers are paid the minimum wage.

Which one of the following, if true, (most helps to) (explain) why the increase in the minimum wage did not affect the number of jobs in the fast-food industry?

(A)     After the recent increase in the minimum wage, decreased job turnover in the fast-food industry allowed employers of fast-food workers to save enough on recruiting costs to cover the cost of the wage increase.

(B)     If, in any industry, an increase in the minimum wage leads to the elimination of many jobs that pay the minimum wage, then higher-paying supervisory positions will also be eliminated in that industry.

(C)     With respect to its response to increases in the minimum wage, the fast-food industry does not differ significantly from other industries that employ many workers at the minimum wage.

(D)     A few employees in the fast-food industry were already earning more than the new, higher minimum wage before the new minimum wage was established.

(E)     Sales of fast food to workers who are paid the minimum wage did not increase following the recent change in the minimum wage.[10]

## Step 1. Identify the Question Type

The phrase "most helps to explain" is a classic Paradox indicator. The question stem also identifies the paradox in the stimulus—that an "increase in the minimum wage did not affect the number of jobs in the fast-food industry."

## Step 2. Untangle the Stimulus

Companies often cut the number of employees when an increase in minimum wage would reduce their profits. However, a recent increase in the minimum wage did not result in employee downsizing in the fast-food industry, an industry that employs a lot of minimum-wage workers. As noted in the question stem, the paradox is that despite an increase in the minimum wage, the number of jobs in the fast-food industry did not change.

---

[10]PrepTest 50, Sec. 2, Q 8

### Step 3. Make a Prediction

It's not just an increase in minimum wage that results in a staff cut. It's an increase in minimum wage that reduces profits that results in a staff cut. Because the fast-food industry did not cut their staff, the minimum-wage increase must not have reduced the industry's profit. Look for an answer that provides a way for the fast-food industry to save money in spite of a minimum-wage increase.

### Step 4. Evaluate the Answer Choices

Choice (A) tells you that reduced recruiting costs covered the wage increase. So, profits were not affected by the minimum-wage increase, which explains why jobs were not cut. The paradox is resolved and you have the correct answer.

Choice (B) says supervisory positions are cut when a minimum wage increase leads to a reduction of minimum wage paying jobs. This doesn't explain why the fast-food industry didn't cut any jobs at all.

Choice (C) adds to the paradox. If the fast-food industry is like other industries, you would expect it to cut jobs like those other industries.

Choice (D) discusses a few fast-food employees who earn more than the higher minimum wage. However, according to the stimulus, most fast-food workers are paid minimum wage, so you have no reason to believe that these few higher-paid workers will affect the industry's bottom line.

Choice (E) presents a situation in which sales of fast food did not increase. So, choice (E) eliminates one way to maintain profits in the face of a minimum wage increase, which is the opposite of the answer you want.

## PARADOX REVIEW

Before you proceed to the next chapter, turn to Appendix A and complete the review exercise for Paradox questions. A completed chart is included in Appendix B.

# CHAPTER 15

# POINT AT ISSUE QUESTIONS

Point at Issue questions present a conversation between two speakers and ask you to identify the issue on which they disagree. These questions reflect the common task of law students and lawyers who read cases to identify the point at issue between the two parties. Before you can analyze a case, you must know what the parties are at odds about and what the issue is before the court.

Typically, the LSAT will include one scored Point at Issue question. While not a big point payoff, Point at Issue questions tend to be straightforward, so practicing this question type is a relatively easy way to get a quick point on test day.

## DEFINITION OF POINT AT ISSUE QUESTIONS

Point at Issue questions ask you to determine the point of disagreement between two speakers. So essentially, your job is to identify what the speakers are arguing about. In a very rare instance, you may be asked to identify the point of agreement, so be sure to read the question stem carefully.

# USE THE KAPLAN METHOD TO ANSWER POINT AT ISSUE QUESTIONS

## Identify the Question Type

Read the question stem first to identify the question type and note any relevant clues. Phrases that indicate a Point at Issue question include:

- Disagree over whether
- Point at issue between them is
- Disagree about which one of the following

Here's how some of those phrases could appear in a question stem:

- On the basis of their statements, Price and Albrecht are committed to disagreeing about whether
- The dialogue most strongly supports the claim that Pat and Amar disagree with each other about whether
- Antonio and Marla disagree over

Again, a Point at Issue question rarely asks what the two speakers agree on. In this case, the stem would look like:

- Their dialogue provides the most support for the claim that Denise and Reshmi agree that

## Untangle the Stimulus

A Point at Issue stimulus is always presented in the form of a dialogue. Keep in mind, though, that a dialogue does not always indicate a Point at Issue question; it could be a Method of Argument question, for example. Use the wording of the question to direct you. Read each speaker's argument and briefly summarize it as you go along. As always, bracket the conclusion and identify any indicator words to help you understand the speakers' arguments.

## Make a Prediction

You may be able to predict the point at issue as you read the stimulus. For example, one speaker may say something like "The key to increasing sales is good customer service." The second speaker may respond with "I disagree. Offering products that meet customer needs is the most important factor in raising sales." The speakers are telling you directly that they disagree about the key factor to raise product sales.

## Evaluate the Answer Choices

If you were able to form a prediction, compare it to the answer choices and find the match. If not, find the answer that describes a point addressed by **both** speakers and about which the speakers hold conflicting views. The trick is to stay within the scope of both speakers' arguments; the point at issue can't be something that one speaker raises, but the other doesn't address at all.

Watch out for common wrong answer choices for Point at Issue questions, which include statements on which only one speaker comments or statements on which the speakers agree.

# THE KAPLAN METHOD IN ACTION

Now I'll walk you through a couple examples to show you how the Kaplan Method can help you efficiently solve any Point at Issue question you'll see on test day.

1.  Aaron: A prominent judge, criticizing "famous lawyers who come before courts ill-prepared to argue their cases," recently said, "This sort of cavalier attitude offends the court and can do nothing but harm to the client's cause." <I find the judge's remarks irresponsible.>

    Belinda: I find it natural and an admirable display of candor. <Letting people know of the damage their negligence causes is responsible behavior.>

    The point at issue between Aaron and Belinda is whether

    (A)  ill-prepared lawyers damage their clients' causes
    (B)  the judge's criticism of lawyers is irresponsible
    (C)  a lawyer's being ill-prepared to argue a client's case constitutes negligence
    (D)  famous lawyers have a greater responsibility to be well prepared than do lawyers who are not famous
    (E)  it is to be expected that ill-prepared lawyers would offend the court in which they appear[1]

## Step 1. Identify the Question Type

The phrase "the point at issue" tells you directly that this is a Point at Issue question.

## Step 2. Untangle the Stimulus

Aaron calls a judge's criticism of famous, ill-prepared lawyers "irresponsible." Belinda supports the judge's remarks and calls them "responsible."

## Step 3. Make a Prediction

The speakers disagree over whether the judge's disapproval of certain lawyers was responsible or not.

---

[1]PrepTest 47, Sec. 1, Q 4

## Step 4. Evaluate the Answer Choices

Choice (A) gets Belinda's support. She indicates that negligent lawyers damage their clients, which is her reason for concluding the judge was responsible. Aaron, however, directs his opinion to the judge who commented on ill-prepared lawyers without revealing his own opinion about ill-prepared lawyers damaging their clients' cases. Move on to the next choice.

Choice (B) matches the prediction exactly. Both speakers address the judge's criticism of lawyers and disagree on whether the action is irresponsible. This is the correct answer.

Choice (C) might get Belinda's support but Aaron does not discuss whether being unprepared for a client's case constitutes negligence.

Choice (D) gets no attention from either speaker. The level of responsibility owed to clients by famous versus little-known attorneys is outside the scope.

Choice (E) may get Belinda's agreement, but Aaron does not give any indication of whether ill-prepared lawyers would offend the court in which they appear.

2.  Mark: To convey an understanding of past events, <a historian should try to capture what it was like to experience those events.> For instance, a foot soldier in the Battle of Waterloo knew through direct experience what the battle was like, and it is this kind of knowledge that the historian must capture.

    Carla: But how do you go about choosing whose perspective is the valid one? Is the foot soldier's perspective more valid than that of a general? Should it be a French or an English soldier? Your approach would generate a biased version of history, and to avoid that, <historians must stick to general and objective characterizations of the past.>

    Mark's and Carla's positions indicate that they disagree about the truth of which one of the following?

    (A)   The purpose of writing history is to convey an understanding of past events.
    (B)   The participants in a battle are capable of having an objective understanding of the ramifications of the events in which they are participating.
    (C)   Historians can succeed in conveying a sense of the way events in the distant past seemed to someone who lived in a past time.
    (D)   Historians should aim to convey past events from the perspective of participants in those events.
    (E)   Historians should use fictional episodes to supplement their accounts of past events if the documented record of those events is incomplete.[2]

---

[2]PrepTest 37, Sec. 2, Q 11

## Step 1. Identify the Question Type

This stem asks for what Mark and Carla "disagree about" so it's a Point at Issue question.

## Step 2. Untangle the Stimulus

Mark concludes that historians should convey history through the perspective of those who lived it. Carla voices her concern that such an approach would result in a biased version of history and concludes that historians should present history through a general and objective perspective.

## Step 3. Make a Prediction

Mark and Carla's conclusions tell you they are talking about how best to present history. Mark supports a personalized viewpoint, while Carla endorses a more general approach.

## Step 4. Evaluate the Answer Choices

Choice (A) presents a point of agreement for Mark and Carla, so this choice is out.

Choice (B) is about whether participants can have an objective understanding of the events they live through. This is not discussed by either speaker. Mark offers a participant in battle as an example of someone who could best convey history through personal experience. While you may infer that Mark considers the participant's account to be subjective, he doesn't directly address whether the participant can be objective. Carla raises the difficulty of deciding whose perspective is the most appropriate to use in conveying history and the bias of whoever is chosen. She wants history to be presented objectively, but does not address who can be objective.

Choice (C) says that it's possible for historians to convey history through someone who lived it. While this may be a tempting answer choice, the speakers don't address this possibility; their arguments are focused on whether it's a good idea to take that approach. Eliminate this choice.

Choice (D) identifies the point at issue: Mark thinks historians should convey past events from the participants' perspectives, while Carla disagrees because the approach would generate a biased version of history. This is the correct answer.

Choice (E) is outside the scope. Neither speaker addresses the possibility of using fictional episodes to supplement incomplete historical accounts.

# POINT AT ISSUE QUESTIONS: NOW YOU TRY IT

It's now your turn to try a Point at Issue question on your own. Use the template I've provided after the question to guide you through the four-step Kaplan Method. (Note: On test day, you won't be writing out all the steps as you are in this exercise. However, as you are learning the Method, it's good practice to help it become second nature.) Remember to bracket conclusions and circle Keywords.

1. Davis: The only relevant factor in determining appropriate compensation for property damage or theft is the value the property loses due to damage or the value of the property stolen; the harm to the victim is directly proportional to the pertinent value.

   Higuchi: I disagree. More than one factor must be considered: A victim who recovers the use of personal property after two years is owed more than a victim who recovers its use after only one year.

   Davis's and Higuchi's statements most strongly support the view that they would disagree with each other about which one of the following?

   (A) It is possible to consistently and reliably determine the amount of compensation owed to someone whose property was damaged or stolen.
   (B) Some victims are owed increased compensation because of the greater dollar value of the damage done to their property.
   (C) Victims who are deprived of their property are owed compensation in proportion to the harm they have suffered.
   (D) Some victims are owed increased compensation because of the greater amount of time they are deprived of the use of their property.
   (E) The compensation owed to victims should be determined on a case-by-case basis rather than by some general rule.[3]

---

[3]PrepTest 43, Sec. 2, Q 13

**Step 1. Identify the Question Type**

_____

**Step 2. Untangle the Stimulus**

_____

**Step 3. Make a Prediction**

_____

**Step 4. Evaluate the Answer Choices**

_____

# Explanations

### 1. **(D)**

Davis: <The only relevant factor in determining appropriate compensation for property damage or theft is the value the property loses due to damage or the value of the property stolen;> the harm to the victim is directly proportional to the pertinent value.

Higuchi: <I disagree. More than one factor must be considered:> A victim who recovers the use of personal property after two years is owed more than a victim who recovers its use after only one year.

Davis's and Higuchi's statements most strongly support the view that they would disagree with each other about which one of the following?

(A)  It is possible to consistently and reliably determine the amount of compensation owed to someone whose property was damaged or stolen.

(B)  Some victims are owed increased compensation because of the greater dollar value of the damage done to their property.

(C)  Victims who are deprived of their property are owed compensation in proportion to the harm they have suffered.

(D)  Some victims are owed increased compensation because of the greater amount of time they are deprived of the use of their property.

(E)  The compensation owed to victims should be determined on a case-by-case basis rather than by some general rule.[4]

## Step 1. Identify the Question Type

The phrase "disagree with each other" tells you directly this is a Point at Issue question.

## Step 2. Untangle the Stimulus

When it comes to assessing compensation for property damage or theft, Davis argues there is only one factor to consider: the property value lost due to damage or the value of the property stolen. Higuchi argues for more than one factor, such as the length of time the victim is left without his property.

## Step 3. Make a Prediction

The speakers are talking about how to determine compensation for property damage or theft. Davis identifies one factor to consider and Higuchi thinks more than one factor must be considered.

---

[4]PrepTest 43, Sec. 2, Q 13

### Step 4. Evaluate the Answer Choices

Choice (A) is outside the scope. Neither speaker addresses the possibility of a consistent and reliable determination of compensation. Eliminate this choice.

Choice (B) reflects Davis's view, but Higuchi doesn't voice an opinion on this specific consideration for compensation. You just know that she thinks more than one factor must be considered. So, this choice is out.

Choice (C) has the same problem as choice (B): It echoes Davis's viewpoint, but Higuchi doesn't address it. Move on to the next choice.

Choice (D) is the correct answer. Davis limits determination of compensation to one factor, the value of the property lost. Higuchi says consider other factors and gives one such factor, the length of time the victim is deprived of the property.

Choice (E) presents a point of agreement, not disagreement, between Davis and Higuchi. Rather than specify one rule, both speakers identify a factor or factors to consider for compensation. Thus, they both imply that determination must be made on a case-by-case basis.

# DRILL: PRACTICING POINT AT ISSUE QUESTIONS

Use the Kaplan Method to answer the following Point at Issue questions. Take this opportunity to practice and apply the steps in the Method so you are comfortable using them on test day. Be sure to circle conclusion and evidence Keywords and bracket the conclusion. Check your responses against the full explanations provided after the Drill.

1. Constance: The traditional definition of full employment as a 5 percent unemployment rate is correct, because at levels below 5 percent, inflation rises.

   Brigita: That traditional definition of full employment was developed before the rise of temporary and part-time work and the fall in benefit levels. When people are juggling several part-time jobs with no benefits, or working in a series of temporary assignments, as is now the case, 5 percent unemployment is not full employment.

   The dialogue most strongly supports the claim that Constance and Brigita disagree with each other about which one of the following?

   (A) what definition of full employment is applicable under contemporary economic conditions
   (B) whether it is a good idea, all things considered, to allow the unemployment level to drop below 5 percent
   (C) whether a person with a part-time job should count as fully employed
   (D) whether the number of part-time and temporary workers has increased since the traditional definition of full employment was developed
   (E) whether unemployment levels above 5 percent can cause inflation levels to rise[5]

2. Samuel: Because communication via computer is usually conducted privately and anonymously between people who would otherwise interact in person, it contributes to the dissolution, not the creation, of lasting communal bonds.

   Tova: You assume that communication via computer replaces more intimate forms of communication and interaction, when more often it replaces asocial or even antisocial behavior.

   On the basis of their statements, Samuel and Tova are committed to disagreeing about which one of the following?

   (A) A general trend of modern life is to dissolve the social bonds that formerly connected people.
   (B) All purely private behavior contributes to the dissolution of social bonds.
   (C) Face-to-face communication is more likely to contribute to the creation of social bonds than is anonymous communication.
   (D) It is desirable that new social bonds be created to replace the ones that have dissolved.
   (E) If people were not communicating via computer, they would most likely be engaged in activities that create stronger social bonds.[6]

---

[5]PrepTest 51, Sec. 1, Q 23      [6]PrepTest 52, Sec. 3, Q 10

3. Antonio: One can live a life of moderation by never
   deviating from the middle course. But then one
   loses the joy of spontaneity and misses the
   opportunities that come to those who are
   occasionally willing to take great chances, or to
   go too far.

   Marla: But one who, in the interests of moderation,
   never risks going too far is actually failing to live
   a life of moderation: one must be moderate even
   in one's moderation.

   Antonio and Marla disagree over

   (A)   whether it is desirable for people occasionally
         to take great chances in life
   (B)   what a life of moderation requires of a person
   (C)   whether it is possible for a person to embrace
         other virtues along with moderation
   (D)   how often a person ought to deviate from the
         middle course in life
   (E)   whether it is desirable for people to be
         moderately spontaneous[7]

---

[7]PrepTest June 2007, Sec. 3, Q 7

# Explanations

## 1. **(A)**

Constance: <The traditional definition of full employment as a 5 percent unemployment rate is correct,> (because) at levels below 5 percent, inflation rises.

Brigita: That traditional definition of full employment was developed before the rise of temporary and part-time work and the fall in benefit levels. When people are juggling several part-time jobs with no benefits, or working in a series of temporary assignments, as is now the case, <5 percent unemployment is not full employment.>

The dialogue most strongly supports the claim that Constance and Brigita (disagree with each other about) which one of the following?

- (A) what definition of full employment is applicable under contemporary economic conditions
- (B) whether it is a good idea, all things considered, to allow the unemployment level to drop below 5 percent
- (C) whether a person with a part-time job should count as fully employed
- (D) whether the number of part-time and temporary workers has increased since the traditional definition of full employment was developed
- (E) whether unemployment levels above 5 percent can cause inflation levels to rise[8]

## Step 1. Identify the Question Type

The phrase "disagree with each other about" tells you this is a Point at Issue question.

## Step 2. Untangle the Stimulus

Constance concludes that the traditional definition of full employment (5 percent unemployment rate) is correct. Brigita disagrees and argues the traditional definition is not correct because it doesn't consider additional factors.

## Step 3. Make a Prediction

Constance and Brigita disagree over the definition of full employment.

## Step 4. Evaluate the Answer Choices

Choice (A) is a match, and is the correct answer. Both speakers address the definition of full employment and disagree about whether to apply contemporary economic conditions.

---

[8]PrepTest 51, Sec. 1, Q 23

Choice (B) is outside the scope. Neither speaker discusses the consequences of allowing the unemployment level to drop below 5 percent or whether it's a good idea.

Choice (C) presents information addressed by Brigita but never discussed by Constance.

Choice (D) is wrong for the same reason as choice (D).

Choice (E) is wrong because neither speaker talks about what happens above 5 percent unemployment.

2.  **(E)**

Samuel: (Because) communication via computer is usually conducted privately and anonymously between people who would otherwise interact in person, <it contributes to the dissolution, not the creation, of lasting communal bonds.>

Tova: You assume that communication via computer replaces more intimate forms of communication and interaction, when <more often it replaces asocial or even antisocial behavior.>

On the basis of their statements, Samuel and Tova are (committed to disagreeing about) which one of the following?

(A)   A general trend of modern life is to dissolve the social bonds that formerly connected people.
(B)   All purely private behavior contributes to the dissolution of social bonds.
(C)   Face-to-face communication is more likely to contribute to the creation of social bonds than is anonymous communication.
(D)   It is desirable that new social bonds be created to replace the ones that have dissolved.
(E)   If people were not communicating via computer, they would most likely be engaged in activities that create stronger social bonds.[9]

## Step 1. Identify the Question Type

The question stem asks for what Samuel and Tova are "committed to disagreeing about," so this is a Point at Issue question.

## Step 2. Untangle the Stimulus

Samuel argues that communication by computer helps dissolve, rather than develop, lasting communal bonds. He bases his conclusion on the evidence that the private, anonymous communication takes the place of in-person interaction. Tova claims that communication via computer replaces asocial or even antisocial behavior.

---

[9]PrepTest 52, Sec. 3, Q 10

## Step 3. Make a Prediction

Both speakers discuss the impact of communication by computer on interpersonal relationships. Samuel says that form of communication is destructive to positive relations while Tova says it replaces negative relations.

## Step 4. Evaluate the Answer Choices

Choice (A) discusses a general trend of modern life, something neither speaker addresses. Actually, they talk about one phenomenon, communication via computer. So, you can cross this choice out.

Choice (B) is too extreme. The speakers talk about one type of behavior, not all private behavior. This choice is also out.

Choice (C) is something Samuel agrees with, but it's hard to get an exact read on Tova's thinking on it. If anything, she might agree with choice (C) based on her "more intimate forms of communication" statement that implies in-person communication provides better bonding opportunities. You can eliminate this choice.

Choice (D) is incorrect for two reasons. Neither speaker discusses the creation of new bonds nor do they talk about the desirability of one condition over another.

Choice (E) is weighed in on by both speakers and their positions conflict. Samuel thinks computer interaction keeps people from other interaction that develops bonds. Tova thinks it replaces nonbonding interaction. Choice (E) is the correct answer.

3.  **(B)**

Antonio: <One can live a life of moderation by never deviating from the middle course.> But then one loses the joy of spontaneity and misses the opportunities that come to those who are occasionally willing to take great chances, or to go too far.

Marla: But one who, in the interests of moderation, never risks going too far is actually failing to live a life of moderation: <one must be moderate even in one's moderation.>

Antonio and Marla (disagree over)

(A)   whether it is desirable for people occasionally to take great chances in life
(B)   what a life of moderation requires of a person
(C)   whether it is possible for a person to embrace other virtues along with moderation
(D)   how often a person ought to deviate from the middle course in life
(E)   whether it is desirable for people to be moderately spontaneous[10]

---

[10]PrepTest June 2007, Sec. 3, Q 7

### Step 1. Identify the Question Type

The phrase "disagree over" is a common Point at Issue indicator.

### Step 2. Untangle the Stimulus

Antonio defines a life of moderation as "never deviating from the middle course." Marla says never taking risks is really not a life of moderation.

### Step 3. Make a Prediction

Antonio and Marla disagree about the nature of a life of moderation.

### Step 4. Evaluate the Answer Choices

Choice (A) is discussed by Antonio when he says people miss the joy of spontaneity when they don't take chances. But Marla limits her discussion to the definition of a moderate life and takes no position on desirability. So, cross this choice out.

Choice (B) is the correct answer. Both speakers define a life of moderation, but they differ on its meaning.

Choice (C) is outside the scope of both speakers. Neither one mentions embracing other virtues.

Choice (D) presents the same problem. Neither speaker talks about how often a person should deviate from the middle of the road.

Choice (E) adds a new topic to the speakers' conversation. Neither speaker brings up moderate spontaneity, so they can't take a position on its desirability.

## POINT AT ISSUE REVIEW

Before you proceed to the next chapter, turn to Appendix A and complete the review exercise for Point at Issue questions. A completed chart is included in Appendix B.

# CHAPTER 16

# ROLE OF A STATEMENT QUESTIONS

Role of a Statement questions ask you to identify the function served by a specific assertion in a stimulus. This question type is yet another way in which the LSAT tests your ability to analyze an argument and identify its parts.

You will see about two scored Role of a Statement questions on an LSAT. Take advantage of the straightforward nature of these questions and earn these points quickly and confidently.

## DEFINITION OF ROLE OF A STATEMENT QUESTIONS

Role of a Statement question stems include a statement from the stimulus (usually verbatim) and ask you to determine the role it plays in the argument.

## USE THE KAPLAN METHOD TO ANSWER ROLE OF A STATEMENT QUESTIONS

### Identify the Question Type

Read the question stem first to identify the question type and note any relevant clues. You can identify a Role of a Statement question from words and phrases like:

- Plays which one of the following roles
- Figures in the argument
- Plays which part

Here's how some of those phrases could appear in a question stem:

- Which one of the following most accurately expresses the role played in the argument by the observation that attending a live musical performance is a richer experience than is listening to recorded music?
- The statement that human food-producing capacity has increased more rapidly than human population plays which one of the following roles in the argument?
- The statement that the educational use of computers enables schools to teach far more courses with far fewer teachers figures in the argument in which one of the following ways?

### Untangle the Stimulus

To untangle the stimulus of a Role of a Statement question, you need to find the phrase that appears in both the question stem and the stimulus, and then determine the role it plays in the argument. (I also recommend that you underline the statement so you can quickly refer to it if you need to.) Then, locate the components of the argument: Find and bracket the conclusion, and then find and summarize the evidence.

### Make a Prediction

Your prediction is the part of the argument in which you locate the statement in question. Additionally, think about what the author is trying to do with the statement (e.g., support a particular claim, rebut a certain hypothesis, or reach a specific conclusion). This consideration is also helpful if you can't classify the repeated statement as part of the arguments' conclusion or as part of the evidence

### Evaluate the Answer Choices

Determine an answer that matches your prediction. Remember, the answer may not be as explicit as "conclusion" or "evidence." Instead, it may be presented as a definition of those terms.

# THE KAPLAN METHOD IN ACTION

Now I'll walk you through an example to show you how the Kaplan Method can help you efficiently solve any Role of a Statement question you'll see on test day.

1.  Teacher: Participating in organized competitive athletics may increase a child's strength and coordination. As critics point out, however, it also instills in those children who are not already well developed in these respects a feeling of inferiority that never really disappears. Yet, since research has shown that adults with feelings of inferiority become more successful than those free of such anxieties, funding for children's athletic programs should not be eliminated.

    Which one of the following most accurately describes the role played in the teacher's argument by the assertion that participating in organized competitive athletics may increase a child's strength and coordination?

    (A)    It is mentioned as one possible reason for adopting a policy for which the teacher suggests an additional reason.
    (B)    It is a claim that the teacher attempts to refute with counterarguments.
    (C)    It is a hypothesis for which the teacher offers additional evidence.
    (D)    It is cited as an insufficient reason for eliminating funding for children's athletic programs.
    (E)    It is cited as an objection that has been raised to the position that the teacher is supporting.[1]

## Step 1. Identify the Question Type

The question asks you to describe the "role played" by an assertion made in the teacher's argument. This is standard language for a Role of a Statement question. The statement, the role of which you must identify, is, "participating in organized competitive athletics may increase a child's strength and coordination." Underline this statement in the question stem (you will also underline it in the stimulus in the next step).

## Step 2. Untangle the Stimulus

Read the stimulus and look for the conclusion, evidence, and the specific assertion in the question. The statement you underlined in the question stem—in which the teacher asserts a benefit of organized athletics—appears right away in the first sentence. Underline it. Then, note that the teacher also points to a criticism of organized athletics, but rebuts it providing an additional benefit. The teacher then concludes with a recommendation to keep funding for children's athletics.

---

[1]PrepTest 42, Sec. 4, Q 3

### Step 3. Make a Prediction

The assertion is one piece of evidence provided to support the teacher's recommendation.

### Step 4. Evaluate the Answer Choices

Choice (A) matches the prediction and is the correct answer. The assertion is one of two reasons the teacher mentions for the recommendation.

Choice (B) is wrong because the teacher doesn't attack the notion that organized athletics makes children stronger and more coordinated. In fact, she provides it in support of her conclusion.

Choice (C) is wrong. It suggests that the teacher returns to the assertion to offer additional evidence for it as if it was the conclusion; however, the teacher never goes back to the assertion. She adds another piece of evidence in support of the conclusion in the final sentence.

Choice (D) is also wrong. The assertion is presented as a sufficient reason to continue funding for children's athletics.

Choice (E) is wrong as well. The critics' objection is in the second sentence. The assertion is offered in support of the teacher's position.

# ROLE OF A STATEMENT QUESTIONS: NOW YOU TRY IT

It's now your turn to try a Role of a Statement question on your own. Use the template I've provided after the question to guide you through the four-step Kaplan Method. (Note: On test day, you won't be writing out all the steps as you are in this exercise. However, as you are learning the Method, it's good practice to help it become second nature.) Remember to bracket conclusions and circle Keywords.

1. It would not be surprising to discover that the trade routes between China and the West were opened many centuries, even millennia, earlier than 200 B.C., contrary to what is currently believed. After all, what made the Great Silk Road so attractive as a trade route linking China and the West—level terrain, easily traversable mountain passes, and desert oases—would also have made it an attractive route for the original emigrants to China from Africa and the Middle East, and this early migration began at least one million years ago.

   That a migration from Africa and the Middle East to China occurred at least one million years ago figures in the above reasoning in which one of the following ways?

   (A) It is cited as conclusive evidence for the claim that trade links between China and the Middle East were established long before 200 B.C.

   (B) It is an intermediate conclusion made plausible by the description of the terrain along which the migration supposedly took place.

   (C) It is offered as evidence in support of the claim that trade routes between China and the West could easily have been established much earlier than is currently believed.

   (D) It is offered as evidence against the claim that trade routes between China and Africa preceded those eventually established between China and the Middle East.

   (E) It is the main conclusion that the argument attempts to establish about intercourse between China and the West.[2]

---

[2]PrepTest 51, Sec. 1, Q 14

**Step 1. Identify the Question Type**

_____

**Step 2. Untangle the Stimulus**

_____

**Step 3. Make a Prediction**

_____

**Step 4. Evaluate the Answer Choices**

_____

# Explanations

## 1. **(C)**

<It would not be surprising to discover that the trade routes between China and the West were opened many centuries, even millennia, earlier than 200 B.C., contrary to what is currently believed.>(After all,) what made the Great Silk Road so attractive as a trade route linking China and the West—level terrain, easily traversable mountain passes, and desert oases—would also have made it an attractive route for the original emigrants to China from Africa and the Middle East, and this early migration began at least one million years ago.

That a migration from Africa and the Middle East to (China occurred at least one million) years ago figures in the above reasoning in which one of the following ways?

(A)  It is cited as conclusive evidence for the claim that trade links between China and the Middle East were established long before 200 B.C.

(B)  It is an intermediate conclusion made plausible by the description of the terrain along which the migration supposedly took place.

(C)  It is offered as evidence in support of the claim that trade routes between China and the West could easily have been established much earlier than is currently believed.

(D)  It is offered as evidence against the claim that trade routes between China and Africa preceded those eventually established between China and the Middle East.

(E)  It is the main conclusion that the argument attempts to establish about intercourse between China and the West.[3]

## Step 1. Identify the Question Type

This stem includes a statement taken from the stimulus along with the phrase "figures in the above reasoning," which indicates that this a Role of the Statement question.

## Step 2. Untangle the Stimulus

The conclusion—that it would not be a surprise to learn that trade routes between China and the West were much older than currently believed—appears in the first sentence in the form of the author's opinion. The words "After all" point to the evidence that backs up her thinking, which states that the trade route is probably much older because the features that made it an attractive trade route would have also been attractive to emigrants from a much earlier time period.

---

[3]PrepTest 51, Sec. 1, Q 14

## Step 3. Make a Prediction

The information in question is the evidence in the last sentence of the argument, which provides support for the conclusion that the China-West trade route opened earlier than is currently believed.

## Step 4. Evaluate the Answer Choices

Choice (A) is extreme. The author does not present the information as conclusive evidence but rather as a possibility in support of an alternative theory. Eliminate this choice.

Choice (B) is wrong. The information is not an intermediary conclusion, it's part of the evidence.

Choice (C) is the correct answer. It is evidence that supports the possibility that trade routes between China and the West were in place much earlier than is now thought. Notice that to identify choice (C) as the correct answer, you needed to identify the statement as a piece of evidence and also to be clear as to the conclusion it supported. Often, every answer choice will correctly identify the statement as a piece of evidence, and you will need to select the one that correctly describes the conclusion it supports.

Choice (D) has it backward. The information in question is evidence, but it is offered in support of the author's conclusion, not against it.

Choice (E) misidentifies the statement in question. The statement is evidence located at the end of the stimulus, not the conclusion, which is in the first sentence.

# DRILL: PRACTICING ROLE OF A STATEMENT QUESTIONS

Use the Kaplan Method to answer the following Role of a Statement questions. Take this opportunity to practice and apply the steps in the Method so you are comfortable using them on test day. Be sure to circle conclusion and evidence Keywords, bracket the conclusion, and underline the statement. Check your responses against the full explanations provided after the Drill.

1. When a major record label signs a contract with a band, the label assumes considerable financial risk. It pays for videos, album art, management, and promotions. Hence, the band does not need to assume nearly as much risk as it would if it produced its own records independently. For this reason, it is only fair for a major label to take a large portion of the profits from the record sales of any band signed with it.

Which one of the following most accurately describes the role played in the argument by the claim that a band signed with a major label does not need to assume nearly as much risk as it would if it produced its own records independently?

(A) It is the only conclusion that the argument attempts to establish.

(B) It is one of two unrelated conclusions, each of which the same premises are used to support.

(C) It is a general principle from which the argument's conclusion follows as a specific instance.

(D) It describes a phenomenon for which the rest of the argument offers an explanation.

(E) Premises are used to support it, and it is used to support the main conclusion.[4]

2. It is primarily by raising interest rates that central bankers curb inflation, but an increase in interest rates takes up to two years to affect inflation. Accordingly, central bankers usually try to raise interest rates before inflation becomes excessive, at which time inflation is not yet readily apparent either. But unless inflation is readily apparent, interest rate hikes generally will be perceived as needlessly restraining a growing economy. Thus, central bankers' success in temporarily restraining inflation may make it harder for them to ward off future inflation without incurring the public's wrath.

Which one of the following most accurately describes the role played in the argument by the claim that it is primarily by raising interest rates that central bankers curb inflation?

(A) It is presented as a complete explanation of the fact that central bankers' success in temporarily restraining inflation may make it harder for them to ward off future inflation without incurring the public's wrath.

(B) It is a description of a phenomenon for which the claim that an increase in interest rates takes up to two years to affect inflation is offered as an explanation.

(C) It is a premise offered in support of the conclusion that central bankers' success in temporarily restraining inflation may make it harder for them to ward off future inflation without incurring the public's wrath.

(D) It is a conclusion for which the statement that an increase in interest rates takes up to two years to affect inflation is offered as support.

(E) It is a premise offered in support of the conclusion that unless inflation is readily apparent, interest rate hikes generally will be perceived as needlessly restraining a growing economy.[5]

3. Philosopher: Graham argues that since a person is truly happy only when doing something, the best life is a life that is full of activity. But we should not be persuaded by Graham's argument. People sleep, and at least sometimes when sleeping, they are truly happy, even though they are not doing anything.

Which one of the following most accurately describes the role played in the philosopher's argument by the claim that at least sometimes when sleeping, people are truly happy, even though they are not doing anything?

(A) It is a premise of Graham's argument.

(B) It is an example intended to show that a premise of Graham's argument is false.

(C) It is an analogy appealed to by Graham but that the philosopher rejects.

(D) It is an example intended to disprove the conclusion of Graham's argument.

(E) It is the main conclusion of the philosopher's argument.[6]

---

[6]PrepTest 52, Sec. 3, Q 17

# Explanations

## 1. (E)

When a major record label signs a contract with a band, the label assumes considerable financial risk. It pays for videos, album art, management, and promotions. (Hence,) the band does not need to assume nearly as much risk as it would if it produced its own records independently. ⟨For this reason,⟩ it is only fair for a major label to take a large portion of the profits from the record sales of any band signed with it.⟩

Which one of the following most accurately describes the (role played) in the argument by the claim that a band signed with a major label does not need to assume nearly as much risk as it would if it produced its own records independently?

(A)   It is the only conclusion that the argument attempts to establish.

(B)   It is one of two unrelated conclusions, each of which the same premises are used to support.

(C)   It is a general principle from which the argument's conclusion follows as a specific instance.

(D)   It describes a phenomenon for which the rest of the argument offers an explanation.

(E)   Premises are used to support it, and it is used to support the main conclusion.[7]

## Step 1. Identify the Question Type

The question mentions a claim from the argument and asks what role it played, which indicates a Role of a Statement question.

## Step 2. Untangle the Stimulus

At first glance, the claim in the question stem—that bands signed by major record labels don't assume as much risk as they would by producing their own records independently—appears to be the conclusion of the argument because it follows the word "hence." If you stopped your analysis here and went right to the answer choices, you would lose a point. While the claim is a conclusion, it is not the primary conclusion of the argument.

The stimulus begins with evidence that the record label assumes great risk when it signs a band and therefore a band need not assume as much risk. The words "For this reason" indicate the conclusion—that the record labels are justified in taking a big portion of the proceeds.

## Step 3. Make a Prediction

The claim identified in the question stem is a subsidiary conclusion that serves as evidence and supports the main conclusion.

---

[7]PrepTest 51, Sec. 3, Q 11

## Step 4. Evaluate the Answer Choices

Choice (A) is wrong. The claim is not the only conclusion in the argument.

Choice (B) is also wrong. The claim is related to the other conclusion and, in fact, supports it.

Choice (C) is wrong for two reasons: The claim is not a general principle, and the conclusion is not a specific example of the claim.

Choice (D) suggests that the claim is the primary conclusion and the rest of the argument is evidence in support of it, which is not the case. This choice is also wrong.

Choice (E) is the correct answer. Evidence supports the claim as a subsidiary conclusion and it provides support for the primary conclusion.

2.   **(C)**

It is primarily by raising interest rates that central
bankers curb inflation, but an increase in interest
rates takes up to two years to affect inflation.
Accordingly, central bankers usually try to raise
interest rates before inflation becomes excessive, at
which time inflation is not yet readily apparent
either. But unless inflation is readily apparent,
interest rate hikes generally will be perceived as
needlessly restraining a growing economy. ⟨Thus,⟩
central bankers' success in temporarily restraining
inflation may make it harder for them to ward off
future inflation without incurring the public's wrath.⟩

Which one of the following most accurately describes
the ⟨role played⟩ in the argument by the claim that it is
primarily by raising interest rates that central
bankers curb inflation?

(A)   It is presented as a complete explanation of the
      fact that central bankers' success in
      temporarily restraining inflation may make it
      harder for them to ward off future inflation
      without incurring the public's wrath.
(B)   It is a description of a phenomenon for which
      the claim that an increase in interest rates
      takes up to two years to affect inflation is
      offered as an explanation.
(C)   It is a premise offered in support of the
      conclusion that central bankers' success in
      temporarily restraining inflation may make it
      harder for them to ward off future inflation
      without incurring the public's wrath.
(D)   It is a conclusion for which the statement that
      an increase in interest rates takes up to two
      years to affect inflation is offered as support.
(E)   It is a premise offered in support of the
      conclusion that unless inflation is readily
      apparent, interest rate hikes generally will be
      perceived as needlessly restraining a growing
      economy.[8]

### Step 1. Identify the Question Type

The question asks for the role played by a claim in the stimulus, signaling a Role of a Statement question.

### Step 2. Untangle the Stimulus

The stimulus starts with the claim identified in the question stem that explains raising interest
rates is the primary tool central bankers use to curb inflation. It continues with a discussion of

---

the impact of its implementation. The stimulus ends with the argument's conclusion identified by "Thus." Restraining inflation in the short term makes it harder to ward off in the long run.

## Step 3. Make a Prediction

The claim is part of the chain of evidence that results in the conclusion.

## Step 4. Evaluate the Answer Choices

Choice (A) is too extreme in calling the initial clause a complete explanation when it is just an introduction of the mechanism used by bankers to curb inflation. It does not address the other issues of short-term versus long-term success or the public's reaction.

Choice (B) is wrong; the "But" says the phenomenon and the claim contrast each other, not support each other.

Choice (C) correctly identifies the initial claim as supporting evidence for the conclusion regarding the short-term versus long-term impact of curbing inflation.

Choice (D) misidentifies the claim as a conclusion supported by the second clause in the sentence. Just as in choice (B), the contrast word "But" puts the two clauses in opposition to each other.

Choice (E) incorrectly identifies the third sentence as the conclusion.

3.   **(B)**

Philosopher: Graham argues that (since) a person is truly happy only when doing something, the best life is a life that is full of activity. <(But) we should not be persuaded by Graham's argument.> People sleep, and at least sometimes when sleeping, they are truly happy, even though they are not doing anything.

Which one of the following most accurately describes the (role played) in the philosopher's argument by the claim that at least sometimes when sleeping, people are truly happy, even though they are not doing anything?

(A)   It is a premise of Graham's argument.
(B)   It is an example intended to show that a premise of Graham's argument is false.
(C)   It is an analogy appealed to by Graham but that the philosopher rejects.
(D)   It is an example intended to disprove the conclusion of Graham's argument.
(E)   It is the main conclusion of the philosopher's argument.[9]

---

[9]PrepTest 52, Sec. 3, Q 17

### Step 1. Identify the Question Type

The phrase "role played," along with a claim from the stimulus, both indicate a Role of a Statement question. Note that you are looking for the role of the claim in the philosopher's argument, an important point because the stimulus presents two arguments: one from the philosopher and one from Graham.

### Step 2. Untangle the Stimulus

The philosopher starts with Graham's argument that the best life is one full of activity because people are only happy when they do something. He follows it with "But," which signals that he is about to disagree. The philosopher concludes you shouldn't be swayed by Graham's assertion because people can be happy when they're sleeping and not doing anything. This evidence is the claim referred to in the question stem.

### Step 3. Make a Prediction

The philosopher's evidence obviously supports his conclusion, but it also rebuts Graham's evidence.

### Step 4. Evaluate the Answer Choices

Choice (A) credits the evidence to the wrong person. This choice is out.

Choice (B) correctly identifies the evidence as an example intended to attack Graham's evidence. This is the correct answer.

Choice (C) incorrectly identifies the evidence as an analogy and attributes it to the wrong person.

Choice (D) is directed at the wrong part of Graham's argument.

Choice (E) mislabels the philosopher's evidence as his conclusion.

## ROLE OF A STATEMENT REVIEW

Before you proceed to the next chapter, turn to Appendix A and complete the review exercise for Role of a Statement questions. A completed chart is included in Appendix B.

# CHAPTER 17

# MAIN POINT QUESTIONS

Of all the question types on the LSAT, Main Point questions will probably seem the most familiar to you. They are exactly what they sound like: They ask you to find the central claim in the argument. You will see about two scored Main Point questions on test day. Go after them.

## DEFINITION OF MAIN POINT QUESTIONS

Simply enough, Main Point questions ask you to identify the conclusion of the the author's argument.

## USE THE KAPLAN METHOD TO ANSWER MAIN POINT QUESTIONS

### Identify the Question Type

Read the question stem first to identify the question type and note any relevant clues. You can identify a Main Point question from words and phrases like:

- Conclusion
- Main idea
- Main point

Here's how some of those phrases could appear in a question stem:

- Which one of the following most accurately expresses the main conclusion drawn in the above argument?
- The main point of the argument is

## Untangle the Stimulus

All stimuli for Main Point questions present an argument. Your task is to identify the conclusion, so read the argument to break it down to it components: the evidence and the conclusion.

Main Point questions rarely include clear conclusion indicator words, making it a bit more difficult to find the conclusion. However, the test makers will often still give you evidence keywords, and identifying the evidence will help you to identify the conclusion it supports.

There are other ways you can find the conclusion. One way is to look for a disagreement in the stimulus; LSAT arguments often present a claim by one person or group followed by the author's conclusion that refutes the other view. So, if you find the author refuting a claim, there's a good chance that it's part of the conclusion.

You can also try using the "one-sentence test." Eliminate all extra information and keep the one sentence the author would need to keep to express her point. Hone in on emphatic statements and remember the conclusion types you learned about in the chapter on Parallel Reasoning questions. Recommendations, value judgments, and predictions will trump mundane assertions of fact and generally point to the author's big idea.

Another tool to find the conclusion is to determine whether the statement answers the question "why," making it evidence, or if the statement is supported by other information that answers the question "why," making it the conclusion.

## Make a Prediction

Paraphrase the main idea without getting bogged down in the details of the argument. Remember, the author's conclusion is the part of the stimuli that you bracket, as you have now done for dozens of arguments; the conclusion is NOT a summary of everything going on in the argument.

## Evaluate the Answer Choices

Find the answer choice that matches your summary of the author's conclusion.

# THE KAPLAN METHOD IN ACTION

Now I'll walk you through an example to show you how the Kaplan Method can help you efficiently solve any Main Point question you'll see on test day.

1.  Industrial engineer: Some people have suggested that the problem of global warming should be addressed by pumping some of the carbon dioxide produced by the burning of fossil fuels into the deep ocean. Many environmentalists worry that this strategy would simply exchange one form of pollution for an equally destructive form. This worry is unfounded, however; much of the carbon dioxide now released into the atmosphere eventually ends up in the ocean anyway, where it does not cause environmental disturbances as destructive as global warming.

    Which one of the following most accurately expresses the conclusion of the industrial engineer's argument as a whole?

    (A)  Global warming from the emission of carbon dioxide into the atmosphere could be reduced by pumping some of that carbon dioxide into the deep ocean.

    (B)  Environmentalists worry that the strategy of pumping carbon dioxide into the deep ocean to reduce global warming would simply exchange one form of pollution for another, equally destructive one.

    (C)  Worrying that pumping carbon dioxide into the deep ocean to reduce global warming would simply exchange one form of pollution for another, equally destructive, form is unfounded.

    (D)  Much of the carbon dioxide now released into the atmosphere ends up in the ocean where it does not cause environmental disturbances as destructive as global warming.

    (E)  To reduce global warming, the strategy of pumping into the deep ocean at least some of the carbon dioxide now released into the atmosphere should be considered.[1]

## Step 1. Identify the Question Type

The term "conclusion" tells you this is a Main Point question.

## Step 2. Untangle the Stimulus

The industrial engineer first tells you what some people think about how to address global warming, and then adds that many environmentalists object to the strategy. When an author

---

[1]PrepTest 50, Sec. 2, Q 20

describes what "some people" think, be on the lookout for the author to rebut that statement, which is exactly what happens here. The engineer gives his opinion, set off by the contrast word "however." The author believes that the worry is unfounded because much of the carbon dioxide now released into the atmosphere eventually ends up in the ocean anyway. Bracket "This worry is unfounded." Those four words are the conclusion.

### Step 3. Make a Prediction

The correct answer will match the statement that you should bracket as the conclusion. However, note that the word "this" in the conclusion refers back to the prior sentence; the author's conclusion is that the worry about exchanging one form of pollution for another is unfounded.

### Step 4. Evaluate the Answer Choices

Choice (A) supports the suggestion that "some people" make in the first sentence. However, the engineer never endorses the strategy; he just says the environmentalists shouldn't worry about it. Eliminate this choice.

Choice (B) reiterates the environmentalists' concerns, not the engineer's conclusion. Cross this choice out.

Choice (C) correctly paraphrases the engineer's conclusion and is the correct answer.

Choice (D) comes from the evidence cited by the engineer at the end of the last sentence, not from the conclusion.

Choice (E) has the same problem as choice (A). The engineer never backs a strategy to address global warming. He says that one particular objection is unfounded.

# MAIN POINT QUESTIONS: NOW YOU TRY IT

It's now your turn to try a Main Point question on your own. Use the template I've provided after the question to guide you through the four-step Kaplan Method. (Note: On test day, you won't be writing out all the steps as you are in this exercise. However, as you are learning the Method, it's good practice to help it become second nature.) Remember to bracket conclusions and circle Keywords.

1.  Tallulah: The columnist attributes the decline of interest in novels to consumerism, technology, and the laziness of people who prefer watching television to reading a novel. However, in reaching this conclusion, the columnist has overlooked important evidence. It is surely relevant that contemporary fiction is frequently of poor quality—indeed, much of it is meaningless and depressing—whereas many good newspapers, magazines, professional journals, and books of other types are currently available.

    Which one of the following most accurately expresses the main conclusion of Tallulah's argument?

    (A) Contemporary fiction is unpopular because it is meaningless, depressing, and of poor overall quality.
    (B) The columnist's claim that novels are being displaced by consumerism, technology, and television is false.
    (C) The view expressed by the columnist was formed without considering all of the pertinent evidence.
    (D) People read as much as they used to, but most of the works they now read are not novels.
    (E) A large number of high-quality newspapers, magazines, professional journals, and nonfiction books are currently published.[2]

## Step 1. Identify the Question Type

_____

## Step 2. Untangle the Stimulus

_____

## Step 3. Make a Prediction

_____

## Step 4. Evaluate the Answer Choices

_____

_____

[2]PrepTest 41, Sec. 3, Q 18

# Explanations

### 1. (C)

Tallulah: The columnist attributes the decline of interest in novels to consumerism, technology, and the laziness of people who prefer watching television to reading a novel. ⟨However, in reaching this conclusion, the columnist has overlooked important evidence.⟩ It is surely relevant that contemporary fiction is frequently of poor quality—indeed, much of it is meaningless and depressing—whereas many good newspapers, magazines, professional journals, and books of other types are currently available.

Which one of the following most accurately expresses the main conclusion of Tallulah's argument?

(A)   Contemporary fiction is unpopular because it is meaningless, depressing, and of poor overall quality.

(B)   The columnist's claim that novels are being displaced by consumerism, technology, and television is false.

(C)   The view expressed by the columnist was formed without considering all of the pertinent evidence.

(D)   People read as much as they used to, but most of the works they now read are not novels.

(E)   A large number of high-quality newspapers, magazines, professional journals, and nonfiction books are currently published.[3]

## Step 1. Identify the Question Type

The question asks for the "main conclusion," which indicates a Main Point question.

## Step 2. Untangle the Stimulus

The author begins with a statement of someone else's thinking. Here, Tallulah states the columnist's explanation for the decline of interest in novels. She concludes—set off by the contrast Keyword "However"—that the columnist overlooked important information in reaching his conclusion. Tallulah then supports her conclusion with the evidence she thinks the columnist overlooked.

## Step 3. Make a Prediction

The correct answer choice will summarize Tallulah's belief that the columnist overlooked evidence in reaching his conclusion about the decline of interest in novels.

---

[3]PrepTest 41, Sec. 3, Q 18

### Step 4. Evaluate the Answer Choices

Choice (A) points out Tallulah's evidence that the columnist's appraisal is deficient, and doesn't mention the conclusion. Cross this choice out.

Choice (B) is extreme. Tallulah never says the columnist is wrong, she just says that the columnist's assessment is incomplete. Eliminate this choice as well.

Choice (C) properly captures Tallulah's conclusion, so it is the correct answer.

Choice (D) is incorrect for two reasons. First, Tallulah does not address whether people read as much as they did before. Second, it's an issue taken up by the columnist—not Tallulah—and he limits his discussion to reading novels—not other reading.

Choice (E) presents Tallulah's evidence, not her conclusion.

# DRILL: PRACTICING MAIN POINT QUESTIONS

Use the Kaplan Method to answer the following Main Point questions. Take this opportunity to practice and apply the steps in the Method so you are comfortable using them on test day. Be sure to circle conclusion and evidence Keywords and bracket the conclusion. Check your responses against the full explanations provided after the Drill.

1. Double-blind techniques should be used whenever possible in scientific experiments. They help prevent the misinterpretations that often arise due to expectations and opinions that scientists already hold, and clearly scientists should be extremely diligent in trying to avoid such misinterpretations.

   Which one of the following most accurately expresses the main conclusion of the argument?

   (A) Scientists' objectivity may be impeded by interpreting experimental evidence on the basis of expectations and opinions that they already hold.

   (B) It is advisable for scientists to use double-blind techniques in as high a proportion of their experiments as they can.

   (C) Scientists sometimes neglect to adequately consider the risk of misinterpreting evidence on the basis of prior expectations and opinions.

   (D) Whenever possible, scientists should refrain from interpreting evidence on the basis of previously formed expectations and convictions.

   (E) Double-blind experimental techniques are often an effective way of ensuring scientific objectivity.[4]

2. A strong correlation exists between what people value and the way they act. For example, those who value wealth tend to choose higher-paying jobs in undesirable locations over lower-paying jobs in desirable locations. Thus, knowing what people value can help one predict their actions.

   Which one of the following most accurately expresses the conclusion of the argument?

   (A) Knowing how people behave allows one to infer what they value.

   (B) People's claims concerning what they value are symptomatic of their actions.

   (C) No two people who value different things act the same way in identical circumstances.

   (D) People who value wealth tend to allow their desire for it to outweigh other concerns.

   (E) What people value can be a reliable indicator of how they will act.[5]

3. Publisher: The new year is approaching, and with it the seasonal demand for books on exercise and fitness. We must do whatever it takes to ship books in that category on time; our competitors have demonstrated a high level of organization, and we cannot afford to be outsold.

   Which one of the following most accurately expresses the main conclusion drawn in the publisher's argument?

   (A) The company should make shipping books its highest priority.

   (B) By increasing its efficiency, the company can maintain its competitive edge.

   (C) The company will be outsold if it does not maintain its competitors' high level of organization.

   (D) It is imperative that the company ship fitness and exercise books on time.

   (E) The company should do whatever is required in order to adopt its competitors' shipping practices.[6]

---

[4]PrepTest June 2007, Sec. 2, Q 10

[5]PrepTest 50, Sec. 2, Q 4
[6]PrepTest 51, Sec. 3, Q 16

**Answer Explanations follow on the next page.**

## Explanations

### 1.  (B)

<Double-blind techniques should be used whenever possible in scientific experiments.> They help prevent the misinterpretations that often arise due to expectations and opinions that scientists already hold, and clearly scientists should be extremely diligent in trying to avoid such misinterpretations.

Which one of the following most accurately expresses the main conclusion of the argument?

(A)     Scientists' objectivity may be impeded by interpreting experimental evidence on the basis of expectations and opinions that they already hold.

(B)     It is advisable for scientists to use double-blind techniques in as high a proportion of their experiments as they can.

(C)     Scientists sometimes neglect to adequately consider the risk of misinterpreting evidence on the basis of prior expectations and opinions.

(D)     Whenever possible, scientists should refrain from interpreting evidence on the basis of previously formed expectations and convictions.

(E)     Double-blind experimental techniques are often an effective way of ensuring scientific objectivity.[7]

### Step 1. Identify the Question Type

The question asks for the "main conclusion," which indicates a Main Point question.

### Step 2. Untangle the Stimulus

Because this is a Main Point question, it's unlikely that the stimulus will include a conclusion Keyword. However, this stimulus includes the word "clearly." Don't let it fool you, though. In this case, "clearly" is part of the evidence, not the conclusion.

The argument starts with a recommendation to use double-blind techniques in scientific experiments. The next sentence tells you why—because they help prevent misinterpretations and avoiding misinterpretations is important.

Remember that recommendations are important LSAT conclusion types, and the word "should" indicates a recommendation. If you are unsure whether the recommendation in the first sentence of the stimulus is the conclusion or the recommendation at the end is the conclusion, you can test which one supports the other by sticking the word "because" between them. For example, read the following two sentences. Which one makes sense?

---

[7]PrepTest June 2007, Sec. 2, Q 10

Double-blind techniques should be used whenever possible in scientific experiments BECAUSE scientists should be extremely diligent in trying to avoid such misinterpretations.

Scientists should be extremely diligent in trying to avoid such misinterpretations BECAUSE double-blind techniques should be used whenever possible in scientific experiments.

The first sentence puts the two statements in their proper claim and support format. Claim: Use Double-blind techniques. Why use them? Reason: want to avoid misinterpretations. It doesn't work the other way around.

### Step 3. Make a Prediction

Scientists should use double-blind techniques wherever possible. The rest of the argument is evidence for that conclusion.

### Step 4. Evaluate the Answer Choices

Choice (A) restates the evidence, so it is wrong. Cross it out.

Choice (B) reiterates the conclusion, so it is the correct answer.

Choice (C) is not mentioned in the argument, but adds evidence to institute double-blind techniques.

Choice (D), like choice (A), repeats the evidence.

Choice (E) may be true, but the conclusion goes beyond *recognizing* the effectiveness of double-blind procedures. It *recommends* them.

### 2.   (E)

A strong correlation exists between what people value and the way they act. For example, those who value wealth tend to choose higher-paying jobs in undesirable locations over lower-paying jobs in desirable locations. <Thus,> knowing what people value can help one predict their actions.>

Which one of the following most accurately expresses the (conclusion) of the argument?

(A)   Knowing how people behave allows one to infer what they value.
(B)   People's claims concerning what they value are symptomatic of their actions.
(C)   No two people who value different things act the same way in identical circumstances.
(D)   People who value wealth tend to allow their desire for it to outweigh other concerns.
(E)   What people value can be a reliable indicator of how they will act.[8]

---

[8]PrepTest 50, Sec. 2, Q 4

### Step 1. Identify the Question Type

The word "conclusion" tells you that this is a Main Point question.

### Step 2. Untangle the Stimulus

Unlike most Main Point questions, this argument does include a conclusion Keyword—"Thus," in the last sentence. The author states that knowing what people value helps predict what they'll do. The author points out a correlation between what people value and the way they act and gives an example to support the conclusion.

### Step 3. Make a Prediction

The correct answer will summarize the last sentence of the stimulus.

### Step 4. Evaluate the Answer Choices

Choice (A) get the terms backward. The conclusion says people's values predict their behavior. Because you were given a clear conclusion Keyword, expect the wrong answer choices to closely mimic—but be slightly off—the correct match to your bracketed statement. This answer has all the right words, but it takes the logic in the wrong direction. Cross this choice out.

Choice (B) also misses the mark. The conclusion talks about what people value, not what they claim they value. Move on to the next choice.

Choice (C) is extreme as well as outside the scope of the argument. The author claims that values predict behavior, not that values tell you exactly how someone or a group of people will act in any particular situation. Eliminate this choice.

Choice (D) is outside the scope. The conclusion refers to values generally and not to any specific value. With this choice out, that leaves only one.

Choice (E) presents a correct summary of the conclusion and is the correct answer.

## 3. **(D)**

Publisher: The new year is approaching, and with it the seasonal demand for books on exercise and fitness. <We must do whatever it takes to ship books in that category on time;> our competitors have demonstrated a high level of organization, and we cannot afford to be outsold.

Which one of the following most accurately expresses the (main conclusion) drawn in the publisher's argument?

(A)   The company should make shipping books its highest priority.

(B)   By increasing its efficiency, the company can maintain its competitive edge.

(C)   The company will be outsold if it does not maintain its competitors' high level of organization.

(D)   It is imperative that the company ship fitness and exercise books on time.

(E)   The company should do whatever is required in order to adopt its competitors' shipping practices.[9]

### Step 1. Identify the Question Type

The phrase "main conclusion" indicates that this is a Main Point question.

### Step 2. Untangle the Stimulus

The publisher recognizes a demand for certain books. She knows the competitors are ready and organized, and she cannot let them outsell her. These facts support the publisher's conclusion that her team must do whatever it takes to ship the books on time.

You can also use the "one-sentence test" to find the conclusion. In this case, the only sentence that can stand on its own as the main point is, "We must do whatever it takes to ship books in that category on time."

### Step 3. Make a Prediction

Find the answer choice that best matches the conclusion you bracketed.

### Step 4. Evaluate the Answer Choices

Choice (A) is too broad. The argument doesn't advise making book shipping the highest priority. Rather, the publisher insists that exercise and fitness books be shipped by whatever means necessary and on time. Eliminate this choice.

Choice (B) is outside the scope of the argument. The publisher doesn't discuss efficiency. This choice is out.

---

[9]PrepTest 51, Sec. 3, Q 16

Choice (C) is extreme. You know the publisher can't afford to be outsold, but you don't know she will be outsold if her team doesn't maintain its competitors' high level of organization. Go on to the next choice.

Choice (D) correctly rephrases the publisher's main point. This is the correct answer.

Choice (E) is outside the scope of the argument. The publisher concludes the exercise and fitness books must be shipped on time. She doesn't talk about how to accomplish that directive.

## MAIN POINT REVIEW

Before you proceed to the next chapter, turn to Appendix A and complete the review exercise for Main Point questions. A completed chart is included in Appendix B.

# CHAPTER 18

# RECENT TRENDS

With all the effort you're putting into your test preparation, it makes sense that you keep up to date on the most recent trends appearing in the Logical Reasoning sections. While the exact distribution of question types isn't set in stone, there are patterns that contribute to the predictability of the LSAT. In this brief chapter, I'll review the structural trends on the most recent LSATs with you.

## LOGICAL REASONING ON RECENT LSATS: BREAKDOWN BY QUESTION TYPE

Table 18.1 shows the question breakdown of the four most recent tests at the time of this writing, along with the average number of questions per question type.

Please note that no February tests are included because the LSAC does not regularly release them.

**Table 18.1**

| Question Types | PrepTests | | | |
|---|---|---|---|---|
| | 61<br>Oct. '10 | 60<br>June '10 | 59<br>Dec. '09 | 58<br>Oct. '09 |
| Assumption | 6 | 7 | 7 | 12 |
| Weaken/Strengthen | 10 | 9 | 9 | 6 |
| Flaw | 6 | 7 | 10 | 7 |
| Inference | 7 | 6 | 7 | 7 |
| Principle | 5 | 5 | 4 | 7 |
| Method of Argument | 1 | 2 | 2 | 3 |
| Parallel Reasoning | 3 | 4 | 3 | 2 |
| Paradox | 5 | 3 | 4 | 5 |
| Point at Issue | 2 | 1 | 1 | 0 |
| Role of a Statement | 3 | 3 | 2 | 0 |
| Main Point | 3 | 2 | 2 | 2 |
| Total Logical Reasoning Questions | 51 | 49* | 51 | 51 |

*One question was removed from scoring by LSAC

# PREDICTABILITY IS THE TREND

The good news about the Logical Reasoning sections is they've remained consistent over the last few years. Generally speaking, the two scored Logical Reasoning sections per test represent 50 to 51 questions on the LSAT, with each section having 24 to 26 questions.

Assumption, Weaken, Strengthen, and Flaw questions make up half the Logical Reasoning questions and thus demand most of your attention. While an individual question type may have a few more or a few less questions in the mix, the Logical Reasoning section has not been a surprise for test takers. In addition to consistent numbers, the question types have remained the same.

Since this is the LSAT, you know you can't infer what is not provided to you. So, predictability doesn't guarantee that the test won't change at all. However, predictability, combined with the slow rate of changes made to the LSAT, indicate that Logical Reasoning is unlikely to present big surprises on test day.

# THE IMPORTANCE OF THE KAPLAN METHOD

In this book, you have learned the Kaplan Method, a proven approach to efficiently and accurately navigate the Logical Reasoning sections on the LSAT. And you know the LSAT and each section are predictable. Use that to your advantage on test day and in your preparation.

# PART III

# FULL-SECTION PRACTICE

# CHAPTER 19

# Timing and Section Management in a Nutshell

In Parts I and II, you learned the Kaplan Method for Logical Reasoning and applied it to the twelve question types. While familiarity with the questions and mastery of the logical reasoning skills will help you score points on test day, your preparation is incomplete without training in section timing and management. In Part III, I'll introduce you to some basic concepts to help you manage the section most efficiently and maximize your score. Then, you'll have a chance to take two complete Logical Reasoning sections.

I want to offer one bit of caution before you proceed. Don't take a timed section until you've completed Parts I and II in this book. Remember we talked in the beginning about treating LSAT preparation like learning a skill. Timed training without adequate preparation doesn't make sense. You wouldn't run a race without practicing the fundamentals and conditioning. Don't do it on the LSAT either.

# EFFICIENCY, NOT SPEED

Every LSAT student I've ever taught wished they had more time on each section or wished they had no time restriction at all. However, every section is strictly timed at 35 minutes, so you need to learn to work within that time frame and use every minute to get as much out of every section as you can. Your goal is not to finish a section but rather to get as many right answers as you can in the time allotted. So, you must strategically decide how you can get the most points in your limited time.

As I tell my students, I don't care how fast you got it wrong because the LSAT only gives points for correct answers. As you become more proficient at the Kaplan Method, practice more questions, and make strategic section decisions, you will become more efficient and accurate in your work. You can measure your progress by an increase in the number of questions you get to in 35 minutes and in the number you get correct—not by your speed.

# OPTIMAL TIMING

Ideally, you will process and answer each of the approximately 25 Logical Reasoning questions in a section in 75 to 90 seconds to stay within the 35-minute time limit. A practiced strategy is essential to achieve this pace and maintain the necessary focus. While finishing the section with efficiency and accuracy is the goal, I also know that you may not complete every section. To maximize your score, approach that situation with control and strategic thinking.

## Strategic Guessing

The last thing you want to do is run out of time on a section with blank answers on your test grid. Unlike the SAT, the LSAT has no penalty for wrong answers. So, be sure to enter an answer for every question. If you know you will not get to every question, set aside time at the end of the 35 minutes to fill in the blanks with your guess. I recommend picking a letter and using that same letter as your fall back. Using a consistent letter to guess actually takes less time than if you try to think about it. You're also more likely to get something right than if you switch it up. No letter is more likely to be the answer than any other so pick your own lucky letter and stick with it.

Just remember, this is a competition and you need to maximize the value of every second of the test. If you are running out of time, fill in those other bubbles with a guess, but continue working until the very second that the proctor calls "pencils down." Then, immediately put your pencil down.

What can you do in very limited time at the end of sections? Well, Parallel Reasoning questions are often a time drain, but if you save them for last, remember that you can make a lot of progress toward honing in on the right answer just by comparing conclusion types between the stimulus and the answer choices. An educated guess from one of three remaining choices is much better odds than a blind one of five.

If you don't have enough time to work a problem, but have 15 seconds to scan the choices, then generally you are better off with a more modest-sounding answer and should eliminate the extreme sounding answers, especially on an Inference or a Necessary Assumption question. Of course, you have seen plenty of exceptions to this rule, so don't think you can just skip reading the problem when you have the time to do so!

If you only have 30 seconds to work on a Strengthen or Weaken question, then try to immediately hone in on the conclusion. It's the most important component of the argument. Scan the choices for the one that is either most in line with the conclusion (Strengthen) or opposed to the conclusion (Weaken).

The main point is that there is always something that you can do to try to improve your score in every second of those limited 35 minutes of a Logical Reasoning section, even if you don't have the normal minute and a half to work the problem fully. The LSAT tests your competitive drive and efficiency, as well as your logic skills.

# SECTION MANAGEMENT: YOU'RE IN CONTROL
## Basic Anatomy of a Logical Reasoning Section

By understanding the basic anatomy of a Logical Reasoning section, you can take more control of it and spend your time more efficiently.

Take a look at Kaplan's Logical Reasoning: Typical Question Difficulties Chart.

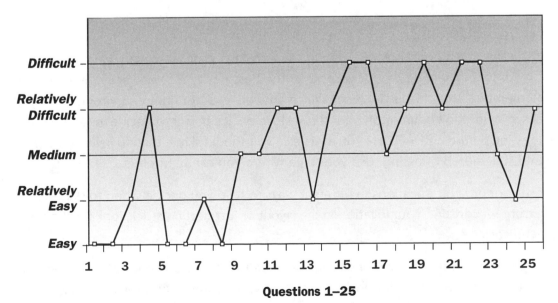

**The Logical Reasoning Section: The Inside Story**

Questions 1–25

Notice the questions generally go from less difficult to more difficult as you proceed through a section. Of course, you'll find a difficult question or two early in the section. Such placement rewards test takers who answer skillfully or skip a tough question and punishes test takers who insist on sticking with a question regardless of the amount of time they've wasted on it. You'll also find easier questions toward the end of the section, rewarding those who get there and penalizing those who get bogged down and never get to the end.

One more point about the typical layout of a Logical Reasoning section: The difficulty level tends to spike from around questions 14 to 22, in what we at Kaplan call the "danger zone." Practice working up to question 13, 14, or 15 (wherever there is a natural page break) and then turn to the end of the section and work back from there. For example, you can work through the first four pages then turn to the last page and the last question of the section and begin working from the last question in to the middle. Be sure you stay within the section and do not accidentally turn to the following section—that could result in a penalty. Taking the questions in the manner described will get you to the "danger zone" at the end of your 35 minutes. If you are running out of time, you want to run out of time where the questions are harder and you might do just as well to guess anyway.

Understanding the anatomy of a Logical Reasoning section helps you set a pace for yourself. Although you need to be aware of where you are in the 35 minutes, it's a waste of time and energy to track your time on individual questions. Set a goal of 15 minutes for the first fifteen questions. The difficulty level generally builds through the section so you want to set a brisker pace in the beginning and bank some time for the more difficult questions in the danger zone. If you find that a question is bogging you down, skip it and come back to it at the end. Use the next 15 minutes to work from the last question back toward question 15. Use the final five minutes to make a guess with your lucky letter on all the questions you skipped and to revisit any answers you are not confident about.

## Strategic Skipping

Because each question is worth the same value toward your score, you want to manage the Logical Reasoning section to put yourself in the best position to get as many points as you can. Remember, law schools don't see which answers you get right and wrong. They just get a final score, so don't belabor one question. Move on. It's better to decide in ten seconds that the question is hard and will take you a while so you should skip it than to invest three minutes in it and still end up guessing. Use your time where you can get points.

You can spot difficult questions in different ways to help you decide when to skip a question. Aside from recognizing your location in the layout or just getting stuck, look for the following characteristics.

- Longer stimulus and/or answers: The more text there is, the longer it can take to get through the material. Principle and Parallel Reasoning questions typically fall in this category. The Kaplan Method will help you work through the text more efficiently. However, longer text is one way to make a question objectively more difficult.

- General language: Language that is not specific to the content of the stimulus but describes it in general terms can also be difficult to wade through.
- Similar answer choices: Each choice may use similar wording from the stimulus making it more difficult to distinguish between them.
- Formal logic: While formal logic is a useful tool to simplify a stimulus and you want to embrace it as such, it does add a layer of work until you're comfortable with it.
- Difficult topic: The LSAT does not require any outside knowledge, but some topics like science and economics can be difficult for some students. If you find yourself confused by the text because of the topic and you're on your second read yet no closer to untangling the stimulus, move on.
- Unknown question type: If you can't determine the question type, you can't know your task. Working through the stimulus without that direction will just slow you down and waste your time.
- Historically tough question type: Certainly, you can't skip every Assumption question, for example, if that's your toughest type. However, use that knowledge when you run in to your toughest type in the danger zone or when you're down to minimal time and you can only get to one more question.

The important lesson is that you recognize questions that are more challenging for you and use that knowledge to decide whether to skip a question or not. You're not admitting defeat, just making a strategic choice to keep moving and return to it if you have time. Remember to circle a question you skip so you can refer to it later. Also, make sure you bubble your answers properly on the grid sheet. If you skip a question in your test booklet, be sure to skip it on the bubble sheet.

# COMMON WRONG ANSWER TYPES

The most direct route to finding the correct answer to a Logical Reasoning question is to predict the answer and find a match in the answer choices. Sometimes, however, your prediction is wrong, you can't find a match, or you get down to two or three answers and can't decide between them. Being familiar with the common wrong answer types will help you sort through the remaining answers. If nothing else, you can eliminate answers that fall into these categories to improve your chance of picking the right answer.

## Extreme Answers

Extreme answers include words like "always," "must," "will," "never," "all," "none," and "every."

Extreme language is not problematic if the language in the stimulus matches the extreme nature of the answer choice. However, extreme language often indicates a wrong answer.

The correct answer for most question types can never be more extreme than the stimulus. In general, more modest is better, especially for Necessary Assumption and Inference questions.

Here's an example:

Braille is a method of producing text by means of raised dots that can be read by touch. A recent development in technology will allow flat computer screens to be made of a material that can be heated in patterns that replicate the patterns used in braille. (Since) the thermal device will utilize the same symbol system as braille, <it follows that anyone who is accustomed to reading braille can easily adapt to the use of this electronic system.>

Which one of the following is an (assumption) on which the conclusion (depends)?

(A)  Braille is the only symbol system that can be readily adapted for use with the new thermal screen. (*Extreme answer*)

(C)  People with the tactile ability to discriminate symbols in braille have an ability to discriminate similar patterns on a flat heated surface.[1] (*Correct assumption*)

## Out of Scope Answers

Out of scope answers bring in new information that is immaterial or irrelevant to the stimulus.

Don't be fooled by new information not included in the stimulus; it may or may not be outside the scope of the argument depending on the question type. For example, Strengthen and Weaken answers often present new information to the argument to make the argument more or less likely to be true. Here's an example:

The people most likely to watch a televised debate between political candidates are the most committed members of the electorate and thus the most likely to have already made up their minds about whom to support. Furthermore, following a debate, uncommitted viewers are generally undecided about who won the debate. <(Hence,) winning a televised debate does little to bolster one's chances of winning an election.>

The reasoning in the argument is most (vulnerable to) (criticism) because the argument (fails to consider) the possibility that

(B)  the voting behavior of people who do not watch a televised debate is influenced by reports about the debate (*Correct answer that describes the flaw in the argument*)

(C)  there are differences of opinion about what constitutes winning or losing a debate[2] (*Out of scope answer*)

---

[1]PrepTest 22, Sec. 2, Q 1

[2]PrepTest 41, Sec. 1, Q 20

## 180 Answers

A 180 answer is the opposite answer to the correct choice. It can appear in all question types, but is especially prevalent in Strengthen and Weaken questions.

For example, a 180 answer to a Strengthen question will weaken the argument, and vice versa. What makes 180s so tricky is that they typically include terms or ideas that are similar to the correct answer, but take the argument in the wrong direction.

Here's an example:

Several companies will soon offer personalized electronic news services, delivered via cable or telephone lines and displayed on a television. People using these services can view continually updated stories on those topics for which they subscribe. (Since) these services will provide people with the information they are looking for more quickly and efficiently than printed newspapers can, <newspaper sales will decline drastically if these services become widely available.>

Which one of the following, if true, most seriously (weakens) the argument?

(A)   In reading newspapers, most people not only look for stories on specific topics but also like to idly browse through headlines or pictures for amusing stories on unfamiliar or unusual topics. (*Correct answer weakens the argument*)

(D)   The average monthly cost of subscribing to several channels on a personalized electronic news service will approximately equal the cost of a month's subscription to a newspaper.[3] (*180 answer strengthens the argument*)

---

[3]PrepTest 36, Sec. 3, Q 2

## Distorted Answers

A distorted answer will use language or concepts from the stimulus but misapply them in some way.

Here's an example:

<Publicity campaigns for endangered species are unlikely to have much impact on the most important environmental problems,> for while the ease of attributing feelings to large mammals facilitates evoking sympathy for them, it is more difficult to elicit sympathy for other kinds of organisms, such as the soil microorganisms on which large ecosystems and agriculture depend.

Which one of the following is an assumption on which the argument depends?

(A)  The most important environmental problems involve endangered species other than large mammals.  (*Correct assumption*)

(B)  Microorganisms cannot experience pain or have other feelings.[4]  (*Distorted answer*)

## Irrelevant Comparisons

Irrelevant comparisons will compare two things that are unrelated or don't affect the argument. If the argument is comparative, however, it's likely that the correct answer will be comparative in nature as well.

Here's an example:

Barnes:  The two newest employees at this company have salaries that are too high for the simple tasks normally assigned to new employees and duties that are too complex for inexperienced workers. Hence, <the salaries and the complexity of the duties of these two newest employees should be reduced.>

Which one of the following is an assumption on which Barnes's argument depends?

(C)  The two newest employees are not experienced at their occupations.  (*Correct assumption*)

(E)  The salaries of the two newest employees are no higher than the salaries that other companies pay for workers with a similar level of experience.[5]  (*Irrelevant comparison*)

---

[4]PrepTest 35, Sec. 4, Q 16

[5]PrepTest 29, Sec. 1, Q 5

## TAKE CONTROL WITH THE KAPLAN METHOD

Of course, the best approach is to improve your logical reasoning skills and practice the Kaplan Method. But it's inevitable that everyone runs into questions they need to let go of, so practice it.

The best test takers take control of the Logical Reasoning sections and strategically use the time available to make accurate choices and get the most points possible. If you follow the Kaplan Method, you can be one of them.

# CHAPTER 20

# HOW TO USE THE
# PRACTICE SECTION

The following two chapters include the two full-length Logical Reasoning sections as they appeared on the December 2007 LSAT (now called PrepTest 53). Set aside 35 minutes for each section and take them in a place where you won't be interrupted. If you can access the building in which you'll take your actual test, consider going there for practice. You'll want to time yourself strictly and follow the test instructions to the letter, just as you'll have to on test day.

## TAKE THE PRACTICE SECTIONS

As I cautioned earlier, don't take a full-length section before you've completed the first two parts of this book. Full-length section practice is about "putting it all together" and pacing. It's not for learning the fundamentals of question types and methods, but rather for improving your ability to quickly and efficiently apply best practices to each question. Of course, you'll conduct a review of your performance using the explanations that follow each section and use that information to hone your skills.

With timed, section-length practice, your goal is to get as many points as possible. Skip and guess as needed to maximize your efficiency and increase the overall number of correct answers you can produce. Use the tools you will use on test day—a number 2 pencil and an analog watch. Also, clear your desk of all prohibited test day items including food, drinks, and cell phones.

Remember that there is no "guessing penalty," so fill in an answer for every question. Don't leave an answer blank because you want to see what you would get without guessing. You should guess on test day, so it's unrealistic not to do it in practice. If you can eliminate two or three of the wrong answers, guess from the remaining choices. When you review the section, you can look to see how you would be able to answer the question quickly and effectively, but don't let that deter you from guessing and skipping when it's in your interest to do so.

On test day, you will get credit only for the answers on your bubble sheet. No one will look in your test booklet to see what you've circled or the work you've done. So, practice now by scoring your section based only on what you bubbled into the grid.

## CALCULATE YOUR SCORE

Use the answer key that follows each section to determine your score. Mark each of the answers you got right or wrong. There's no way to determine your overall LSAT score from any single section. Test scores are produced based on the overall number of correct answers you produced.

Here are a couple of score conversion tables from recently-released LSATs. There are almost always 101 scored questions per LSAT, of which 24–26 come from the Logical Reasoning section.

---

### SCORING WORKSHEET

1. Enter the number of questions you answered correctly in each section

   NUMBER CORRECT

   SECTION I . . . . . . . . . . _____

   SECTION II . . . . . . . . . _____

   SECTION III . . . . . . . . _____

   SECTION IV . . . . . . . . _____

2. Enter the sum here: _____  THIS IS YOUR RAW SCORE.

| **CONVERSION CHART** | | |
|---|---|---|
| For converting Raw Score to the 120–180 LSAT Scaled Score LSAT Prep Test 47 | | |
| REPORTED SCORE | LOWEST RAW SCORE | HIGHEST RAW SCORE |
| 180 | 99 | 100 |
| 179 | 98 | 98 |
| 178 | 97 | 97 |
| 177 | 96 | 96 |
| 176 | --* | --* |
| 175 | 95 | 95 |
| 174 | 94 | 94 |
| 173 | 93 | 93 |
| 172 | 92 | 92 |
| 171 | 91 | 91 |
| 170 | 90 | 90 |
| 169 | 89 | 89 |
| 168 | 88 | 88 |
| 167 | 87 | 87 |
| 166 | 85 | 86 |
| 165 | 84 | 84 |
| 164 | 83 | 83 |
| 163 | 81 | 82 |
| 162 | 80 | 80 |
| 161 | 78 | 79 |
| 160 | 77 | 77 |
| 159 | 75 | 76 |
| 158 | 73 | 74 |
| 157 | 72 | 72 |
| 156 | 70 | 71 |
| 155 | 68 | 69 |
| 154 | 66 | 67 |
| 153 | 65 | 65 |
| 152 | 63 | 64 |
| 151 | 61 | 63 |
| 150 | 59 | 60 |
| 149 | 57 | 58 |
| 148 | 55 | 56 |
| 147 | 54 | 54 |
| 146 | 52 | 53 |
| 145 | 50 | 51 |
| 144 | 48 | 49 |
| 143 | 46 | 47 |
| 142 | 45 | 45 |
| 141 | 43 | 44 |
| 140 | 41 | 42 |
| 139 | 40 | 40 |
| 138 | 38 | 39 |
| 137 | 36 | 37 |
| 136 | 35 | 35 |
| 135 | 33 | 34 |
| 134 | 32 | 32 |
| 133 | 30 | 31 |
| 132 | 29 | 29 |
| 131 | 27 | 28 |
| 130 | 26 | 26 |
| 129 | 25 | 25 |
| 128 | 24 | 24 |
| 127 | 22 | 23 |
| 126 | 21 | 21 |
| 125 | 20 | 20 |
| 124 | 19 | 19 |
| 123 | 18 | 18 |
| 122 | 17 | 17 |
| 121 | 16 | 16 |
| 120 | 0 | 15 |

*There is no raw score that will produce this scaled score for the test.

| **CONVERSION CHART** | | |
|---|---|---|
| For converting Raw Score to the 120–180 LSAT Scaled Score LSAT Prep Test 50 | | |
| REPORTED SCORE | LOWEST RAW SCORE | HIGHEST RAW SCORE |
| 180 | 98 | 100 |
| 179 | 97 | 97 |
| 178 | --* | --* |
| 177 | 96 | 96 |
| 176 | 95 | 95 |
| 175 | 94 | 94 |
| 174 | --* | --* |
| 173 | 93 | 93 |
| 172 | 92 | 92 |
| 171 | 91 | 91 |
| 170 | 90 | 90 |
| 169 | 89 | 89 |
| 168 | 88 | 88 |
| 167 | 86 | 87 |
| 166 | 85 | 85 |
| 165 | 84 | 84 |
| 164 | 83 | 83 |
| 163 | 81 | 82 |
| 162 | 80 | 80 |
| 161 | 78 | 79 |
| 160 | 77 | 77 |
| 159 | 75 | 76 |
| 158 | 73 | 74 |
| 157 | 72 | 72 |
| 156 | 70 | 71 |
| 155 | 68 | 69 |
| 154 | 66 | 67 |
| 153 | 64 | 65 |
| 152 | 63 | 63 |
| 151 | 61 | 62 |
| 150 | 59 | 60 |
| 149 | 57 | 58 |
| 148 | 55 | 56 |
| 147 | 53 | 54 |
| 146 | 52 | 52 |
| 145 | 50 | 51 |
| 144 | 48 | 49 |
| 143 | 46 | 47 |
| 142 | 45 | 45 |
| 141 | 43 | 44 |
| 140 | 41 | 42 |
| 139 | 40 | 40 |
| 138 | 38 | 39 |
| 137 | 36 | 37 |
| 136 | 35 | 35 |
| 135 | 33 | 34 |
| 134 | 32 | 32 |
| 133 | 30 | 31 |
| 132 | 29 | 29 |
| 131 | 27 | 28 |
| 130 | 26 | 26 |
| 129 | 25 | 25 |
| 128 | 23 | 24 |
| 127 | 22 | 22 |
| 126 | 21 | 21 |
| 125 | 20 | 20 |
| 124 | 18 | 19 |
| 123 | 17 | 17 |
| 122 | 16 | 16 |
| 121 | 15 | 15 |
| 120 | 0 | 14 |

*There is no raw score that will produce this scaled score for the test.

By estimating the number of correct responses you'd generate from the remaining sections of the test, you can gain an idea of the impact that your Logical Reasoning performance will have on your score.

To improve your performance on the other sections of the test, study this book's companion volumes, *LSAT Reading Comprehension: Strategies and Tactics* and *LSAT Logic Games: Strategies and Tactics*.

If you haven't done so already, register for the Kaplan LSAT Experience test for additional section practice at www.kaptest.com/LSAT.

The Kaplan LSAT Experience provides you with the chance to take the most recently released, full-length LSAT under all of the proctoring conditions and rules that will apply on test day. You'll receive your score and a detailed performance analysis, answers and explanations for all of the questions, and access to an On Demand review of the test's most difficult questions (as determined by aggregate test-taker performance) delivered by some of Kaplan's most experienced LSAT instructors. Register at www.kaplanlsat.com/lsatexperience.

I recommend that you get as much full-length test practice and additional Logical Reasoning section practice as you can. The more questions you see, and the more familiar and proficient you become with the Kaplan Method, the better prepared you'll be on test day.

## LEARN FROM YOUR PERFORMANCE

Most importantly, put time aside to review your performance. You need to go back to each question whether you got it right or wrong and review the Kaplan Method as well as the reason why the right answer is right and why the other four are wrong. You don't have to do it all in one sitting. What's important is that you do it. Think of this exercise like a project debriefing or watching game film to review your performance. What do you see that you want to make sure you do again or change? What do you need to practice?

Proceed with calm, focus, confidence, and patience. You need to find your LSAT zone and practice what you've learned. Good luck!

# CHAPTER 21

# FULL-LENGTH SECTION I[1]

Section I
Time—35 minutes
25 Questions

<u>Directions:</u> The questions in this section are based on the reasoning contained in brief statements or passages. For some questions, more than one of the choices could conceivably answer the question. However, you are to choose the <u>best</u> answer; that is, the response that most accurately and completely answers the question. You should not make assumptions that are by commonsense standards implausible, superfluous, or incompatible with the passage. After you have chosen the best answer, blacken the corresponding space on your answer sheet.

[1]PrepTest 53, Sec. 1

1. Consumer advocate: Businesses are typically motivated primarily by the desire to make as great a profit as possible, and advertising helps businesses to achieve this goal. But it is clear that the motive of maximizing profits does not impel businesses to present accurate information in their advertisements. It follows that consumers should be skeptical of the claims made in advertisements.

Each of the following, if true, would strengthen the consumer advocate's argument EXCEPT:

(A) Businesses know that they can usually maximize their profits by using inaccurate information in their advertisements.

(B) Businesses have often included inaccurate information in their advertisements.

(C) Many consumers have a cynical attitude toward advertising.

(D) Those who create advertisements are less concerned with the accuracy than with the creativity of advertisements.

(E) The laws regulating truth in advertising are not applicable to many of the most common forms of inaccurate advertising.

2. Elaine: The purpose of art museums is to preserve artworks and make them available to the public. Museums, therefore, should seek to acquire and display the best examples of artworks from each artistic period and genre, even if some of these works are not recognized by experts as masterpieces.

Frederick: Art museums ought to devote their limited resources to acquiring the works of recognized masters in order to ensure the preservation of the greatest artworks.

Elaine's and Frederick's statements provide the most support for the claim that they would disagree about whether

(A) many artistic masterpieces are not recognized as such by art experts

(B) museums should seek to represent all genres of art in their collections

(C) art museums should seek to preserve works of art

(D) an art museum ought to acquire an unusual example of a period or genre if more characteristic examples are prohibitively expensive

(E) all of the artworks that experts identify as masterpieces are actually masterpieces

3. Science columnist: It is clear why humans have so many diseases in common with cats. Many human diseases are genetically based, and cats are genetically closer to humans than are any other mammals except nonhuman primates. Each of the genes identified so far in cats has an exact counterpart in humans.

Which one of the following, if true, most weakens the science columnist's explanation for the claim that humans have so many diseases in common with cats?

(A) Cats have built up resistance to many of the diseases they have in common with humans.

(B) Most diseases that humans have in common with cats have no genetic basis.

(C) Cats have more diseases in common with nonhuman primates than with humans.

(D) Many of the diseases humans have in common with cats are mild and are rarely diagnosed.

(E) Humans have more genes in common with nonhuman primates than with cats.

4. This region must find new ways to help business grow. After all, shoe manufacturing used to be a major local industry, but recently has experienced severe setbacks due to overseas competition, so there is a need for expansion into new manufacturing areas. Moreover, our outdated public policy generally inhibits business growth.

Which one of the following most accurately expresses the main conclusion drawn in the argument?

(A) The region needs to find new ways to enhance business growth.

(B) Shoe manufacturing is no longer a major source of income in the region.

(C) Shoe manufacturing in the region has dramatically declined due to overseas competition.

(D) Business in the region must expand into new areas of manufacturing.

(E) Outdated public policy inhibits business growth in the region.

5. As a result of modern medicine, more people have been able to enjoy long and pain-free lives. But the resulting increase in life expectancy has contributed to a steady increase in the proportion of the population that is of advanced age. This population shift is creating potentially devastating financial problems for some social welfare programs.

   Which one of the following propositions is most precisely exemplified by the situation presented above?

   (A) Technical or scientific innovation cannot be the solution to all problems.
   (B) Implementing technological innovations should be delayed until the resulting social changes can be managed.
   (C) Every enhancement of the quality of life has unavoidable negative consequences.
   (D) All social institutions are affected by a preoccupation with prolonging life.
   (E) Solving one set of problems can create a different set of problems.

6. Since Jackie is such a big fan of Moral Vacuum's music, she will probably like The Cruel Herd's new album. Like Moral Vacuum, The Cruel Herd on this album plays complex rock music that employs the acoustic instrumentation and harmonic sophistication of early sixties jazz. The Cruel Herd also has very witty lyrics, full of puns and sardonic humor, like some of Moral Vacuum's best lyrics.

   Which one of the following, if true, most strengthens the argument?

   (A) Jackie has not previously cared for The Cruel Herd, but on the new album The Cruel Herd's previous musical arranger has been replaced by Moral Vacuum's musical arranger.
   (B) Though The Cruel Herd's previous albums' production quality was not great, the new album is produced by one of the most widely employed producers in the music industry.
   (C) Like Moral Vacuum, The Cruel Herd regularly performs in clubs popular with many students at the university that Jackie attends.
   (D) All of the music that Jackie prefers to listen to on a regular basis is rock music.
   (E) Jackie's favorite Moral Vacuum songs have lyrics that are somber and marked by a strong political awareness.

7. Superconductors are substances that conduct electricity without resistance at low temperatures. Their use, however, will never be economically feasible, unless there is a substance that superconducts at a temperature above minus 148 degrees Celsius. If there is such a substance, that substance must be an alloy of niobium and germanium. Unfortunately, such alloys superconduct at temperatures no higher than minus 160 degrees Celsius.

   If the statements above are true, which one of the following must also be true?

   (A) The use of superconductors will never be economically feasible.
   (B) If the alloys of niobium and germanium do not superconduct at temperatures above minus 148 degrees Celsius, then there are other substances that will do so.
   (C) The use of superconductors could be economically feasible if there is a substance that superconducts at temperatures below minus 148 degrees Celsius.
   (D) Alloys of niobium and germanium do not superconduct at temperatures below minus 160 degrees Celsius.
   (E) No use of alloys of niobium and germanium will ever be economically feasible.

8.  Doctor: In three separate studies, researchers compared children who had slept with night-lights in their rooms as infants to children who had not. In the first study, the children who had slept with night-lights proved more likely to be nearsighted, but the later studies found no correlation between night-lights and nearsightedness. However, the children in the first study were younger than those in the later studies. This suggests that if night-lights cause nearsightedness, the effect disappears with age.

Which one of the following, if true, would most weaken the doctor's argument?

(A)   A fourth study comparing infants who were currently sleeping with night-lights to infants who were not did not find any correlation between night-lights and nearsightedness.

(B)   On average, young children who are already very nearsighted are no more likely to sleep with night-lights than young children who are not already nearsighted.

(C)   In a study involving children who had not slept with night-lights as infants but had slept with night-lights when they were older, most of the children studied were not nearsighted.

(D)   The two studies in which no correlation was found did not examine enough children to provide significant support for any conclusion regarding a causal relationship between night-lights and nearsightedness.

(E)   In a fourth study involving 100 children who were older than those in any of the first three studies, several of the children who had slept with night-lights as infants were nearsighted.

9.  Global surveys estimate the earth's population of nesting female leatherback turtles has fallen by more than two-thirds in the past 15 years. Any species whose population declines by more than two-thirds in 15 years is in grave danger of extinction, so the leatherback turtle is clearly in danger of extinction.

Which one of the following is an assumption that the argument requires?

(A)   The decline in the population of nesting female leatherback turtles is proportional to the decline in the leatherback turtle population as a whole.

(B)   If the global population of leatherback turtles falls by more than two-thirds over the next 15 years, the species will eventually become extinct.

(C)   The global population of leatherback turtles consists in roughly equal numbers of females and males.

(D)   Very few leatherback turtles exist in captivity.

(E)   The only way to ensure the continued survival of leatherback turtles in the wild is to breed them in captivity.

10.  Public health experts have waged a long-standing educational campaign to get people to eat more vegetables, which are known to help prevent cancer. Unfortunately, the campaign has had little impact on people's diets. The reason is probably that many people simply dislike the taste of most vegetables. Thus, the campaign would probably be more effective if it included information on ways to make vegetables more appetizing.

Which one of the following, if true, most strengthens the argument?

(A)   The campaign to get people to eat more vegetables has had little impact on the diets of most people who love the taste of vegetables.

(B)   Some ways of making vegetables more appetizing diminish vegetables' ability to help prevent cancer.

(C)   People who find a few vegetables appetizing typically do not eat substantially more vegetables than do people who dislike the taste of most vegetables.

(D)   People who dislike the taste of most vegetables would eat many more vegetables if they knew how to make them more appetizing.

(E)   The only way to make the campaign to get people to eat more vegetables more effective would be to ensure that anyone who at present dislikes the taste of certain vegetables learns to find those vegetables appetizing.

11. Pure science—research with no immediate commercial or technological application—is a public good. Such research requires a great amount of financial support and does not yield profits in the short term. Since private corporations will not undertake to support activities that do not yield short-term profits, a society that wants to reap the benefits of pure science ought to use public funds to support such research.

The claim about private corporations serves which one of the following functions in the argument?

(A) It expresses the conclusion of the argument.

(B) It explains what is meant by the expression "pure research" in the context of the argument.

(C) It distracts attention from the point at issue by introducing a different but related goal.

(D) It supports the conclusion by ruling out an alternative way of achieving the benefits mentioned.

(E) It illustrates a case where unfortunate consequences result from a failure to accept the recommendation offered.

12. Melinda: Hazard insurance decreases an individual's risk by judiciously spreading the risk among many policyholders.

Jack: I disagree. It makes sense for me to buy fire insurance for my house, but I don't see how doing so lessens the chances that my house will burn down.

Jack's response most clearly trades on an ambiguity in which one of the following expressions used by Melinda?

(A) judiciously spreading

(B) many policyholders

(C) risk

(D) decreases

(E) hazard insurance

13. Some doctors believe that a certain drug reduces the duration of episodes of vertigo, claiming that the average duration of vertigo for people who suffer from it has decreased since the drug was introduced. However, during a recent three-month shortage of the drug, there was no significant change in the average duration of vertigo. Thus, we can conclude that the drug has no effect on the duration of vertigo.

Which one of the following is an assumption required by the argument?

(A) If a drug made a difference in the duration of vertigo, a three-month shortage of that drug would have caused a significant change in the average duration of vertigo.

(B) If there were any change in the average duration of vertigo since the introduction of the drug, it would have demonstrated that the drug has an effect on the duration of vertigo.

(C) A period of time greater than three months would not have been better to use in judging whether the drug has an effect on the duration of vertigo.

(D) Changes in diet and smoking habits are not responsible for any change in the average duration of vertigo since the introduction of the drug.

(E) There are various significant factors other than drugs that decrease the duration of vertigo for many people who suffer from it.

14. It has been suggested that a television set should be thought of as nothing more than "a toaster with pictures" and that since we let market forces determine the design of kitchen appliances we can let them determine what is seen on television. But that approach is too simple. Some governmental control is needed, since television is so important politically and culturally. It is a major source of commercial entertainment. It plays an important political role because it is the primary medium through which many voters obtain information about current affairs. It is a significant cultural force in that in the average home it is on for more than five hours a day.

Which one of the following most accurately expresses the role played in the argument by the claim that television is so important politically and culturally?

(A) It states a view that the argument as a whole is designed to discredit.

(B) It is an intermediate conclusion that is offered in support of the claim that a television set should be thought of as nothing more than "a toaster with pictures" and for which the claim that we can let market forces determine what is seen on television is offered as support.

(C) It is a premise that is offered in support of the claim that we let market forces determine the design of kitchen appliances.

(D) It is an intermediate conclusion that is offered in support of the claim that some governmental control of television is needed and for which the claim that the television is on for more than five hours a day in the average home is offered as partial support.

(E) It is a premise that is offered in support of the claim that television is the primary medium through which many voters obtain information about current affairs.

15. Earthworms, vital to the health of soil, prefer soil that is approximately neutral on the acid-to-alkaline scale. Since decomposition of dead plants makes the top layer of soil highly acidic, application of crushed limestone, which is highly alkaline, to the soil's surface should make the soil more attractive to earthworms.

Which one of the following is an assumption on which the argument depends?

(A) As far as soil health is concerned, aiding the decomposition of dead plants is the most important function performed by earthworms.

(B) After its application to the soil's surface, crushed limestone stays in the soil's top layer long enough to neutralize some of the top layer's acidity.

(C) Crushed limestone contains available calcium and magnesium, both of which are just as vital as earthworms to healthy soil.

(D) By itself, acidity of soil does nothing to hasten decomposition of dead plants.

(E) Alkaline soil is significantly more likely to benefit from an increased earthworm population than is highly acidic soil.

16. Jurist: A nation's laws must be viewed as expressions of a moral code that transcends those laws and serves as a measure of their adequacy. Otherwise, a society can have no sound basis for preferring any given set of laws to all others. Thus, any moral prohibition against the violation of statutes must leave room for exceptions.

Which one of the following can be properly inferred from the jurist's statements?

(A) Those who formulate statutes are not primarily concerned with morality when they do so.

(B) Sometimes criteria other than the criteria derived from a moral code should be used in choosing one set of laws over another.

(C) Unless it is legally forbidden ever to violate some moral rules, moral behavior and compliance with laws are indistinguishable.

(D) There is no statute that a nation's citizens have a moral obligation to obey.

(E) A nation's laws can sometimes come into conflict with the moral code they express.

17. An association between two types of conditions does not establish that conditions of one type cause conditions of the other type. Even persistent and inviolable association is inconclusive; such association is often due to conditions of both types being effects of the same kind of cause.

Which one of the following judgments most closely conforms to the principle stated above?

(A) Some people claim that rapid growth of the money supply is what causes inflation. But this is a naive view. What these people do not realize is that growth in the money supply and inflation are actually one and the same phenomenon.

(B) People who have high blood pressure tend to be overweight. But before we draw any inferences, we should consider that an unhealthy lifestyle can cause high blood pressure, and weight gain can result from living unhealthily.

(C) In some areas, there is a high correlation between ice cream consumption and the crime rate. Some researchers have proposed related third factors, but we cannot rule out that the correlation is purely coincidental.

(D) People's moods seem to vary with the color of the clothes they wear. Dark colors are associated with gloomy moods, and bright colors are associated with cheerful moods. This correlation resolves nothing, however. We cannot say whether it is the colors that cause the moods or the converse.

(E) Linguists propose that the similarities between Greek and Latin are due to their common descent from an earlier language. But how are we to know that the similarities are not actually due to the two languages having borrowed structures from one another, as with the languages Marathi and Telegu?

18. Salesperson: When a salesperson is successful, it is certain that that person has been in sales for at least three years. This is because to succeed as a salesperson, one must first establish a strong client base, and studies have shown that anyone who spends at least three years developing a client base can eventually make a comfortable living in sales.

The reasoning in the salesperson's argument is vulnerable to criticism on the grounds that it fails to consider the possibility that

(A) salespeople who have spent three years developing a client base might not yet be successful in sales

(B) some salespeople require fewer than three years in which to develop a strong client base

(C) a salesperson who has not spent three years developing a client base may not succeed in sales

(D) it takes longer than three years for a salesperson to develop a strong client base

(E) few salespeople can afford to spend three years building a client base

19. People who have habitually slept less than six hours a night and then begin sleeping eight or more hours a night typically begin to feel much less anxious. Therefore, most people who sleep less than six hours a night can probably cause their anxiety levels to fall by beginning to sleep at least eight hours a night.

The reasoning in which one of the following arguments is most similar to that in the argument above?

(A) When a small company first begins to advertise on the Internet, its financial situation generally improves. This shows that most small companies that have never advertised on the Internet can probably improve their financial situation by doing so.

(B) Certain small companies that had never previously advertised on the Internet have found that their financial situations began to improve after they started to do so. So, most small companies can probably improve their financial situations by starting to advertise on the Internet.

(C) It must be true that any small company that increases its Internet advertising will improve its financial situation, since most small companies that advertise on the Internet improved their financial situations soon after they first began to do so.

(D) Usually, the financial situation of a small company that has never advertised on the Internet will improve only if that company starts to advertise on the Internet. Therefore, a typical small company that has never advertised on the Internet can probably improve its financial situation by doing so.

(E) A small company's financial situation usually improves soon after that company first begins to advertise on the Internet. Thus, most small companies that have never advertised on the Internet could probably become financially strong.

20. Biologist: Lions and tigers are so similar to each other anatomically that their skeletons are virtually indistinguishable. But their behaviors are known to be quite different: tigers hunt only as solitary individuals, whereas lions hunt in packs. Thus, paleontologists cannot reasonably infer solely on the basis of skeletal anatomy that extinct predatory animals, such as certain dinosaurs, hunted in packs.

The conclusion is properly drawn if which one of the following is assumed?

(A) The skeletons of lions and tigers are at least somewhat similar in structure in certain key respects to the skeletons of at least some extinct predatory animals.

(B) There have existed at least two species of extinct predatory dinosaurs that were so similar to each other that their skeletal anatomy is virtually indistinguishable.

(C) If skeletal anatomy alone is ever an inadequate basis for inferring a particular species' hunting behavior, then it is never reasonable to infer, based on skeletal anatomy alone, that a species of animals hunted in packs.

(D) If any two animal species with virtually indistinguishable skeletal anatomy exhibit quite different hunting behaviors, then it is never reasonable to infer, based solely on the hunting behavior of those species, that the two species have the same skeletal anatomy.

(E) If it is unreasonable to infer, solely on the basis of differences in skeletal anatomy, that extinct animals of two distinct species differed in their hunting behavior, then the skeletal remains of those two species are virtually indistinguishable.

21. The trees always blossom in May if April rainfall exceeds 5 centimeters. If April rainfall exceeds 5 centimeters, then the reservoirs are always full on May 1. The reservoirs were not full this May 1 and thus the trees will not blossom this May.

   Which one of the following exhibits a flawed pattern of reasoning most similar to the flawed pattern of reasoning in the argument above?

   (A) If the garlic is in the pantry, then it is still fresh. And the potatoes are on the basement stairs if the garlic is in the pantry. The potatoes are not on the basement stairs, so the garlic is not still fresh.

   (B) The jar reaches optimal temperature if it is held over the burner for 2 minutes. The contents of the jar liquefy immediately if the jar is at optimal temperature. The jar was held over the burner for 2 minutes, so the contents of the jar must have liquefied immediately.

   (C) A book is classified "special" if it is more than 200 years old. If a book was set with wooden type, then it is more than 200 years old. This book is not classified "special," so it is not printed with wooden type.

   (D) The mower will operate only if the engine is not flooded. The engine is flooded if the foot pedal is depressed. The foot pedal is not depressed, so the mower will operate.

   (E) If the kiln is too hot, then the plates will crack. If the plates crack, then the artisan must redo the order. The artisan need not redo the order. Thus, the kiln was not too hot.

22. Doctor: Being overweight has long been linked with a variety of health problems, such as high blood pressure and heart disease. But recent research conclusively shows that people who are slightly overweight are healthier than those who are considerably underweight. Therefore, to be healthy, it suffices to be slightly overweight.

   The argument's reasoning is flawed because the argument

   (A) ignores medical opinions that tend to lead to a conclusion contrary to the one drawn

   (B) never adequately defines what is meant by "healthy"

   (C) does not take into account the fact that appropriate weight varies greatly from person to person

   (D) holds that if a person lacks a property that would suffice to make the person unhealthy, then that person must be healthy

   (E) mistakes a merely relative property for one that is absolute

23. Robust crops not only withstand insect attacks more successfully than other crops, they are also less likely to be attacked in the first place, since insects tend to feed on weaker plants. Killing insects with pesticides does not address the underlying problem of inherent vulnerability to damage caused by insect attacks. Thus, a better way to reduce the vulnerability of agricultural crops to insect pest damage is to grow those crops in good soil—soil with adequate nutrients, organic matter, and microbial activity.

   Which one of the following is an assumption on which the argument depends?

   (A) The application of nutrients and organic matter to farmland improves the soil's microbial activity.

   (B) Insects never attack crops grown in soil containing adequate nutrients, organic matter, and microbial activity.

   (C) The application of pesticides to weak crops fails to reduce the extent to which they are damaged by insect pests.

   (D) Crops that are grown in good soil tend to be more robust than other crops.

   (E) Growing crops without the use of pesticides generally produces less robust plants than when pesticides are used.

24. People perceive color by means of certain photopigments in the retina that are sensitive to certain wavelengths of light. People who are color-blind are unable to distinguish between red and green, for example, due to an absence of certain photopigments. What is difficult to explain, however, is that in a study of people who easily distinguish red from green, 10 to 20 percent failed to report distinctions between many shades of red that the majority of the subjects were able to distinguish.

Each of the following, if true, helps to explain the result of the study cited above EXCEPT:

(A) People with abnormally low concentrations of the photopigments for perceiving red can perceive fewer shades of red than people with normal concentrations.

(B) Questions that ask subjects to distinguish between different shades of the same color are difficult to phrase with complete clarity.

(C) Some people are uninterested in fine gradations of color and fail to notice or report differences they do not care about.

(D) Some people are unable to distinguish red from green due to an absence in the retina of the photopigment sensitive to green.

(E) Some people fail to report distinctions between certain shades of red because they lack the names for those shades.

25. Occultist: The issue of whether astrology is a science is easily settled: it is both an art and a science. The scientific components are the complicated mathematics and the astronomical knowledge needed to create an astrological chart. The art is in the synthesis of a multitude of factors and symbols into a coherent statement of their relevance to an individual.

The reasoning in the occultist's argument is most vulnerable to criticism on the grounds that the argument

(A) presumes, without providing justification, that any science must involve complicated mathematics

(B) incorrectly infers that a practice is a science merely from the fact that the practice has some scientific components

(C) denies the possibility that astrology involves components that are neither artistic nor scientific

(D) incorrectly infers that astronomical knowledge is scientific merely from the fact that such knowledge is needed to create an astrological chart

(E) presumes, without providing justification, that any art must involve the synthesis of a multitude of factors and symbols

**Answer Explanations follow on the next page.**

# ANSWER KEY

1. C

2. B

3. B

4. A

5. E

6. A

7. A

8. D

9. A

10. D

11. D

12. C

13. A

14. D

15. B

16. E

17. B

18. B

19. A

20. C

21. A

22. E

23. D

24. D

25. B

# SECTION TRIAGE

Section management means taking control of the test. You want to answer the easier questions with efficiency so you bank some time for the more difficult questions at the end. If you do run out of time on a section, you want to run out on the most difficult questions on which you might have had to guess anyway.

Remember that you don't have to answer each question in the order in which it is presented. However, ordering each question individually as you would with Reading Comprehension passages and Logic Games is time consuming. So, you'll use your knowledge of the general flow of difficulty across the section to guide your section-management decisions.

The following table lists the difficulty level (as reported by Kaplan students) of each question from the first Logical Reasoning section in PrepTest 53. One star indicates the lowest difficulty and four stars represent the highest difficulty. Of course, the actual difficulty level for you can be higher or lower; however, it's important for you to be aware of the general trends.

The level of difficulty generally progresses from beginning to end with some tougher questions scattered in the beginning and some moderate questions tucked in the back. Note what I call the "danger zone"—a stretch of tough questions that shows up in every Logical Reasoning section and, In this case, from question 16 to 22. Based on this consistent pattern, I recommend that you work through about four pages of the section and then turn to the end of the section and answer questions from the end, working your way backward toward the middle.

Pay attention to the factors that make a question difficult for you. For example, question 16 is an Inference question with a relatively short stimulus and answer choices. However, the abstract nature of the text might have caused you some difficulty. Sometimes just the question type is enough to make a question difficult. Knowing that a question is difficult for you allows you to make a quick decision on whether to skip it or attack it immediately.

But always remember the bulk of the easier questions, regardless of question type, are in the first dozen or so questions. You need those points. So while there is great strategic advantage in skipping a question that you recognize quickly as highly difficult and moving on through the section, just attack in order most of the early questions. Also, pick up any easy to moderate points tucked into the back. And, finally, be selective and strategic in the danger zone, based on objective difficulty and also your question type preferences. The ultimate, and only, goal is maximizing the number of correct answers.

Use this table as a guide to review your own section management, to assess the questions that were difficult for you, and to recognize there are other questions up ahead with points. Keep moving through the section!

**Table 21.1**

| PrepTest 53: Section 1 | | |
|---|---|---|
| Question | Question Type | Difficulty Level |
| 1 | Strengthen | * |
| 2 | Point at Issue | *** |
| 3 | Weaken | * |
| 4 | Main Point | * |
| 5 | Principle | * |
| 6 | Strengthen | * |
| 7 | Inference | ** |
| 8 | Weaken | ** |
| 9 | Assumption | ** |
| 10 | Strengthen | * |
| 11 | Role of a Statement | * |
| 12 | Flaw | * |
| 13 | Assumption | ** |
| 14 | Role of a Statement | ** |
| 15 | Assumption | ** |
| 16 | Inference | **** |
| 17 | Principle | *** |
| 18 | Flaw | **** |
| 19 | Parallel Reasoning | **** |
| 20 | Assumption | *** |
| 21 | Parallel Reasoning | **** |
| 22 | Flaw | *** |
| 23 | Assumption | ** |
| 24 | Paradox | ** |
| 25 | Flaw | ** |

## Explanations

1. **(C)**

> Consumer advocate: Businesses are typically motivated primarily by the desire to make as great a profit as possible, and advertising helps businesses to achieve this goal. But it is clear that the motive of maximizing profits does not impel businesses to present accurate information in their advertisements. <It follows that consumers should be skeptical of the claims made in advertisements.>

> Each of the following, if true, would strengthen the consumer advocate's argument EXCEPT:

(A) Businesses know that they can usually maximize their profits by using inaccurate information in their advertisements.

(B) Businesses have often included inaccurate information in their advertisements.

(C) Many consumers have a cynical attitude toward advertising.

(D) Those who create advertisements are less concerned with the accuracy than with the creativity of advertisements.

(E) The laws regulating truth in advertising are not applicable to many of the most common forms of inaccurate advertising.

### Step 1. Identify the Question Type

The word "strengthen" tells you directly this is a Strengthen question. Because this is an "EXCEPT" question, be sure to characterize the answer choices: the four wrong answers will strengthen the argument, while the one correct answer will either weaken the argument or have no effect on it.

### Step 2. Untangle the Stimulus

The consumer advocate generalizes that businesses are motivated by profit, and profit, not accuracy, drives their advertising. Using "It follows that" to signal the conclusion, the advocate warns consumers to be wary of advertising claims. In other words, be careful because they might lie.

### Step 3. Make a Prediction

The advocate assumes that because businesses could lie, they will. Anything that validates this assumption will strengthen the argument. Find them and cross them out. Remember, you're looking for the answer that weakens the argument or makes no impact.

### Step 4. Evaluate the Answer Choices

Choice (A) states that inaccurate ads can increase profits and thus provide incentive to businesses to use inaccurate ads. Choice (A) supports the assumption that businesses will cheat and consumers should be skeptical. Therefore, cross it out.

Choice (B) provides specific evidence of the advocate's claim and makes it more convincing. The message is if they've done it before, they'll do it again. Eliminate this choice.

Choice (C) raises the notion that many consumers are already cynical toward advertising. While this is in line with the author's recommendation, this answer choice, unlike the other four, doesn't provide any concrete reason or evidence supporting the claim against the businesses' integrity. The consumers' attitude has no impact on the advocate's assumption that those with a motive to lie will or can act on it. So, choice (C) does not strengthen the argument and is therefore the right answer.

Choice (D) indicates that accuracy is not a priority in advertising, strengthening the argument that ads should be questioned.

Choice (E) suggests that businesses are more likely to present inaccurate advertising because there is little regulation of it, thus strengthening the argument.

2.   **(B)**

Elaine: The purpose of art museums is to preserve artworks and make them available to the public. <Museums, (therefore,) should seek to acquire and display the best examples of artworks from each artistic period and genre,> even if some of these works are not recognized by experts as masterpieces.

Frederick: <Art museums ought to devote their limited resources to acquiring the works of recognized masters in order to ensure the preservation of the greatest artworks.>

Elaine's and Frederick's statements provide the most support for the claim that they would (disagree about) whether

(A)   many artistic masterpieces are not recognized as such by art experts

(B)   museums should seek to represent all genres of art in their collections

(C)   art museums should seek to preserve works of art

(D)   an art museum ought to acquire an unusual example of a period or genre if more characteristic examples are prohibitively expensive

(E)   all of the artworks that experts identify as masterpieces are actually masterpieces

### Step 1. Identify the Question Type

This question asks for what the two speakers "disagree about" and is therefore a Point at Issue question.

### Step 2. Untangle the Stimulus

Elaine concludes that museums should acquire and display art from every artistic period and genre to preserve art and expose the public to a broad range of artwork. Frederick recommends that museums acquire masterpieces to preserve the greatest artwork.

### Step 3. Make a Prediction

The speakers obviously agree that museums should acquire and preserve art. They differ on the reason for it and the type of art to be collected: Elaine seeks to preserve examples of all the different genres, while Frederick believes that preservation efforts should be restricted to the greatest artwork.

### Step 4. Evaluate the Answer Choices

Choice (A) is outside the scope of both speakers' arguments. Neither suggests any failure to recognize masterpieces by experts. Although Frederick does suggest that museums should focus their collections on "recognized masters," he doesn't discuss whether masterpieces are overlooked by art experts. Elaine's recommendation to preserve other works of art is based on a goal of preserving genres, not necessarily any implied failure to recognize the greatness of them.

Choice (B) correctly identifies the point at issue. It focuses on the type of art museums should acquire. Elaine would agree that collections should broadly represent all genres of art. Frederick would disagree and focus collections on masterpieces regardless of genre.

Choice (C) presents a point of agreement for Elaine and Frederick. While they agree on preservation, they disagree on the type of art to preserve.

Choice (D), like (A) is outside the score of both speakers' arguments. While Frederick does raise the issue of limited resources, neither speaker advocates this course of action of preserving "unusual" examples. Frederick does not believe in preserving all periods and genres, while Elaine explicitly advocates preserving the best examples of all genres.

Choice (E), like choice (A), raises the issue of whether you can trust an expert to identify a masterpiece. Again, neither speaker suggests any failure by experts to recognize masterpieces.

3.   **(B)**

Science columnist: (It is clear why) humans have so
many diseases in common with cats. <Many human
diseases are genetically based>, and cats are
genetically closer to humans than are any other
mammals except nonhuman primates. Each of the
genes identified so far in cats has an exact
counterpart in humans.

Which one of the following, if true, most (weakens) the
science columnist's explanation for the claim that
humans have so many diseases in common with cats?

(A)   Cats have built up resistance to many of the
diseases they have in common with humans.

(B)   Most diseases that humans have in common with
cats have no genetic basis.

(C)   Cats have more diseases in common with
nonhuman primates than with humans.

(D)   Many of the diseases humans have in common
with cats are mild and are rarely diagnosed.

(E)   Humans have more genes in common with
nonhuman primates than with cats.

## Step 1. Identify the Question Type

The question stem specifically identifies this as a Weaken question with the term "weaken."
As with many Strengthen and Weaken questions, the question stem tells you what you need
to use as the conclusion. In this case, you are tasked with weakening the science columnist's
explanation.

## Step 2. Untangle the Stimulus

The author's "explanation" for the number of diseases shared by humans and cats is that many
human diseases are genetically based. The author supports this explanation by documenting
the genetic closeness of humans and cats.

## Step 3. Make a Prediction

On the LSAT, words like "some," "many," "few," and "often" simply mean "at least one." So
when the author puts forward "many" human genetic based diseases as the explanation for
the shared disease between cats and humans, it should strike you as a potentially limited
explanation. The scope shift here is from an undefined number of genetic-based diseases in
humans to the better defined genetic commonalities. The science columnist assumes lots of
shared genes indicate lots of shared genetic diseases. Weaken this argument with an answer
that indicates that shared genes do not necessarily mean shared genetic diseases or that provides an alternative explanation for why cats and humans share diseases.

The other important pattern to recognize here is that this is a causal argument. The way to
weaken a causal argument is to break the connection between the science columnist's proposed cause (genetic diseases) and the effect (shared diseased among humans and cats), or
to provide an alternative cause for the shared diseases.

### Step 4. Evaluate the Answer Choices

Choice (A) has no effect on the argument because it does not address the issue of why cats and humans share diseases in common. The question stem clearly identifies the central issue as explaining why cats and humans share diseases. Any answer that does not attack the science columnist's explanation of genetics or provide an alternative explanation (cause) is wrong.

Choice (B) negates the assumption and therefore weakens the argument. This is the correct answer.

Choice (C) makes an irrelevant comparison and, like choice (A), has no bearing on the central issue of explaining "why" cats and humans share a certain number of diseases.

Choice (D) exposes the mild nature and low diagnosis rate of the diseases shared by humans and cats. While it identifies common characteristics, it does nothing to explain the commonalities or weaken the argument.

Choice (E), like choice (C), makes an irrelevant comparison and provides no explanation for why cats and humans share diseases in common.

4. **(A)**

<This region must find new ways to help business grow.> (After all,) shoe manufacturing used to be a major local industry, but recently has experienced severe setbacks due to overseas competition, so there is a need for expansion into new manufacturing areas. (Moreover,) our outdated public policy generally inhibits business growth.

Which one of the following most accurately expresses the (main conclusion) drawn in the argument?

(A)  The region needs to find new ways to enhance business growth.
(B)  Shoe manufacturing is no longer a major source of income in the region.
(C)  Shoe manufacturing in the region has dramatically declined due to overseas competition.
(D)  Business in the region must expand into new areas of manufacturing.
(E)  Outdated public policy inhibits business growth in the region.

### Step 1. Identify the Question Type

The question stem asks for the "main conclusion" making this a Main Point question.

### Step 2. Untangle the Stimulus

The conclusion is stated right away: This region must find new ways to support the growth of businesses. She presents her evidence using Keywords: She starts her second sentence with "after all" and her third sentence with "moreover" indicating the information will support her conclusion. While you will usually not be given clear conclusion Keywords on a Main Point question, you may well be provided with evidence Keywords.

### Step 3. Make a Prediction

The correct answer will paraphrase the conclusion, the sentence you bracketed.

### Step 4. Evaluate the Answer Choices

Choice (A) is the correct answer as it repeats the first sentence almost word for word.

Choice (B) might be implied in the evidence, but it's definitely not the argument conclusion.

Choices (C), (D), and (E) repeat evidence provided to support the conclusion. They don't state the conclusion itself.

5.  **(E)**

As a result of modern medicine, more people have been able to enjoy long and pain-free lives. But the resulting increase in life expectancy has contributed to a steady increase in the proportion of the population that is of advanced age. <This population shift is creating potentially devastating financial problems for some social welfare programs.>

Which one of the <u>following</u> (propositions) is most precisely exemplified by the situation presented above?

(A)  Technical or scientific innovation cannot be the solution to all problems.
(B)  Implementing technological innovations should be delayed until the resulting social changes can be managed.
(C)  Every enhancement of the quality of life has unavoidable negative consequences.
(D)  All social institutions are affected by a preoccupation with prolonging life.
(E)  Solving one set of problems can create a different set of problems.

### Step 1. Identify the Question Type

The term "propositions" signals a Principle question, and the word "following" tells you the principle is in the answer choice. Your task is to find the broad rule that is exemplified by the specific example in the stimulus.

### Step 2. Untangle the Stimulus

People are living longer, pain-free lives because of modern medicine creating a larger proportion of older people in the population. Consequently, some social welfare programs are facing major financial problems.

### Step 3. Make a Prediction

Take the narrow situation and generalize it. Solving one problem (shorter, more painful lives) can contribute to another problem (financial crisis for some social welfare programs).

## Step 4. Evaluate the Answer Choices

Choice (A) is not a good match. The technical innovations in the stimulus solved some problems, but an important contrast is that they created other problems rather than simply failing to solve all problems.

Choice (B) recommends delaying innovation to avoid resulting social problems. But the stimulus doesn't include a recommendation to manage problems. In fact, it says dealing with one issue creates another. This is a common type of out-of-scope answer that takes the logic of the argument another step forward to what may seem like an entirely reasonable next step. Recognize that the author is simply saying what has happened and is not recommending what to do in response to this information. Resist the urge to take that next step.

Choice (C) is extreme. The stimulus does not address every enhancement of the quality of life and does not suggest whether or not the problems created are avoidable.

Choice (D) is extreme on the other end. The stimulus specifically says that some social institutions are affected, not all.

Choice (E) matches the prediction and is the correct answer.

6. **(A)**

(Since) Jackie is such a big fan of Moral Vacuum's music, <she will probably like The Cruel Herd's new album.> Like Moral Vacuum, The Cruel Herd on this album plays complex rock music that employs the acoustic instrumentation and harmonic sophistication of early sixties jazz. The Cruel Herd also has very witty lyrics, full of puns and sardonic humor, like some of Moral Vacuum's best lyrics.

Which one of the following, if true, most (strengthens) the argument?

(A) Jackie has not previously cared for The Cruel Herd, but on the new album The Cruel Herd's previous musical arranger has been replaced by Moral Vacuum's musical arranger.

(B) Though The Cruel Herd's previous albums' production quality was not great, the new album is produced by one of the most widely employed producers in the music industry.

(C) Like Moral Vacuum, The Cruel Herd regularly performs in clubs popular with many students at the university that Jackie attends.

(D) All of the music that Jackie prefers to listen to on a regular basis is rock music.

(E) Jackie's favorite Moral Vacuum songs have lyrics that are somber and marked by a strong political awareness.

**Step 1. Identify the Question Type**

Since the question asks for something that "most strengthens" the argument, this is a Strengthen question.

**Step 2. Untangle the Stimulus**

Presented in the first sentence, the conclusion states that Jackie will probably like The Cruel Herd's new album. This qualified prediction ("will probably") is based on evidence, signaled by "since," that Jackie likes Moral Vacuum's music. The argument then details characteristics shared by the bands: complex rock music, acoustic instrumentation, harmonic sophistication, and witty lyrics.

**Step 3. Make a Prediction**

The author provides some similarities between The Cruel Herd and Moral Vacuum and assumes that such similarities indicate she will like both bands. The correct answer will confirm the assumption, provide another reason why the two bands are similar, or eliminate some potential difference between the bands that might have prevented Jackie from liking The Cruel Herd despite the similarities to Moral Vacuum.

**Step 4. Evaluate the Answer Choices**

Choice (A) supports the assumption indicating that The Cruel Herd's music will likely further resemble Moral Vacuum's now that The Cruel Herd has enlisted Moral Vacuum's musical arranger. Therefore, this is the correct answer. Most importantly, notice that only choices (A) and (B) focus on The Cruel Herd's new album, which is the real subject of the author's conclusion. The author does not claim that Jackie will like the band generally, just the new album. Staying on topic with the conclusion is one of the most important things you can do on the Logical Reasoning section of the LSAT.

Choice (B) tells you that The Cruel Herd's production quality will probably improve, but there is no indication that Jackie favors production quality. More importantly, this argument is based on an analogy or comparison between the two bands. To strengthen an analogy or comparison, you need either another similarity or to eliminate a potential difference.

Choice (C) fails to directly connect the music of the two bands, especially The Cruel Herd's new album. The fact that both bands play in clubs popular with university students doesn't address similarity of musical elements, nor the music on the new album.

Choice (D) adds nothing to the argument by indicating a general preference for rock music, since the stimulus provides far more detailed information on the types of rock music that Jackie likes. Just because she only likes rock would not dictate that she likes all rock music; in fact, the stimulus indicates she has specific tastes in rock music.

Choice (E) may weaken the argument. By identifying things that Jackie likes about Moral Vacuum songs and not connecting them back to The Cruel Herd, (E) suggests why Jackie would like Moral Vacuum and not The Cruel Herd. Since, there is no connection to The Cruel Herd's new album, this answer cannot strengthen the author's argument.

7. **(A)**

Superconductors are substances that conduct electricity without resistance at low temperatures. Their use, however, will (never) be economically feasible, (unless) there is a substance that superconducts at a temperature above minus 148 degrees Celsius. If there is such a substance, that substance must be an alloy of niobium and germanium. Unfortunately, such alloys superconduct at temperatures no higher than minus 160 degrees Celsius.

If the statements above are true, which one of the following (must also be true)?

(A)  The use of superconductors will never be economically feasible.

(B)  If the alloys of niobium and germanium do not superconduct at temperatures above minus 148 degrees Celsius, then there are other substances that will do so.

(C)  The use of superconductors could be economically feasible if there is a substance that superconducts at temperatures below minus 148 degrees Celsius.

(D)  Alloys of niobium and germanium do not superconduct at temperatures below minus 160 degrees Celsius.

(E)  No use of alloys of niobium and germanium will ever be economically feasible.

## Step 1. Identify the Question Type

The phrase "must also be true" identifies this is an Inference question. The correct answer must be true based on the information in the stimulus.

## Step 2. Untangle the Stimulus

The LSAT does not test your knowledge of content, so don't let the technical science language throw you off. Instead, use the formal logic language in the stimulus to help you get a handle on the material so you can spot an answer that must be true based on it. Remember, the correct answer to an Inference question that includes formal logic often comes from the statement's contrapositive.

The stimulus starts with a definition of superconductors and then doubts their economic feasibility unless there's a substance that superconducts above –148 degrees Celsius. "Never … unless" signals formal logic, so you can translate this sentence using the "No X unless Y" equation, then into an "If X, then Y," and then form the contrapositive. Here is what the progression looks like:

**Table 21.2**

| | |
|---|---|
| Never economically feasible unless superconducts above −148 degrees Celsius<br><br>If economically feasible then superconducts above −148 degrees Celsius | On test day, you will not want to take the time to write out this part of the formal logic. As you practice, though, it's important to think it through and write it out to improve your accuracy and efficiency. |
| Econ feas → sc above −148<br><br>Not sc above −148 → not econ feasible | On test day, consider jotting down the basic X → Y statement and its contrapositive so you don't have to reread any information and you have something to compare to the answer choices. |

The stimulus then says that the only substances that superconduct above −148 Celsius are alloys of niobium and germanium. Finally, you learn that the alloys can't superconduct at temperatures above −160 Celsius. Notice you can combine the last two statements. If niobium and germanium alloys can't superconduct above −160, they can't superconduct above −148, and that triggers the contrapositive. Therefore, superconductors can't be economically feasible.

### Step 3. Make a Prediction

Once you have a handle on an Inference stimulus, go right to the answer choices. In this case, you've translated the formal logic and combined statements where possible. You're ready to move to the answers with the understanding that there is a necessary condition for economic feasibility; that condition can't be met; so, superconductors are not economically feasible.

### Step 4. Evaluate the Answer Choices

Choice (A) *must be true*. The first formal logic statement told you that economic feasibility required conduction at certain temperatures. Later, you were told that such conduction was not possible. Thus, without the necessary prerequisite, economic feasibility is not possible.

Choice (B) contradicts the stimulus. The stimulus specifically states that the only substances that can superconduct above −148 degrees must be an alloy of niobium and germanium. Therefore, if they don't superconduct above −148 degrees, then there are no other substances that will do so.

Choice (C) confuses necessity and sufficiency. You know that economic feasibility requires conductivity at such temperatures, but that does not mean that conductivity at such temperatures will allow for economic feasibility. This answer changes the direction of the arrow in your formal logic, making it an incomplete contrapositive.

Choice (D) also contradicts the stimulus that says the alloys of niobium and germanium do not superconduct at temperatures higher than –160, which means that they must superconduct below –160.

Choice (E) is tempting, but you only know that these elements will not be economically feasible as superconductors, not that they will never have any other economically viable uses.

8. **(D)**

> Doctor: In three separate studies, researchers compared children who had slept with night-lights in their rooms as infants to children who had not. In the first study, the children who had slept with night-lights proved more likely to be nearsighted, but the later studies found no correlation between night-lights and nearsightedness. However, the children in the first study were younger than those in the later studies. <This suggests that if night-lights cause nearsightedness, the effect disappears with age.>

Which one of the following, if true, would most weaken the doctor's argument?

(A)    A fourth study comparing infants who were currently sleeping with night-lights to infants who were not did not find any correlation between night-lights and nearsightedness.

(B)    On average, young children who are already very nearsighted are no more likely to sleep with night-lights than young children who are not already nearsighted.

(C)    In a study involving children who had not slept with night-lights as infants but had slept with night-lights when they were older, most of the children studied were not nearsighted.

(D)    The two studies in which no correlation was found did not examine enough children to provide significant support for any conclusion regarding a causal relationship between night-lights and nearsightedness.

(E)    In a fourth study involving 100 children who were older than those in any of the first three studies, several of the children who had slept with night-lights as infants were nearsighted.

## Step 1. Identify the Question Type

The term "weaken" tells you directly that this is a Weaken question.

## Step 2. Untangle the Stimulus

The doctor's conclusion appears at the end of the stimulus, signaled by the phrase "This suggests that." It says that if night-lights cause nearsightedness, the effect disappears with age. It's based on the results of three different studies. The first study reported that children who slept with night-lights were more likely to be nearsighted. The two later studies found no correlation between sleeping with night-lights and nearsightedness. Because the children were older in the last two studies than in the first study, the doctor determines that nearsightedness must go away with age.

### Step 3. Make a Prediction

Any argument based on a study assumes the study is valid. To weaken such an argument, you need to attack the assumption and identify a problem with the research. Not every Weaken question involving a study will have a correct answer that identifies a problem with the study itself, but it is a common pattern on LSAT Weaken questions to watch out for.

### Step 4. Evaluate the Answer Choices

Choice (A) introduces a study group that is not representative of the original research population. The doctor is only interested in testing children who slept or didn't sleep with night-lights when they were infants. The fourth study deals with infants who currently sleep with night-lights. Therefore, this sample can't be used to weaken (or strengthen for that matter) a study to determine if night-light sleepers outgrow nearsightedness. Eliminate this choice.

Choice (B) does not attack the argument either. It deals with children who are already nearsighted, so knowing whether they sleep with night-lights will not be helpful.

Choice (C) also reaches outside the scope of the argument by introducing an unrepresentative study group. This group of children did not sleep with night-lights until they were older.

Choice (D) attacks the validity of the two later studies saying the sample size was too small to support the doctor's conclusion. Choice (D) weakens the argument and is the correct answer.

Choice (E) indicates a correlation between night-lights and nearsightedness but doesn't address the doctor's conclusion that if night-lights cause nearsightedness, the effect disappears with age.

9. **(A)**

Global surveys estimate the earth's population of <u>nesting female leatherback turtles</u> has fallen by more than two-thirds in the past 15 years. Any species whose population declines by more than two-thirds in 15 years is in grave danger of extinction, <(so) the <u>leatherback turtle</u> is clearly in danger of extinction.>

Which one of the following is an (assumption) that the argument requires?

(A)   The decline in the population of nesting female leatherback turtles is proportional to the decline in the leatherback turtle population as a whole.

(B)   If the global population of leatherback turtles falls by more than two-thirds over the next 15 years, the species will eventually become extinct.

(C)   The global population of leatherback turtles consists in roughly equal numbers of females and males.

(D)   Very few leatherback turtles exist in captivity.

(E)   The only way to ensure the continued survival of leatherback turtles in the wild is to breed them in captivity.

## Step 1. Identify the Question Type

The term "assumption" makes this an Assumption question.

## Step 2. Untangle the Stimulus

The author draws a conclusion in the last sentence, set off by "so," that the leatherback turtle is in danger of extinction. Her evidence is that the nesting female leatherback turtle population has dropped by more than two-thirds in the past fifteen years, a sure indicator the group is in danger of extinction.

## Step 3. Make a Prediction

The author uses evidence about the nesting female leatherbacks to reach a conclusion about all leatherbacks. To make that jump, the author must assume the nesting female population is representative of the whole group.

## Step 4. Evaluate the Answer Choices

Choice (A) correctly indicates that the decline of the nesting female leatherback turtle population is proportional to and therefore representative of the leatherback turtle population decline.

Choice (B) is an extreme distortion of the evidence in saying that the species will become extinct. The argument says a species is in grave danger of extinction. The result is not certain. Also, even if this answer more accurately restated that evidence, the correct assumption answer choice cannot simply restate a piece of evidence. Watch out for this type of wrong answer trap specific to Assumption questions.

Choice (C) does not make any connection between the population decline of nesting female leatherbacks and the whole leatherback population. Instead it adds another factor, the general female leatherback population.

Choice (D) strengthens the author's claim of imminent extinction, but is not a necessary assumption of the author's argument that a decline in nesting females indicates a danger of extinction of the species. Use the denial test: denied, this choice indicates that more than a few turtles exist in captivity. The existence of more than a few turtles in captivity does not prevent the author from being right that the species is in danger of extinction. A Necessary Assumption answer cannot bring in out of scope information or concepts, even if it seems to support the conclusion.

Choice (E) is also outside the scope by discussing captive breeding. It is extreme in indicating that it is the only way to prevent extinction. Again, use the denial test. Denied, this answer indicates that captive breeding is not the only possible way to prevent extinction. Just because there are more than one possible way, even multiple ways, to potentially prevent extinction does not mean that any will be implemented or will ultimately work. Denying this choice does not destroy the author's claim that the turtles are in danger of extinction.

10. **(D)**

Public health experts have waged a long-standing educational campaign to get people to eat more vegetables, which are known to help prevent cancer. Unfortunately, the campaign has had little impact on people's diets. The reason is probably that many people simply dislike the taste of most vegetables. ⟨Thus,⟩ the campaign would probably be more effective if it included information on ways to make vegetables more appetizing.⟩

Which one of the following, if true, most ⟨strengthens⟩ the argument?

(A)   The campaign to get people to eat more vegetables has had little impact on the diets of most people who love the taste of vegetables.

(B)   Some ways of making vegetables more appetizing diminish vegetables' ability to help prevent cancer.

(C)   People who find a few vegetables appetizing typically do not eat substantially more vegetables than do people who dislike the taste of most vegetables.

(D)   People who dislike the taste of most vegetables would eat many more vegetables if they knew how to make them more appetizing.

(E)   The only way to make the campaign to get people to eat more vegetables more effective would be to ensure that anyone who at present dislikes the taste of certain vegetables learns to find those vegetables appetizing.

### Step 1. Identify the Question Type

The word "strengthens" in the stem tells you this is a Strengthen question.

### Step 2. Untangle the Stimulus

A public health campaign to encourage people to eat more vegetables is not working. The author surmises that people just don't like the taste of vegetables. "Thus," the author concludes, the campaign should tell people how to make their vegetables more appetizing so they're more likely to eat them.

### Step 3. Make a Prediction

To reach that conclusion, the author must assume that people don't know how to prepare their vegetables so that they like the taste. A strengthener will confirm that assumption.

### Step 4. Evaluate the Answer Choices

Choice (A) talks about people who love the taste of vegetables, while the stimulus deals with people who don't like the taste of vegetables. Choice (A) goes beyond the scope of the argument, so it's out.

Choice (B) creates a conundrum. The whole purpose of the campaign to eat more vegetables is to prevent cancer. Choice (B) would threaten the value of the campaign, so you can cross it out.

Choice (C) makes an irrelevant comparison between people who like a few vegetables and those who don't like most vegetables. The author focuses the argument on people who don't like the taste of vegetables. Move on to the next choice.

Choice (D) confirms the assumption by making the argument more likely. Once people who don't like vegetables learn how to make them more tasty, they'll eat them. This is the correct answer.

Choice (E) reverses the logic, so it's incorrect.

11.  **(D)**

> Pure science—research with no immediate commercial
> or technological application—is a public good. Such
> research requires a great amount of financial support
> and does not yield profits in the short term. (Since)
> <u>private corporations will not undertake to support</u>
> <u>activities that do not yield short-term profits</u>, &lt;a society
> that wants to reap the benefits of pure science ought to
> use public funds to support such research.&gt;

> The <u>claim about private corporations</u> (serves which one)
> (of the following functions) in the argument?

(A)   It expresses the conclusion of the argument.
(B)   It explains what is meant by the expression "pure
      research" in the context of the argument.
(C)   It distracts attention from the point at issue by
      introducing a different but related goal.
(D)   It supports the conclusion by ruling out an
      alternative way of achieving the benefits
      mentioned.
(E)   It illustrates a case where unfortunate
      consequences result from a failure to accept
      the recommendation offered.

## Step 1. Identify the Question Type

The phrases "claim about private corporations" and "serves which one of the following functions" indicate that this is a Role of the Statement question.

## Step 2. Untangle the Stimulus

The stimulus begins with some background information that defines "pure science" as research with no prospects for short-term profits. It's followed by the claim in question: that private corporations won't support activities that don't have short-term profitability. The word "Since" indicates that the claim is evidence. It supports the final clause, the conclusion.

## Step 3. Make a Prediction

The correct answer will identify the claim as evidence in the argument.

## Step 4. Evaluate the Answer Choices

Choice (A) is wrong. The claim is the evidence, not the conclusion.

Choice (B) misattributes the definition of pure research to the claim in question. The term is explained in the background information immediately preceding the claim.

Choice (C) also gets it wrong. The claim in question is relevant to the point at issue and does not introduce any other goals.

Choice (D) correctly identifies the claim as evidence by defining evidence as support for the conclusion and more specifically defining its purpose.

Choice (E) misdirects attention to the recommendation made in the conclusion to use public funds to support pure science and adds information about consequences for ignoring the recommendation not in the argument at all.

12. **(C)**

> Melinda: Hazard insurance decreases an individual's risk by judiciously spreading the risk among many policyholders.
>
> Jack: I disagree. It makes sense for me to buy fire insurance for my house, but I don't see how doing so lessens the chances that my house will burn down.

Jack's response most clearly trades on an ambiguity in which one of the following expressions used by Melinda?
(A) judiciously spreading
(B) many policyholders
(C) risk
(D) decreases
(E) hazard insurance

### Step 1. Identify the Question Type

This question has no clear Keywords to help you identify the question type. But stop and think what it's really asking. You are tasked with identifying how Jack responds to Melinda, specifically to an ambiguity in one of Melinda's expressions. So, this is a Method of Argument question with a twist. You need to identify the expression that is used by Melinda with two different meanings or connotations.

### Step 2. Untangle the Stimulus

Read both speakers' statements looking for the ambiguous term. Melinda says that hazard insurance decreases individual risk by spreading risk among lots of policyholders. Jack disagrees and claims that insurance doesn't reduce the risk his house will burn down.

### Step 3. Make a Prediction

Jack and Melinda are both talking about risk, but the term is not specifically defined. Melinda talks about spreading the risk of disaster among insurance policyholders, which indicates concern for financial loss, while Jack's response focuses on the chances of something bad happening. Melinda never asserts that buying insurance reduces the risk of her house burning down. So, Jack's method of argument is to play word games with the term "risk."

### Step 4. Evaluate the Answer Choices

Choice (A) does not have ambiguity. Jack may disagree that hazard insurance judiciously spreads risk, but Melinda's use of the phrase is clear.

Choice (B) is overlooked by Jack. He's not focused on others, just his own insurance and his own risk. So, he can't trade on an ambiguity of a term he ignores.

Choice (C) matches the prediction and is the correct answer.

Choice (D) is used by both speakers in the same way.

Choice (E) is also consistently understood by Jack and Melinda as a type of insurance policy.

13. **(A)**

Some doctors believe that a certain drug reduces the duration of episodes of vertigo, claiming that the average duration of vertigo for people who suffer from it has decreased since the drug was introduced. (However,) during a recent three-month shortage of the drug, there was no significant change in the average duration of vertigo. <(Thus,) we can (conclude) that the drug has no effect on the duration of vertigo.>

Which one of the following is an (assumption) required by the argument?

(A) If a drug made a difference in the duration of vertigo, a three-month shortage of that drug would have caused a significant change in the average duration of vertigo.

(B) If there were any change in the average duration of vertigo since the introduction of the drug, it would have demonstrated that the drug has an effect on the duration of vertigo.

(C) A period of time greater than three months would not have been better to use in judging whether the drug has an effect on the duration of vertigo.

(D) Changes in diet and smoking habits are not responsible for any change in the average duration of vertigo since the introduction of the drug.

(E) There are various significant factors other than drugs that decrease the duration of vertigo for many people who suffer from it.

### Step 1. Identify the Question Type

This question specifically asks for the argument's assumption, so it's an Assumption question.

### Step 2. Untangle the Stimulus

The stimulus begins with some background information about what some doctors believe—that a certain drug cuts the length of time of vertigo episodes. The contrast Keyword "However" tells you that the author is about to disagree. He offers evidence that limited availability of the drug over a three-month period did not result in a significant change in the duration of a vertigo episode. The conclusion appears in the last sentence, signaled by "Thus" and "conclude." In it, the author determines that the drug has no effect on the length of time of a vertigo episode. In other words, the author argues that since there is no increase in the duration of a vertigo episode after a three-month absence of the drug, the drug has no effect.

## Step 3. Make a Prediction

Because the drug was not used for three months, the author determines that the drug has no effect. The author must assume then that three months without the drug is enough time for the duration of the vertigo episodes to increase again. Maybe the episodes increase after a longer period.

Generally speaking, if an author relies on a certain duration of time in the evidence, she must assume it was enough time to prove her conclusion.

## Step 4. Evaluate the Answer Choices

Choice (A) is phrased as a conditional statement, but don't let that throw you off. It's just another way of saying that three months should have been enough time for a change to occur. In making an argument, the author assumes that "If I have this evidence, then I can reach this conclusion." Here the evidence is: no change in three months, and the conclusion is: the drug has no effect. So the author assumes:

No change in 3 months → no effect

And the contrapositive is:

Effect → change within 3 months

Choice (A) is the contrapositive form of: If evidence, then conclusion. So, choice (A) is the correct answer.

Choice (B) is also in conditional statement form, but it commits a classic formal logic flaw. This choice takes the conditional, if evidence, then conclusion, and negates both sides without reversing the sides.

This choice in short says:

Change → effect rather than no change → no effect

Choice (C) is tempting. The author must assume that three months is a sufficient amount of time in which to make a judgment whether the drug has any effect on vertigo. So, it is not a great leap to think that the author assumes that a longer test would not be any better judge of the effect, or lack thereof, of the drug. This choice certainly strengthens the argument. But it is not necessary to the author's argument that three months is the ideal length of study, that no longer length would be a better test. All that is necessary to the author's argument is that three months is a sufficient length of time for the study. Again, the denial test can help you eliminate Assumption answer choices that support the conclusion but are not essential to the argument. Here, denying this choice indicates that a longer time period would be a better judge of the effects of the drug on vertigo, but that in no way tells you that a longer test would reach a different conclusion than the three-month test or contradict the author's claim.

Choice (D) eliminates another cause for any changes in the duration of vertigo. The elimination of other possibilities is a common Assumption answer pattern. This would be an attractive answer if the author had, in fact, concluded that the drugs DID cause a change in the duration of vertigo. With such a causal conclusion, the author would have assumed there were no other causes. Here the author does the opposite and concludes that the drug does NOT cause a change in the duration of vertigo. So, you are not looking for an answer that eliminates other potential causes.

Choice (E) brings in out of scope factors. It adds "various significant factors" not included in the argument. The answer to an assumption will never reach beyond the scope of the argument.

14. **(D)**

It has been suggested that a television set should be thought of as nothing more than "a toaster with pictures" and that since we let market forces determine the design of kitchen appliances we can let them determine what is seen on television. But that approach is too simple. <Some governmental control is needed, > (since) television is so important politically and culturally. It is a major source of commercial entertainment. It plays an important political role because it is the primary medium through which many voters obtain information about current affairs. It is a significant cultural force in that in the average home it is on for more than five hours a day.

Which one of the following most accurately expresses the (role played) in the argument by the claim that television is so important politically and culturally?

(A) It states a view that the argument as a whole is designed to discredit.

(B) It is an intermediate conclusion that is offered in support of the claim that a television set should be thought of as nothing more than "a toaster with pictures" and for which the claim that we can let market forces determine what is seen on television is offered as support.

(C) It is a premise that is offered in support of the claim that we let market forces determine the design of kitchen appliances.

(D) It is an intermediate conclusion that is offered in support of the claim that some governmental control of television is needed and for which the claim that the television is on for more than five hours a day in the average home is offered as partial support.

(E) It is a premise that is offered in support of the claim that television is the primary medium through which many voters obtain information about current affairs.

### Step 1. Identify the Question Type

The question identifies a specific claim in the stimulus and asks for the "role played" by it. This is a Role of a Statement question.

### Step 2. Untangle the Stimulus

The stimulus begins with one school of thought that television programming should be determined by market forces. Just like other LSAT arguments, you can expect the author's disagreement when an argument introduces how some people think. The author concludes that some government control is needed and goes on to explain why in the evidence signaled by "since." And that's where you'll find the claim in question.

If you stop your stimulus review here and proceed to the answer choices, you'll be looking for an answer that identifies the claim as evidence that supports the conclusion. While it is, you won't find that answer as one of the choices. You need to untangle the whole stimulus.

The rest of the argument explains why television is so important politically and culturally— because it entertains us, informs us about current affairs, and provides a cultural presence in our homes. The last few sentences are evidence of the claim of television's political and cultural importance.

### Step 3. Make a Prediction

The claim in question is support for the conclusion, but also has its own evidentiary support. Thus, it is a subsidiary conclusion.

### Step 4. Evaluate the Answer Choices

Choice (A) is a 180. You know the argument is not intended to discredit the claim because the author spends the last half of the argument supporting it.

Choice (B) should get your attention, but it falls short. The claim is an intermediate conclusion, but it does not support the thought that television is a toaster with pictures. The author disagrees with that thought and uses the claim in question to discredit that idea.

Choice (C) is convoluted and wrong. The claim is a premise, but it's certainly not offered to support the notion that market forces determine the design of kitchen appliances. That idea is part of the school of thought with which the author disagrees.

Choice (D) correctly defines the role of the claim in question.

Choice (E) gets it backward. The claim that television is the primary medium through which many voters obtain information about current affairs supports the claim that television is politically and culturally important, not the other way around.

15. **(B)**

Earthworms, vital to the health of soil, prefer soil that is approximately neutral on the acid-to-alkaline scale. (Since) decomposition of dead plants makes the top layer of soil highly acidic, <application of crushed limestone, which is highly alkaline, to the soil's surface should make the soil more attractive to earthworms.>

Which one of the following is an (assumption) on which the argument depends?

(A) As far as soil health is concerned, aiding the decomposition of dead plants is the most important function performed by earthworms.

(B) After its application to the soil's surface, crushed limestone stays in the soil's top layer long enough to neutralize some of the top layer's acidity.

(C) Crushed limestone contains available calcium and magnesium, both of which are just as vital as earthworms to healthy soil.

(D) By itself, acidity of soil does nothing to hasten decomposition of dead plants.

(E) Alkaline soil is significantly more likely to benefit from an increased earthworm population than is highly acidic soil.

## Step 1. Identify the Question Type

The word "assumption" tells you that this is an Assumption question.

## Step 2. Untangle the Stimulus

The author concludes in the last sentence that crushed limestone should be added to soil to attract earthworms. The evidence says that decomposing plants make soil acidic and earthworms prefer soil that is acid-to-alkaline neutral.

## Step 3. Make a Prediction

Limestone is discussed in the conclusion, but not in the evidence. There must be something about the limestone that the author assumes will solve the problem of the high acid content of the soil and attract earthworms.

## Step 4. Evaluate the Answer Choices

Choice (A) is stuck on the background information that earthworms are vital to soil health, which has nothing to do with whether adding limestone will make soil more attractive to earthworms, as the author concludes. Knowing that earthworms' most important function is to aid decomposing plants does nothing to tie together the evidence and conclusion. Also, be wary of extreme answers like this one, which says something is the "most" important factor.

Choice (B) works because it explains that limestone neutralizes some of the soil's acidity which makes the soil more attractive to the earthworms. This is the correct answer. If you are unsure, use the denial test and it should become clear that this answer is necessary to the author's recommendation. If the limestone does not stay in the soil long enough to reduce the acidity, then the recommendation to add it to attract earthworms holds no merit.

Choice (C) does not address the high acidity level of the soil. So, even if limestone offers vital nutrients to earthworms, the acid in the soil will keep them away.

Choice (D) doesn't address limestone, which is what you want to connect the evidence and conclusion. Whether soil acidity does anything to hasten plant decomposition has no impact on the argument.

Choice (E) misses the point. The author doesn't care about the type of soil that will benefit from a larger earthworm population but rather how crushed limestone will make the soil more attractive to earthworms.

16. **(E)**

> Jurist: A nation's laws must be viewed as expressions of a moral code that transcends those laws and serves as a measure of their adequacy. Otherwise, a society can have no sound basis for preferring any given set of laws to all others. Thus, any moral prohibition against the violation of statutes must leave room for exceptions.

Which one of the following can be properly (inferred) from the jurist's statements?

(A) Those who formulate statutes are not primarily concerned with morality when they do so.
(B) Sometimes criteria other than the criteria derived from a moral code should be used in choosing one set of laws over another.
(C) Unless it is legally forbidden ever to violate some moral rules, moral behavior and compliance with laws are indistinguishable.
(D) There is no statute that a nation's citizens have a moral obligation to obey.
(E) A nation's laws can sometimes come into conflict with the moral code they express.

### Step 1. Identify the Question Type

Because the stem asks for something that can be "inferred" from the jurist's statement, this is an Inference question.

## Step 2. Untangle the Stimulus

This atypical Inference stimulus presents an argument. The evidence states that a nation's laws are based on a moral code, supporting the conclusion that any moral ban on breaking the law must allow for exceptions.

## Step 3. Make a Prediction

The argument deals with two things: law and morality. The jurist largely equates the two, but by saying that there must be room for exceptions, there must be some differences. Also remember that even though the statements in the stimulus are largely absolute and forceful, a modest-sounding answer is usually the one that must be true. Scan the answers for the choice that generally indicates that morality and law are not exactly in sync.

## Step 4. Evaluate the Answer Choices

Choice (A) is nowhere to be found in the stimulus, which is concerned with what the jurist believes should be the case in formulating law. It never describes the concerns lawmakers have or don't have.

Choice (B) distorts the stimulus by adding additional criteria to the moral code that is necessary to choose a set of laws.

Choice (C) contradicts the stimulus by saying moral behavior and legal compliance are the same thing. The last sentence of the stimulus suggests otherwise.

Choice (D) conflicts with the jurist's statements. If laws are expressions of a moral code, there are many statutes that citizens have a moral obligation to obey.

Choice (E) can be inferred from the last sentence of the stimulus. If a moral ban on lawbreaking must have exceptions, there must be times when the law and the moral code don't agree. This is the correct answer.

17. **(B)**

An association between two types of conditions does not establish that conditions of one type cause conditions of the other type. Even persistent and inviolable association is inconclusive; such association is often due to conditions of both types being effects of the same kind of cause.

Which one of the following judgments most closely conforms to the (principle) stated above?

(A)  Some people claim that rapid growth of the money supply is what causes inflation. But this is a naive view. What these people do not realize is that growth in the money supply and inflation are actually one and the same phenomenon.

(B)  People who have high blood pressure tend to be overweight. But before we draw any inferences, we should consider that an unhealthy lifestyle can cause high blood pressure, and weight gain can result from living unhealthily.

(C)  In some areas, there is a high correlation between ice cream consumption and the crime rate. Some researchers have proposed related third factors, but we cannot rule out that the correlation is purely coincidental.

(D)  People's moods seem to vary with the color of the clothes they wear. Dark colors are associated with gloomy moods, and bright colors are associated with cheerful moods. This correlation resolves nothing, however. We cannot say whether it is the colors that cause the moods or the converse.

(E)  Linguists propose that the similarities between Greek and Latin are due to their common descent from an earlier language. But how are we to know that the similarities are not actually due to the two languages having borrowed structures from one another, as with the languages Marathi and Telegu?

## Step 1. Identify the Question Type

The word "principle" identifies the stem as a Principle question. The stem also tells you the principle is "stated above" in the stimulus and your task is to apply it to a parallel situation in the answer.

## Step 2. Untangle the Stimulus

This is a classic LSAT pattern. A correlation between two conditions does not necessarily mean that one condition caused the other. Even a long-standing correlation can be due to both conditions having a common cause.

### Step 3. Make a Prediction

Look for an answer that presents a strong correlation and no causation between two conditions and shows they have the same cause.

### Step 4. Evaluate the Answer Choices

Choice (A) denies causation between growth of the money supply and inflation by saying they are the same thing. This is not a match.

Choice (B) conforms to the principle. It acknowledges a correlation between having high blood pressure and being overweight, and warns against drawing an inference about whether one caused the other. Instead, it says both conditions are probably the result of a common cause, unhealthy living. This is the correct answer.

Choice (C) considers whether the correlation between ice cream consumption and the crime rate is coincidental. Coincidental correlation is not part of the principle.

Choice (D) identifies a correlation between clothing color and mood and says one causes the other, but it's not clear which one is the cause and which one is the effect. Eliminate this choice.

Choice (E) looks promising by proposing a common cause of Greek and Latin similarities (common descent from an earlier language). But choice (E) dismisses the common cause theory by wondering whether the two languages are similar because they borrowed structures from each other.

18.  **(B)**

> Salesperson: ⟨When⟩ a salesperson is successful, it is certain that person has been in sales for at least three years.⟩ ⟨This is because⟩ to succeed as a salesperson, one ⟨must⟩ first establish a strong client base, and studies have shown that ⟨anyone⟩ who spends at least three years developing a client base can eventually make a comfortable living in sales.

> The reasoning in the salesperson's argument is ⟨vulnerable to criticism⟩ on the grounds that it ⟨fails to⟩ ⟨consider the possibility that⟩

(A)    salespeople who have spent three years developing a client base might not yet be successful in sales
(B)    some salespeople require fewer than three years in which to develop a strong client base
(C)    a salesperson who has not spent three years developing a client base may not succeed in sales
(D)    it takes longer than three years for a salesperson to develop a strong client base
(E)    few salespeople can afford to spend three years building a client base

### Step 1. Identify the Question Type

The phrase "vulnerable to criticism" makes this a Flaw question, and "fails to consider the possibility that" identifies the flaw as an overlooked possibility. Your task is to describe what the salesperson overlooks in his argument.

### Step 2. Untangle the Stimulus

The second sentence begins with "This is because," which indicates that the conclusion preceded the statement and the evidence will follow. Note the formal logic language in the stimulus, and use it to translate the statements. The conclusion says that if a salesperson is successful, he's been in sales for at least three years. The evidence tells you that if a salesperson is successful, he has a strong customer base and that if he spends at least three years developing that customer base, he'll make a comfortable living.

### Step 3. Make a Prediction

The evidence says that three years in sales is *sufficient* to be successful in sales. The conclusion says that three years in sales is *necessary* to be successful in sales. The salesperson confuses a sufficient condition with a necessary condition, which can always be expressed as an ignored possibility flaw. The salesperson does not consider other ways to be successful in sales, besides three years at the job. When the salesperson concludes that it is absolutely necessary to have three years at the job, then he ignores the possibility that a salesperson might not need those three years to be successful.

### Step 4. Evaluate the Answer Choices

Choice (A) talks about salespeople who are not successful in sales, which is beyond the scope of the argument.

Choice (B) is correct. It presents an overlooked way for a salesperson to be successful (in two years instead of three).

Choice (C) is not overlooked by the salesperson. He argues three years is necessary for success.

Choice (D) is not overlooked either. The salesperson says it takes at least three years to develop a client base which leaves room for the possibility that salespeople may need longer than three years to develop that client base.

Choice (E) is irrelevant to the argument. Whether salespeople can afford to spend three years developing a client base, the salesperson deems it necessary.

19. **(A)**

People who have habitually slept less than six hours a night and then begin sleeping eight or more hours a night typically begin to feel much less anxious. <Therefore, most people who sleep less than six hours a night can probably cause their anxiety levels to fall by beginning to sleep at least eight hours a night.>

The reasoning in which one of the following arguments is most similar to that in the argument above?

(A) When a small company first begins to advertise on the Internet, its financial situation generally improves. This shows that most small companies that have never advertised on the Internet can probably improve their financial situation by doing so.

(B) Certain small companies that had never previously advertised on the Internet have found that their financial situations began to improve after they started to do so. So, most small companies can probably improve their financial situations by starting to advertise on the Internet.

(C) It must be true that any small company that increases its Internet advertising will improve its financial situation, since most small companies that advertise on the Internet improved their financial situations soon after they first began to do so.

(D) Usually, the financial situation of a small company that has never advertised on the Internet will improve only if that company starts to advertise on the Internet. Therefore, a typical small company that has never advertised on the Internet can probably improve its financial situation by doing so.

(E) A small company's financial situation usually improves soon after that company first begins to advertise on the Internet. Thus, most small companies that have never advertised on the Internet could probably become financially strong.

## Step 1. Identify the Question Type

The phrase "most similar to" tells you that this is a Parallel Reasoning question.

## Step 2. Untangle the Stimulus

The conclusion appears in the second sentence, indicated by "Therefore." It's a prediction that most people who sleep less than six hours a night can probably reduce their anxiety levels by sleeping at least eight hours a night. What else can help you focus the description before you check the answers? It covers a majority of the subjects ("most people"), the prediction is qualified ("can probably"), and it's based on behaving in a new way ("sleeping at least eight hours a night"). The evidence appears in the first sentence and says that sleeping eight hours instead of six (the new behavior) reduces anxiety (is typically successful).

### Step 3. Make a Prediction

The correct answer will account for all features of the conclusion: a qualified prediction that a majority will improve from behaving in a new way. If more than one answer has a similar conclusion to the stimulus, compare the evidence.

### Step 4. Evaluate the Answer Choices

Choice (A) correctly parallels the stimulus. It predicts that most small companies that don't advertise on the Internet can probably help their financial situations by doing so. The evidence provides that the new behavior of advertising on the Internet does work.

Choice (B) is close, but leaves out one important distinction. The conclusion talks about most small companies, not most small companies that have not used Internet advertising. The course of action the companies take must be new.

Choice (C) uses extreme language ("It must be true") that differentiates if from the stimulus. Another problem with choice (C) is that it refers to companies that increase their Internet advertising, rather than companies that have never advertised on the Internet before. The majority must be trying new behavior to match the stimulus.

Choice (D), like choice (A), has a conclusion similar to the stimulus'. It predicts that a typical small company that has never advertised on the Internet can probably improve its financial situation by doing so. However, the difference arises in the evidence. The stimulus' evidence states that new behavior typically produces improvement. Choice (D) distorts this by saying that improvement comes "only if" the new behavior is followed.

Choice (E) is missing an important feature from the stimulus' conclusion. Choice (E)'s conclusion predicts that most small companies that have never advertised on the Internet could probably become financially strong. The problem is the conclusion doesn't attribute the improvement to the new behavior.

20. **(C)**

> Biologist: Lions and tigers are so similar to each other anatomically that their skeletons are virtually indistinguishable. But their behaviors are known to be quite different: tigers hunt only as solitary individuals, whereas lions hunt in packs. <Thus, paleontologists cannot reasonably infer solely on the basis of skeletal anatomy that extinct predatory animals, such as certain dinosaurs, hunted in packs.>

The conclusion is properly drawn if which one of the following is assumed?

(A) The skeletons of lions and tigers are at least somewhat similar in structure in certain key respects to the skeletons of at least some extinct predatory animals.

(B) There have existed at least two species of extinct predatory dinosaurs that were so similar to each other that their skeletal anatomy is virtually indistinguishable.

(C) If skeletal anatomy alone is ever an inadequate basis for inferring a particular species' hunting behavior, then it is never reasonable to infer, based on skeletal anatomy alone, that a species of animals hunted in packs.

(D) If any two animal species with virtually indistinguishable skeletal anatomy exhibit quite different hunting behaviors, then it is never reasonable to infer, based solely on the hunting behavior of those species, that the two species have the same skeletal anatomy.

(E) If it is unreasonable to infer, solely on the basis of differences in skeletal anatomy, that extinct animals of two distinct species differed in their hunting behavior, then the skeletal remains of those two species are virtually indistinguishable.

## Step 1. Identify the Question Type

Because the question asks "which one of the following is assumed," it is an Assumption question. Moreover, it is a Sufficient Assumption question, so the correct answer choice *must be true*. The correct answer to a Sufficient Assumption question is likely to be very forceful and absolute, as opposed to Necessary Assumption correct answers, which tend to be more modest.

## Step 2. Untangle the Stimulus

The biologist explains that lions and tigers are almost anatomically identical and can't be distinguished by their skeletons. Yet their hunting behaviors are quite different. "Thus," she concludes, paleontologists can't just use the skeletal anatomy of extinct predatory animals, such as certain dinosaurs, to determine they hunted in packs.

## Step 3. Make a Prediction

The biologist makes quite a scope shift. The evidence is based on lions and tigers and the conclusion refers to extinct predatory animals. The assumption will need to bridge the gap between the two. Here, the biologist assumes that if skeletal anatomy can't be used to determine the hunting behavior of lions and tigers, then it can't be used to determine the hunting behavior of any set of animals, past or present.

## Step 4. Evaluate the Answer Choices

Choice (A) makes an irrelevant comparison between the skeletons of lions and tigers to some extinct predatory animals. The similarities between them does nothing to connect the skeleton of one group to its hunting behavior. Eliminate this choice.

Choice (B) compares the skeletons of two species of dinosaurs, but does not tie the experience of lions and tigers to the extinct predatory animals. Cross out this choice.

When (C) is added to the biologist's argument, it becomes ironclad. Choice (C) confirms the biologist's assumption: that an inability to infer hunting behavior from skeletal anatomy in just one case makes it impossible to do so in any other case. This is the correct answer.

Choice (D) is wrong because it uses the hunting behavior to infer something about the skeletal anatomy. Actually, the biologist uses the skeletal anatomy to infer something about the hunting behavior.

Choice (E) goes off track in two ways. First, it focuses on differences in skeletal anatomy rather than similarities. Second, it uses hunting behavior to determine skeletal anatomy rather than the other way around.

21. **(A)**

The trees always blossom in May if April rainfall exceeds 5 centimeters. If April rainfall exceeds 5 centimeters, then the reservoirs are always full on May 1. The reservoirs were not full this May 1 and <thus the trees will not blossom this May.>

Which one of the following exhibits a flawed pattern of reasoning most similar to the flawed pattern of reasoning in the argument above?

(A) If the garlic is in the pantry, then it is still fresh. And the potatoes are on the basement stairs if the garlic is in the pantry. The potatoes are not on the basement stairs, so the garlic is not still fresh.

(B) The jar reaches optimal temperature if it is held over the burner for 2 minutes. The contents of the jar liquefy immediately if the jar is at optimal temperature. The jar was held over the burner for 2 minutes, so the contents of the jar must have liquefied immediately.

(C) A book is classified "special" if it is more than 200 years old. If a book was set with wooden type, then it is more than 200 years old. This book is not classified "special," so it is not printed with wooden type.

(D) The mower will operate only if the engine is not flooded. The engine is flooded if the foot pedal is depressed. The foot pedal is not depressed, so the mower will operate.

(E) If the kiln is too hot, then the plates will crack. If the plates crack, then the artisan must redo the order. The artisan need not redo the order. Thus, the kiln was not too hot.

## Step 1. Identify the Question Type

The question asks for the "flawed pattern of reasoning most similar to the flawed pattern of reasoning" in the stimulus, making this a Parallel Flaw question.

## Step 2. Untangle the Stimulus

Translate the formal logic language in Parallel Reasoning arguments to make it easier to compare the stimulus with the answer choices.

**Table 21.3**

| | Statement | Translation |
|---|---|---|
| Evidence | If April rainfall exceeds 5 centimeters, then the trees always blossom in May. | X → Y |
| | If April rainfall exceeds 5 centimeters, then the reservoirs are always full on May 1. | X → Z |
| Conclusion | The reservoirs were not full this May 1 and thus the trees will not blossom this May. | not Z → not Y |

The flaw in the argument comes from the formal logic. The absence of one result (Z) does not guarantee the absence of the other (Y), as stated in the conclusion.

### Step 3. Make a Prediction

The correct answer will follow the same flawed formal logic.

### Step 4. Evaluate the Answer Choices

Once you find a discrepancy in the formal logic, move on to the next answer. For purposes of explanation, the full translations are provided.

Table 21.4

| Choice (A) | Statement | Translation |
|---|---|---|
| Evidence | If the garlic is in the pantry, then it is still fresh. | X → Y |
| | If the garlic is in the pantry, then the potatoes are on the basement stairs. | X → Z |
| Conclusion | The potatoes are not on the basement stairs, so the garlic is not still fresh. | not Z → not Y |

Choice (A) is the correct answer, matching the stimulus point by point.

For the record:

Table 21.5

| Choice (B) | Statement | Translation |
|---|---|---|
| Evidence | If it is held over the burner for 2 minutes, then the jar reaches optimal temperature. | X → Y |
| | If the jar is at optimal temperature, then the contents of the jar liquefy immediately. | Y → Z |
| Conclusion | The jar was held over the burner for 2 minutes, so the contents of the jar must have liquefied immediately. | X → Z |

Choice (B) does not match the logic of the stimulus nor does it contain a flaw in the reasoning.

Table 21.6

| Choice (C) | Statement | Translation |
|---|---|---|
| Evidence | If it is more than 200 years old, then a book is classified "special." | X → Y |
| | If a book was set with wooden type, then it is more than 200 years old. | Z → X |
| Conclusion | This book is not classified "special," so it is not printed with wooden type. | not Y → not Z |

Choice (C) does not match the logic of the stimulus either nor does it contain a flaw in the reasoning.

**Table 21.7**

| Choice (D) | Statement | Translation |
|---|---|---|
| Evidence | If the mower operates, then the engine is not flooded. | X → not Y |
| | If the foot pedal is depressed, the engine is flooded. | Z → Y |
| Conclusion | The foot pedal is not depressed, so the mower will operate. | Not Z → X |

Choice (D) does not match the formal logic of the stimulus. It is flawed, but not in the same way as the stimulus. From the evidence, you have no way to know what happens if the foot pedal is not depressed.

**Table 21.8**

| Choice (E) | Statement | Translation |
|---|---|---|
| Evidence | If the kiln is too hot, then the plates will crack. | X → Y |
| | If the plates crack, then the artisan must redo the order. | Y → Z |
| Conclusion | The artisan need not redo the order. Thus, the kiln was not too hot. | Not Z → not X |

Choice (E) does not match the logic of the stimulus, and like (C), does not have a flaw.

22. **(E)**

> Doctor: Being overweight has long been linked with a variety of health problems, such as high blood pressure and heart disease. But recent research conclusively shows that people who are slightly overweight are healthier than those who are considerably underweight. <Therefore, to be healthy, it suffices to be slightly overweight.>

The argument's reasoning is flawed because the argument

(A) ignores medical opinions that tend to lead to a conclusion contrary to the one drawn

(B) never adequately defines what is meant by "healthy"

(C) does not take into account the fact that appropriate weight varies greatly from person to person

(D) holds that if a person lacks a property that would suffice to make the person unhealthy, then that person must be healthy

(E) mistakes a merely relative property for one that is absolute

## Step 1. Identify the Question Type

The term "flawed" tells you this is a Flaw question.

### Step 2. Untangle the Stimulus

Signaled by "Therefore," the doctor concludes in the last sentence that you can be slightly overweight and be healthy. She bases her statement on recent research that showed slightly overweight people were healthier than considerably underweight people.

### Step 3. Make a Prediction

The argument says that slightly overweight people are healthier than considerably underweight people, so slightly overweight people are healthy. The scope shift here is from evidence that discusses becoming "healthier" to a conclusion about what it takes to be "healthy." The doctor jumps from a relative condition (healthier) to a discrete condition (healthy). Comparative healthiness does not establish health. The correct answer will make that point.

### Step 4. Evaluate the Answer Choices

Choice (A) contradicts the stimulus. The doctor does pay attention to the medical research and cites it in her argument.

Choice (B) is irrelevant. The flaw in the argument is the doctor's faulty assumption that being healthier than someone else means being healthy, not the absent definition of healthy.

Choice (C) adds information not raised in the stimulus. You don't know whether the doctor accounted for weight variations or not.

Choice (D) goes beyond the scope of the argument. The doctor doesn't argue that lacking weight suffices to make someone unhealthy. She argues that having a few extra pounds suffices to make someone healthy.

Choice (E) may not jump out to you as the correct answer because it's presented in abstract terms, but it is. The doctor argues that relative health (slightly overweight is healthier than considerably underweight) establishes the health of the slightly overweight.

23. **(D)**

> Robust crops not only withstand insect attacks more successfully than other crops, they are also less likely to be attacked in the first place, since insects tend to feed on weaker plants. Killing insects with pesticides does not address the underlying problem of inherent vulnerability to damage caused by insect attacks. ⟨Thus,⟩ a better way to reduce the vulnerability of agricultural crops to insect pest damage is to grow those crops in good soil—soil with adequate nutrients, organic matter, and microbial activity.⟩

Which one of the following is an ⟨assumption⟩ on which the argument depends?

(A) The application of nutrients and organic matter to farmland improves the soil's microbial activity.

(B) Insects never attack crops grown in soil containing adequate nutrients, organic matter, and microbial activity.

(C) The application of pesticides to weak crops fails to reduce the extent to which they are damaged by insect pests.

(D) Crops that are grown in good soil tend to be more robust than other crops.

(E) Growing crops without the use of pesticides generally produces less robust plants than when pesticides are used.

### Step 1. Identify the Question Type

The word "assumption" identifies this as an Assumption question.

### Step 2. Untangle the Stimulus

"Thus" points to the conclusion: grow crops in good soil to reduce the crops' vulnerability to insect damage. The author backs up the recommendation with evidence that robust crops are more resistant to insect attacks and less likely to be attacked at all.

### Step 3. Make a Prediction

The evidence refers to robust crops and the conclusion talks about crops grown in good soil. The author must assume a connection between the two unmatched terms—that crops grown in good soil are more robust.

### Step 4. Evaluate the Answer Choices

Choice (A) explains what makes good soil, but doesn't link good soil to robustness. This choice is out.

Choice (B) is extreme in saying insects never attack crops grown in good soil. Move on to the next choice.

Choice (C) refers to a side point in the evidence, not a connection between the evidence and the conclusion. Eliminate this choice.

Choice (D) is a perfect match of the prediction.

Choice (E) conflicts with the argument. If crops are less robust without pesticides, then pesticides should make them more robust.

24. **(D)**

> People perceive color by means of certain photopigments in the retina that are sensitive to certain wavelengths of light. People who are color-blind are unable to distinguish between red and green, for example, due to an absence of certain photopigments. What is difficult to explain, however, is that in a study of people who easily distinguish red from green, 10 to 20 percent failed to report distinctions between many shades of red that the majority of the subjects were able to distinguish.

> Each of the following, if true, ⟨helps to explain⟩ the result of the study cited above ⟨EXCEPT⟩:

> (A) People with abnormally low concentrations of the photopigments for perceiving red can perceive fewer shades of red than people with normal concentrations.
> (B) Questions that ask subjects to distinguish between different shades of the same color are difficult to phrase with complete clarity.
> (C) Some people are uninterested in fine gradations of color and fail to notice or report differences they do not care about.
> (D) Some people are unable to distinguish red from green due to an absence in the retina of the photopigment sensitive to green.
> (E) Some people fail to report distinctions between certain shades of red because they lack the names for those shades.

## Step 1. Identify the Question Type

"Helps to explain" identifies a Paradox question. The "EXCEPT" tells you that the correct answer will not resolve the paradox and that the four wrong answers will.

## Step 2. Untangle the Stimulus

Color-blind people can't distinguish between red and green due to the lack of certain photopigments. Yet in a study of people who easily distinguish red from green (and therefore not color-blind), 10–20% of the subjects failed to report distinctions between shades of red.

### Step 3. Make a Prediction

The paradox is that some people who are not color-blind don't report distinction between shades of red, and therefore appear to show signs of colorblindness. Four answers will help explain this paradox. The correct answer will not.

### Step 4. Evaluate the Answer Choices

Choice (A) explains that some people, color-blind or not, have trouble perceiving different shades of red. They just have abnormally low concentrations of the photopigments that would typically allow them to differentiate reds. They may be able to distinguish red from green due to the presence of photopigments for green, but lack the pigments for reds. Eliminate this choice.

Choice (B) explains that subjects might have been able to distinguish between different shades of red, but may not have been able to articulate the differences.

Choice (C) explains that some people just aren't interested in fine color distinctions. So, even if they see them, they don't report them. This choice is out.

Choice (D) takes the discussion outside the scope and is therefore the right answer. It gives an explanation for why some color-blind people can't tell the difference between red and green. You are looking for an explanation of why some people who are not color-blind can't distinguish some shades of red.

Choice (E) provides one more reason why some of the subjects didn't report distinctions. Without names for certain shades of red, they could not accurately report their differences.

25. **(B)**

> Occultist: The issue of whether astrology is a science is easily settled: <it is both an art and a science.> The scientific components are the complicated mathematics and the astronomical knowledge needed to create an astrological chart. The art is in the synthesis of a multitude of factors and symbols into a coherent statement of their relevance to an individual.

The reasoning in the occultist's argument is (most) (vulnerable to criticism) on the grounds that the argument

(A)  presumes, without providing justification, that any science must involve complicated mathematics

(B)  incorrectly infers that a practice is a science merely from the fact that the practice has some scientific components

(C)  denies the possibility that astrology involves components that are neither artistic nor scientific

(D)  incorrectly infers that astronomical knowledge is scientific merely from the fact that such knowledge is needed to create an astrological chart

(E)  presumes, without providing justification, that any art must involve the synthesis of a multitude of factors and symbols

## Step 1. Identify the Question Type

The "most vulnerable to criticism" language indicates a Flaw question.

## Step 2. Untangle the Stimulus

The occultist concludes that astrology is both science and an art. The reason, the occultist says, is because astrology has both scientific and artistic components.

## Step 3. Make a Prediction

Notice the shift in terms between the evidence (scientific components and artistic components) and conclusion (a science and an art). The faulty assumption is that because astrology has features of science and art, it actually *is* a science and an art.

## Step 4. Evaluate the Answer Choices

Choice (A) is too broad. The occultist doesn't presume anything about all science. He merely states that complicated math is one of the scientific components of astrology. Move on to the next choice.

Choice (B) correctly identifies the faulty assumption made by the occultist.

Choice (C) is never addressed in the argument. The occultist says that astrology is a science and an art. He doesn't reject the possibility that astrology includes non-scientific and non-artistic components.

Choice (D) reverses the occultist's reasoning. He doesn't say that astronomy is scientific because it's used in astrology. Rather, astrology is scientific because it uses astronomy.

Choice (E), like choice (A), is too broad. The occultist doesn't presume anything about all art. He simply states that the synthesis of multiple factors and symbols is one of the artistic elements of astrology.

# CHAPTER 22

# FULL-LENGTH SECTION II[1]

Section II
Time—35 minutes
25 Questions

<u>Directions:</u> The questions in this section are based on the reasoning contained in brief statements or passages. For some questions, more than one of the choices could conceivably answer the question. However, you are to choose the <u>best</u> answer; that is, the response that most accurately and completely answers the question. You should not make assumptions that are by commonsense standards implausible, superfluous, or incompatible with the passage. After you have chosen the best answer, blacken the corresponding space on your answer sheet.

[1]PrepTest 53, Sec. 3

1. At many electronics retail stores, the consumer has the option of purchasing product warranties that extend beyond the manufacturer's warranty. However, consumers are generally better off not buying extended warranties. Most problems with electronic goods occur within the period covered by the manufacturer's warranty.

   Which one of the following, if true, most strengthens the argument?

   (A) Problems with electronic goods that occur after the manufacturer's warranty expires are generally inexpensive to fix in comparison with the cost of an extended warranty.
   (B) Because problems are so infrequent after the manufacturer's warranty expires, extended warranties on electronic goods are generally inexpensive.
   (C) Most of those who buy extended warranties on electronic goods do so because special circumstances make their item more likely to break than is usually the case.
   (D) Some extended warranties on electronic goods cover the product for the period covered by the manufacturer's warranty as well as subsequent years.
   (E) Retail stores sell extended warranties in part because consumers who purchase them are likely to purchase other products from the same store.

2. Since the 1970s, environmentalists have largely succeeded in convincing legislators to enact extensive environmental regulations. Yet, as environmentalists themselves not only admit but insist, the condition of the environment is worsening, not improving. Clearly, more environmental regulations are not the solution to the environment's problems.

   The argument's reasoning is flawed because the argument

   (A) attacks the environmentalists themselves instead of their positions
   (B) presumes, without providing warrant, that only an absence of environmental regulations could prevent environmental degradation
   (C) fails to consider the possibility that the condition of the environment would have worsened even more without environmental regulations
   (D) fails to justify its presumption that reducing excessive regulations is more important than preserving the environment
   (E) fails to consider the views of the environmentalists' opponents

3. Although it is unwise to take a developmental view of an art like music—as if Beethoven were an advance over Josquin, or Miles Davis an advance over Louis Armstrong—there are ways in which it makes sense to talk about musical knowledge growing over time. We certainly know more about certain sounds than was known five centuries ago; that is, we understand how sounds that earlier composers avoided can be used effectively in musical compositions. For example, we now know how the interval of the third, which is considered dissonant, can be used in compositions to create consonant musical phrases.

   Which one of the following most accurately expresses the main conclusion of the argument?

   (A) Sounds that were never used in past musical compositions are used today.
   (B) Sounds that were once considered dissonant are more pleasing to modern listeners.
   (C) It is inappropriate to take a developmental view of music.
   (D) It is unwise to say that one composer is better than another.
   (E) Our understanding of music can improve over the course of time.

4. A recent test of an electric insect control device discovered that, of the more than 300 insects killed during one 24-hour period, only 12 were mosquitoes. Thus this type of device may kill many insects, but will not significantly aid in controlling the potentially dangerous mosquito population.

   Which one of the following, if true, most seriously weakens the argument?

   (A) A careful search discovered no live mosquitoes in the vicinity of the device after the test.
   (B) A very large proportion of the insects that were attracted to the device were not mosquitoes.
   (C) The device is more likely to kill beneficial insects than it is to kill harmful insects.
   (D) Many of the insects that were killed by the device are mosquito-eating insects.
   (E) The device does not succeed in killing all of the insects that it attracts.

5. Brain-scanning technology provides information about processes occurring in the brain. For this information to help researchers understand how the brain enables us to think, however, researchers must be able to rely on the accuracy of the verbal reports given by subjects while their brains are being scanned. Otherwise brain-scan data gathered at a given moment might not contain information about what the subject reports thinking about at that moment, but instead about some different set of thoughts.

Which one of the following most accurately expresses the main conclusion of the argument?

(A) It is unlikely that brain-scanning technology will ever enable researchers to understand how the brain enables us to think.

(B) There is no way that researchers can know for certain that subjects whose brains are being scanned are accurately reporting what they are thinking.

(C) Because subjects whose brains are being scanned may not accurately report what they are thinking, the results of brain-scanning research should be regarded with great skepticism.

(D) Brain scans can provide information about the accuracy of the verbal reports of subjects whose brains are being scanned.

(E) Information from brain scans can help researchers understand how the brain enables us to think only if the verbal reports of those whose brains are being scanned are accurate.

6. Ornithologist: This bird species is widely thought to subsist primarily on vegetation, but my research shows that this belief is erroneous. While concealed in a well-camouflaged blind, I have observed hundreds of these birds every morning over a period of months, and I estimate that over half of what they ate consisted of insects and other animal food sources.

The reasoning in the ornithologist's argument is most vulnerable to criticism on the grounds that the argument

(A) assumes, without providing justification, that the feeding behavior of the birds observed was not affected by the ornithologist's act of observation

(B) fails to specify the nature of the animal food sources, other than insects, that were consumed by the birds

(C) adopts a widespread belief about the birds' feeding habits without considering the evidence that led to the belief

(D) neglects the possibility that the birds have different patterns of food consumption during different parts of the day and night

(E) fails to consider the possibility that the birds' diet has changed since the earlier belief about their diet was formed

7. Educator: Only those students who are genuinely curious about a topic can successfully learn about that topic. They find the satisfaction of their curiosity intrinsically gratifying, and appreciate the inherent rewards of the learning process itself. However, almost no child enters the classroom with sufficient curiosity to learn successfully all that the teacher must instill. A teacher's job, therefore, _____.

Which one of the following most logically completes the educator's argument?

(A) requires for the fulfillment of its goals the stimulation as well as the satisfaction of curiosity

(B) necessitates the creative use of rewards that are not inherent in the learning process itself

(C) is to focus primarily on those topics that do not initially interest the students

(D) is facilitated by students' taking responsibility for their own learning

(E) becomes easier if students realize that some learning is not necessarily enjoyable

8. Environmentalist: When bacteria degrade household cleaning products, vapors that are toxic to humans are produced. Unfortunately, household cleaning products are often found in landfills. Thus, the common practice of converting landfills into public parks is damaging human health.

Which one of the following is an assumption the environmentalist's argument requires?

(A) In at least some landfills that have been converted into public parks there are bacteria that degrade household cleaning products.

(B) Converting a landfill into a public park will cause no damage to human health unless toxic vapors are produced in that landfill and humans are exposed to them.

(C) If a practice involves the exposure of humans to vapors from household cleaning products, then it causes at least some damage to human health.

(D) When landfills are converted to public parks, measures could be taken that would prevent people using the parks from being exposed to toxic vapors.

(E) If vapors toxic to humans are produced by the degradation of household cleaning products by bacteria in any landfill, then the health of at least some humans will suffer.

9. Tea made from camellia leaves is a popular beverage. However, studies show that regular drinkers of camellia tea usually suffer withdrawal symptoms if they discontinue drinking the tea. Furthermore, regular drinkers of camellia tea are more likely than people in general to develop kidney damage. Regular consumption of this tea, therefore, can result in a heightened risk of kidney damage.

Which one of the following, if true, most seriously weakens the argument?

(A) Several other popular beverages contain the same addictive chemical that is found in camellia tea.

(B) Addictive chemicals are unlikely to cause kidney damage solely by virtue of their addictive qualities.

(C) Some people claim that regular consumption of camellia tea helps alleviate their stress.

(D) Most people who regularly drink camellia tea do not develop kidney damage.

(E) Many people who regularly consume camellia tea also regularly consume other beverages suspected of causing kidney damage.

10. Artist: Avant-garde artists intend their work to challenge a society's mainstream beliefs and initiate change. And some art collectors claim that an avant-garde work that becomes popular in its own time is successful. However, a society's mainstream beliefs do not generally show any significant changes over a short period of time. Therefore, when an avant-garde work becomes popular it is a sign that the work is not successful, since it does not fulfill the intentions of its creator.

The reference to the claim of certain art collectors plays which one of the following roles in the artist's argument?

(A) It serves to bolster the argument's main conclusion.

(B) It identifies a view that is ultimately disputed by the argument.

(C) It identifies a position supported by the initial premise in the argument.

(D) It provides support for the initial premise in the argument.

(E) It provides support for a counterargument to the initial premise.

11. A recent epidemiological study found that businesspeople who travel internationally on business are much more likely to suffer from chronic insomnia than are businesspeople who do not travel on business. International travelers experience the stresses of dramatic changes in climate, frequent disruption of daily routines, and immersion in cultures other than their own, stresses not commonly felt by those who do not travel. Thus, it is likely that these stresses cause the insomnia.

Which one of the following would, if true, most strengthen the reasoning above?

(A) Most international travel for the sake of business occurs between countries with contiguous borders.

(B) Some businesspeople who travel internationally greatly enjoy the changes in climate and immersion in another culture.

(C) Businesspeople who already suffer from chronic insomnia are no more likely than businesspeople who do not to accept assignments from their employers that require international travel.

(D) Experiencing dramatic changes in climate and disruption of daily routines through international travel can be beneficial to some people who suffer from chronic insomnia.

(E) Some businesspeople who once traveled internationally but no longer do so complain of various sleep-related ailments.

12. Many mountain climbers regard climbing Mount Everest as the ultimate achievement. But climbers should not attempt this climb since the risk of death or serious injury in an Everest expedition is very high. Moreover, the romantic notion of gaining "spiritual discovery" atop Everest is dispelled by climbers' reports that the only profound experiences they had at the top were of exhaustion and fear.

Which one of the following principles, if valid, most helps to justify the reasoning above?

(A) Projects undertaken primarily for spiritual reasons ought to be abandoned if the risks are great.
(B) Dangerous activities that are unlikely to result in significant spiritual benefits for those undertaking them should be avoided.
(C) Activities that are extremely dangerous ought to be legally prohibited unless they are necessary to produce spiritual enlightenment.
(D) Profound spiritual experiences can be achieved without undergoing the serious danger involved in mountain climbing.
(E) Mountain climbers and other athletes should carefully examine the underlying reasons they have for participating in their sports.

13. Each of the smallest particles in the universe has an elegantly simple structure. Since these particles compose the universe, we can conclude that the universe itself has an elegantly simple structure.

Each of the following arguments exhibits flawed reasoning similar to that in the argument above EXCEPT:

(A) Each part of this car is nearly perfectly engineered. Therefore this car is nearly perfect, from an engineering point of view.
(B) Each part of this desk is made of metal. Therefore this desk is made of metal.
(C) Each brick in this wall is rectangular. Therefore this wall is rectangular.
(D) Each piece of wood in this chair is sturdy. Therefore this chair is sturdy.
(E) Each sentence in this novel is well constructed. Therefore this is a well-constructed novel.

14. Criminologist: A judicial system that tries and punishes criminals without delay is an effective deterrent to violent crime. Long, drawn-out trials and successful legal maneuvering may add to criminals' feelings of invulnerability. But if potential violent criminals know that being caught means prompt punishment, they will hesitate to break the law.

Which one of the following, if true, would most seriously weaken the criminologist's argument?

(A) It is in the nature of violent crime that it is not premeditated.
(B) About one-fourth of all suspects first arrested for a crime are actually innocent.
(C) Many violent crimes are committed by first-time offenders.
(D) Everyone accused of a crime has the right to a trial.
(E) Countries that promptly punish suspected lawbreakers have lower crime rates than countries that allow long trials.

15. Journalist: Many people object to mandatory retirement at age 65 as being arbitrary, arguing that people over 65 make useful contributions. However, if those who reach 65 are permitted to continue working indefinitely, we will face unacceptable outcomes. First, young people entering the job market will not be able to obtain decent jobs in the professions for which they were trained, resulting in widespread dissatisfaction among the young. Second, it is not fair for those who have worked 40 or more years to deprive others of opportunities. Therefore, mandatory retirement should be retained.

The journalist's argument depends on assuming which one of the following?

(A) Anyone who has worked 40 years is at least 65 years old.
(B) All young people entering the job market are highly trained professionals.
(C) It is unfair for a person not to get a job in the profession for which that person was trained.
(D) If people are forced to retire at age 65, there will be much dissatisfaction among at least some older people.
(E) If retirement ceases to be mandatory at age 65, at least some people will choose to work past age 65.

16. Editorial: Contrary to popular belief, teaching preschoolers is not especially difficult, for they develop strict systems (e.g., for sorting toys by shape), which help them to learn, and they are always intensely curious about something new in their world.

Which one of the following, if true, most seriously weakens the editorial's argument?

(A) Preschoolers have a tendency to imitate adults, and most adults follow strict routines.

(B) Children intensely curious about new things have very short attention spans.

(C) Some older children also develop strict systems that help them learn.

(D) Preschoolers ask as many creative questions as do older children.

(E) Preschool teachers generally report lower levels of stress than do other teachers.

17. Lawyer: A body of circumstantial evidence is like a rope, and each item of evidence is like a strand of that rope. Just as additional pieces of circumstantial evidence strengthen the body of evidence, adding strands to the rope strengthens the rope. And if one strand breaks, the rope is not broken nor is its strength much diminished. Thus, even if a few items of a body of circumstantial evidence are discredited, the overall body of evidence retains its basic strength.

The reasoning in the lawyer's argument is most vulnerable to criticism on the grounds that the argument

(A) takes for granted that no items in a body of circumstantial evidence are significantly more critical to the strength of the evidence than other items in that body

(B) presumes, without providing justification, that the strength of a body of evidence is less than the sum of the strengths of the parts of that body

(C) fails to consider the possibility that if many items in a body of circumstantial evidence were discredited, the overall body of evidence would be discredited

(D) offers an analogy in support of a conclusion without indicating whether the two types of things compared share any similarities

(E) draws a conclusion that simply restates a claim presented in support of that conclusion

18. Ethicist: Many environmentalists hold that the natural environment is morally valuable for its own sake, regardless of any benefits it provides us. However, even if nature has no moral value, nature can be regarded as worth preserving simply on the grounds that people find it beautiful. Moreover, because it is philosophically disputable whether nature is morally valuable but undeniable that it is beautiful, an argument for preserving nature that emphasizes nature's beauty will be less vulnerable to logical objections than one that emphasizes its moral value.

The ethicist's reasoning most closely conforms to which one of the following principles?

(A) An argument in favor of preserving nature will be less open to logical objections if it avoids the issue of what makes nature worth preserving.

(B) If an argument for preserving nature emphasizes a specific characteristic of nature and is vulnerable to logical objections, then that characteristic does not provide a sufficient reason for preserving nature.

(C) If it is philosophically disputable whether nature has a certain characteristic, then nature would be more clearly worth preserving if it did not have that characteristic.

(D) Anything that has moral value is worth preserving regardless of whether people consider it to be beautiful.

(E) An argument for preserving nature will be less open to logical objections if it appeals to a characteristic that can be regarded as a basis for preserving nature and that philosophically indisputably belongs to nature.

19. An editor is compiling a textbook containing essays by several different authors. The book will contain essays by Lind, Knight, or Jones, but it will not contain essays by all three. If the textbook contains an essay by Knight, then it will also contain an essay by Jones.

If the statements above are true, which one of the following must be true?

(A) If the textbook contains an essay by Lind, then it will not contain an essay by Knight.

(B) The textbook will contain an essay by only one of Lind, Knight, and Jones.

(C) The textbook will not contain an essay by Knight.

(D) If the textbook contains an essay by Lind, then it will also contain an essay by Jones.

(E) The textbook will contain an essay by Lind.

20. The ability of mammals to control their internal body temperatures is a factor in the development of their brains and intelligence. This can be seen from the following facts: the brain is a chemical machine, all chemical reactions are temperature dependent, and any organism that can control its body temperature can assure that these reactions occur at the proper temperatures.

Which one of the following is an assumption on which the argument depends?

(A) Organisms unable to control their body temperatures do not have the capacity to generate internal body heat without relying on external factors.

(B) Mammals are the only animals that have the ability to control their internal body temperatures.

(C) The brain cannot support intelligence if the chemical reactions within it are subject to uncontrolled temperatures.

(D) The development of intelligence in mammals is not independent of the chemical reactions in their brains taking place at the proper temperatures.

(E) Organisms incapable of controlling their internal body temperatures are subject to unpredictable chemical processes.

21. People who object to the proposed hazardous waste storage site by appealing to extremely implausible scenarios in which the site fails to contain the waste safely are overlooking the significant risks associated with delays in moving the waste from its present unsafe location. If we wait to remove the waste until we find a site certain to contain it safely, the waste will remain in its current location for many years, since it is currently impossible to guarantee that any site can meet that criterion. Yet keeping the waste at the current location for that long clearly poses unacceptable risks.

The statements above, if true, most strongly support which one of the following?

(A) The waste should never have been stored in its current location.

(B) The waste should be placed in the most secure location that can ever be found.

(C) Moving the waste to the proposed site would reduce the threat posed by the waste.

(D) Whenever waste must be moved, one should limit the amount of time allotted to locating alternative waste storage sites.

(E) Any site to which the waste could be moved will be safer than its present site.

22. A recent survey indicates that the average number of books read annually per capita has declined in each of the last three years. However, it also found that most bookstores reported increased profits during the same period.

Each of the following, if true, helps to resolve the survey's apparently paradoxical results EXCEPT:

(A) Recent cutbacks in government spending have forced public libraries to purchase fewer popular contemporary novels.

(B) Due to the installation of sophisticated new antitheft equipment, the recent increase in shoplifting that has hit most retail businesses has left bookstores largely unaffected.

(C) Over the past few years many bookstores have capitalized on the lucrative coffee industry by installing coffee bars.

(D) Bookstore owners reported a general shift away from the sale of inexpensive paperback novels and toward the sale of lucrative hardback books.

(E) Citing a lack of free time, many survey respondents indicated that they had canceled magazine subscriptions in favor of purchasing individual issues at bookstores when time permits.

23. Naturalist: A species can survive a change in environment, as long as the change is not too rapid. Therefore, the threats we are creating to woodland species arise not from the fact that we are cutting down trees, but rather from the rate at which we are doing so.

The reasoning in which one of the following is most similar to that in the naturalist's argument?

(A) The problem with burning fossil fuels is that the supply is limited; so, the faster we expend these resources, the sooner we will be left without an energy source.

(B) Many people gain more satisfaction from performing a job well—regardless of whether they like the job—than from doing merely adequately a job they like; thus, people who want to be happy should choose jobs they can do well.

(C) Some students who study thoroughly do well in school. Thus, what is most important for success in school is not how much time a student puts into studying, but rather how thoroughly the student studies.

(D) People do not fear change if they know what the change will bring; so, our employees' fear stems not from our company's undergoing change, but from our failing to inform them of what the changes entail.

(E) Until ten years ago, we had good soil and our agriculture flourished. Therefore, the recent decline of our agriculture is a result of our soil rapidly eroding and there being nothing that can replace the good soil we lost.

24. Professor: A person who can select a beverage from among 50 varieties of cola is less free than one who has only these 5 choices: wine, coffee, apple juice, milk, and water. It is clear, then, that meaningful freedom cannot be measured simply by the number of alternatives available; the extent of the differences among the alternatives is also a relevant factor.

The professor's argument proceeds by

(A) supporting a general principle by means of an example

(B) drawing a conclusion about a particular case on the basis of a general principle

(C) supporting its conclusion by means of an analogy

(D) claiming that whatever holds for each member of a group must hold for the whole group

(E) inferring one general principle from another, more general, principle

25. Principle: Meetings should be kept short, addressing only those issues relevant to a majority of those attending. A person should not be required to attend a meeting if none of the issues to be addressed at the meeting are relevant to that person.

Application: Terry should not be required to attend today's two o'clock meeting.

Which one of the following, if true, most justifies the stated application of the principle?

(A) The only issues on which Terry could make a presentation at the meeting are issues irrelevant to at least a majority of those who could attend.

(B) If Terry makes a presentation at the meeting, the meeting will not be kept short.

(C) No issue relevant to Terry could be relevant to a majority of those attending the meeting.

(D) If Terry attends the meeting a different set of issues will be relevant to a majority of those attending than if Terry does not attend.

(E) The majority of the issues to be addressed at the meeting are not relevant to Terry.

**Answer Explanations follow on the next page.**

## ANSWER KEY

| | |
|---|---|
| 1. A | 14. A |
| 2. C | 15. E |
| 3. E | 16. B |
| 4. A | 17. A |
| 5. E | 18. E |
| 6. D | 19. A |
| 7. A | 20. D |
| 8. A | 21. C |
| 9. E | 22. B |
| 10. B | 23. D |
| 11. C | 24. A |
| 12. B | 25. C |
| 13. B | |

# SECTION TRIAGE

Be sure to evaluate the section-management decisions you made just as you did on the previous full-length section. Using the table below, review the difficulty levels of the questions. (One star indicates the lowest difficulty and four stars represent the highest difficulty.) Remember that the actual difficulty level for you can be higher or lower, but you should be aware of the general trends in the section.

This section started with an easier set of questions and a tough assumption question thrown in the mix, became more difficult in an expanded "danger zone" from question 13 to 22, and ended with a lower difficulty question set. Again, I recommend that you work through about four pages of the section and then turn to the end of the section and answer questions from the end, working your way backward toward the middle. It's imperative that you use your knowledge of the Logical Reasoning section anatomy to help guide you through the questions so you don't get bogged down by individual questions or leave easier questions behind.

**Table 22.1**

| PrepTest 53: Section 3 | | |
|---|---|---|
| Question | Question Type | Difficulty Level |
| 1 | Strengthen | * |
| 2 | Flaw | * |
| 3 | Main Point | * |
| 4 | Weaken | ** |
| 5 | Main Point | ** |
| 6 | Flaw | * |
| 7 | Inference | ** |
| 8 | Assumption | *** |
| 9 | Weaken | ** |
| 10 | Role of a Statement | * |
| 11 | Strengthen | ** |
| 12 | Principle | *** |
| 13 | Parallel Reasoning | **** |
| 14 | Weaken | ** |
| 15 | Assumption | ** |
| 16 | Weaken | ** |
| 17 | Flaw | **** |
| 18 | Principle | **** |
| 19 | Inference | *** |
| 20 | Assumption | ** |
| 21 | Inference | *** |

(continued)

| Question | Question Type | Difficulty Level |
|---|---|---|
| 22 | Paradox | *** |
| 23 | Parallel Reasoning | ** |
| 24 | Method of Argument | ** |
| 25 | Principle | ** |

## Explanations

1. **(A)**

At many electronics retail stores, the consumer has the option of purchasing product warranties that extend beyond the manufacturer's warranty. <However, consumers are generally better off not buying extended warranties.> Most problems with electronic goods occur within the period covered by the manufacturer's warranty.

Which one of the following, if true, most strengthens the argument?

(A) Problems with electronic goods that occur after the manufacturer's warranty expires are generally inexpensive to fix in comparison with the cost of an extended warranty.

(B) Because problems are so infrequent after the manufacturer's warranty expires, extended warranties on electronic goods are generally inexpensive.

(C) Most of those who buy extended warranties on electronic goods do so because special circumstances make their item more likely to break than is usually the case.

(D) Some extended warranties on electronic goods cover the product for the period covered by the manufacturer's warranty as well as subsequent years.

(E) Retail stores sell extended warranties in part because consumers who purchase them are likely to purchase other products from the same store.

### Step 1. Identify the Question Type

The word "strengthens" identifies this as a Strengthen question.

### Step 2. Untangle the Stimulus

The author's main point, noted by the contrast Keyword "However," is that consumers are generally better off not buying extended warranties. The evidence follows in the last sentence and explains that most problems with electronics happen in the period covered by the manufacturer's warranty.

### Step 3. Make a Prediction

Focus on the qualifying language in the evidence: "Most." Most problems occur during the covered time period. What about the ones that don't? The author must assume that the few problems that happen after the warranty expires aren't bad enough to justify purchasing the extended warranty. A valid strengthener will confirm the assumption and thereby make the conclusion more likely to follow from the evidence.

### Step 4. Evaluate the Answer Choices

Choice (A) strengthens the argument by supporting the assumption. If post-warranty problems are inexpensive compared to the cost of an extended warranty, the author's conclusion makes even more sense. This is the correct answer.

Choice (B) is an ambivalent answer choice that you should watch out for on Strengthen and Weaken questions. Sure, emphasizing the infrequency of post-warranty problems strengthens the argument, but mentioning the low cost of extended warranties could support purchasing the extension. While a Strengthen answer choice need not prove the conclusion true, it does have to unequivocally make the conclusion at least a little more likely to be true. Choice (A) does that, while it is debatable whether choice (B) makes the conclusion more or less likely.

Choice (C) is compatible with the author's recommendation to generally not buy the extension by explaining that people who do buy extended warranties have special circumstances under which they make that purchase. But, though compatible with the author's reasoning, this information does nothing to bolster an argument against buying an extension.

Choice (D) misses the point. The overlap of coverage does nothing to make the extension more, or less, valuable to the buyer. Therefore, it does not weaken, nor strengthen the argument against purchasing extensions.

Choice (E) presents a rationale for stores to sell the extended warranties but it doesn't address whether consumers should buy them.

2. **(C)**

Since the 1970s, environmentalists have largely succeeded in convincing legislators to enact extensive environmental regulations. Yet, as environmentalists themselves not only admit but insist, the condition of the environment is worsening, not improving. <(Clearly,) more environmental regulations are not the solution to the environment's problems.>

The argument's reasoning is (flawed) because the argument

(A) attacks the environmentalists themselves instead of their positions

(B) presumes, without providing warrant, that only an absence of environmental regulations could prevent environmental degradation

(C) fails to consider the possibility that the condition of the environment would have worsened even more without environmental regulations

(D) fails to justify its presumption that reducing excessive regulations is more important than preserving the environment

(E) fails to consider the views of the environmentalists' opponents

### Step 1. Identify the Question Type

The term "flawed" clearly tells you that this is a Flaw question.

### Step 2. Untangle the Stimulus

"Clearly" points to the conclusion in the last sentence, which says more regulation will not solve environmental problems. The evidence provided states that environmental problems keep getting worse despite the enactment of extensive regulations.

### Step 3. Make a Prediction

The author must assume that environmental regulation does not work, at least not well, since there have been environmental regulations yet the situation has still deteriorated. However, maybe the environment would have more problems without the regulations. That's the possibility the author fails to consider and the classic flaw he commits.

### Step 4. Evaluate the Answer Choices

Choice (A) describes an ad hominem, which is a type of flaw, but not the flaw in this argument. The author never makes a personal attack on the environmentalists. Cross out this choice.

Choice (B) is extreme. The author says more regulation is not the answer to environmental problems, not that eliminating all regulation is the only way to prevent further problems. Move on to the next choice.

Choice (C) correctly identifies the flaw in the argument and is the correct answer.

Choice (D) raises an irrelevant comparison between the importance of reducing excessive regulations and preserving the environment. The author doesn't assume anything about this comparison, only that reducing regulation will not preserve the environment.

Choice (E) is a 180 answer. Does the author really ignore environmental opponents? No way, the author is an opponent of environmental regulations.

3.  **(E)**

    (Although) it is unwise to take a developmental view of an art like music—as if Beethoven were an advance over Josquin, or Miles Davis an advance over Louis Armstrong—<there are ways in which it makes sense to talk about musical knowledge growing over time.> We certainly know more about certain sounds than was known five centuries ago; that is, we understand how sounds that earlier composers avoided can be used effectively in musical compositions. (For example,) we now know how the interval of the third, which is considered dissonant, can be used in compositions to create consonant musical phrases.

    Which one of the following most accurately expresses the (main conclusion) of the argument?

    (A)   Sounds that were never used in past musical
            compositions are used today.
    (B)   Sounds that were once considered dissonant are
            more pleasing to modern listeners.
    (C)   It is inappropriate to take a developmental view
            of music.
    (D)   It is unwise to say that one composer is better
            than another.
    (E)   Our understanding of music can improve over
            the course of time.

## Step 1. Identify the Question Type

"Main conclusion" signals that this is a Main Point question.

## Step 2. Untangle the Stimulus

The argument begins with "Although" signaling a concession by the author. He acknowledges it's not a good idea to think of music in developmental terms, but, he says, it does make sense to talk about musical knowledge expanding over time. The rest of the argument supports this statement with information and examples of how we know more about sound today than we did five centuries ago.

### Step 3. Make a Prediction

Like most Main Point questions, the stimulus offers no conclusion Keywords to direct you to the conclusion. Instead use the evidence Keywords and the author's opinion. Here, the correct answer will identify the main point as the notion that musical knowledge can expand over time.

### Step 4. Evaluate the Answer Choices

Choice (A) is an example of our expanding musical knowledge, and as so, is part of the evidence not the conclusion. Eliminate this choice.

Choice (B) offers a statement that is part of the sentence that begins with "For example," an indication of evidence not the conclusion. Move on to the next choice.

Choice (C) presents the information conceded by the author as part of the "Although" phrase at the beginning of the argument. This choice is out.

Choice (D) is another point of concession for the author.

Choice (E), the remaining choice, captures the first sentence and is the correct answer.

4.  **(A)**

    A recent test of an electric insect control device discovered that, of the more than 300 insects killed during one 24-hour period, only 12 were mosquitoes. ⟨Thus⟩ this type of device may kill many insects, but will not significantly aid in controlling the potentially dangerous mosquito population.⟩

    Which one of the following, if true, most seriously ⟨weakens⟩ the argument?

    (A)  A careful search discovered no live mosquitoes in the vicinity of the device after the test.
    (B)  A very large proportion of the insects that were attracted to the device were not mosquitoes.
    (C)  The device is more likely to kill beneficial insects than it is to kill harmful insects.
    (D)  Many of the insects that were killed by the device are mosquito-eating insects.
    (E)  The device does not succeed in killing all of the insects that it attracts.

### Step 1. Identify the Question Type

The term "weaken" is classic language for a Weaken question

### Step 2. Untangle the Stimulus

The author concludes (note the indicator "Thus") that the electric insect control device kills insects but won't really help control the mosquito population. The author supports this conclusion with test results that found only 12 mosquitoes were killed out of more than 300 insects in a 24-hour period.

### Step 3. Make a Prediction

The author determines that the device doesn't work well enough to control the mosquito population based on the number of mosquitoes killed. He assumes the 12 killed is a low number in relation to the mosquito population. So, to weaken the argument and make it less likely that the device won't control the mosquito population, find an answer that attacks the assumption.

### Step 4. Evaluate the Answer Choices

Choice (A) challenges the assumption and weakens the argument by suggesting the device got rid of all the mosquitoes in the vicinity and therefore controlled the mosquito population. In this case, 12 mosquitoes is the whole population. This is the correct answer.

Choice (B) does not address the proportion of mosquitoes killed by the device, so it cannot weaken the argument. In fact, choice (B) may strengthen the argument that the device doesn't control the mosquito population if a large portion of the mosquito population is not attracted to it.

Choice (C), far from weakening the argument, is in line with the author's claim that at least one harmful insect, the mosquito, will not be controlled by the device.

Choice (D) strengthens the argument that the device will not control mosquitoes by indicating that in addition to the apparent anemic effect on mosquitoes, it also eliminates mosquito predators.

Choice (E) is too broad in referencing all insects attracted to the device but also provides a deficiency in its killing power. So, choice (E) also marginally strengthens, not weakens the argument.

5. **(E)**

Brain-scanning technology provides information about processes occurring in the brain. <For this information to help researchers understand how the brain enables us to think, (however,) researchers must be able to rely on the accuracy of the verbal reports given by subjects while their brains are being scanned.> Otherwise brain-scan data gathered at a given moment might not contain information about what the subject reports thinking about at that moment, but instead about some different set of thoughts.

Which one of the following most accurately expresses the (main conclusion) of the argument?

(A)   It is unlikely that brain-scanning technology will ever enable researchers to understand how the brain enables us to think.

(B)   There is no way that researchers can know for certain that subjects whose brains are being scanned are accurately reporting what they are thinking.

(C)   Because subjects whose brains are being scanned may not accurately report what they are thinking, the results of brain-scanning research should be regarded with great skepticism.

(D)   Brain scans can provide information about the accuracy of the verbal reports of subjects whose brains are being scanned.

(E)   Information from brain scans can help researchers understand how the brain enables us to think only if the verbal reports of those whose brains are being scanned are accurate.

### Step 1. Identify the Question Type

The phrase "main conclusion" tells you that this is a Main Point question.

### Step 2. Untangle the Stimulus

The stimulus begins with a statement of the information provided by a brain scan. As background information, it sets the stage for the author's strong opinion highlighted by "however" in the next sentence. It says that for brain scans to be helpful, researchers must rely on the reports of the subjects as they are scanned. The next sentence, starting with "Otherwise," tells you the result if they don't.

### Step 3. Make a Prediction

Without conclusion Keywords, look for opinion and other Keywords to help you determine the author's main point. Here, the second sentence gives the author's point and receives support from the statements around it. The correct answer will paraphrase that sentence.

**Step 4. Evaluate the Answer Choices**

Choice (A) distorts information in the stimulus. The author identifies a necessary condition for the scans to be helpful. He doesn't conclude that brain scans are unlikely to be helpful.

Choice (B) is not mentioned in the stimulus. The author says that researchers must be able to trust the subjects' reports. He never questions whether researchers can know for sure that subjects can accurately report their thinking during a scan.

Choice (C) isn't discussed in the stimulus either. The author doesn't mention the possibility of inaccurate reports from subjects nor does he conclude that brain-scan research should be regarded with skepticism.

Choice (D) reverses the information. Brain scans don't shed light on the verbal reports of subjects being scanned. It's the other way around. The verbal reports are necessary for the researchers to use brain scans to help them understand how we think.

Choice (E) correctly states the author's main point. Remember, the phrase "only if" indicates a necessary condition, just like the word "must" in the sentence of the stimulus bracketed as the conclusion. So, this answer choice matches perfectly. Fluency in the language of necessity and sufficiency is invaluable on the Logical Reasoning section.

6.  **(D)**

Ornithologist: This bird species is widely thought to subsist primarily on vegetation, <but my research shows that this belief is erroneous.> While concealed in a well-camouflaged blind, I have observed hundreds of these birds every morning over a period of months, and I estimate that over half of what they ate consisted of insects and other animal food sources.

The reasoning in the ornithologist's argument is most vulnerable to criticism on the grounds that the argument

(A) assumes, without providing justification, that the feeding behavior of the birds observed was not affected by the ornithologist's act of observation

(B) fails to specify the nature of the animal food sources, other than insects, that were consumed by the birds

(C) adopts a widespread belief about the birds' feeding habits without considering the evidence that led to the belief

(D) neglects the possibility that the birds have different patterns of food consumption during different parts of the day and night

(E) fails to consider the possibility that the birds' diet has changed since the earlier belief about their diet was formed

### Step 1. Identify the Question Type

The phrase "most vulnerable to criticism" indicates that this is a Flaw question.

### Step 2. Untangle the Stimulus

When a stimulus begins with a widely held belief, expect the author to disagree. Here, the ornithologist presents a common belief that certain bird species primarily eat vegetation. In her disagreement, signaled by "but," she states the belief is false and tells you specifically she bases her conclusion on her research. She observed hundreds of the birds each morning over a period of months and estimates that over half their diet consisted of insects and other animals.

### Step 3. Make a Prediction

When a Flaw question includes research or a study, consider the common flaw of representativeness. While the number of birds observed sounds like it might be a large enough sample, notice the ornithologist observed the birds in the morning only, which may not represent their day-long eating habits. She overlooks the possibility that they eat differently—specifically different vegetation—during the rest of the day.

### Step 4. Evaluate the Answer Choices

Choice (A) accuses the ornithologist of not providing justification for the assumption, which she does make—she claims she was well-concealed. Do not try to argue, especially from outside knowledge, whether such camouflage would work. The only relevant question is "does the ornithologist really do this?" Does the ornithologist really not provide justification? No.

Choice (B) is irrelevant. What's important is that the non-insect animal food sources were not vegetation.

Choice (C) contradicts the stimulus. Remember on Flaw questions your task is to describe the author's logic, particularly its flawed logic. Your task is not to weaken the argument or dispute the author's claims. The ornithologist disagrees with the widespread belief, so this choice doesn't describe her argument at all.

Choice (D) correctly points out that the birds' morning eating habits may not represent their general eating habits and the ornithologist failed to consider that possibility.

Choice (E) is not at issue in the stimulus. Whether the birds changed their diet is of no consequence in the ornithologist's quest to disprove the widely held belief that the birds currently eat mostly vegetation. The ornithologist does not assert what was or was not the case in the past.

7.　**(A)**

Educator: (Only) those students who are genuinely curious about a topic can successfully learn about that topic. They find the satisfaction of their curiosity intrinsically gratifying, and appreciate the inherent rewards of the learning process itself. However, almost no child enters the classroom with sufficient curiosity to learn successfully all that the teacher must instill. A teacher's job, therefore, _____.

Which one of the following (most logically completes) the educator's argument?

(A)　requires for the fulfillment of its goals the stimulation as well as the satisfaction of curiosity

(B)　necessitates the creative use of rewards that are not inherent in the learning process itself

(C)　is to focus primarily on those topics that do not initially interest the students

(D)　is facilitated by students' taking responsibility for their own learning

(E)　becomes easier if students realize that some learning is not necessarily enjoyable

## Step 1. Identify the Question Type

Because this question asks for a statement that "most logically completes" the argument, it is an Inference question. Recognizing this as an Inference question should be a reminder to not get creative in tagging on a "conclusion" to this argument that goes beyond what *must be true* based on the information already provided.

## Step 2. Untangle the Stimulus

When an inference stimulus includes formal logic, translate the statement to help you understand the argument. "Only" signals formal logic in this case, so translate the statement from its "Only Y are X" form to "X → Y." "Only curious students can learn" becomes "Learn → curious." Then you find out that being curious means students are gratified by curiosity and appreciate the rewards of the learning process. The stimulus ends with a problem: Most students enter the classroom without enough curiosity to sustain learning. So, what's a teacher to do to instill learning?

## Step 3. Make a Prediction

Some Inference questions are not susceptible to prediction. In this case, however, you are asked for the logical conclusion to a formal logic chain of reasoning, so a prediction is possible. And here is what you know: Curiosity is necessary for learning and most students don't have enough curiosity. Therefore, a teacher's job must be to stimulate curiosity.

### Step 4. Evaluate the Answer Choices

Choice (A) correctly defines a teacher's responsibility to arouse curiosity.

Choice (B) distorts the stimulus. It says that a curious student will appreciate the inherent rewards of the learning process, not that a teacher must use rewards that are not inherent in the learning process.

Choice (C) is a reasonable potential course of action based on the information provided, but such speculation, no matter how reasonable, must be resisted. This is precisely the type of answer that requires thinking of this as an Inference question, whose answer *must be true* based on the information in the stimulus, rather than feeling free to tag on a reasonable conclusion that *could be true* from this information.

Choice (D) must not be true based on the stimulus. Student responsibility is never discussed. Besides, how can students take responsibility for their own learning if they lack the curiosity needed to learn?

Choice (E) also reaches beyond the stimulus and therefore cannot be true based on it. The stimulus never says that a teacher's job will be easier if students understand that learning is not always enjoyable.

8.  **(A)**

Environmentalist: When bacteria degrade household cleaning products, vapors that are toxic to humans are produced. Unfortunately, household cleaning products are often found in landfills. <Thus,> the common practice of converting landfills into public parks is damaging human health.>

Which one of the following is an (assumption) the environmentalist's argument requires?

(A) In at least some landfills that have been converted into public parks there are bacteria that degrade household cleaning products.

(B) Converting a landfill into a public park will cause no damage to human health unless toxic vapors are produced in that landfill and humans are exposed to them.

(C) If a practice involves the exposure of humans to vapors from household cleaning products, then it causes at least some damage to human health.

(D) When landfills are converted to public parks, measures could be taken that would prevent people using the parks from being exposed to toxic vapors.

(E) If vapors toxic to humans are produced by the degradation of household cleaning products by bacteria in any landfill, then the health of at least some humans will suffer.

### Step 1. Identify the Question Type

Because the stem specifically asks for an "assumption," this is an Assumption question.

### Step 2. Untangle the Stimulus

"Thus" in the last sentence identifies the conclusion: The common practice of turning landfills into public parks damages human health. To support his conclusion, the environmentalist offers evidence that toxic vapors are produced when bacteria degrade household cleaning products which are often found in landfills.

### Step 3. Make a Prediction

With an Assumption question, you know a gap exists between the conclusion and the evidence. Your task is to bridge that gap. Here, you have mismatched terms in the conclusion and evidence. The conclusion mentions converting landfills to public parks, while the evidence says that toxic vapors are released when bacteria degrade household cleaning products. Connect these terms and you will have a prediction for the assumption: The environmentalist must assume that converting landfills into parks must result in bacterial degradation of household cleaning products.

### Step 4. Evaluate the Answer Choices

Choice (A) matches the prediction and is the correct answer.

Choice (B) distorts the stimulus by saying toxic vapors are the only way to harm human health in the conversion of a landfill to a public park.

Choice (C) connects vapor exposure to damaged health, but never makes the connection back to the conversion of landfills to parks in the conclusion.

Choice (D) attempts to solve the problem of exposure to toxic vapors, which goes beyond the scope of the argument.

Choice (E) has the same problem as choice (C) by not linking to the conclusion.

9. **(E)**

Tea made from camellia leaves is a popular beverage.
However, studies show that regular drinkers of camellia
tea usually suffer withdrawal symptoms if they
discontinue drinking the tea. Furthermore, regular
drinkers of camellia tea are more likely than people in
general to develop kidney damage. <Regular
consumption of this tea, (therefore,) can result in a
heightened risk of kidney damage.>

Which one of the following, if true, most seriously
(weakens) the argument?

(A)  Several other popular beverages contain the
     same addictive chemical that is found in
     camellia tea.
(B)  Addictive chemicals are unlikely to cause
     kidney damage solely by virtue of their
     addictive qualities.
(C)  Some people claim that regular consumption of
     camellia tea helps alleviate their stress.
(D)  Most people who regularly drink camellia tea do
     not develop kidney damage.
(E)  Many people who regularly consume camellia
     tea also regularly consume other beverages
     suspected of causing kidney damage.

### Step 1. Identify the Question Type

The term "weaken" makes this a Weaken question.

### Step 2. Untangle the Stimulus

The stimulus indicates that regular drinkers of camellia tea are more likely than people in general to develop kidney damage. Based on that, the author concludes with "therefore" that regular consumption of this tea can result in a heightened risk of kidney damage. The phrase "can result in" indicates a causal relationship between tea and kidney damage. The problem is that it's based on evidence of a correlation.

### Step 3. Make a Prediction

There are three possibilities to weaken a causal argument: reverse the causation (maybe kidney damage caused people to drink the tea), offer an alternative cause (maybe the tea drinkers consume or do something else that causes kidney damage), or write it off as coincidence.

### Step 4. Evaluate the Answer Choices

Choice (A) doesn't weaken the argument by any of the three stated methods. Even if camellia tea contains the same addictive chemical as other popular beverages, that doesn't make the tea less likely to cause kidney damage. Eliminate this choice.

Choice (B) focuses on addictive chemicals, not on weakening the causal connection between camellia tea and kidney damage. Move on to the next choice.

Choice (C) says camellia tea may relieve stress. But, it could do that and still cause kidney damage. Choice (C) does nothing to weaken the relationship between the tea and kidney damage.

Choice (D) may be tempting, but remember to check the three standard methods for weakening a causal argument. Choice (D) doesn't fit. The author simply claims some causal connection between the tea and a heightened risk of kidney damage. An answer that indicates a majority, meaning at least 51%, of tea drinkers do NOT get kidney damage, does not undermine the author's modest conclusion of some causal connection. This answer allows for up to 49% of tea drinkers having kidney damage, which could very well be considered a heightened risk.

Choice (E) correctly offers an alternative cause: other beverages that could increase the risk of kidney damage.

10. **(B)**

> Artist: Avant-garde artists intend their work to challenge a society's mainstream beliefs and initiate change. And some art collectors claim that an avant-garde work that becomes popular in its own time is successful. However, a society's mainstream beliefs do not generally show any significant changes over a short period of time. Therefore, when an avant-garde work becomes popular it is a sign that the work is not successful, > since it does not fulfill the intentions of its creator.

The reference to the claim of certain art collectors plays which one of the following roles in the artist's argument?

(A) It serves to bolster the argument's main conclusion.

(B) It identifies a view that is ultimately disputed by the argument.

(C) It identifies a position supported by the initial premise in the argument.

(D) It provides support for the initial premise in the argument.

(E) It provides support for a counterargument to the initial premise.

## Step 1. Identify the Question Type

The question refers to a claim in the stimulus and asks for the role the claim plays. Therefore, this stem is a Role of a Statement question.

### Step 2. Untangle the Stimulus

The claim in question is in the second sentence; it says that avant-garde art that becomes popular in its own time is successful. The next sentence, which starts with "However," signals a contrast ahead. The artist presents her shift in the conclusion marked by "Therefore" and says that the popularity of avant-garde work is not a sign of success. Her evidence follows in the clause that starts with "since."

### Step 3. Make a Prediction

The claim is not part of the argument's conclusion or evidence. It's the target of the artist's disagreement.

### Step 4. Evaluate the Answer Choices

Choice (A) has it backward; the claim contrasts the conclusion, it doesn't support it.

Choice (B) is a perfect match and is the correct answer.

Choice (C) doesn't work. The initial premise that avant-garde artists intend their work to challenge society has no clear connection to the claim made by some art collectors that an avant-garde work that becomes popular in its own time is successful.

Choice (D) has the same problem. The initial premise doesn't support or isn't supported by the claim in question.

Choice (E) references a counterargument not included in the stimulus.

11. **(C)**

A recent epidemiological study found that businesspeople who travel internationally on business are much more likely to suffer from chronic insomnia than are businesspeople who do not travel on business. International travelers experience the stresses of dramatic changes in climate, frequent disruption of daily routines, and immersion in cultures other than their own, stresses not commonly felt by those who do not travel. <(Thus,) it is likely that these stresses <u>cause</u> the insomnia.>

Which one of the following would, if true, most (strengthen) the reasoning above?

(A)   Most international travel for the sake of business occurs between countries with contiguous borders.

(B)   Some businesspeople who travel internationally greatly enjoy the changes in climate and immersion in another culture.

(C)   Businesspeople who already suffer from chronic insomnia are no more likely than businesspeople who do not to accept assignments from their employers that require international travel.

(D)   Experiencing dramatic changes in climate and disruption of daily routines through international travel can be beneficial to some people who suffer from chronic insomnia.

(E)   Some businesspeople who once traveled internationally but no longer do so complain of various sleep-related ailments.

## Step 1. Identify the Question Type

This is a Strengthen question, signaled by "strengthen" in the question stem.

## Step 2. Untangle the Stimulus

The author concludes at the end of the stimulus that the stresses associated with international business travel cause travelers to suffer from insomnia. This claim of causation is based on a correlation found in a study that said international business travelers are more likely to be chronic insomniacs than those businesspeople who do not travel on business.

## Step 3. Make a Prediction

Causal arguments can be strengthened in three different ways: by confirming the causality, by eliminating an alternative cause for the stated result (or eliminating the possibility of reverse causation), or by reducing the possibility of coincidence. Look for an answer that fits into one of these categories.

## Step 4. Evaluate the Answer Choices

Choice (A) has no impact on the argument. The specific destination of international business travel doesn't affect a relationship between international business travel and insomnia.

Choice (B) contradicts the stimulus by calling some factors of international business travel enjoyable, while the author considers them stressors.

Choice (C) strengthens the argument by making it less likely that causation is reversed. In other words, choice (C) confirms the causal relationship from the stress of international travel to insomnia by pointing out that it's unlikely that the reverse is true, that insomnia causes the stress of international business travel. Choice (C) is the correct answer.

Choice (D) weakens the causal link between the stresses of international travel and insomnia by suggesting the so-called stresses may be beneficial to insomnia sufferers.

Choice (E) broadens the argument beyond insomnia to include various sleep-related ailments.

12. **(B)**

Many mountain climbers regard climbing Mount Everest as the ultimate achievement. But <climbers should not attempt this climb> (since) the risk of death or serious injury in an Everest expedition is very high. (Moreover,) the romantic notion of gaining "spiritual discovery" atop Everest is dispelled by climbers' reports that the only profound experiences they had at the top were of exhaustion and fear.

Which one of the <u>following</u> (principles,) if valid, <u>most helps to justify</u> the reasoning above?

(A) Projects undertaken primarily for spiritual reasons ought to be abandoned if the risks are great.

(B) Dangerous activities that are unlikely to result in significant spiritual benefits for those undertaking them should be avoided.

(C) Activities that are extremely dangerous ought to be legally prohibited unless they are necessary to produce spiritual enlightenment.

(D) Profound spiritual experiences can be achieved without undergoing the serious danger involved in mountain climbing.

(E) Mountain climbers and other athletes should carefully examine the underlying reasons they have for participating in their sports.

## Step 1. Identify the Question Type

The term "principles" tells you that this is a Principle question, and "following" tells you to find the principle in the answer choices. Because of the phrase "most helps to justify," you also know that the principle will act like a strengthener for the specific situation in the stimulus.

## Step 2. Untangle the Stimulus

The author warns against climbing Mount Everest because it's very dangerous and dismisses any notion of spiritual discovery with reports of exhaustion and fear at the peak.

## Step 3. Make a Prediction

The correct answer will take this specific situation and broaden it to a general rule, such as: Don't bother with dangerous activities that hold no spiritual reward.

## Step 4. Evaluate the Answer Choices

Choice (A) distorts the argument by contorting it into a balance of risk versus spiritual reward and coming down on the side of safety. However, the author's recommendation is limited to endeavors that are both risky and do not provide the spiritual reward anticipated.

Choice (B) matches the prediction and is the correct answer.

Choice (C) is extreme in recommending legal prohibition for extremely dangerous activities. The stimulus never mentions what the law should or should not permit.

Choice (D) is out because the author never discusses achieving profound spiritual experiences. Rather, he talks about one activity in which spiritual discovery is unlikely.

Choice (E) does not match up with the author's recommendation to avoid the activity, not just think about it first.

13. **(B)**

> Each of the smallest particles in the universe has an elegantly simple structure. (Since) these particles compose the universe, <we can (conclude that) the universe itself has an elegantly simple structure.>
>
> Each of the following arguments exhibits (flawed) (reasoning similar to) that in the argument above (EXCEPT:)

(A)   Each part of this car is nearly perfectly engineered. Therefore this car is nearly perfect, from an engineering point of view.

(B)   Each part of this desk is made of metal. Therefore this desk is made of metal.

(C)   Each brick in this wall is rectangular. Therefore this wall is rectangular.

(D)   Each piece of wood in this chair is sturdy. Therefore this chair is sturdy.

(E)   Each sentence in this novel is well constructed. Therefore this is a well-constructed novel.

### Step 1. Identify the Question Type

The phrase "flawed reasoning similar to" denotes a Parallel Flaw question. "EXCEPT" means that the four wrong answers will share a similar type of argument with a similar flaw with the stimulus, while the correct answer will not.

### Step 2. Untangle the Stimulus

The conclusion at the end of the stimulus asserts that the universe has a simple structure. The evidence, noted by "since," explains that the particles that make up the universe have the same structure.

### Step 3. Make a Prediction

A quick check of the answer choices shows that the conclusions are all assertions of fact like the stimulus. So, move on and compare the flaws. The argument commits a classic flaw by assuming that what is true of the parts is true of the whole. The four wrong answers will have the same flaw. The one right answer will have a different flaw or will not have a flaw at all.

### Step 4. Evaluate the Answer Choices

Choice (A) has a parallel flaw because it claims that perfect engineering of each car part means a perfectly engineered car. The flaw arises in the process of putting the parts together. The car is not just the sum of its parts, but also the process of putting the parts together. The argument does not account for that. Eliminate this choice.

Choice (B) has a superficially similar structure as the stimulus, but it is not flawed. Consequently, (B) is the correct answer. If every part of a desk is metal, the whole desk really is metal. On Parallel Flaw questions, it is common for one or more answers to not contain a logic flaw. On a Parallel Flaw EXCEPT question, there can be only one, and it will be the correct answer.

Choice (C) commits the same flaw as the stimulus and can therefore be eliminated. Each brick in the wall may be rectangular, but the bricks can be arranged to form different shapes. The wall does not necessarily have to be rectangular.

Choice (D) runs into the same flaw as the stimulus. With poor construction, you can create a not-so-sturdy chair with sturdy individual pieces.

You can eliminate choice (E) as well because it has a parallel flaw. Well-constructed sentences don't guarantee a well-constructed novel, especially if the sentences have no logical relationship to each other.

14. **(A)**

> Criminologist: <A judicial system that tries and punishes criminals without delay is an effective deterrent to violent crime.> Long, drawn-out trials and successful legal maneuvering may add to criminals' feelings of invulnerability. But if potential violent criminals know that being caught means prompt punishment, they will hesitate to break the law.

> Which one of the following, if true, would most seriously (weaken) the criminologist's argument?

(A)   It is in the nature of violent crime that it is not premeditated.

(B)   About one-fourth of all suspects first arrested for a crime are actually innocent.

(C)   Many violent crimes are committed by first-time offenders.

(D)   Everyone accused of a crime has the right to a trial.

(E)   Countries that promptly punish suspected lawbreakers have lower crime rates than countries that allow long trials.

### Step 1. Identify the Question Type

The question asks you to "weaken" the criminologist's argument, so it's a Weaken question.

### Step 2. Untangle the Stimulus

The criminologist concludes that prompt punishment helps prevent violent crime. He bases this on the evidence that lengthy trials and legal maneuvering make criminals feel like they can work the system to their own benefit. But, people thinking of committing a crime will hesitate if they know punishment will be swift.

### Step 3. Make a Prediction

If knowledge of swift punishment will deter crime, the criminologist must assume that would-be criminals can consider the consequences. If they can't do that, the argument is weaker. In other words, attack the assumption to weaken the argument.

### Step 4. Evaluate the Answer Choices

Choice (A) weakens the argument. If violent crime is not premeditated, then criminals don't stop to consider the consequences. This is the correct answer.

Choice (B) does not impact the argument, which is about whether speedy trials deter violent crime, not the guilt or innocence of suspects when they're first arrested.

Choice (C) brings in the history of violent criminals and does not address whether someone can think about the consequences of his crime before he commits it.

Choice (D) doesn't work either. The criminologist isn't talking about a right to trial, but rather a quick trial as a deterrent.

Choice (E) strengthens the argument by suggesting that speedy trials do reduce the crime rate.

15. **(E)**

> Journalist: Many people object to mandatory retirement at age 65 as being arbitrary, arguing that people over 65 make useful contributions. However, if those who reach 65 are permitted to continue working indefinitely, we will face unacceptable outcomes. First, young people entering the job market will not be able to obtain decent jobs in the professions for which they were trained, resulting in widespread dissatisfaction among the young. Second, it is not fair for those who have worked 40 or more years to deprive others of opportunities. <(Therefore,) mandatory retirement should be retained.>

The journalist's argument (depends) on (assuming) which one of the following?

(A)    Anyone who has worked 40 years is at least 65 years old.
(B)    All young people entering the job market are highly trained professionals.
(C)    It is unfair for a person not to get a job in the profession for which that person was trained.
(D)    If people are forced to retire at age 65, there will be much dissatisfaction among at least some older people.
(E)    If retirement ceases to be mandatory at age 65, at least some people will choose to work past age 65.

## Step 1. Identify the Question Type

The word "assuming" identifies the stem as an Assumption question. "Depends" indicates a necessary assumption.

## Step 2. Untangle the Stimulus

The journalist concludes that the mandatory retirement age should be preserved because allowing people to work past the age of 65 will produce unacceptable outcomes.

## Step 3. Make a Prediction

The journalist is assuming that the downside of older people continuing to work is outweighed by the rights of older people or benefits of them continuing to work.

## Step 4. Evaluate the Answer Choices

Choice (A) refers to details in the argument and just confuses them. Eliminate this choice.

Choice (B) is too extreme in referring to all young people entering the job market and is not mentioned in the stimulus. Cross out this choice.

Choice (C) distorts the details of the unacceptable outcomes outlined in the stimulus. Move on.

Choice (D) doesn't make sense in light of the fact the journalist wants to maintain mandatory retirement for people over 65. So, she wouldn't assume that older people will be dissatisfied with it.

Choice (E) was a tough one to predict in advance because it is so basic and not at all profound. But anytime the journalist makes a recommendation, the journalist inherently assumes that the proposal is not impossible and that there is some point to the proposal. Use the denial test, and see how if nobody will continue working, then the author's claim that mandatory retirement provisions should be retained is pointless.

16. **(B)**

Editorial: Contrary to popular belief, <teaching preschoolers is not especially difficult,> for they develop strict systems (e.g., for sorting toys by shape), which help them to learn, and they are always intensely curious about something new in their world.

Which one of the following, if true, most seriously weakens the editorial's argument?

(A) Preschoolers have a tendency to imitate adults, and most adults follow strict routines.
(B) Children intensely curious about new things have very short attention spans.
(C) Some older children also develop strict systems that help them learn.
(D) Preschoolers ask as many creative questions as do older children.
(E) Preschool teachers generally report lower levels of stress than do other teachers.

### Step 1. Identify the Question Type

The term "weakens" in the stem tells you that this is a Weaken question.

### Step 2. Untangle the Stimulus

According to the editorial, a common belief holds that preschoolers are hard to teach. However, the editorial disagrees and says preschoolers are actually easier to teach because they have strict systems to help them learn and because they are very curious.

### Step 3. Make a Prediction

To jump from learning systems and curiosity to easy to teach, the editorial must assume that students who learn with strict systems and are curious are easier to teach. The correct answer will invalidate the assumption, suggesting that these qualities make the preschoolers less easy to teach.

## Step 4. Evaluate the Answer Choices

Choice (A) connects preschoolers to adults, but does not address whether they are easier to teach. Move on to the next choice.

Choice (B) weakens the argument by suggesting that children who are curious might not be easy to teach. This is the correct answer.

Choice (C) veers outside the scope of the argument introducing older children. The argument is only concerned with preschoolers.

Choice (D) provides an irrelevant comparison between preschoolers and older children. While choice (D) might suggest that preschoolers are curious, it doesn't break the connection between curiosity and preschoolers being easy to teach.

Choice (E) focuses on the teachers and doesn't address the relationship between preschoolers' learning characteristics and the ease of teaching them.

17. **(A)**

Lawyer: A body of circumstantial evidence is like a rope, and each item of evidence is like a strand of that rope. Just as additional pieces of circumstantial evidence strengthen the body of evidence, adding strands to the rope strengthens the rope. And if one strand breaks, the rope is not broken nor is its strength much diminished. <Thus, even if a few items of a body of circumstantial evidence are discredited, the overall body of evidence retains its basic strength.>

The reasoning in the lawyer's argument is most vulnerable to criticism on the grounds that the argument

(A) takes for granted that no items in a body of circumstantial evidence are significantly more critical to the strength of the evidence than other items in that body

(B) presumes, without providing justification, that the strength of a body of evidence is less than the sum of the strengths of the parts of that body

(C) fails to consider the possibility that if many items in a body of circumstantial evidence were discredited, the overall body of evidence would be discredited

(D) offers an analogy in support of a conclusion without indicating whether the two types of things compared share any similarities

(E) draws a conclusion that simply restates a claim presented in support of that conclusion

### Step 1. Identify the Question Type

The phrase "most vulnerable to criticism" signals a Flaw question.

### Step 2. Untangle the Stimulus

Be on the lookout for classic flaws when you read a Flaw stimulus. Here, the lawyer makes an analogy between a body of circumstantial evidence and a rope. The lawyer concludes that a body of evidence remains strong even if a few pieces are discredited because a rope remains strong even if a few strands break.

### Step 3. Make a Prediction

An analogy is based on the assumption that what's being analogized is comparable. In a Flaw question, that assumption is faulty. So, the correct answer will draw a distinction between rope and circumstantial evidence.

### Step 4. Evaluate the Answer Choices

Choice (A) correctly points out that individual pieces of circumstantial evidence may have different levels of importance to the body of evidence, unlike strands of rope that are equally important.

Choice (B) gets it backward. The lawyer says the strength of a body of evidence is more than the sum of the parts because you can sacrifice some of the parts without compromising the strength of the whole.

Choice (C) need not be considered because the lawyer's conclusion concerns discrediting a few items of circumstantial evidence, not many.

Choice (D) ignores the lawyer's attempts to describe similarities between rope and a body of evidence. While, the lawyer does offer an analogy in support of the conclusion, she then attempts to support a comparison between a rope and a body of evidence by describing how adding each new piece of circumstantial evidence strengthens the whole, just like adding a strand strengthens the rope.

Choice (E) defines the flaw as circular reasoning, but the evidence and conclusion are not the same in this argument.

18. **(E)**

> Ethicist: Many environmentalists hold that the natural environment is morally valuable for its own sake, regardless of any benefits it provides us. However, even if nature has no moral value, nature can be regarded as worth preserving simply on the grounds that people find it beautiful. Moreover, because it is philosophically disputable whether nature is morally valuable but undeniable that it is beautiful, <an argument for preserving nature that emphasizes nature's beauty will be less vulnerable to logical objections than one that emphasizes its moral value.>

The ethicist's reasoning most closely conforms to which one of the following principles?

(A) An argument in favor of preserving nature will be less open to logical objections if it avoids the issue of what makes nature worth preserving.

(B) If an argument for preserving nature emphasizes a specific characteristic of nature and is vulnerable to logical objections, then that characteristic does not provide a sufficient reason for preserving nature.

(C) If it is philosophically disputable whether nature has a certain characteristic, then nature would be more clearly worth preserving if it did not have that characteristic.

(D) Anything that has moral value is worth preserving regardless of whether people consider it to be beautiful.

(E) An argument for preserving nature will be less open to logical objections if it appeals to a characteristic that can be regarded as a basis for preserving nature and that philosophically indisputably belongs to nature.

## Step 1. Identify the Question Type

The stem specifically asks you to pick a principle, so this is a Principle question. Your task is to identify the broad rule in the answers that conforms to the specific situation, or in this case the argument, laid out in the stimulus. The reference to "reasoning" in the question stem, indicates that the stimulus is an argument with evidence and a conclusion, rather than just a factual situation.

## Step 2. Untangle the Stimulus

The stimulus is dense and abstract, so slow down if you need to and take it one sentence at a time:

It is widely held amongst environmentalists that the natural world is morally valuable. Even if it's not, some believe nature should be preserved because it's beautiful. Nature's moral value is disputable, but its beauty is not. Therefore, a preservation argument based on beauty will face fewer objections than an argument based on moral value.

### Step 3. Make a Prediction

The ethicist is saying that an argument is less objectionable if it is based on an indisputable trait.

### Step 4. Evaluate the Answer Choices

Choice (A) is wrong because it talks about avoiding the issue. Actually, the ethicist supports emphasizing what makes nature worth preserving.

Choice (B) distorts the ethicist's reasoning. The ethicist reasons that an argument in favor of preserving nature that emphasizes nature's moral value may be more logically vulnerable than one emphasizing nature's beauty, but that's different from saying that moral value is not a sufficient reason for preserving nature.

Choice (C) ignores the ethicist's principle about what makes an argument more or less defensible.

Choice (D) goes too far. The ethicist says that beauty, not moral value, is sufficient grounds for arguing for the preservation of nature. The ethicist never says that anything morally valuable is worth preserving.

Choice (E) matches the prediction and is the correct answer.

19. **(A)**

An editor is compiling a textbook containing essays by several different authors. The book will contain essays by Lind, Knight, or Jones, but it will not contain essays by all three. (If) the textbook contains an essay by Knight, (then) it will also contain an essay by Jones.

If the statements above are true, which one of the following (must be true)?

(A)   If the textbook contains an essay by Lind, then it will not contain an essay by Knight.
(B)   The textbook will contain an essay by only one of Lind, Knight, and Jones.
(C)   The textbook will not contain an essay by Knight.
(D)   If the textbook contains an essay by Lind, then it will also contain an essay by Jones.
(E)   The textbook will contain an essay by Lind.

### Step 1. Identify the Question Type

The question asks what "must be true," so it is an Inference question.

## Step 2. Untangle the Stimulus

The issue is which authors will be included in the textbook. Lind, Knight, and Jones are three authors who may be included in the book, but the book will never contain all three. Also, if Knight's included, then Jones is included.

Write out the formal logic statement to help you know what must be true in the stimulus. You already know that K → J, so you also know the contrapositive, Not J → not K.

## Step 3. Make a Prediction

When you have formal logic in an Inference stimulus, be on the lookout for a contrapositive or a combined statement in the correct answer choice. Here you have additional information to combine with the formal logic statements you already have. You know all three authors will never be together in a book. So if K is in the book and then J is in the book, then L must not be included. In other words, K → no L. The contrapositive is L → no K. Since you do have a prediction, scan the answer choices for your prediction before you analyze the answer choices in more detail.

## Step 4. Evaluate the Answer Choices

Notice the answer choices are all presented in formal logic language. Translate them quickly if necessary and compare them to what you know from the stimulus.

Choice (A) gives the correct answer (L → no K). Notice it matches the contrapositive of the combined statement from the stimulus.

Choice (B) doesn't have to be true because according to the stimulus, one textbook could include essays from Knight and Jones or Jones and Lind.

Choice (C) also contradicts the stimulus. Knight could have an essay in the textbook as long as Jones did too.

Choice (D) translates to L → J, which cannot be inferred from the stimulus. If Lind has an essay in the textbook, you know from the contraposed statement that Knight will not. The stimulus gives no indication of whether or not Jones will have an essay in the book.

Choice (E) incorrectly states that the textbook must always include an essay by Lind. The stimulus indicates otherwise. The textbook can contain an essay by Knight and one by Jones, or just Jones.

20. **(D)**

<The ability of mammals to control their internal body temperatures is a factor in the development of their brains and intelligence.> This can be seen from the following facts: the brain is a chemical machine, all chemical reactions are temperature dependent, and any organism that can control its body temperature can assure that these reactions occur at the proper temperatures.

Which one of the following is an assumption on which the argument depends?

(A)   Organisms unable to control their body temperatures do not have the capacity to generate internal body heat without relying on external factors.

(B)   Mammals are the only animals that have the ability to control their internal body temperatures.

(C)   The brain cannot support intelligence if the chemical reactions within it are subject to uncontrolled temperatures.

(D)   The development of intelligence in mammals is not independent of the chemical reactions in their brains taking place at the proper temperatures.

(E)   Organisms incapable of controlling their internal body temperatures are subject to unpredictable chemical processes.

## Step 1. Identify the Question Type

The stem asks for an "assumption," so it's an Assumption question.

## Step 2. Untangle the Stimulus

In the first sentence, the conclusion says that mammals' ability to control their internal body temperatures influences the development of their brains and intelligence. The evidence, clearly identified by "this can be seen from," says the brain is a chemical machine and chemical reactions must occur at proper temperatures. The ability to control body temperature ensures that the chemical reactions occur at the proper temperatures.

## Step 3. Make a Prediction

The development of brains and intelligence is nowhere to be found in the evidence, and the conclusion ignores chemical reactions. The assumption will make the connection and provide that development of brains and intelligence is influenced by chemical reactions in the brain occurring at the right temperatures.

## Step 4. Evaluate the Answer Choices

Choice (A) talks about organisms that can't control their internal body temperature, which are not discussed in this stimulus and are therefore outside the scope of the argument.

Choice (B) is extreme because the argument says that mammals have the ability to control their body temperatures. It doesn't say they are the only animals that can do so. So, this choice is out.

Choice (C) is also extreme. The author indicates that the regulation of chemical reaction temperatures is a factor in the development of intelligence, but doesn't say that intelligence can't develop without such regulation.

Choice (D) presents the correct assumption, just with negative wording. The notion that the development of intelligence is not independent of the temperature of chemical reactions means that it *is* influenced by the temperature of chemical reactions.

Choice (E) has the same problem as choice (A). Organisms incapable of controlling their internal body temperatures are outside the scope.

21. **(C)**

People who object to the proposed hazardous waste storage site by appealing to extremely implausible scenarios in which the site fails to contain the waste safely are overlooking the significant risks associated with delays in moving the waste from its present unsafe location. If we wait to remove the waste until we find a site certain to contain it safely, the waste will remain in its current location for many years, since it is currently impossible to guarantee that any site can meet that criterion. Yet keeping the waste at the current location for that long clearly poses unacceptable risks.

The statements above, if true, most strongly support which one of the following?

(A) The waste should never have been stored in its current location.
(B) The waste should be placed in the most secure location that can ever be found.
(C) Moving the waste to the proposed site would reduce the threat posed by the waste.
(D) Whenever waste must be moved, one should limit the amount of time allotted to locating alternative waste storage sites.
(E) Any site to which the waste could be moved will be safer than its present site.

## Step 1. Identify the Question Type

Since the statements in the stimulus "most strongly support" a certain answer choice, the stem is an Inference question.

### Step 2. Untangle the Stimulus

The author says that objecting to a proposed hazardous waste site poses risks by delaying movement of the waste. Waiting for a location certain to contain all the waste ensures the waste will remain in its current site for many years, a situation that the author says poses "unacceptable risks."

### Step 3. Make a Prediction

The stimulus offers no formal logic or statements to combine, so there is no prediction to be made. Proceed to the answer choices with an understanding of what the stimulus says. The correct answer to an Inference question *must be true* based on the stimulus.

### Step 4. Evaluate the Answer Choices

Choice (A) is extreme and is not addressed in the stimulus. The current location may have been the best option at the time, but the stimulus provides no background information.

Choice (B) is wrong because the author says we can't afford to wait to find the most secure location that can ever be found.

Choice (C) *must be true* based on the stimulus because the author eliminates the possibility of keeping the waste where it is. Notice that this answer choice is the most modest of the choices, as the correct Inference answer choice often is. This choice simply indicates that moving the waste reduces the risk, not that it is the best solution or the only solution or that it will completely eliminate the risk.

Choice (D) is extreme in saying that time used to locate alternative waste sites should be limited whenever waste must be moved. The author might agree in this specific instance, but you don't know about every other situation.

Choice (E) is problematic because you don't know whether the author believes every single alternative site would be safer than the current site, just the site to which the author advocates moving the waste.

22. **(B)**

> A recent survey indicates that the average number of books read annually per capita has declined in each of the last three years. However, it also found that most bookstores reported increased profits during the same period.
>
> Each of the following, if true, helps to resolve the survey's apparently paradoxical results EXCEPT:

(A) Recent cutbacks in government spending have forced public libraries to purchase fewer popular contemporary novels.

(B) Due to the installation of sophisticated new antitheft equipment, the recent increase in shoplifting that has hit most retail businesses has left bookstores largely unaffected.

(C) Over the past few years many bookstores have capitalized on the lucrative coffee industry by installing coffee bars.

(D) Bookstore owners reported a general shift away from the sale of inexpensive paperback novels and toward the sale of lucrative hardback books.

(E) Citing a lack of free time, many survey respondents indicated that they had canceled magazine subscriptions in favor of purchasing individual issues at bookstores when time permits.

### Step 1. Identify the Question Type

The phrase "resolve the survey's apparently paradoxical results" identifies a Paradox question, and "EXCEPT" indicates that the four wrong answers will resolve the paradox and that the one right answer will not.

### Step 2. Untangle the Stimulus

Reading is declining yet bookstore profits are up. That doesn't seem to make sense.

### Step 3. Make a Prediction

The correct answer will not explain this conundrum. Maybe the fewer books sold are more expensive or something other than books accounts for the higher profits. Check the answers and eliminate the four that resolve the paradox.

### Step 4. Evaluate the Answer Choices

Choice (A) suggests that libraries have less-popular books, so readers may have to buy them at the bookstore. However, purchasing the books, and thus raising bookstore profits, doesn't necessarily mean the customers are reading them. Choice (A) gives one explanation for how bookstore profits could go up while reading declines. Therefore, it resolves the paradox and is not the correct answer choice.

Choice (B) explains why bookstores may have seen higher profits relative to other retail businesses, but that's not the paradox in question. Because choice (B) doesn't explain how bookstores are making more money while people read less, it is the correct answer.

Choice (C) accounts for the higher profits with higher sales of coffee not books.

Choice (D) explains the higher profits with the sale of higher priced books. A higher price point makes up for lower sales.

Choice (E) offers another income source in the form of magazine sales.

23. **(D)**

> Naturalist: A species can survive a change in environment, as long as the change is not too rapid. <Therefore, the threats we are creating to woodland species arise not from the fact that we are cutting down trees, but rather from the rate at which we are doing so.>

The reasoning in which one of the following is most similar to that in the naturalist's argument?

(A) The problem with burning fossil fuels is that the supply is limited; <so, the faster we expend these resources, the sooner we will be left without an energy source.>

(B) Many people gain more satisfaction from performing a job well—regardless of whether they like the job—than from doing merely adequately a job they like; <thus, people who want to be happy should choose jobs they can do well.>

(C) Some students who study thoroughly do well in school. <Thus, what is most important for success in school is not how much time a student puts into studying, but rather how thoroughly the student studies.>

(D) People do not fear change if they know what the change will bring; <so, our employees' fear stems not from our company's undergoing change, but from our failing to inform them of what the changes entail.>

(E) Until ten years ago, we had good soil and our agriculture flourished. <Therefore, the recent decline of our agriculture is a result of our soil rapidly eroding and there being nothing that can replace the good soil we lost.>

## Step 1. Identify the Question Type

The phrase "most similar to" tells you that this is a Parallel Reasoning question.

## Step 2. Untangle the Stimulus

The naturalist states a basic principle that a species can survive a change of environment if the change is not too quick. Then, he applies the principle to a specific species and concludes that the woodland species isn't in danger because its environment is changing, but because its environment is changing too quickly.

## Step 3. Make a Prediction

The naturalist claims with an assertion of fact that it's not the cutting down of trees in general, but the rate of cutting down trees that is harming the species. Generally, the naturalist is asserting that it's not the thing *itself* that is causing the problem, but something about *how that thing is done* that is causing the problem. Look for a similar conclusion in the answer choices, and if necessary, compare the evidence to find a parallel argument.

## Step 4. Evaluate the Answer Choices

Choice (A)'s conclusion is a prediction, not an assertion of fact. Eliminate this choice.

Choice (B) is wrong because the conclusion is a recommendation, not an assertion of fact.

Choice (C) weighs the importance of two factors (time and thoroughness of studying) to achieve success in school. Move on to the next choice.

Choice (D) correctly matches the stimulus because it is not the change itself that is causing the problem but how the change is undertaken (without informing the employees).

Choice (E) is not similar. It asserts two causes for a negative result and doesn't dismiss one in favor of the other.

24. **(A)**

> Professor: A person who can select a beverage from among 50 varieties of cola is less free than one who has only these 5 choices: wine, coffee, apple juice, milk, and water. It is clear, then, that meaningful freedom cannot be measured simply by the number of alternatives available;> the extent of the differences among the alternatives is also a relevant factor.

The professor's argument proceeds by

(A)  supporting a general principle by means of an example

(B)  drawing a conclusion about a particular case on the basis of a general principle

(C)  supporting its conclusion by means of an analogy

(D)  claiming that whatever holds for each member of a group must hold for the whole group

(E)  inferring one general principle from another, more general, principle

### Step 1. Identify the Question Type

The phrase "argument proceeds by" means this is a Method of Argument question.

### Step 2. Untangle the Stimulus

The phrase "It is clear, then" at the start of the second sentence points to the professor's conclusion that freedom can't be measured by the number of alternatives available. The professor supports her conclusion with an example about the freedom of a person selecting among beverages.

### Step 3. Make a Prediction

The professor makes a broad statement in the conclusion and backs it up with an example of that principle. The correct answer will match this prediction.

### Step 4. Evaluate the Answer Choices

Choice (A) correctly restates the prediction and is the correct answer.

Choice (B) is backward. The professor's conclusion is general, and she supports it with a specific example, not the other way around.

Choice (C) adds an analogy to the answer not mentioned in the stimulus. The professor uses an example, not an analogy, to support the conclusion.

Choice (D) is wrong because the professor doesn't claim any properties are true for "each member of a group."

Choice (E) adds a second principle which is not mentioned in the stimulus. The professor's conclusion is a principle, but the professor never claims it's derived from another principle.

25. **(C)**

> Principle: Meetings should be kept short, addressing only those issues relevant to a majority of those attending. A person should not be required to attend a meeting if none of the issues to be addressed at the meeting are relevant to that person.

> Application: <Terry should not be required to attend today's two o'clock meeting.>

Which one of the following, if true, most <u>justifies</u> the stated application of the (principle)?

(A) The only issues on which Terry could make a presentation at the meeting are issues irrelevant to at least a majority of those who could attend.

(B) If Terry makes a presentation at the meeting, the meeting will not be kept short.

(C) No issue relevant to Terry could be relevant to a majority of those attending the meeting.

(D) If Terry attends the meeting a different set of issues will be relevant to a majority of those attending than if Terry does not attend.

(E) The majority of the issues to be addressed at the meeting are not relevant to Terry.

### Step 1. Identify the Question Type

This is a Principle question, signaled by "principle." In this case, the principle is in the stimulus and you're asked to justify, or strengthen, its application. So, the principle is the evidence, and the application is the conclusion.

### Step 2. Untangle the Stimulus

The principle says that meetings should cover issues relevant to a majority of attendees and if the issues are not relevant to a person, that person shouldn't have to attend. The application of the principle concludes that Terry shouldn't have to attend today's meeting.

### Step 3. Make a Prediction

So if the issues are not relevant, you don't have to attend the meeting. And if you're Terry, you don't have to attend the meeting. Therefore, the argument assumes that the issues are not relevant to Terry. The correct answer will confirm the assumption.

### Step 4. Evaluate the Answer Choices

Choice (A) contradicts the stimulus. According to the principle, if the issues are irrelevant, the person shouldn't have to attend the meeting.

Choice (B) doesn't work. The principle says meetings should be kept short, but it doesn't connect back to Terry and let him out of the meeting.

Choice (C) is the correct answer. If an issue is relevant to Terry, then it is not relevant to the meeting majority. Contrapose the statement and you learn that if meeting issues are relevant to the meeting majority, they are not relevant to Terry. Therefore, he is not required to attend.

Choice (D) suggests Terry may decide to attend the meeting even though he's not required to be in attendance. However, his voluntary attendance would not have any impact on the meeting agenda.

Choice (E) requires a close read. The principle allows a person to skip a meeting if none of the issues are relevant to him. It doesn't allow a person to skip the meeting if a majority of the issues are not relevant to him. "Majority" in the stimulus refers to the attendees, not the issues.

# PART IV

# THE TEST DAY EXPERIENCE

# CHAPTER 23

# GET READY FOR TEST DAY

Congratulations. Your work with the Kaplan Method and strategies gives you the knowledge and practice you need for LSAT success. Now, it's time for you to schedule a test date, register for the exam (if you haven't done so already), and put yourself in the right frame of mind to take the next step on the road to law school.

The details of registering for the test are covered in "An Introduction to the LSAT" at the beginning of the book. Follow the steps and recommendations mentioned there to ensure that you have a spot at the next test administration or on the test date that's best for you. In the remainder of this chapter, I'll cover what you need to do to have yourself mentally and emotionally ready for the rigors and rewards of test day.

## YOU ARE PREPARED

First, remember (and remind yourself) that you are prepared. By learning the lessons and doing the work from this book, you can know, with confidence, that there is nothing else you need to *know* about LSAT Logical Reasoning. The Kaplan Method, the specific strategies, and their application to specific question types that I've presented in this book are the result not only of my own 9-year tenure as an LSAT instructor; they're the summation of five decades of Kaplan expertise and research. Hundreds of great LSAT minds—including those of perfect scorers, legal scholars, and psychometricians—have contributed to the development, testing, and refinement of Kaplan's LSAT pedagogy. If we know it, you now know it. So strike from your mind any concern that there's one more secret to uncover or a mysterious LSAT Rosetta Stone to search for. You have the most complete, proven system for LSAT Logical Reasoning success available. If you've already studied and practiced from this book's companion volumes—*Kaplan LSAT Reading Comprehension: Strategies and Tactics* and *Kaplan LSAT Logic Games: Strategies and Tactics*—you can say the same thing about the entire exam.

Now, saying that you *know* everything you need to about the Logical Reasoning section doesn't mean you're ready to *do* everything you need to do to achieve your goal score. You need to continue to practice and review. Indeed, I'll cover that in the next section of this chapter. But first, I want to make sure you're translating your comprehensive knowledge of logical reasoning into confidence on test day. From now until the day you sit for your official administration of the LSAT, you need to exhibit the confidence your preparation has earned you.

There are some very practical steps you can take to reinforce your test day confidence. Once you're registered for the test, visit your test site. You may even want to take some logical reasoning questions to practice in the very room where you'll be sitting for the real test. At a minimum, know where you're going to be, how you'll get there, and where you'll park or where public transportation will drop you off. You want no surprises on the morning of your official LSAT.

The day before your test, relax. There's no way to cram for a skills-based exam. While your competition is scrambling and fretting, go to the gym, watch your favorite movie, or have a nice dinner. Gather what you need for the next day, and keep yourself one step ahead of everything you need to do. It sounds a little corny, but acting confident will actually make you feel more confident. Get to bed relatively early, have a good night's sleep, and wake ready to have the best day of your (test-taking) life.

The following is a list of what you'll need to have with you on test day:

# LSAT SURVIVAL KIT

**You MUST have the following:**
- Admissions ticket
- Photo ID
- Several sharpened #2 pencils
- 1-gallon transparent zip-top bag

**You SHOULD also have:**
- Pencil sharpener
- Eraser
- Analog wristwatch
- Aspirin
- Snack and drink for the break

**You CANNOT have:**
- Cell phone
- MP3 player
- Computer or electronic reader
- Electronic or digital timers
- Weapons
- Papers other than your admission ticket

That list conforms to the rules for the test site as they stand at the time of this writing. You should check www.lsac.org periodically before your test date to make sure there haven't been any changes or amendments to the Law School Administration Council's (LSAC) policies.

Of course, the "MUSTs" are non-negotiable. You need those to be allowed entry to the testing room. Some of the "SHOULDs," on the other hand, you may not need at all. But if you begin to feel a little headache coming on, or if you find your stomach grumbling midway through Section 3 of the test, you'll be awfully glad you took along those "just in case" items. As for the "CANNOTs," do yourself a favor and avoid any conflict with the proctors or test administrators. Just leave your phone or electronics in the car or at home.

One other very practical thing you can do is to dress in layers. The LSAT is usually administered during the weekend and almost always in a large, institutional building. It's really tough to predict whether the room will be too hot or too cold or whether it will fluctuate throughout the day. Take the Goldilocks approach and make sure the temperature is always "just right" for you by wearing or taking the kind of sweater or light jacket that's easy (and quiet) to slip on or off.

The stress levels of test takers around you will be high. But if you demonstrate nothing but preparation and confidence on the morning of the test, you'll feel calmer, more clear-headed, and ready for the real challenges of the test itself.

## CHAMPIONS PRACTICE. VIRTUOSOS PRACTICE. YOU PRACTICE.

To put my earlier point about practice into formal logic terms, knowledge of the test is necessary, but not sufficient, for test day success. Mistaking this relationship is something that leads a lot of test takers off track. They haven't achieved the score they want, so they say, "There must be something I don't know yet," or, "What am I missing?" The fact is that many of these test takers know all about the test, but they haven't practiced taking the test. Ask almost any great performer, musician, public speaker, or athlete and they'll tell you that the key to their success is practice. A great violinist may study a composer's compositional theory, historical context, or even personal life in order to better understand a piece before performing it. But all of that will mean little if the performer hasn't practiced. The audience would be pretty disappointed if the violinist showed up to give a lecture about the composer instead of playing a concert. It's the same with the LSAT. Your audience, law school admissions officers, won't care what you know about the exam, just how well you perform on it.

So how can you best practice? First, lay out a study and practice schedule for yourself that runs from now until test day—one that's ambitious but practical. Fill in as much as you can about which sections or question types you'll be practicing each day or week. If you're working on different parts of the test, vary the sections you're practicing and the materials you're using.

If you haven't completed and reviewed the full-section practice in this book, make sure you do so. Leave time for review of your work. Remember that you're not just checking to see whether you produced the correct answer, you're asking whether you did so as efficiently and effectively as you could have. That means that you should always be reviewing the questions you got right as well as those you got wrong. Look for what features and patterns in a question you're likely to see again on test day. You won't see the questions from this book on your test, but every question on your test will have similarities to those you've practiced here.

If you're looking for additional practice, consider the following additional resources:

## OTHER KAPLAN LSAT RESOURCES

*Logic Games On Demand*
*Logical Reasoning On Demand*
*Reading Comprehension On Demand*
Comprehensive, section-specific courses for in-depth instruction and targeted practice.

*LSAT Advantage—On Site, Anywhere or On Demand*
Our most popular option—complete, targeted, and focused prep designed for busy students.

*LSAT Advanced—On Site or Anywhere*
Fast-paced for high-scorers focusing on the most advanced content. (158+ required to enroll.)

*LSAT Extreme—On Site or Anywhere*
Maximum in-class instruction plus tutoring for students who want extra time, review, and more practice.

*LSAT One on One—On Site or Anywhere*
An expert tutor designs a one-on-one, custom program around your individual needs, goals, and schedule.

*LSAT Summer Intensive*
Six weeks of total LSAT immersion in a residential academic program at Boston University

Check out *www.kaplanlsat.com* for courses and free events in live, online and in your area.

All of those additional resources will provide the outstanding instruction, coaching, and practice you expect from Kaplan test prep. Consider which ones work best for your schedule, learning style, and admissions timeline. Kaplan is committed to helping you achieve your educational and career goals.

# THE PSYCHOLOGICAL DIMENSIONS OF TEST DAY

There's no doubt that taking your official LSAT is one of the most important steps (maybe *the* most important) you'll take on the road to law school. That's a lot of pressure. It's natural to have a little excitement and some extra adrenaline for such a big event. Those are actually healthy things to feel, provided that you channel your emotions into energy and concentration, rather than anxiety and confusion. I'd be pretty disappointed if, after weeks or months of practice and preparation, one of my students said, "Eh, I don't really care what happens on the test." Of course you care. That's why you're reading this book and working so hard. So embrace the big day.

I've already talked about how you can begin to foster an attitude of confidence and act in ways that support and sustain it. Here are a couple of practical steps you can take to carry your confidence right into the testing room.

## Know What to Expect

It is easy to lay out the order of events on test day. Here's a chart that shows you what will happen from the time you arrive at the test site.

| Event | What Happens | Time |
|---|---|---|
| Check-In | Show admissions ticket, ID, fingerprints, room and seat assignment | 10–30 minutes |
| Rules and Procedures | Test booklets distributed, proctor reads the rules, test takers fill out grid information | 30 minutes |
| LSAT Administration | | |
| Section 1 | Logic Games, Logical Reasoning, or Reading Comprehension Section | 35 minutes |
| Section 2 | Logic Games, Logical Reasoning, or Reading Comprehension Section | 35 minutes |
| Section 3 | Logic Games, Logical Reasoning, or Reading Comprehension Section | 35 minutes |

| Break | Test booklets and grids collected, test takers have break, return to seats, booklets and grids redistributed | 12–20 minutes (10 minute break with additional time for administrative tasks) |
|---|---|---|
| Section 4 | Logic Games, Logical Reasoning, or Reading Comprehension Section | 35 minutes |
| Section 5 | Logic Games, Logical Reasoning, or Reading Comprehension Section | 35 minutes |
| Prepare for Writing Sample | Test booklets and grids collected, test takers given a chance to cancel scores, Writing Sample booklets distributed | 5–10 minutes |
| Writing Sample | Test takers produce Writing Samples | 35 minutes |

You can see that even if everything goes as smoothly as possible, you're in for around five hours from start to finish. This is another reason that it's so important to be rested, comfortable, and nourished. Students who are too groggy to be at their best in Section 1 or too exhausted and hungry to keep up their performance in Section 5 will have trouble competing with someone like you, who's prepared for the entire testing day, from start to finish.

One thing that star performers do—I don't care if you're thinking of singers, actors, athletes, or even great trial lawyers—is to warm up before they "go on." You can do the same on the morning of your test by reviewing a Logic Game, Logical Reasoning question, or Reading Comprehension passage that you've done before. As you revisit the game or question, go over the steps in the Kaplan Method that allowed you to be successful with the item before. This will get your brain warmed up just as a quarterback would loosen his arm or a singer would warm up her vocal cords. Don't try new material, and certainly don't try a full section. Just start reading and thinking—calmly and confidently—in the LSAT way. You'll be miles ahead of the unprepared test taker who looks shell-shocked for most of Section 1.

In order to maintain a high level of performance, it's important to stay hydrated and nourished. Mental work makes most people hungry. So drink water at the break and have a small, healthy snack. Don't, however, eat a sleep-inducing turkey sandwich or gobble sugar that will have you crashing out during Section 5.

Knowing what to expect also helps you manage your mental preparation for test day in other small, but important, ways. A lot of test takers don't know that the proctors will ask whether anyone in the room wants to cancel his or her score right after Section 5 is completed and the test booklets are collected. If you're not expecting that question, it can throw you into a moment of self-doubt. It's human nature to underestimate your performance on the test. You will remember the handful of questions that gave you trouble while ignoring the dozens of questions you answered routinely with no problem. I've personally known students who canceled their scores when they shouldn't have. The LSAC allows you a number of days after the test to cancel your score, so don't worry about it during the exam. Complete the Writing Sample to the best of your ability. You can always consider things that might have caused you to underperform—illness, a personal crisis—after you've completed the test.

## You Will Panic, but Don't Panic

Over the course of four to five hours of rigorous, detailed, strictly timed test taking, you're going to reach a point at which you lose focus, feel overwhelmed, or just downright panic for a moment. It's normal. So first thing, don't feed the panic by blaming yourself or saying, "Oh, I knew this would happen." There's nothing wrong with you for having those feelings. In fact, panic is a physical response to high-pressure situations. It's related to the autonomic nervous system, the "flight or fight" response we've adapted to survive danger. Your heart beats faster; blood leaves your brain to go to your extremities; your breathing gets rapid and shallow. That's all very important when the danger you face is a predator or enemy. It's just not very helpful when you're facing a standardized test.

If—when—you face a point of doubt, confusion, or panic on test day, take a moment. Collect yourself physically first. Take a deep breath; sit up in a straight, comfortable posture; put both feet flat on the floor and lower your shoulders; even close your eyes for a second while you breathe. Then open your eyes and remind yourself that whatever you're looking at, it's just an LSAT question. The fact is that you've seen one like it and done one like it before. You know that's the case because of your preparation. Get your concentration back by reciting the Kaplan Method as you work through the problem. You know that will provide a strategic, purposeful approach every time.

## Worry Only about What's in Your Control

When I have students in LSAT prep courses, they often ask a lot of questions about what to do if things go wrong on test day. "What if the proctor doesn't give us a verbal five minute warning?" "What if someone is being noisy right behind me?" "What if the school marching band is rehearsing in the courtyard under the window?" All of those and a few weirder, more distracting things have happened to test takers. But my students' concern about such occurrences before test day is misplaced. They should be taking care of the things that are within their control—learning the Kaplan Method, practicing logical reasoning questions—not worrying about the things that aren't. The vast majority of LSAT administrations go off without more than a minor hitch. Your job is to be ready to have a peak performance on a routine test day.

When the unexpected happens, stay calm. If there is something that you notice before the test begins—a window is open, letting in cold air or street noise; the lights in the back of the room aren't turned on, making it dark where you're sitting—just let the proctor know (politely) and ask if it can be remedied. If something happens during a section—another test taker is unconsciously tapping his pencil; the proctor forgets the five-minute announcement—keep working. Raise your hand and get a proctor's attention. When they come to your seat, quickly and quietly explain the situation. Most of the time, they'll take action to remedy the situation. But don't let those things throw you off your game. If something truly bizarre happens that seriously impedes your performance—a fire alarm goes off, a wrecking crew starts to jack-hammer the building—follow the proctor's instructions, keep a record of what happened, and follow up with the LSAC by telephone or in writing after the test concludes. You are welcome to contact 1-800-KAPTEST and ask for advice from one of our LSAT experts, too. A word to the wise: The LSAC will not add points to a score as a remedy for a distracting test administration, but they have found other ways to accommodate test takers who, through no fault of their own, have been unable to complete the test or who encountered unmanageable distractions.

## GET READY FOR TEST DAY

This chapter really boils down to one message: Prepare yourself for the perfect test day. Display confidence and preparation in all that you do. Get ready for a consistent, focused performance from start to finish. When that's the attitude you take into the test, you're more likely to outperform your competition and have your best day regardless of what else does or doesn't happen.

# CHAPTER 24

# SECRETS OF THE LSAT

The "secrets" of the LSAT aren't really secrets at all. They're well-known facts that many test takers fail to take full advantage of. The best test takers use the structure and format of the test to their advantage. Just as a great football or basketball coach adjusts the team's strategy when time is running out on the clock, or just as a great conductor rearranges an orchestra to take advantage of the acoustics in a new venue, you can learn to adjust your approach to the test you're taking. We might well laud the insightful coach or conductor by saying, "Wow, he really knows the 'secrets' of this game (or stadium or theater)." But in fact, he's simply taking account of all the circumstances and making the right strategic decisions for that time and place. Consider a handful of facts that make the LSAT a unique testing experience, and see how you can use them to your advantage.

## EVERY QUESTION IS WORTH THE SAME AMOUNT TO YOUR SCORE

Many tests you've taken (even some standardized tests) rewarded you more for certain questions or sections than for others. In school, it's common for a professor to say, "The essay counts for half of your score," or to make a section of harder questions worth five points each while easier ones are worth less. With such exams, you may simply be unable to get a top score without performing well on a given question or topic. It makes sense, then, to target the areas the professor will reward most highly.

As you well know, that's not the case on the LSAT. Every question—easy or hard, short or long, common or rare—is worth exactly the same amount as every other question. That means that you should seek out the questions, games, and passages that are the easiest for you to handle. Far too many test takers get their teeth into a tough question and won't let go. That hurts them in two ways. First, they spend too much time—sometimes three or four minutes—on such a question, sacrificing their chances with other, easier questions. Second, since questions like these are tough or confusing, they're less likely to produce a right answer no matter how much time you spend. Learn to skip questions when it's in your interest to do so. Mark questions that you skip by circling the entire question in your test booklet. That way, those questions will be easy to spot if you have time left after you complete the other questions in the section. If you've eliminated one or two obviously incorrect answer choicess, strike them through completely so that you don't spend time rethinking them when you come back to the question.

When schools receive your score report, the only thing they see is your score. They don't know—and they don't care—whether you've answered the easiest or the toughest questions on the LSAT. They only care that you answered more questions correctly than the other applicants. Becoming a good manager of the test sections is invaluable. You'll do that, in part, by triaging the games or passages and choosing to put off the toughest for last. Even more often, you'll manage the section by skipping and guessing strategically. Don't slug it out with a tough question for minutes and then grudgingly move on. Boldly seek out questions on which you can exert your strengths, and be clearheaded and decisive in your decisions to move past questions you know are targeted at your weaknesses. Take the test; don't let it take you.

## ONE RIGHT, FOUR ROTTEN

I'm sure you've had the experience, on a multiple-choice test in school, of having a teacher tell you, "More than one answer may be correct, but pick the best answer for each question." Given that you're a future law student, I wouldn't be surprised to learn that you may even have debated with your instructor, making a case for why a certain answer should receive credit. As a result, you're used to comparing answer choices to one another. On the LSAT, however, that's a recipe for wasted time and effort. The test makers design the correct answer to be unequivocally correct; it will respond to the call of the question stem precisely. Likewise, the four wrong answers are demonstrably wrong, not just "less good."

For the well-trained test taker—for you, that is—this leads to an important, practical adjustment in strategy. Throughout the test, you should seek to predict the correct answer before assessing the answer choices. In Logical Reasoning, you will, on most questions, be able to anticipate the content of the correct answer, sometimes almost word for word. In Reading Comprehension and Logic Games, you should spend the time up front to have a clear passage road map or game sketch. At a minimum, you must characterize the correct and incorrect answers (if the correct answer *must be true*, for example, each of the wrong answers *could be false*). Then seek out the one answer that matches your prediction or characterization.

The bottom line is that, on the LSAT, you are always comparing the answers against what you know must be correct, not against one another. When locating the correct choice is difficult or time-consuming, you can always turn the tables on the test maker and eliminate the wrong ones with your knowledge of common wrong answer traps. Because you know that there will always be one correct choice and that you can always identify the characteristics that make wrong answers wrong, you can always take the most direct route to the LSAT point.

## THERE'S NO WRONG-ANSWER PENALTY

This point is easy to understand, but sometimes hard to remember when you're working quickly through an LSAT section. The LSAT is scored only by counting the number of correct responses you bubble in. Unlike some standardized tests—the SAT is the most notorious example—you're not penalized for marking incorrect responses. Simply put, there's nothing to lose, so mark a response, even if it's a blind guess, for every answer.

Of course, strategic guessing is better than just taking a wild stab at the correct answer. Even if a question gives you a lot of trouble, see if you can eliminate one or more answer choices as clearly wrong. When you can, take your guess from the remaining choices. Removing even one clearly incorrect choice improves your chances of hitting on the right one from 20 percent to 25 percent; getting rid of two wrong answers, of course, gives you a one-in-three chance of guessing correctly. Provided that you do it quickly (not taking time away from questions you can handle with little trouble), strategic guessing can improve your score.

Students ask another question related to this point about the answer choices. They want to know if a particular answer choice—(A), (B), (C), (D), or (E)—shows up more often than others, or whether it's better, when guessing, to pick a particular choice for all guesses. The answer to both questions is no. Over the course of a full LSAT, all five answer choices show up just about equally. There's no pattern associated with particular question types. You're no more likely to see any particular answer early or late in a section. Thus, when you're blind guessing, you have a one-in-five chance of hitting the correct answer whatever you choose. And there's no benefit from guessing choice (C) or choice (D) over and over. It's far more valuable to spend your limited time trying to eliminate one or more wrong answers than it is to fret over any illusory patterns within the choices.

## THE LSAT IS A MARATHON . . . MADE UP OF SPRINTS

At this point in your academic career, you've had long tests and you've had tests that put time pressure on you. But chances are, you've never encountered as intense a combination of the two as you will on the LSAT. In the last chapter, I already talked about the importance of stamina. Including the administrative tasks at the beginning, the breaks, and the collection and distribution of your testing materials, you're in for around a five-hour test day. It's important to remember that, over the course of that marathon, the first and fifth sections are just as valuable as those in the middle. Unsurprisingly, Kaplan's research has shown that, for the untrained test taker, those sections are likely to produce the poorest performance. You can counteract the inherent difficulties in the schedule by doing a little warm-up so that you're ready to hit the ground running at the start of Section 1, and by staying relaxed and having a healthy snack at the break so that you're still going strong at the end of Section 5. Just taking these simple steps could add several points to your score.

At the same time that you're striving to maintain focus and sustain your performance, you're trying to manage a very fast 35 minutes in each section. I've talked already about how you can triage a section to maximize your opportunity to attack the easiest questions up front and save the danger zone for the end. Combine that with confident, strategic guessing and you'll be outperforming many test takers who succumb to the "ego battle" with tough or time-consuming questions. But there's one more thing that you have to add to your repertoire of test day tactics: You have to learn to not look back. Over the years, I've talked to many students who could tell me how they thought they performed on each of the test's sections. To be honest with you, I find that a little disappointing. Sure, you may remember that the game with the Cowboys and Horses or the passage on Nanotechnology was really challenging, but it's a waste of time and mental capacity to try and assess your performance as you're taking the test. Once you've answered a question, leave it behind. Give your full concentration to what you're working on. This is even more important when it comes to sections. Once time is called, you may no longer work on the section, not even to bubble in the answers to questions you completed in your test booklet. If a proctor sees you continuing to work on a section for which the time has expired, he or she can issue you a misconduct slip, and the violation will be reported to all of the schools to which you apply. More importantly, you're harming your work on the current section.

There's no rearview mirror on the LSAT. Work diligently, mark the correct answers, and move on to the next question. Keep this in mind: Even if you could accurately assess your performance as you worked (you can't, but imagine it for a moment), it wouldn't change anything. You'd still need to get the remaining questions right. So learn this lesson—and the other "secrets" of the LSAT—now. Be like those seemingly brilliant coaches and performers. By knowing how the LSAT test day works, you can gain an edge over test takers who treat this just as they have every other exam in their academic careers.

# CHAPTER 25

# LSAT STRATEGIES AND TACTICS

At last, I'll bring you full circle back to the premise at the start of this book. The LSAT may be unlike any other test you've studied or prepared for, but it need not be mysterious or overwhelming. The underlying principle that has informed this book is that **every question has an answer**. The twist is that you're not expected to know the answers. How could you? This is a test that rewards what you can do, not what you've learned. In that sense, you can't *study* for the test. And you certainly can't cram for it. What you can do, indeed what you've been doing throughout this book, is to *practice* for the test. Instead of thinking of the LSAT as a test, think of it as your law school audition or tryout. A play's director or a team's coach doesn't ask you what you know; she wants to see what you can do. And just as the director or coach will give you everything you need to demonstrate your skill, the test makers always give you everything you need to produce the correct answers on the LSAT.

## THE LSAT REWARDS THE CORE 4 SKILLS

Law schools don't expect incoming students to know the law. Indeed, much as the LSAT does, your professors may try to use your outside knowledge and assumptions against you. What the schools are looking for is incoming students who have the skills they'll need to succeed through the coming three years of rigorous legal training. That, at least in part, is what they're looking for your LSAT score to indicate. That's why the LSAT is a skills-based, rather than a knowledge-based, exam. Back near the beginning of this book, you learned the central skills rewarded on the test.

## THE CORE 4 LSAT SKILLS

1. **Strategic Reading**
2. **Analyzing Arguments**
3. **Understanding Formal Logic**
4. **Making Deductions**

# USE WHAT YOU'VE LEARNED THROUGHOUT THE TEST

One nice thing to realize is that much of the work you've done here, preparing for the Logical Reasoning sections specifically, will translate to exceptional performance throughout the test. Your understanding of the sufficient-necessary relationship highlighted by formal logic rules will be rewarded in the Logic Games sections. Your ability to analyze arguments and draw valid inferences will support your strategic reading skills. And, of course, to be successful on the Reading Comprehension section, you will use your reasoning strategy and skill to answer specific logical reasoning questions.

So let me leave you with this: The LSAT is designed to reward the skills that will make you a successful law student. You know that you have those skills. You are, after all, seeking this path with passion and focus. The work you've done in this book is all about honing your skills and preparing you for a successful test day. Take the insights you've gathered about LSAT logical reasoning and apply them throughout the exam. Take what you've learned about yourself as a test taker, and use it not only for a stronger, more confident performance on test day, but also throughout your law school endeavor, during your bar exam, and into your legal career. Best of luck to you. Now, go out and accomplish great things.

# PART V

# APPENDICES

# APPENDIX A

# KAPLAN METHOD FOR LOGICAL REASONING: REVIEW SHEET EXERCISE

Directions: At the end of every chapter in Part II of this book, review the Kaplan Method for Logical Reasoning by answering the questions in the first column and entering your responses under the designated question type. Consider this sheet your "playbook" and use it to answer other practice questions as you learn the Kaplan Method.

**Table Appendix A.1**

Question Types

| Method | Assumption | Strengthen | Weaken | Flaw | Inference | Principle | Method of Argument | Parallel Reasoning | Paradox | Point at Issue | Role of a Statement | Main Point |
|---|---|---|---|---|---|---|---|---|---|---|---|---|
| Step 1. Identify the Question Type<br><br>What words and phrases tell you the question type? | | | | | | | | | | | | |
| Step 2. Untangle the Stimulus<br><br>How do you unpack the stimulus for the particular question type? | | | | | | | | | | | | |

(continued)

| | |
|---|---|
| | |
| | |
| | |
| | |
| | |
| | |
| | |
| | |
| | |
| | |
| Step 3. Make a Prediction<br><br>What do you do with the information gathered in Step 2? | Step 4. Evaluate the Answer Choices<br><br>How do you compare your prediction with the answer choices? |

# KAPLAN METHOD FOR LOGICAL REASONING: REVIEW SHEET

Directions: Do NOT read this chart until you refer to the review exercise in Appendix A and complete the blank Review Sheet on your own. Use this sheet to check your work and supplement it as appropriate. Keep your sheet in front of you as you practice questions so you can learn and apply the Kaplan Method correctly. The more you can refer to it in the beginning of your practice, the more comfortable and efficient you can become in implementing it.

### Table Appendix B.1

#### Question Types

| Method | Assumption | Strengthen | Weaken | Flaw | Inference | Principle | Method of Argument | Parallel Reasoning | Paradox | Point at Issue | Role of a Statement | Main Point |
|---|---|---|---|---|---|---|---|---|---|---|---|---|
| Step 1. Identify the Question Type<br><br>What words and phrases tell you the question type? | Assumes<br>Assumption<br>Presupposes<br>Added to the premise<br>Depends on<br>If assumed ... conclusion follows logically | Strengthen<br>Support (answer supports stimulus)<br>Justify | Weaken<br>Calls into question<br>Casts doubt on<br>Undermine<br>Counter<br>Damages | Flaw<br>Vulnerable to criticism<br>Questionable because<br>Error in reasoning<br>Overlooks the possibility<br>Fails to demonstrate | Must be true<br>Logically follows from<br>Can be inferred<br>Support (stimulus supports answer)<br>Logically completes the passage | Principle<br>Policy<br>Proposition<br>Generalization | Argumentative technique<br>Method<br>Process<br>Argumentative strategy<br>Responds to... by | Parallel to<br>Similar to<br>Pattern of reasoning | Solve the apparent paradox<br>Resolve the discrepancy<br>Explain<br>Solve the mystery | Disagree over whether<br>Point at issue between them is<br>Disagree about which one of the following | Plays which one of the following roles<br>Figures in the argument<br>Plays which part | Conclusion<br>Main idea<br>Main point |
| Step 2. Untangle the Stimulus<br><br>How do you unpack the stimulus for the particular question type? | Identify the conclusion and summarize the evidence in the argument. | Identify the conclusion and summarize the evidence in the argument. | Identify the conclusion and summarize the evidence in the argument. | Identify the conclusion and summarize the evidence in the argument. | Get the gist of each statement and accept as true. | Identify the conclusion and evidence or untangle the stimulus as you would for the question type it mimics. | Identify the conclusion and the evidence. | Identify the conclusion and its type, check the evidence, characterize the stimulus, and look for flaws. | Identify the discrepancy. | Summarize each speaker's argument. | Find the phrase noted in the question, conclusion, and evidence. | Identify the conclusion using Keywords, disagreement, or the one-sentence test. |

(continued)

| | Assumption | Strengthen | Weaken | Flaw | Inference | Principle | Method of Argument | Parallel Reasoning | Paradox | Point at Issue | Role of a Statement | Main Point |
|---|---|---|---|---|---|---|---|---|---|---|---|---|
| **Step 3. Make a Prediction** — What do you do with the information gathered in Step 2? | Bridge the gap between evidence and conclusion. Necessary assumption will be core and basic to the argument, usually modestly phrased. Sufficient assumption will be forceful and guarantee that conclusion is true. | Confirm the assumption, affirm the conclusion, or eliminate a plausible alternative to make the argument more likely. | Reject the assumption, contradict the conclusion, or propose a plausible alternative to make the argument less likely. | Describe the disconnect between the conclusion and evidence, consider the classic flaws, or identify the possibility overlooked by the author. | Translate any formal logic statements and combine statements with shared terms. Otherwise, do not predict. | Predict the answer as you would for the question type it mimics in terms of a broad principle or a specific situation depending on what is asked for in the question. | Describe the argument in abstract terms and characterize the evidence. | Compare conclusions, and if necessary, evidence, flaw or entire stimulus. | Determine an explanation that reconciles the discrepancy and makes the statements consistent. | Determine the issue both speakers address and on which they disagree. | Characterize the function of the identified statement in the argument. | Paraphrase the conclusion. |
| **Step 4. Evaluate the Answer Choices** — How do you compare your prediction with the answer choices? | Find the answer that matches your prediction. Beware of common wrong answers. | Find the answer that matches your prediction. Beware of "EXCEPT" questions and common wrong answers. Answer can be modest or forceful, making the conclusion a little more likely or absolutely proving the conclusion. | Find the answer that matches your prediction. Beware of "EXCEPT" questions and common wrong answers. Answer can be modest or forceful, making the conclusion a little less likely or absolutely disproving conclusion. | Find the answer that matches your prediction. Beware of "EXCEPT" questions and common wrong answers. | Find the answer that must be true based on the stimulus. Be especially wary of extreme and out of scope answers. Correct answer must be as extreme or less extreme than stimulus. Usually more modest is better. | Find the answer that matches your prediction. Beware of "EXCEPT" questions and common wrong answers. | Find the answer that matches your prediction. Beware of "EXCEPT" questions and common wrong answers. | Find the answer that matches your prediction. Beware of "EXCEPT" questions and common wrong answers. | Find the answer that matches your prediction. Beware of "EXCEPT" questions and common wrong answers. | Find the answer that matches your prediction. Beware of "EXCEPT" questions and common wrong answers. | Find the answer that matches your prediction. Beware of "EXCEPT" questions and common wrong answers. | Find the answer that matches your prediction. Beware of "EXCEPT" questions and common wrong answers. |

# APPENDIX C

# DRILL: IDENTIFY THE QUESTION TYPE

The first step in the Kaplan Method for Logical Reasoning is to identify the question type. You must be able to instantly recognize each question type so you can move quickly to the next step of untangling the stimulus—and know what to do when you get there.

Directions: In the following question stems, circle the words and phrases that indicate a particular question type and write the question type on the line provided. For additional practice, you can make flashcards with question stems on them and test yourself. Once you've mastered the question stems, create another set of flashcards with the question types on the front and strategy tips for that question type on the back.

**Table Appendix C.1**

| | Question Stem | Question Type |
|---|---|---|
| 1. | The reasoning in the argument is in error because | _____ |
| 2. | The conclusion drawn above would be most undermined if it were true that | _____ |
| 3. | Henry responds to Anne by | _____ |

4.     Which one of the following, if true, most strongly supports Eleanor's argument?

_____

5.     Which one of the following logically follows from the statement above?

_____

6.     Which one of the following principles most helps to justify Patrick's argument?

_____

7.     Which one of the following states an assumption on which the argument depends?

_____

8.     Which one of the following most accurately expresses the main conclusion of the historian's argument?

_____

9.     Mia and Clint disagree with each other over whether

_____

10     Each of the following, if true, most strengthens the argument EXCEPT:

_____

11.    The reasoning in which one of the following is most similar to the reasoning in the argument above?

_____

12.    If all the statements above are true, which one of the following must also be true?

_____

13.    Derek's reasoning is most vulnerable to criticism that he

_____

14.    The conclusion can be properly drawn if which one of the following is assumed?

_____

15.    Which one of the following, if true, helps to explain the trend in weather patterns?

_____

16.    Which one of the following, if true, would most damage the argument above?

_____

17. The passage provides the most support for which one of the following?   _____

18. The argument depends on which one of the following?   _____

19. Upon which one of the following does the author rely in the passage?   _____

20. The announcement that a new income stream for the university comes as state lawmakers begin to debate a budget bill that would impose deep cuts on higher education funding figures in the argument in which one of the following ways?   _____

21. Shannon's reasoning is questionable in that it fails to consider the possibility that   _____

22. The pattern of flawed reasoning in which one of the following arguments is most similar to that in the advertiser's argument?   _____

23. The argumentative strategy used by Kate is to   _____

24. Which one of the following arguments illustrates a principle most similar to the principle underlying the argument above?   _____

25. Which one of the following, if true, most helps to resolve the apparent discrepancy described above?   _____

26. Which one of the following most seriously calls into question the argument above?   _____

# IDENTIFY THE QUESTION TYPE ANSWERS

**Table Appendix C.2**

| Question Stem | Question Type |
|---|---|
| 1. The (reasoning) in the argument is in (error) because | Flaw |
| 2. The conclusion drawn above would be most (undermined) if it were true that | Weaken |
| 3. Henry (responds to) Anne (by) | Method of Argument |
| 4. Which one of the following, if true, most strongly (supports) Eleanor's (argument?) | Strengthen (answer supports stimulus) |
| 5. Which one of the following (logically) follows from the statement above? | Inference |
| 6. Which one of the following (principles) most helps to justify Patrick's argument? | Principle |
| 7. Which one of the following states an (assumption) on which the argument (depends?) | Assumption (necessary) |
| 8. Which one of the following most accurately expresses the (main conclusion) of the historian's argument? | Main Point |
| 9. Mia and Clint (disagree) with each other (over whether) | Point at Issue |
| 10 Each of the following, if true, most (strengthens) the argument (EXCEPT:) | Strengthen (EXCEPT) |
| 11. The reasoning in which one of the following is (most similar to) the reasoning in the argument above? | Parallel Reasoning |
| 12. If all the statements above are true, which one of the following (must also be true?) | Inference |

13. Derek's reasoning is most (vulnerable to criticism) that he

Flaw

14. The (conclusion) can be properly drawn if which one of the following is (assumed)?

Assumption (sufficient)

15. Which one of the following, if true, helps to (explain) the trend in weather patterns?

Paradox

16. Which one of the following, if true, would most (damage) the argument above?

Weaken

17. The passage provides the most (support) for (which one of the following)?

Inference (stimulus supports answer)

18. The argument (depends on) which one of the following?

Assumption (necessary)

19. Upon which one of the following does the author (rely) in thc passage?

Assumption (necessary)

20. The announcement that a new income stream for the university comes as state lawmakers begin to debate a budget bill that would impose deep cuts on higher education funding (figures in the argument) in which one of the following ways?

Role of a Statement

21. Shannon's reasoning is (questionable) in that it (fails to) (consider the possibility that)

Flaw

22. The (pattern of flawed reasoning) in which one of the following arguments is (most similar to) that in the advertiser's argument?

Parallel Reasoning (Parallel Flaw)

23. The (argumentative strategy) used by Kate is to

Method of Argument

24.     Which one of the following arguments illustrates a
        (principle) most similar to the principle underlying the
        argument above?

        Principle

25.     Which one of the following, if true, most helps to
        (resolve the apparent discrepancy) described above?

        Paradox

26.     Which one of the following most seriously (calls into)
        (question) the argument above?

        Weaken

Test Drive Test Day **For Less** at:

# The LSAT* Experience

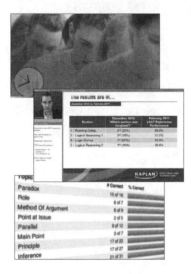

**First, you'll take the most-recently released LSAT either:**
- in a fully-simulated Test Day environment; or
- at home using our self-proctoring tool

**Then, watch a comprehensive review class featuring:**
- national performance analysis
- the most missed and representative questions

**Plus, get study tools to aid you the week before Test Day:**
- Smart Reports™ personal performance analysis
- complete answers and explanations to every question

## Register at KaplanLSAT.com/lsatexperience

**1-800-KAP-TEST**
**KaplanLSAT.com**

*LSAT is a registered trademark of the Law School Admission Council, Inc. 11-LSAT-0233

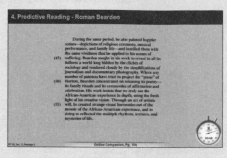

NOTES

NOTES

NOTES

NOTES

NOTES

NOTES

NOTES

NOTES